THE COINAGES OF THE WORLD;

ANCIENT AND MODERN.

BY GEO. D. MATHEWS.

ILLUSTRATED WITH SEVERAL HUNDRED ENGRAVINGS OF THE PRINCIPAL COINS.

New York:
SCOTT & CO., 146 FULTON STREET.

1876.

JOHN POLHEMUS, Printer,
102 Nassau St., N. Y.

INTRODUCTION.

Numismatics, or the science whose aim is the study of coins, might be considered as a branch of Archæology, were its enquiries confined to the coins of by-gone days. As coins of modern periods, however, fall within its range, Numismatics must stand as an independent study. Still, to the student of history, coins are ever of interest. They furnish him with notices of the religious and political systems of ancient nations, as well as of the geography and history of communities of which written traditions give him but the name. The devices on early Greek coins always express some historic or religious tenet in the national belief. A recently discovered series of Bactrian coins tells of a Greek Empire in Central Asia, whose very existence had been previously unknown. "The Roman Imperial coins," says Sir J. Bowring, "in addition to their individual character and interest, possess a general historical interest in consequence of being for the most part struck to commemorate remarkable events. The difficulties of history are consequently cleared up by these contemporary records, which are so complete until the time of Constantine that histories have been compiled from them. They form the most authentic data in the Roman annals, the years of the consular and tribunitian offices held by the Emperors appearing in the front, and on the reverse, representations of the events whose dates are expressed on the other side. The coins of Trajan, of Hadrian and of the Antonines are remarkable for this and for the accurate data which are thereby supplied to history, by which the mistakes of chroniclers are often corrected."

Nor are coins of less value to the artist. To him, as an illustrator of history, they give fairly reliable representations, otherwise unattainable, of persons, places, incidents and objects, to which reference is being continually made, and concerning which men desire to have some authentic information. Who can look on a collection of Roman bronzes without feeling that he has before him the exact likenesses of men, at "whose names the world grew pale"—likenesses whose fidelity is proved by the persistency with which certain features appear, however varied as to metal, size, date, or place of issue, may be the coins themselves? To such an one, coins are also monuments of the art ideas and attainments in mechanical skill of different nations at successive periods in their histories.

To the antiquarian, coins are priceless memorials of the past. They form a genuine portion of that Flotsam and Jetsam of former days which he so loves to gather up. As he contemplates the precious relics, he recalls the national and social circumstances under which they came into existence; he pictures to himself through what endless variety of hands these coins must have passed; what changes in the world's condition they must have witnessed; what desolations they have survived. Such power of suggestion give, in his eyes, a peculiar value to coins and lead to the forming of those collections that are studied with such delight by men of kindred taste.

From whichever of these sources, then, has come that impulse which has awakened in our reader an interest in Numismatics, we shall suppose him to be in possession of a number of coins of different countries, dates and conditions. His first business is, of course, to classify them according to their countries, placing the cities or states of these alphabetically, and arranging the issues of each mint in chronological order.* Next, as opportunity offers, replacing those of an inferior by others of a superior condition or preservation, he will look out for specimens of the different *types* or devices that are sometimes found on pieces of the same issue or series; he will also add *varieties* or coins of a common type, but differing from each other in minute details according to the taste or skill of the different die cutters. Of the American cent of 1793, for example, we have the wreath, the chain, the liberty cap *types*, with trivial differences in their details, giving rise to *varieties*. The young collector should, however, interest himself not so much in the gathering of a full set or series of coins of a particular issue, as in the making of a collection of diverse types. Twenty-five coins of different dates and dissimilar devices will yield vastly more pleasure and instruction than so many all of one date and device, and unlike only in unimportant mechanical details. He should also remember that a small collection of superior pieces is preferable to a larger one of poor and defaced ones. The eye has no pleasure in studying the latter, while the former is a source of constant gratification.

Nor is it wise to run much after *rarities*. Ancient coins are generally found in large masses, the owners of specie in former days hav-

* According to Eckhel, ancient coins should be arranged in the order of the following countries: Spain, France, Great Britain, Italy in its states, Sicily, the Danubian districts of Eastern Europe, Greece, in its kingdoms, with its islands, Asia Minor, Syria, Parthia, Persia, Bactria, Egypt and Northern Africa. Having thus completed a geographical circle we should return to Rome for its *Family* coins, placing next those of the *Emperor's* with their Gothic and Vandal successors in Italy. The Byzantines commence a new line, running out with the fall of Constantinople, and overlapping the coinages of modern civilization which took their rise in the downfall of Rome. In the following pages, while seeing many advantages in the above order, we prefer speaking of coins according to their age, noticing first those of the source of all coinage, Greece and its colonies, till these were all swallowed up by the great Roman people.

ing no other way of hoarding it than by burying it in the ground. In many cases these hoards have lain undisturbed till our own day. When discovered, the pieces on the outside are generally found to be deeply corroded and rust eaten; some farther in have escaped the damp, but have felt the atmosphere and are covered with a greatly admired thin green coating, hard and polished as enamel, called the *patina*, while a small number in the centre, completely protected from the air, may be as bright and clean as on the day that they were buried.* The pieces, therefore, that are rare and costly to-day, may, owing to the discovery of some large collection, become exceedingly common to-morrow and fall proportionately in value. Besides, the fancy prices often paid for "rare" coins is a great inducement to counterfeiting. Some collectors, we may add, confine themselves to the coins of a single country or of a single class, such as the *Autonomous*, or issues of the early free Greek States, or the *Imperial Greek*, the Roman *Family Imperial* or *Colonial* issues, the modern *Obsidional*† or Siege pieces,

---

* A word may be said here about *cleaning* coins. A young collector will often spoil a fine coin by handling it improperly. *Silver* coins should never be touched with any kind of acid. Soap and warm water, with a soft brush, will remove all that should be removed from them. *Copper* coins should have only soap and water applied to them. When the grease and dirt are removed, polish gently with powdered soapstone on flannel. Never use ammonia or acid. *Brass* coins can be cleaned by using a mixture of one part of prepared chalk with two of spirits of hartshorne. Mix these well in a bottle, and apply with flannel or a tooth brush, washing the mixture off with water and polishing with flannel.

† Obsidional or Siege pieces were issued generally in connection with a siege of some town or fortress, to supply the want of a regular coinage. Frequently they were of base metal, in such cases, like the Gun money of James II. of England, bearing values that belong to gold or silver. Their legends, devices and forms are altogether irregular. Our oldest Obsidional are those issued in the beginning of the Fifteenth century, by Francis I., when engaged in his Italian wars. It does not come within the plan of this work to give any account of such special issues, but it may be of interest to our readers to have a list of some of the more common Siege pieces, with the date of their issue.

Place	Date
Aire	1641–1710
Alemaer	1573
Anvers	1814
Baden	1808
Barcelona	1641, 1808–1814
Bearn	
Beeston Castle, England	1645
Bouchain	1702–1710
Carlisle, England	1645
Catalonia (Reals and Liards)	1645
Cisalpine Republic	1800–1802
Cattaro in Albania	1813
Colchester, England	1645
Cracow, with likeness of Napoleon II	1829
Cremona	1526
Dantzic	1813
Egypt	1798–1801
Flanders	
Geneva	1654
Genoa	1813
Gironne (Five Reals)	1641
Harlem	1573
Irvin	1808–1809
Isles of France	1810
Italian Republic	1802–1805
Kampen	1573
[On these pieces were the words: *Extremum subsidium—the last resource*. Hence the phrase—Pieces of Necessity.]	
Kingdom of Italy	1805–1814
Landau	1702–1711
Leyden	1574
Lille	1708
Lyons	
Malta	1799
Mantua	1802
Middleburg	1573
Navarre	
Newark, England	1646
Palma Nova, Italy	1814
Pavia	1524
Perpignan	1641
Pontefract Castle, England	1648
Quesnoy	1712
Rome	1809
Scarborough, England	1645
St. Domingo	
St. Venant	1657
Strasburg	1687, 1814
Tournay	1709
Turin	1808, 1809
Utrecht	1812
Venice	1813
Vichy	1641
Vienna	1529
Walcheren	1813
Zara, in Dalmatia	1813

Pattern pieces, and so on. Others make skeleton collections, filling up the gaps as they have opportunity ; while yet others, of more fastidious tastes, pride themselves on the character and condition of their coins, refusing to admit into their collections any but those of the rarest issues, or of the highest degree of preservation. On such matters each collector must be guided by his own taste or ability.

THE COINAGES OF THE WORLD.

CHAPTER I.

Our earliest coins were evidently *struck*, that is, made by a punch or hammer, driving the metal into a die. As art progressed, a double impression was made ; a die being fastened to either claw of a little instrument resembling a nipper or pincers. The unequal force of the blows of the hammer by which these were closed upon the metal accounts for the great variety in the distinctness or accuracy of the impression, and also for the irregularities and ragged appearances of the edges. Not a few coins were *cast* in moulds ; chiefly, however, it is supposed, by forgers, or, if by authority, by the Roman Emperors themselves when they had debased the coinages. *Plated* coins, fraudulent, of course, and most ingeniously manufactured, are also numerous. The Greeks, the Gauls, the Romans, were all adepts in this business, the temptations to engage in it being very great. The Roman laws punished counterfeiters with infamy and death, but when the State money was itself of mixed metal, how could forgers be detected ?

The hammer and die continued to be the only instruments used in coining until the middle of the Sixteenth century, when the French Mint applied *the screw* in place of the hammer as a power. This change was first adopted in England in the reign of Elizabeth, part of whose money is *hammered* and part *milled* or the result of the screw. Among the advantages of this new method are a smooth edge, a form really circular, and great evenness of impression. To prevent *clipping* or paring the edges of the coin, a common mode of cheating, a circle was now stamped on the coins as near the edge as possible, as may be seen on Elizabeth's early milled money. Another mode of preventing this fraud was the placing a legend on the edge, a plan possible, however, only on the thicker pieces of money. The saw-like edge possessed by modern coins is called the *milling*. On some English coins of last century, the milling is diagonal to the edge, and on others it is at right angles.

The only mode of exchange among the primitive inhabitants of the earth must of course have been simply that of barter—a mere exchanging of articles between individuals. From a very early date, however, there has been employed a metallic medium of exchange, the value of the medium depending on the metal employed, its weight and purity. We do not know when *coins* (from the French *coigner*, to strike with a coigne or wedge),—that is, pieces of metal whose weight and value would be guaranteed by the parties issuing them, and which would therefore be simply *counted* and not *weighed*, —were first used, nor by whom. The credit of inventing such money (from the Latin *moneta*) has been claimed for the Persians, for the Greek Colonists of Asia Minor (who migrated thither from the Peloponnessus about the 11th century B. C.), and for the inhabitants of the island of Ægina ; yet, as the oldest coins we have are the gold pieces issued by the Asiatic Greeks, these may possibly be our earliest coined money. These pieces were called *Staters*,—that is, standards,—and were equal in weight to two, and in value to twenty, drachms of silver. There were also *Di-staters* or two staters, and *Hemi-staters*, or half ones with smaller subdivisions. These coins, as might be expected, are very rude in workmanship, being little more than pieces of metal of a certain weight driven by a strong punch into a mould or die, so that on the one side is the design and on the other the indent of the punch.

Since the earliest coins do not bear the year of their issue, and their devices for the most part are only some national symbol, it is impossible to fix their age with accuracy. Numismatists, however, seek to determine their dates by noting the different styles of the punch mark on the reverses. The oldest coins are supposed to be those on which the punch mark is simply an uneven indent. The next are those on which it is regular in form, and with edges sharply and distinctly cut. Then those on which it is divided into sections. Next, those on which the punch is found to make an incused or bas-relief pattern, and then, the latest, when the indent itself becomes a field, on which important devices or symbols appear. Since the punchmark passed through these changes, at different periods in different countries, we can use these facts to some extent as a guide to the relative ages of coins of the same country, and then, by careful comparison with the coins of other countries, may learn something as to their actual date.

As there can be very little difference of age, if any, between the earliest coinages of Greece and those of Asia Minor, we shall commence with describing, briefly, the coins of some of those States or Cities whose fame has shed a glory on their common Greece. It is impossible, however, for us to describe the coins of every Grecian City or Colony. Many of these States were of very limited extent, and would be content to use the coin of some friendly neighbor, countermarking them with some stamp that proclaimed a new owner, while, on the other hand, every free city in a State might, and often did, exercise the right of coinage, impressing on the coins issued some symbol of local significance. Hence, there exists a far greater variety of devices on Grecian coins than would be possible under our modern system of having a common device for a whole land. On Greek coins, representations of natural objects, such as plants, fishes, animals, birds, that might abound in a locality, be connected with some local incident, or be sacred to some local deity, are among the earliest devices. Sometimes, again, certain attributes, distinctive of their guardian deity, were symbolized to the initiated by figures of animals in which similar characteristics existed. The Bull, for instance, was the symbol for strength; the Eagle, for penetration; the Lion, for courage. These devices were succeeded by ideal representations of the deities themselves. The popular mind was thus prepared for having on the coins the likenesses of their fabled heroes—Hercules, Ajax, Castor, and Pollux. The way was thus opened for the likenesses of living heroes. At first, divine qualities were attributed to these; Alexander was represented as Jupiter; Lysimachus as the horned Bacchus. This class of coins served as a connecting link between the previous classes, to which is given the general name of *Autonomous*, as being the coinage of free States, and those issued subsequently and known as *Regal*, because bearing the effigies of living rulers.

The inhabitants of the island of ÆGINA are supposed to have been the first to issue a *silver* coinage. This they did about the Eighth century B.C., using the device of a tortoise, an animal sacred to Mercury, the God of weights and measures. This remained as their national device for several centuries, while the purity or value of these pieces, familiarly known as "tortoises," soon secured for them so general a circulation as to render it impolitic, if not impossible, to change the symbol. The original device was therefore retained, though with such modifications and changes adopted in the course of time, as reveal a progressively ornate and culti-

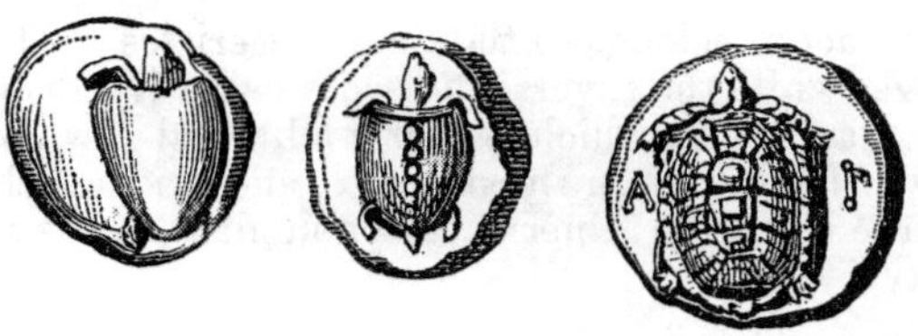

DRACHMS OF ÆGINA.

vated style of art. Our illustrations represent coins of Ægina of different periods, the difference between the rude simplicity of the oldest, and the elaborate and finished appearance of the latest being very great. The *A* and *Γ* on either side of the tortoïse are the first two letters of Ægina.

Few cities have a reputation for artistic taste of culture equal to that of ATHENS,* and yet its early coins, while celebrated for their weight and purity, are by no means attractive. The general device these bear is that of an owl, a bird sacred to Minerva, the patron deity of a city that bore her name, *Αθηνη*—Athens.

ATHENIAN DRACHM OF THE EARLIEST DATE.

The reverse of our illustration has simply a rude indent of irregular shape, caused by the blows of the punch in driving the metal into the die. The knobs or beads on the breast of the owl resemble those on the back of the tortoise of the second period of the coins of Ægina, to the period of whose issue this Athenian coin may therefore be assigned.

ATHENIAN DIDRACHM, 470 B. C.

This didrachm belongs to the time of Pericles. The head is that of Minerva, while the reverse presents us with a deep indent having a circular top, in which is the traditional owl, with the letters *Α Θ Ε* (Athenæ) on the one side, and on the other a sprig of olive, a tree sacred to Minerva, and abundant in the neighborhood of the city.

---

* It may be of service to the Collector to have here a copy of the Greek Alphabet in capitals and small letters, with their English equivalents.

Α—α	A	*Η—η*	Æ	*Ν—ν*	N	*Τ—τ*	T
Β—β	B	*Θ—θ*	Th	*Ξ—ξ*	X	*Υ—υ*	T
Γ—γ	G	*Ι—ι*	I	*Ο—ο*	O	*Φ—φ*	Ph *or* F
Δ—δ	D	*Κ—κ*	K	*Π—π*	P	*Χ—χ*	Ch
Ε—ε	E	*Λ—λ*	L	*Ρ—ρ*	R	*Ψ—ψ*	Ps
Ζ—ζ	Z	*Μ—μ*	M	*Σ—σ*	S	*Ω—ω*	O

On Roman Colonials having Greek legends, K is often used for C, and C for S. See p. 16.

ATHENIAN TETRADRACHM, 230 B. C.

The highest attainment of Athenian art is shown in the above engraving. The head of Minerva is magnificent, while the owl is as ungraceful and uncouth as ever. The olive wreath round the owl, and the vase on which it stands, suggest the olive groves and their famous oil. The small figure represents Æsculapius, the God of Healing, in reference to one of the uses of the oil, and is probably intended as a sort of mint mark, while the incription reads across :

Αθε Μενεδ Επιγενο Οφελο.

meaning Athens (name of issuer). Menedos (possibly name of the mint-master or engraver), son of *Epigenos* and *Ophelon.*

One naturally asks why the Athenian coinages should on one side be so inferior in point of artistic taste, to those of many other less famous localities. Perhaps the commercial inconvenience that would result in such an age, from any change of a national device so well known as the owl, may in part account for the very slight modification allowed during several centuries in its figure. National taste may have had something to do with it, just as on the English florin of the present day, the characters and even the designs of former days reappear. May not the Athenians in like manner have preferred that one side of their coin should retain in all its archaic rudeness, that device which had been so long associated with their national history?

Bæotia, one of the earliest states to issue a silver coinage, had adopted at a remote date as its symbol the device of a shield or buckler.

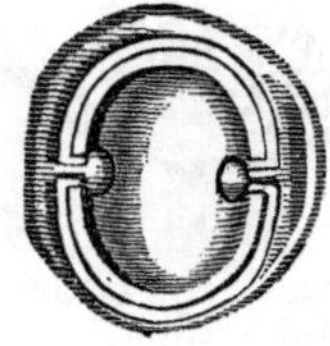

DRACHM OF BÆOTIA, WITH THE HEAD OF THE INDIAN BACCHUS.

To this it adhered through all its history. At first the Bæotian coins bore simply the shield, but subsequently they bore in addition, *Θ*, the initial letter of their chief city, Thebes, while those of the latest date bore the letters *ΘEB*.

None of the Greek coin, however, are so disappointing as those of Corinth, a city of the highest fame for devotion to the fine arts, yet whose numismatic taste or skill was of an exceedingly poor character. The device on Corinthian coins is that of Pegasus, in

EARLY CORINTHIAN DRACHM.

remembrance of the victory over it of Bellerophon, and of his victory again by means of it over the monster, the Chimæra. The designs are exceedingly rude and the execution most wretched, while on the reverse is a series of four punch marks so arranged and of such a shape as to suggest the wards of a key.

Apart from that celebrity which Macedonia possesses because of the fame of Alexander the Great, its coinage entitles it to a special notice. To Macedonia belong the earliest coins on which dates or the names of living monarchs appear, as well as the first gold coins that were issued in Europe. Up to the Sixth century, B. C., the rude punch mark was to be found on the reverse of every coin; but about that period Alexander the First, King of Macedonia, engraved his name round an inner square that was in the centre of the indent. The device on the obverse is the national

TETRADRACHM OF ALEXANDER I. OF MACEDON, 500 B. C.

one of a horse—Macedonia and Thrace being famous for their horses—led by a man wearing a peculiarly shaped head-dress, known as "the Macedonian hat," and carrying two spears, in allusion, it is thought, to the competing, by the King, at the Olympic games.*

The coins of Archelaus, about 400 B. C., resemble, on their obverse, those of Alexander—a horse and a warrior armed with two spears, and wearing the peculiar hat. Now, however, the warrior is mounted and sits with the utmost ease and grace. On the reverse there is still the punch mark, within which, however, is the fore-part of a goat, alluding, it is thought, to the capture of Edessa by Caranus, the founder of the Macedonian dynasty, following a flock of goats, as they entered the city in the dusk of the evening.

DRACHM OF ARCHELAUS OF MACEDONIA, 400 B. C.

In 336 B. C., Alexander III. known as the Great, succeeded his father, Philip II. During the wonderful career of this hero, coins were issued, both in Europe and in Asia, in such abundance that they are still very easily obtained. Our illustration is that of a tetradrachm or four drachma piece, having on the obverse a head, either of Hercules with the skin of the Nemean lion for a head dress, or of Alexander himself. On the reverse is a figure of Jupiter, seated, with the inscription *ΑΛΕΞΑΝΔΡΟΥ* (*money* of Alexander). Jupiter is holding an eagle while the Lyre is the crest or symbol of Colophon in Ionia, part of whose name, *ΚΟΛΟ,* appears.

TETRADRACHM OF ALEXANDER THE GREAT.

---

* The Olympic Games were instituted, it is said, by Heracles or Hercules, about the year 1227 B. C. They took their name from the place where they were held, *Olympus*, a town in the Peloponnessus. For more than 400 years they were held at irregular periods; but in 776 B. C. there commences what is called in history the Era of the Olympiads, the games being held thereafter every fifth year.

The death of Alexander at Babylon in 323 B. C., was followed by a division of the empire among his generals. Macedon itself was seized by Cassander, whom Alexander had left as governor. Cassander's dynasty terminated in Perseus, with whom, after his defeat by the Romans at Pydna, in 168 B. C., the celebrated Macedonian Phalanx—Alexander's great military formation—having broken, the Macedonian monarchy ended, and the country became a Roman Province.

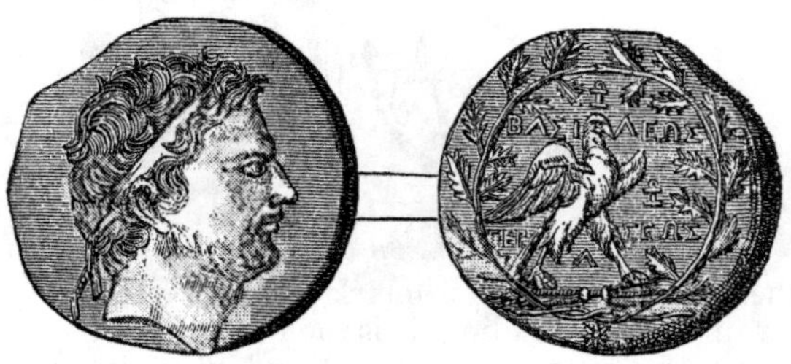

TETRADRACHM OF PERSEUS, THE LAST OF THE KINGS OF MACEDON, 168 B. C.

Many petty kingdoms and independent States lay in the neighborhood of Macedonia, whose coinages greatly resemble those we have already described. About 480 B. C., Getas, King of the *Edoneans*, issued money resembling that of Alexander I., but bearing the inscription *ΒΑΣΙΛΕΥΣ*, the earliest coins on which this word occurs. The Kings of *Thrace*, *Epirus*, *Illyria*, and other less famous districts, all issued coins that from their great rarity have been repeatedly counterfeited. Caution must therefore be exercised in dealing with what appear to be the coins of these localities.

CHAPTER II.

If the coins of *Ægina* are the earliest known of the European series, those of MILETUS in *Ionia* are the earliest of the Asiatic.

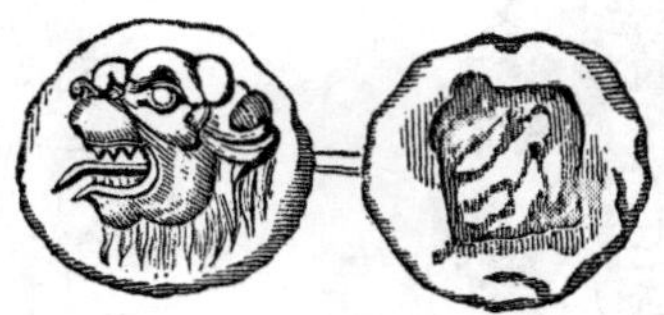

GOLD STATER OF MILETUS, ABOUT 800 B. C.

The device on this stater is that of a lion's head with open mouth, a symbol expressive of strength and courage, in other words, of royalty. The rudeness of the design and execution, reveals a condition of artistic taste not very creditable to the inhabitants of Miletus.

Similar in metal and in weight is the *Daric* or Persian stater, struck by Darius Hystaspes, the Persian conqueror of the Greek colonies. These staters are found in gold, but more frequently in silver. On some the royal archer is represented as kneeling, on

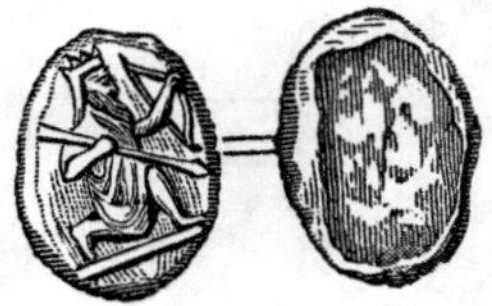

DARIC OR PERSIAN STATER, ABOUT 520 B. C.

others he is standing. It is thought that these staters were struck for the use of the conquered colonists, affording them what they were familiar with—coined money—yet such having, instead of the national or local Grecian devices, the Persian symbol of a crowned archer. The rudeness of the punch mark on the reverse would suggest a remoter date for them, but it is possible that, as elsewhere, commercial and political reasons may have led to a retaining of the early style. In our own day the Austrian Govr nment issues yearly thousands of dollars from the Maria Theresa dies of last century, such alone being freely taken by the inhabitants of her Mediterranean provinces.

Ephesus stands without a peer for its reputation for wealth and culture among the Greek colonies in Asia Minor. It was one of the twelve Ionian cities in Asia Minor of mythic times, having been founded by the Amazons and then taken possession of by colonists from Athens. It is said that the Muses assumed the shape of bees, and, flying before the emigrants, guided their vessels to their future home. In grateful remembrance of this service, the Bee was adopted as the national symbol.

DRACHM OF EPHESUS, ABOUT 330 B. C.

The stag on the reverse of our illustration was sacred to Arterius or Diana, whose worship was so magnificently observed at Ephesus.

On the earliest Ephesian coins we have simply the device of the bee ; on those of a later period, but still autonomous, we have on the reverse the stag, the emblem of Diana the huntress, while on those of the Roman period we have the figure of Diana Multimammia with her stags.

BRONZE COLONIAL OF COMMODUS, STRUCK AT EPHESUS.

Passing over other Grecian colonies, but following up the line along which Greek influence, through the presence of Alexander the Great, would be felt, we come to Bithynia. Nicomedia, the capital of this country, was founded by Nicomedes the First, about 250 B. C. His grandson, Prusias, dared the hostility of the Romans by giving a shelter at his court to Hannibal. The head of Prusias is remarkably life-like, and is evidently a good portrait. The figure on the reverse is that of *Jupiter Soter*—Jupiter, the Saviour—while the Greek inscription is simply (money) " of the King

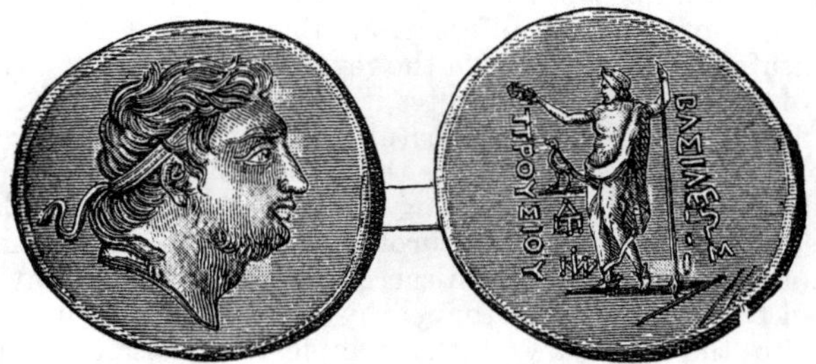

TETRADRACHM OF PRUSIAS, KING OF BITHYNIA, 180 B. C.

Prusias." The other characters are presumably mint marks. Coins of PERGAMUS and of ARMENIA are also found.

EGYPT.

The most illustrious of the Generals of Alexander was Ptolemy Lagus, the son of Arsinöe, a concubine of Philip. On the death of Alexander and the division of the Empire, Ptolemy took possession of EGYPT, and was at first content to rule under the shadow of his great leader's name. He secured that Alexander's funeral should be celebrated at Alexandria, and thus made himself the guardian of his ashes. One of his great works was the formation at Alexandria of its famous library, containing, when burnt about the year 400 A. D., some five hundred thousand volumes. The coins of Ptolemy bore at first the devices of those of Alexander, with his own name added. Next, those on which his own likeness was placed without the title of King. Then, those on which he is styled *ΒΑΣΙΛΕΥΣ*, or King. Afterwards, those struck by his son, and on which his portrait, with or without that of his wife, Berenice, appears,—those bearing the inscription *ΣΩΤΗΡΟΣ*, those struck at Cyrene, in connection with the funeral of Alexander, and those having for a reverse the portrait of Berenice.

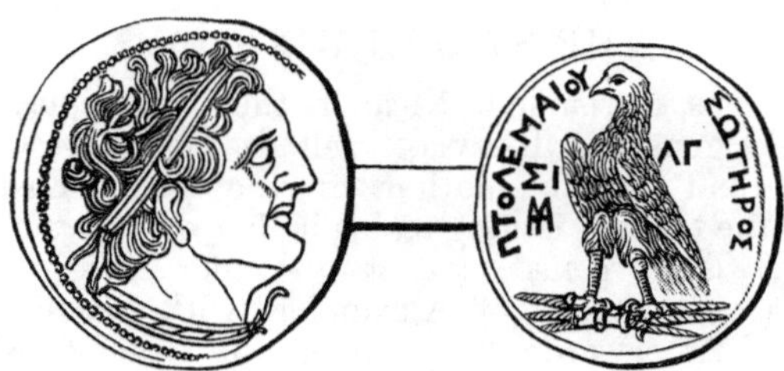

DIDRACHM OF PTOLEMY SOTÆR.

In 285 B. C., his son, Ptolemy Philadelphus, ascended the throne. The effigy on his coins differs from that of his father merely by its youthful appearance. On the reverse is Arsinoë, his wife. The coins of Ptolemy III. Euergetes, the Benefactor, 245 B. C., differ only in the expression of the features from those of his predecessor.

Ptolemy IV., or Philopater, the father-lover, called so in irony, from being suspected of having murdered his father, Euergetes, marked his accession to the throne in 222 B. C. by the murder of his mother, Berenice II. In sacred history this Ptolemy is distinguished for having been stopped by a miracle, when forcing his way into the sanctuary of the temple at Jerusalem. The coins of Ptolemy V., or Epiphanes, 181 B. C., are distinguished by the radiated crown, emblem of divinity.

The course of the Ptolemeian dynasty was soon rapidly downward. In 49 B C., Cleopatra, having quarrelled with her brother Ptolemy XII., invoked and obtained the aid of Julius Cæsar, when Ptolemy was drowned as he sought to swim across the Nile. Cleopatra, now 28 years of age, reigned alone, but after Cæsar's death was summoned by Marc Antony to explain why she had failed to assist the Triumvirs in their struggle. The famous interview took place, at which Cleopatra so fascinated her judge that he became her husband and fled with her to Egypt.

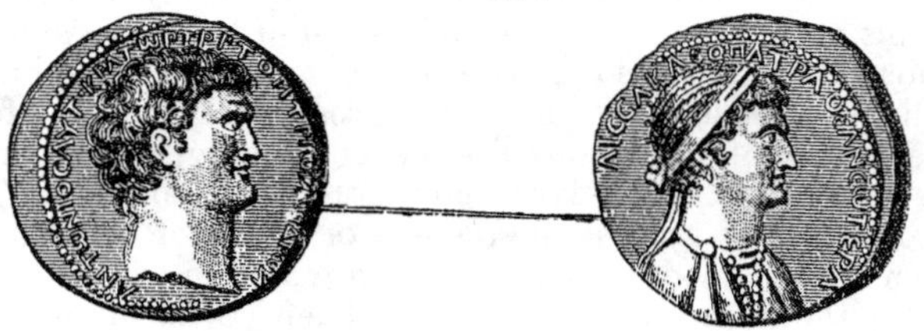

TETRADRACHM OF M. ANTONY AND CLEOPATRA, 33 B. C.

By the death of Cleopatra, who poisoned herself in her 39th year, to avoid capture by Augustus, the line of the Ptolemies became extinct, and Egypt was reduced to a province of Rome.

THE SYRIAN KINGDOM.

To Seleucus, surnamed Nicanor the Victorious, another of Alexander's generals, Babylon fell as his share of territory. There, he laid the foundations of the great Eastern Empire known as the Syrian, issuing coins in his own name in the year 312 B. C. These coins have at first, like those of Ptolemy in Egypt, the usual types of Alexander, with the simple name of Seleucus. Afterwards he assumed the title of *ΒΑΣΙΛΕΥΣ*, or King. On several of his coins the figure of a bull occupies the reverse, in allusion to the overpowering by Seleucus of a bull that had escaped from Alexander when he was about to offer it in sacrifice. In 282 B. C., Seleucus was succeeded by his son Antiochus I., called Soter, from his repelling of the attacks of the Gauls on Asia Minor, who boldly placed his portrait on the coinage, a custom which about this time became very general. In 223 B. C., the throne was occupied by Antiochus III., called The Great, from the wonderful prosperity of the earlier portion of his reign. By sheltering Hannibal, however, and by his unjust war against Ptolemy V., the King of Egypt, he, like Prusias of Bithynia, became involved in war with Rome. This ultimately led to his death in 189 B. C., when plundering the treasures of a temple that he might pay the fines imposed on him by Scipio Asiaticus. This monarch's coins are the first of his dynasty that bear a date. In 176 B. C., Antiochus IV., surnamed Epiphanes the Illustrious, sought to suppress the Jewish mode of worship, and to force the Greek religion on the Jews, thus leading to the great Maccabean rebellion in Judea. On his coins we find not only the name and title of the monarch, but his surname, the first instance of the custom on this series.

Wearied of the wars of their Seleucian Kings, the Syrians, at last, 80 B. C., offered the throne to *Tigranes*, King of Armenia.

TETRADRACHM OF TIGRANES.

For some fifteen years this monarch reigned, when at length he was defeated in 65 B. C., by Pompey the Great, and the throne of the Seleucidæ passed away by the annexation of Syria to Rome.

The dominions of Seleucus had consisted at first only of Babylonia. To this, however, was soon added Susiana. Media was next conquered, and the monarch's power extended to the Oxus and the Indus. After his overthrow in 306 B. C., of Antigones, the most powerful of Alexander's generals, and one that had assumed the title of King of Asia, Asia Minor and the whole of Syria were also added to his territory. The whole Asiatic conquests of Alexander may therefore be held as included in the Kingdom of Syria. The principle, however, on which it was founded—that of establishing a Græco-Macedonian Empire in a foreign country —was fatal to its permanency. Unused to foreign modes of rule and oftentimes ill-treated, the natives of the Eastern portion at length revolted, and under Arsaces, 250 B. C., established the *Parthian* Kingdom. Though Greek rule had so bitterly galled the Parthians, so firmly had Grecian influences affected them, that the inscriptions on the coins now issued were in Greek, the types were from the Greek mythology, and the word *ΦΙΛΕΛΛΗΝΟΣ—lover of the Greeks* oftentimes appeared.

PARTHIA.

One of the most distinguished of these Parthian Kings was Arsaces VI., 150 B. C., known as Mithridates I. Under him Media, Persia and Babylonia were added to the Empire, which thus extended from the Caucasus to the Euphrates. During the reign of Arsaces X., 80 B. C., a great religious revolt took place with a view to the overthrow of the Greek Polytheism and the re-establishment, as the religion of the State, of the ancient faith of Central Asia. Coins of the king's rival—Arsaces Phraates—exist with the inscription on them of *Συνηγοροσ Ζαραστρεωσ—Defender of Zoroaster*. In the year 55 B.C., Arsaces Orodes, one of the most powerful of the line, ascended the throne. Crassus, at the head of 30,000 Roman soldiers, sought the restoration to the throne of an elder brother, but was defeated by Orodes, and his whole army slain or captured.

About the Christian era, Artabanus, king of Media, but one of the Arsacidæ, was called to the Parthian throne, and recovered Armenia from the Romans. The victories of Arsaces XXIII., about 60 A. D., caused such alarm at Rome itself, that eventually Armenia was declared ceded to Arsaces for his brother, a favor acknowledged by an offer from Arsaces to aid Vespasian in his Jewish wars with 40,000 troops. Arsaces XXV., about 120 A. D., became involved in war with Rome, and was ultimately defeated by the Emperor Trajan. For the next hundred years there was a continuous embroilment of Parthia with Rome, till at length its resources were so wasted that in 226 A. D., a revolt of the native Persian population under Ardshir (or Artaxerxes) proved successful, and the Parthian monarchy became merged in the SECOND PERSIAN EMPIRE, under the dynasty of the Sassanidæ.

SECOND PERSIAN EMPIRE.

In this revolt, Artaxerxes obtained the support of the people by claiming to be the heir of the great Cyrus, and by announcing his intention of restoring the national religion—that of Zoroaster. On his coins, therefore, we do not find either Greek characters or

Greek titles, but, in Arian characters, Shahshinsha—the equivalent for the Greek *King of Kings*. The boundaries of this kingdom changed greatly according to the varying fortunes of its monarchs. One while, they embraced the vast region between the shores of the Hellespont, on which, at Chalcedon, the Persians under Chosroes II., 620 A. D., maintained themselves for ten years fighting against the usurper Phocas, and the banks of the Indus. At other times, the Roman eagles were carried triumphantly throughout almost the whole territory. For many years a great struggle was waged between the rising power of Christianity and the national religion, symbolized by the flaming altar of the fire worshippers on the national coinage.

In 640 A. D., the reigning monarch was summoned by the Caliph Abu Bekr, to embrace the Mahommedan religion. War followed on his refusing, and, in the struggle which followed, the monarch of the Second Persian Empire perished, his son fled to China, his territory becoming a province of the Mahommedan dominions.

THE BACTRIAN EMPIRE.

The Syrian Empire, as founded by Seleucus Nicanor, embraced the whole territory from the Hellespont to the Punjaub. The more eastern portion was, however, held by but a feeble tenure, so that Diodotus, the Governor of Bactria, the modern Bokhara, was able, about the year 260 B. C., to make successful his revolt against Antiochus II. For nearly five hundred years the empire thus founded continued in existence. The coinage of its monarchs bore at first inscriptions in Greek alone. Then they became bilingual or Arian words spelt in Grecian characters, with indications of a long struggle for supremacy, when finally all traces of Grecian influence disappeared, so far as characters, titles or symbols are concerned, these being replaced by such as are found on coins of modern date.

These coins have been brought to light only within the last 40 years, and reveal what had been previously unknown to history—the existence of this Græco-Bactrian Empire.

KINGDOM OF PONTUS.

In the extreme south-eastern corner of European Russia is the district now known as the Crimea, but formerly as the Cimmerian Bosphorus. The sovereignty once existing here goes back to the earliest dates of history, or about 480 B. C. Coins have come down to us from Leucon, who lived about the year 390 B. C., bearing on the one side a head of Hercules, and on the other a bow and a club, with the name and title of the monarch in Greek characters.

About the year 300 B. C., owing to its inability to resist and keep back the hordes of warrior emigrants that poured westward from Scythia and Central Asia, the throne of the Bosphorus was yielded to Mithridates, the Satrap or Persian Governor of Pontus. In the break-up of the Persian Empire, consequent on the victories of Alexander, the kingdom of Pontus became fully established, so that about a century before the Christian era, its monarch Mith-

TETRADRACHM OF MITHRIDATES, KING OF PONTUS.

ridates VI., known as the Great, was a formidable rival to Rome for the supremacy of the Eastern World. A series of dealings now ensued between Rome and the sovereigns of Pontus, ending, however, in the reducing of Pontus proper to a Roman province, while the Bosphorus portion was recovered from its Pontic rulers by a descendant of the former native sovereigns. Of this restored monarchy there exists an interesting series of coins, on which, while the names of the native princes appear, there is also the fullest acknowledgment made of Roman sovereignty, by the presence of the likenesses of the Roman emperors, with their names and eras. The Empire maintained its existence down to about the year 330 A. D., the era of Constantine the Great, when it was overthrown by a neighboring barbarous people, and a nationality that had existed for nearly eight hundred years, became obliterated forever.

CHAPTER III.

JUDEA.

IN the earliest account of commerce in PALESTINE, so far back as 1850 B. C., we find that the medium of exchange was silver, not gold, and that this was weighed, not counted. "Abraham weighed to Ephron four hundred shekels of silver current money with the merchant." Gen. 23, 16. The bars or blocks of silver thus used, though not coins in our sense of that word,* would possibly soon come to be of a particular shape or size, or have some stamp or impress on them that would declare their weight and thus secure for them a fixed commercial value. A half shekel piece was the Atonement money, (Exod. 30, 15), while Saul's servant had a quarter shekel, (1 Sam. 9, 8). Such pieces would long supply the few necessities of an agricultural people like the Jews. In David's time, eight hundred years after Abraham, we find silver and gold still weighed, not counted. By degrees, however, the coinage of surrounding countries entered Palestine. The conquest of Israel by Assyria, 721 B. C., led to a considerable circulation of Assyrian money, while Persian money flowed in on the return of Judah from the Babylonian captivity. Cyrus gave large sums from "the king's house," that is, the royal treasury, for the rebuilding of the temple at Jerusalem. These gifts would doubtless be in the form of the thick Persian gold coins called Darics or Archers.

In the year 325 B. C., Alexander the Great took possession of Palestine, when Greek money, consisting of gold staters, and silver drachms and tetradrachms came into use. Many of Alexander's tetradrachms were struck in Palestine and bear the names of the places of their coinage. On the death of Alexander, Palestine became part of the dominion of Seleucus. An interesting series of coins, in many respects resembling the Alexandrine, was issued by the kings of this dynasty, some of which bear the mint mark of *Diospolis*, the Lydda of New Testament times.

About 185 B. C., the Jews rose in revolt, and engaged in a heroic struggle for liberty under the lead of Mattathias of the

*In Gen. 33:19, we read that Jacob bought a field from Hamor for one hundred pieces of money. A similar phrase is found in Job 42:11. The word in these passages translated *pieces* means, properly, *lambs*, and it is now thought denotes pieces of gold with the figure of a lamb stamped on them, denoting that they were of value sufficient to purchase such. Such seems to have been the style of money used in Babylon. It reminds us at once of the figures stamped on the early Roman As.

Asmonean family, and founder of the Maccabean dynasty. In 139 B. C., their independence of the Seleucidæ was practically acknowledged, when Antiochus VII. authorized Simon, successor to Mattathias, "to coin money for the country with thine own stamp," a privilege, however, that Simon is believed to have previously exercised on his own responsibility. Simon now issued the famous shekel, weighing half an ounce, and intrinsically worth about half a dollar, and the half shekel in silver, with quarters and sixths in copper, the first and only national coinage the Jews ever had.

SHEKEL OF SIMON MACCABÆUS, 140 B. C.

These shekels are a little larger than a two cent piece; on the obverse is a cup or chalice, suggesting the water-drawing ceremony at the Feast of Tabernacles, the season of greatest national joy, while the triple lily on the reverse is more suggestive of the Divine promise that "Israel shall bloom as a lily," than of Aaron's almond blossoming rod. Round the cup is the legend, in Samaritan or old Hebrew characters, "Shekel of Israel," a letter over it denoting the year of its issue, while round the lily is the legend, "Jerusalem the holy." Imitations of these shekels, with the legends in square or modern Hebrew characters, are very common. Simon was succeeded in 135 B. C., by John Hyrcanus, on whose coins we find in the legend "Johanan, High Priest, and the Confederation of the Jews," a distinct acknowledgment of a popular sovereignty. The reverses of these pieces have, as a type, a double cornucopia with a poppy head between them. This symbol is found on Egyptian coins of an earlier date, so that Hyrcanus may either have simply borrowed this design, using it as an emblem of national prosperity, or have assumed it to denote some intermarriage, as the coats of arms of allied royal or noble families are frequently quartered on each other's shields.

This double cornucopia remained the type of Jewish coins for about a century, when, in 37 B. C., and by the aid of Roman Legions, the Idumean or Herodian dynasty, in the person of Herod I., or the Great, ascended the throne. Coins were now issued with the legend, for the most part in Greek characters, of "Herod the King," round a caduceus, the emblem of peace, round a helmet, the emblem of war, or most frequently round an anchor, with reference, possibly, to Herod's well known concern for maritime interests. Coins of Herod Archelaus have on them, in part or in whole, the word "*Ethnarch*," a title of less extent than that of king. Those of Antipas have the word *Tetrarch*, denoting that he was governor of but the fourth part of what had once been one kingdom. On the coins of Philip, 34 A. D., we have for the first time in Jewish history, a human effigy, that of the Emperor Tiberius, a daring departure from Jewish law and custom. Herod, however, would readily set such aside that he might flatter a Roman Emperor, or perhaps obey an edict by acknowledging himself a vassal of Rome. Herod Agrippa, grandson of Herod the Great, issued a series of coins purely Jewish, that is, free from any references to a foreign power, having on the obverse an umbrella or canopy, with the legend in Greek characters "*King Agrippa*," and on the reverse, three ears of wheat with date of issue. This monarch outlived the destruction of Jerusalem and the remainder of his coins bear the heads of the Emperors in succession down to Domitian in 96 A. D. Such are the coins that form the Herodian series, and which were struck principally at Cesarea Philippi.

In the year 33 A. D., Judea was reduced to a Province, and came under the control of "Procurators," such as Pontius Pilate, who were appointed by the Roman Emperors. These persons had too great a personal interest in maintaining peace in their territories to allow of any wanton outrages against Jewish feelings or prejudices. They therefore omitted "images," that is, human likenesses, from their coins and placed on these merely some ordinary symbol, the name of the Roman Emperor, and the date of its issue. Such coins were issued down to the year 65 A. D., when there took place that first revolt of the Jews against the Romans which ended in 69 A. D., in the siege and destruction of Jerusalem by Titus. During this four years war, silver and copper shekels were issued by the Jewish leaders, having on them such symbols as a jug or pitcher, a palm tree, a palm branch, a vine leaf, a bunch of grapes,

SHEKEL OF SIMON, PRINCE OF ISRAEL; *round the vine leaf is "First year of the redemption of Israel."*

a lyre or a temple, with the name Simon and the date of its issue, which is described as being such a year of "the deliverance of Israel," or "of the redemption of Israel."

In the year 69 A. D., came the end in the fall of Jerusalem, when a remarkably interesting series of coins known as the *Judæa Capta* series, and referring to this event, was struck at Rome.

In 131 A. D., the Emperor Hadrian resolved to rebuild Jerusalem. The second revolt of the Jews now took place, when Bar-cochab, claiming to be the Messiah, and at the head of 200,000 men, for a time swept all before him. During his power he issued money, for the most part restriking Roman coins, with the symbols

SHEKEL OF SIMON BARCOCHAB, *Second Revolt of the Jews.*

and legends of the coins of the first revolt. After two years this revolt was suppressed, when Hadrian completed his project of restoring Jerusalem, giving to the new city, however, the name of *Ælia Capitolina*, combining his family name of Ælia with that of Jupiter Capitolinus, and thus by rendering the locality profane and polluted in the eyes of the Jews, shattered their hopes of a national kingdom with Jerusalem for its capital.

A new series of coins was now struck at Jerusalem, or rather in *Colonia Ælia Capitolina Commodiana*, the colonial town of Ælia Capitolina Commodiana, with the heads of the respective emperors down to Hostilianus, 251 A. D., when the Imperial Jewish issues ceased, to be succeeded in 695 A. D., by the Cufic coinages of the Mahommedan conquerors. The coins at present in use in Palestine are those issued by the Turkish rulers.

CHAPTER IV.

GRÆCIA MAGNA.

The coins of Macedonia having served as a connecting link between those of Greece and the different Eastern Empires that were more or less affected by its art, we now return to consider those of the Western World, for the maritime and commercial energy of the Greeks had led to a migration in a westerly direction simultaneous with that to Asia Minor. At a very early date, Italy, Sicily, France, Spain, Carthage, had received so many colonies from Greece, that what was till lately the Kingdom of the Two Sicilies, was known formerly as *Græcia Magna*. These colonies soon received additions from the Asiatic settlements, so that the coinages of Græcia Magna, while having features national and distinctive, frequently remind us by their style and devices, not merely of Greece, but of Grecian art as modified by Asiatic influences, some, at times, bearing symbols that are purely of Asiatic origin.

At this distance of time, we are unable to state in every case, the parent land of each of these settlements, but when in the midst of devices known to be local, the well-known symbols of certain Grecian States or Cities appear, we have no hesitation in inferring a connection. Phocis, for instance, in Greece, sent out a colony that founded *Phocea* in Asia Minor. The legend of the shoal of seals or rather of porpoises that attended the ships in their voyage, secured the adoption by the colony of the old name, while as *Φωκη* (Phoce) is the Greek word for a seal, the device of a *seal* stamped on money proclaimed the state by which it had been issued. The presence of the seal or of the porpoise on coinages of Græcia Magna thus tells of connection with Phocis, either direct or indirect, through Phoce. That the Phoceans were a very maritime people is plain also, from the fact that there frequently appears on their coins the figures of the Dioscuri.

The coinage of Græcia Magna is probably the oldest to which dates can with any confidence be assigned. Sybaris, afterwards called Thurium, was founded by a colony from Achaia, about 720 B. C., and destroyed in the year 510 B. C. When destroyed its coinage was of a peculiar style, and one that had long replaced a coinage of a different type. Specimens of this earlier type have come down to us, and we cannot be far wrong in ascribing them to about the year 600 B. C., while those of Alexander I. of Macedon, date only from about 480 B. C.

This earliest known type is thin, flat and large in surface, having the design on the obverse—*incused* or sunk in on the reverse, resulting from the use of a punch on which was the counterpart of the design in the die.

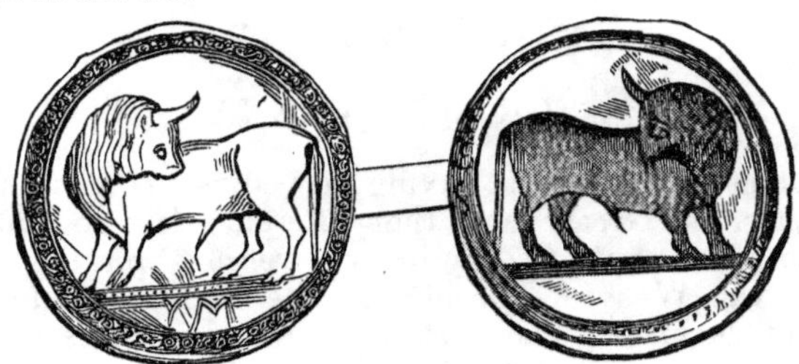

DRACHM OF SYBARIS, 600 B. C.

The bull is the symbol of strength, and appears on all the coins of Thurium, alluding to the river on which the city was built. The city we have said was founded in 721 B. C., about the time of Numa Pompilius in Rome, or the invasion of Judea by Sennacherib, and destroyed in B. C. 510. It was rebuilt in 453 B. C., but destroyed again in 448 B. C., by the Crotonians.

Crotona was another Achaian colony, and founded by Myscellus about 710 B. C. The most frequent of its types is the tripod,

DIDRACHM OF CROTONA.

Apollo having directed Myscellus to the site of the new city.—Hercules is often met with on these coins, because he founded those Olympic games at which the Crotonians had carried off thirteen out of twenty-six prizes. The ancient coinage of Crotona has the tripod with letters *K P O*. On later coins we have no incused designs, but in place thereof a regular reverse, such as an altar with a figure of Hercules beside it.

Metapontum was founded about 710 B. C., by a Pelasgic colony from the north of Greece. The distinguishing symbol on its coins, whether gold or silver, is the full ear of corn, a grateful recognition of Ceres, for the fertility of their soil. Later coins bearing the ancient type, the ear of wheat along with a grasshopper, have a reverse consisting of a bearded figure typical of the river god, with a dolphin beneath, and when used in certain games, the inscription *ΑΧΕΛΟΙΟ ΑΘΛΟΝ*.

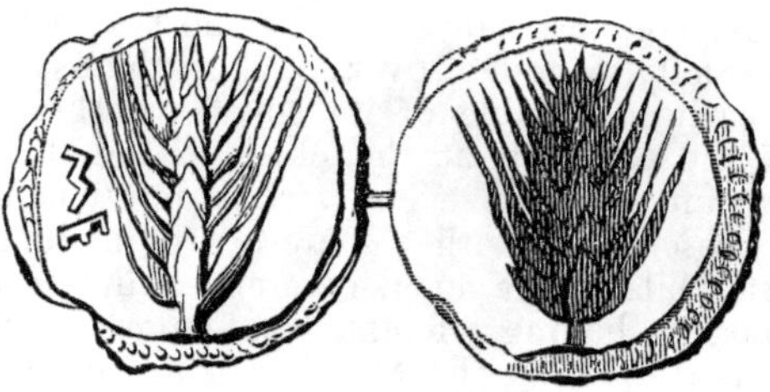

DIDRACHM OF METAPONTUM.

Tarentum lay at the southern extremity of the Italian Peninsula, and was founded by the Lacedemonians about 707 B. C. It was not subject to the Romans until it fell into their hands on the defeat of Pyrrhus in 272 B. C. For long after that change of fortune Tarentum retained its self-government and the use of the Greek language. It is said to have received its name from *Taras*, a son of Neptune, by whom it was founded. The coins of the earliest period have for design a youth kneeling on one knee and striking a lyre, with the inscription *Taras* written reversed so as to appear *ΣΑΡΑΤ*.*

The *first* or ruder period of its coinage extends from 707 B. C.–474 B. C. The *second* or more advanced extends from 474 B. C. down to its capture by the Romans, while the *third* covers its gradual decay under Roman rule. There are two great divisions of the coins of Tarentum ; on the first we have Taras on a dolphin on the obverse, and on the reverse a wheel, symbol of Apollo's tripod ; Taras on a dolphin, and on the reverse a female head encircled by a nimbus—Satyra the mother of Taras ; Taras on a dolphin incused or in bas relief on the one side, and in alto on the

DRACHM OF TARENTUM.

other. On the second, we have Taras on a dolphin, and on the reverse a man seated with a great diversity of objects beside him. These being chiefly the natural products of the locality, the man

*The coins whose inscriptions are so written are known as *Boustrephedon*.

is supposed to represent the People, and all these latter coins are assigned to the second period of Tarentum coinage.

The coinage of Tarentum is next to that of Syracuse in variety of designs, artistic excellence and extent of issues, the known varieties of the silver alone amounting to nearly a thousand.

Of all these colonies, however, the most famous was that of SYRACUSE in Sicily, founded by the Corinthians at a very early date. The earliest reliable of its coins are those issued by the oligarchy of the *Geomori* at the close of the 6th Century B. C. The tetradrachm we engrave was struck previous to the reign of Gelon, and presents us with the design of a quadriga or four-horse chariot, while on the reverse there is an incuse square divided into four quarters, having a female head—possibly that of Proserpine or Koras (Ceres) as the Syracusans called her—in the centre. On these ancient coins the "k" in Syrakosios is represented by the Punic Q.

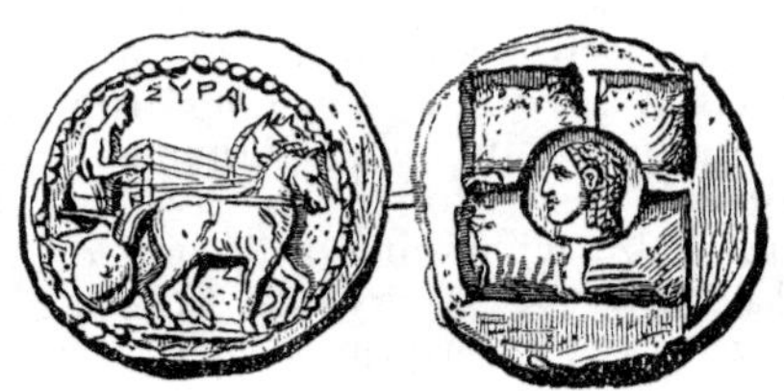

DIDRACHM OF SYRACUSE.

In 488 B. C., Gelon, a citizen of Gela, won the Olympic prize, and having been appointed General in Syracuse, became supreme in 485 B. C. His coins are distinguished by the abandonment of the incused stamp, and the surrounding the enclosed head with dolphins, rendering it the main feature. *Nike* or Victory is now seen crowning either the horses or the charioteer. In 480 B. C., Gelon gained a great naval victory over the Carthaginians. At the solicitation of his wife Demarete, he granted the vanquished more favorable terms than they expected, when they in gratitude presented her with one hundred talents of gold. This Gelon coined into the famous pieces known as *Demaretia*, from his wife's name, or *Pentekontalitra*, from their weight. The head, on the obverse, faces to the right, and is enclosed in a circle, outside of which are dolphins, while on the reverse there is a charioteer and quadriga, Nike crowning the horses, and in the exergue, a lion, possibly as the symbol of a victory in Africa.

In 478 B. C., Gelon was succeeded by his brother Hieron, whose coins have a sea serpent in the exergue in place of the lion, in allusion, it is thought, to his victory in 474 B. C. over the Etruscans,

DRACHM OF HIERON OF SYRACUSE.

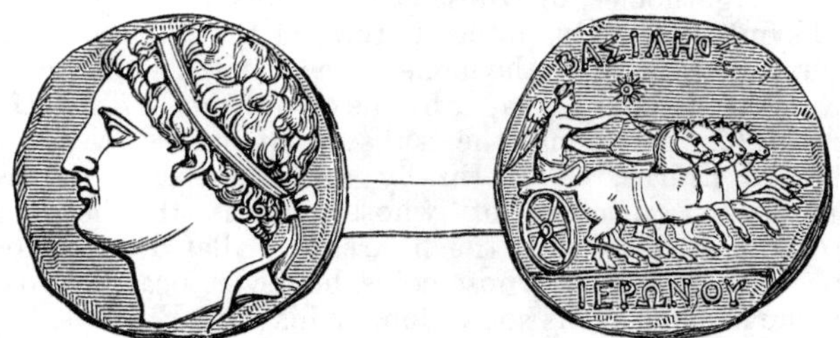

previously the acknowledged rulers of the sea. On the expulsion, in 466 B. C., of the Gelon dynasty, the Democracy was established, lasting until 412 B. C., during which time a number of tetradrachms were issued whose exergues are void of symbols, save one, which has a locust. To this period have been attributed copper coins, supposed to be the first issue in that metal, with a head resembling Hieron's on the obverse and a cuttlefish on the reverse. In 412 B. C. the Athenians besieged Syracuse. Their failure to capture it was marked by the issue of a small gold coinage, with the head of Pallas Athænæ. These coins show a great advance in the style of art. In place of *Συρακοσιον* the final syllable becomes *ων*; the horses in the quadriga are represented as in high action, while the names of the die engravers are signed to their work. In 406 B. C., supreme power was in the hands of Dionysios, who issued the finest specimens we have of the Syracusan coins.

SYRACUSAN TETRADRACHM OF DIONYSIOS, 406 B. C.

In 344, Timoleon was sent from Corinth and the Dionysians expelled, when a large issue of an electrum coinage, that is, of a mixture four-fifths gold and one-fifth silver, was made. These electrum coins resembled and passed for gold staters. On the obverse was the helmeted head of Pallas with *Syracusion*, and on the reverse, the Corinthian Pegasus. Timoleon issued a large sized copper coinage, on whose pieces, as restrikes, are often found the symbols of other colonies.

The Timoleon Democracy or Republic was overthrown in 317 B. C., by Agathocles, on whose earlier coins the triquetra or three-legged symbol of Sicily, similar to that on the coinage of the Isle of Man, first appears, while the name of the city is also found, replaced, however, on his later coinage, by his own name, *ΑΓΑΘΟΚΛΕΟΣ ΒΑΣΙΛΕΥΣ*. Among the subsequent rulers were Hiketas, Pyrrhus of Epirus, called in by the Syracusans to resist the Carthaginians, on many of whose coins is the head of Hercules on the obverse, with the figure of Pallas Promachos on the reverse, and Hieron II., whose coins, however, bear not so often his own name as that of his son Gelon, or his wife Philistis, known by the veiled head with the quadriga drawn by horses walking or galloping. On some coins of this period occur Roman numerals, showing thus early the influence of the Republic, a fact still more clearly shown by the word, *ΣΙΚΙΛΙΩΤΑΝ*, a bravado flung in the face of the rapidly extending control of Sicily by the Romans.

In 214 B. C., Syracuse was besieged by the Romans under Marcellus, and, despite the wonderful mechanical contrivances of Archimedes, was captured 212 B. C. Two years afterwards the whole of Sicily was declared a Roman Province, and the free States of Græcia Magna passed out of existence.

CHAPTER V.

ROME.

Rome was founded by Romulus in the year 753 B. C., and we have every reason to believe that so early as the year 715 B. C. its people were using a metallic currency. The famous copper mines of the Italian peninsula would furnish copper, while the Greek miners seem to have anticipated modern science by discovering such amalgams as rendered this metal suitable for a coinage. At first the Romans made the *Libra* or pound of twelve ounces their standard. A piece of copper of this weight was called an Æs or As, a term afterwards used to denote either the *value*—a pound weight, or the *metal*—bronze. In the time of Servius Tullius, 578 B. C., the As was a rectangular piece of metal, while he is said—though this is doubted—to have been the first to stamp these blocks with the images of domestic animals, a practice that has given us the word *pecunia* (from *pecus*, cattle), money. When these bars were of more than one *As* value, they were suitably stamped. About 395 B. C. the *As* which had hitherto been rectangular and passed by weight, became circular and passed by count. At the same time it was reduced in weight, a usual Roman expedient for meeting hard times. The devices also were changed, and the *As* was divided into the *Semis* or *Semi-As*—the half *As*, bearing generally the head of Jupiter, and stamped with the letter S, and on the reverse, the prow of a ship—common to all the pieces. The *Quincunx*, or five unciæ, with its five dots, unique as a *Roman*, but only scarce as an *Italian* issue. The *Triens*, or third, having generally the head of Minerva, but on the rev. *four* dots to denote the four ounce weight—the third of the twelve ounce pound. The *Quadrans*, having the head of Hercules and three dots to denote the one-fourth of the As. The *Sextans*, with the head of Mercury and two dots, to denote the one-sixth of the As; and the *Uncia*, or ounce, with Minerva's head and one dot, to denote the one-twelfth of the As,—whence the term *Uncial* is used as descriptive of the whole series. A similar division of the bronze money prevailed in the other Italian States, the devices being different.

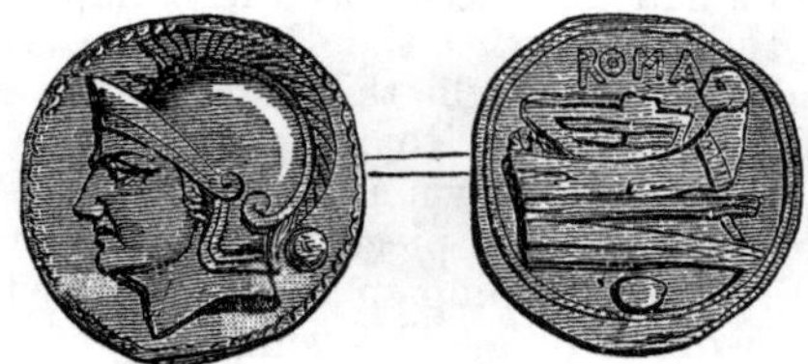

ROMAN UNCIA, OR ONE-TWELFTH OF THE AS.

The first reduction in weight of the As was caused by financial distress, the result of the capture of Rome by the Gauls, 390 B. C. Subsequently further reductions were made, so that at the date of the First Punic war, 264 B. C., the *As* weighed only one ounce, and the national currency was at a sad discount in the money market. In the time of Pompey, 50 B. C., the *As*, weighing about an ounce, resembled in size the pieces known as the First bronze. In the days of Augustus, 27 B. C., the Second bronze was known as the *dupondius* or two *As* piece, and the diminutive Third bronze as the *assarius*, the ancient name for the *As* itself. This copper coinage was adhered to by the Romans through all their history till the Western Empire fell to pieces, the last piece struck at the mint being similar in name and metal to the first.

As this copper coinage was the national money, all its issues were controlled by the Senate, whose authorization was shown by the presence of the letters S. C.—*Senatus Consulto*—by order of the Senate. Then, as now, of course, private individuals or families issued money, but, not bearing these letters, such pieces possessed no legal value, and depended for their circulation on their intrinsic value, or, like our tradesmen's tokens, on the credit of those who issued them. Very interesting collections may, however, be made of these, of which we will speak again.

While thus the copper coinage alone received the national sanction, gold and silver pieces were also used, the issuing of which became afterwards the prerogative of the Emperors.

The intercourse between Rome and those native Italian States in which silver coinages existed, would necessarily lead to the presence of silver money at Rome, yet it was not till the interval between the defeat of Pyrrhus and the engaging in its first Punic war, that Rome adopted a silver currency. In 278 B. C. was issued the *Denarius*—a silver coin equal in weight to the Greek drachm, and in value to ten *As*es, as is shown by its name—*den* or *decem æris;* on the obverse was the head of Pallas, with X, the numeral of value, behind it, and on the reverse generally a likeness of the Dioscuri* with the word *Roe* or *Roma* in the exergue. The *quinarius* or five *As* piece bears the numeral V, and the *sestertius*, or two-and-a-half *As* piece has the stamp SII. The sestertius is really the *semi-tertius*, the Romans describing two-and-a-half as two and half way to the third.

The first appearance of a Roman gold coinage was in the year 207 B. C., when what is known as the *Scrupular* coinage was issued.† The obverse of these pieces bears the head of Mars with the numeral of value according to size, while on the reverse is an eagle with the word ROMA. This simplicity of device, however, soon disappeared, and the name of the moneyer or mint master added to the word *Roma*, or the presence of the Dioscuri made way for some device connected with the moneyer's family—a change, doubtless, partly complimentary and partly precautionary against a debasing of the coinage. These coins were minted at Capua by Greek artists, and were the predecessors of the true Roman *Aureus*, or gold piece. This latter coin resembled the *Scrupulum* in appearance, and weighed about 130 grains, equal to our own five dollar gold piece, though it soon fell short of this weight. The issuing of these pieces was transferred by Constantine to Byzantium. The Eastern Emperors continued the issue, and under the name of Bezants or Byzants, these pieces circulated throughout Europe during all the dark ages, when no other gold coinage existed.

---

*The Dioscuri, Castor and Pollux, twin sons of Jupiter and Leda, were the earliest guardian deities of Rome, so that their figures repeatedly occur on Roman coins, each one generally standing beside a horse. On their removal from earth they were changed into the constellation *Gemini*, hence the star that is seen on their helmets.

†The *Scrupulum* was the one-twenty-fourth part of an ounce. The English Sovereign weighs a little over a quarter of an ounce, so that the *Scrupulum* was a coin worth about one-sixth of a Sovereign, or twenty Sesterces. This valuation is confirmed by our knowledge that in the reign of Augustus, the *Sestertius* was worth about eight farthings and a half, which, multiplied by twenty, gives forty-two pence and a half, or a little over one-sixth of an English Pound. If the Sovereign is worth $4.86 of our money, then the value of the *Scrupulum* would be exactly 61 cents.

The wonderful career of foreign conquest pursued by Rome, is apt to divert attention from the domestic difficulties that oftentimes imperilled her very existence. Among her great struggles must be mentioned, because of its bearing on Italian coinages, the Social or Marsian war of 90 B. C., when the leading Italic States combined to obtain from Rome political rights and powers, equal to those of her own citizens. The dreadful contest lasted for two years, involving the loss of 300,000 of the very flower of the population. Through the generalship of Marius, Sulla and others, it terminated in the triumph of Rome, but was followed by the bestowment, as a favor, of that "Roman Franchise" whose possession had been contended for as a right. During this struggle the allied States issued coins, chiefly silver Denarii, bearing a female head with the national *Italia* in place of the provincial *Roma* in the exergue, and on the reverse eight figures (supposed to represent the States) taking an oath over a sow; with below them the name Q(*uinto Pompædius*) S(*ilo*), the chief leader of the confederacy. Others have the Dioscuri, while on many there are figures of animals used symbolically.

The early coinages of the Republic at first bore simply some national symbol such as Roma, the head of Pallas, or the Dioscuri. After a time, names of individuals appear on the coins. Formerly these names were supposed to be those of the Consuls under whose administration the coins were issued, and the term *Consular* was employed to denote the whole class. The term is still indeed employed as a matter of convenience, though, as many names appear belonging to persons not of consular dignity, it is seen that such a reason for its use has no foundation in fact. It is probable, therefore, that, in some cases, these are the names of the moneyers at the date of issue; that in others they are the names of the persons, Families* or individuals, that had sent to the mint the metal to be coined for their own use; of local officers in some of the provinces, many of the pieces being provincials; while in yet other cases, the pieces may be like our own complimentary or political medals—struck off in connection with some particular incident.

This coinage may be roughly classified as consisting of pieces that bear a name only, without anything to inform us as to the individual, and of such as have, in addition, some significant symbol, or that refer to some well known incident in the history of the individual or family whose name appears on the coin. The First Triumvirate—Crassus, Pompey and J. Cæsar, 60 B. C.—placed their names on the coins they issued, while ten years later, on Cæsar's assumption of supreme power, the Senate placed his portrait there. On Cæsar's assassination, coins were issued bearing the names and

---

* The Roman *Familia*, or Family, was something like a tribe. Its members had a common surname and were supposed to be more or less related by blood.

portraits of Cassius and Brutus, the successful conspirators, and were soon followed by others issued by the second Triumvirate—Antony, Lepidus and Octavius.

GOLD COIN OF BRUTUS.

Brutus and Cassius both struck coins, on the murder of Cæsar; at least coins in silver and gold exist of the above device, and are now generally considered to be genuine.

CHAPTER VI.

Hitherto the distinctive feature of the Roman coinage had been its copper or bronze issues, and, despite the *silver* denarius or the *golden* aureus which in imperial times were freely issued, the *bronze* sestertius, or, as collectors call it, the first Brass, with its divisions, the second and third Brasses, were still the most distinctive features of the national mint. The historic value of the devices and inscriptions on these coins, with their not infrequent high artistic execution, have attracted to them the greatest attention. From such legends as *Ægypta capta, Judea capta, Rex Parthis datus, Rex Armen dat, Germania subacta, Armenia et Mesopotamia in potestatem R. R. redactœ,* we could almost prepare, as Addison has said, a State Gazette.

The Second Triumvirate soon broke up. After triumphing over their opponents, the confederates quarrelled among themselves. This ultimately settled into a contest between Octavius and Antony. Antony united his fortunes with those of Cleopatra, Queen of Egypt, perishing with her in her war with Rome, and thus left Octavius in sole possession of the Empire of the world.

Caius Octavius, grand nephew and adopted heir of Julius Cæsar, was born in 63 B. C. In 27 B. C. the Senate conferred on him that title of Augustus, or "Consecrated," by which he is now personally known. On the earliest sestertius he issued, we find the portrait of Julius Cæsar, with the inscription Divus Julius, while the reverse bore that of Augustus himself, with the legend *Divi Filius*—son of the God, with reference to his adoption by the deified Cæsar. By this politic act he connected himself with the fame of the great Julius, and sheltered the placing of his own portrait on the coin by the precedent of that of Cæsar's.

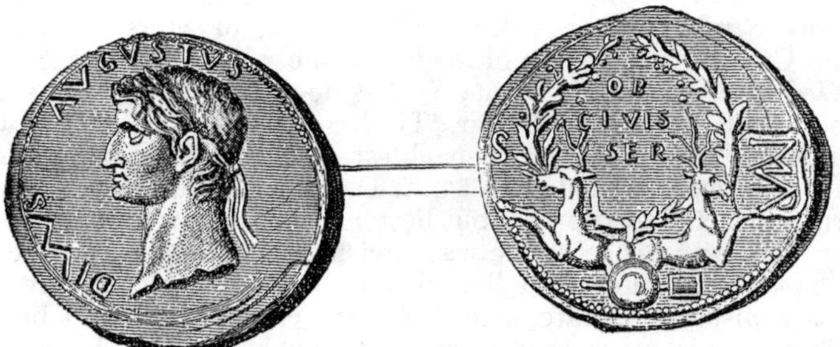

FIRST BRONZE OF AUGUSTUS.

On later issues the inscription is often simply *Divus Augustus*, with head, while the reverses are almost countless. As the inscriptions or legends on the Roman coins consist generally of the names and official titles of the rulers, we place in the Appendix full lists of all these.

Coins were frequently struck during an Emperor's reign bearing the portraits of members of his family, all of which are generally included in the series of the Emperor himself; thus, of Augustus we have coins of his wife, *Livia Drusilla*, who is always called *Julia Augusta* on Latin coins; of *Julia*, his profligate daughter; of *Agrippa*, his son-in-law, and of *Caius* and *Lucius*, his grandsons. After a career of wonderful prosperity, finding Rome, it is said, built of bricks, and leaving it of marble, and having so fostered art and literature that the *Augustan Age* has become a proverbial phrase, Augustus died 14 A. D., aged seventy-seven.

TIBERIUS *Claudius Nero*, son of Augustus' second wife, Livia, succeeded to the empire on his step-father's death. His career was so infamous for its vice and debauchery, that after his death (he was smothered, when 78 years old, by his successor) the Senate called in all the issue of the first bronze, which is, therefore, now

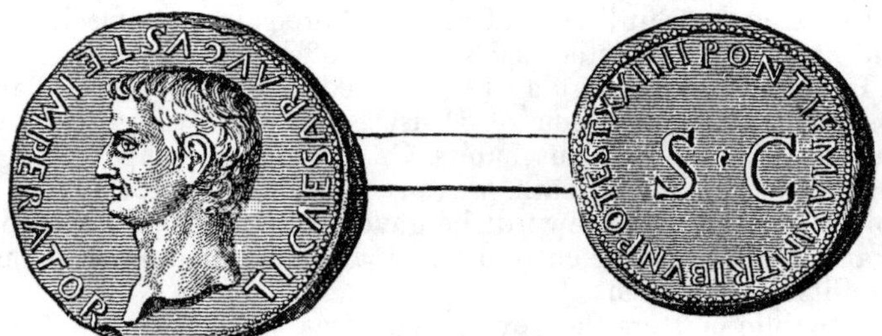

FIRST BRONZE OF TIBERIUS CLAUDIUS, BORN B. C. 42.

rather scarce, though the second and third bronzes are very plentiful. There are also coins of his son, Drusus *Junior*, on whose coins we always read DRUSUS CÆSAR; of the Emperor's brother, Drusus *Senior*, whose titles read DRUSUS, or more frequently, NERO CLAUDIUS DRUSUS; of *Antonia*, the wife of Drusus *Senior;* of *Germanicus*, son of Drusus *Senior*, described on coins as Germ. Cæsar, or Germanicus Cæsar, Ti Aug., and so on; of his wife, *Agrippina* Senior, and of their eldest children, *Nero* and *Drusus*.

Tiberius was succeeded in 37 A. D. by Caius, youngest son of Germanicus and Agrippina, but better known as CALIGULA. In the early period of his reign he was lavishly generous and merciful, but he soon far surpassed Tiberius in his crimes and infamy. In his case, also, the Senate, after his death, called in the first bronze, so that, as his reign was short, but few have come down to us. The one that we engrave has figures of the Emperor's three sisters on the reverse.

FIRST BRONZE OF CALIGULA.

The title *Imperator* as a surname, is found on Caligula's colonial coins.

It was this Emperor who wished that all the Roman people had but one neck that he might decapitate Rome at one blow. In his madness he stabled his favorite horse in the palace, fed it on gilded oats, made it a member of the college of priests, and raised it to the consulship! He afterwards proclaimed himself a god, and had temples erected and sacrifices offered to himself.

In 41 A. D., Caligula was succeeded by Tiberius Claudius Drusus, the youngest son of Drusus *Senior*. Owing to his delicate health and studious habits, CLAUDIUS had escaped Caligula's jealousy, but, on his death, was proclaimed Emperor by the Prætorian guards. The rewards he gave to these troops gave the first example of that fatal custom which afterwards subjected Rome to a military despotism.

In public matters the government was wholly in the hands of the Emperor's infamous wife, *Messalina*, and, on her execution, in those of her as profligate successor, *Agrippina*. During this reign the conquest of Britain was commenced and the great Claudian

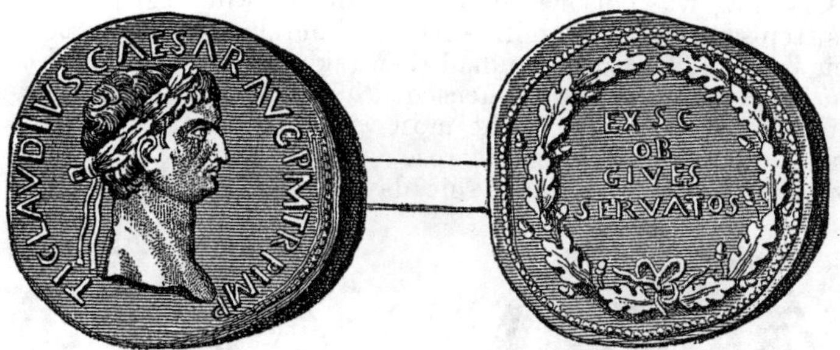

FIRST BRONZE OF TIBERIUS CLAUDIUS DRUSUS.

aqueduct, employing some 30,000 men for ten or twelve years, was pushed forward. On the latin coins of Claudius the legend reads, Ti. Claud. or Claudius Cæsar, with *Imperator* as a surname, while on the Colonials* this title is found only as a prenomen.

---

* The Roman *Colonia* had its origin in the settlement in some conquered country of troops whose military services were requited by grants of land. To encourage emigration into such localities and to attach the inhabitants to Rome, certain political privileges, such as Roman or Italian citizenship, were conferred upon them. The *Colony* means, therefore, the whole district, while the *Municipality* denotes its chief town. Money was issued sometimes in the name of the former, sometimes in that of the latter. The following is a complete list of these places, the Municipalities being in italic:

Abdera.
Acci.
Ælia Capitolina.
Agrigentum.
Agrippina.
Alexandrina.
Antioch (Pisidia.)
" (Syria.)
Aparmœa.
Arva.
Asta.
Asturica.
Babba.
Berytus.
Bilbilis.
Bostra.
Brundusiun.
Burthrotum.
Cabellio.
Cæsaraugusta.
Cæsarea (Libanus.)
Cæsarea (Judea.)
Calagurris.
Carrhæ.
Carteia.
Carthago Nova, Taragon.
Carthago Vetus.
Cascantium.
Cassandræa.
Celsa.
Clunia.
Cœla.
Comana.
Copia.
Corduba.
Corinthus.
Cremna.
Damascus.
Dortosa.
Deuthum.
Dim.
Ebora.
Edessa.
Emerita.
Emisa.
Emporia.
Emia.
Ercavica.
Gades.
Germe.
Graccuris.
Heliopolis.
Junium.
Ilercavonia.
Ilerda.
Ilici.
Italica.
Julia.
Laodicea.
Leptis.
Neapolis.
Nemausus.
Nisibi.
Norba.
Obulco.
Ocea.
Olba.
Osca.
Osicerda.
Pæstum.
Panormus.
Parada.
Parium.
Parlais.
Patra.
Patricia Corduba.
Pax Julia.
Pella.
Philippi.
Philippolis.
Ptolemais.
Rhesæna.
Romula.
Ruscino.
Saguntum.
Sebaste
Sidon.
Singara.
Sinope.
Stobi.
Tarraco.
Thessalonica.
Traducta.
Turiaso.
Tyana.
yrus.
Valentia.
Vienna.
Viminiacum.
Visontim.
Utica.

Claudius was poisoned in 54 A. D. by his wife, Agrippina, when his step-son, Lucius Domitius Nero, whom he had adopted as his heir in 50 A. D., and who had then taken the names of *Tiberius Claudius* NERO *Drusus*, succeeded him. In many respects, the reign of Nero was one of the most wretched that ever Rome endured. At last the legions rose in revolt, and after a reign of fourteen years Nero ended his days by suicide. With all his

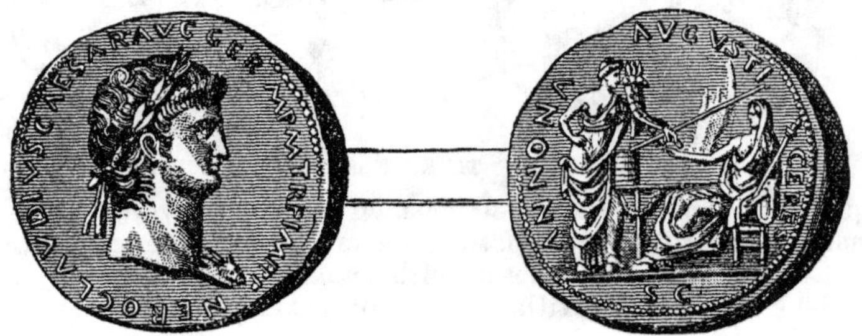

FIRST BRONZE OF TIBERIUS CLAUDIUS NERO DRUSUS.

baseness, Nero was a great lover of the fine arts, and the coinage of his reign is perhaps the best in the whole Roman series, the designs being interesting, the metal hard, and the devices well cut. One of the most interesting of his coins commemorates the great peace in the reign of Augustus, when, for the third time in Roman history, the Temple of Janus was shut. On this coin the Temple is represented with its door shut, the inscription being *Pace P. R. Terra Marique parta Janum clusit*—Peace prevailing on Land and Sea, the Roman People closed the Temple of Janus.

Nero's family coins are those of his wives *Octavia-Poppæa*, and her daughter *Claudia*, and *Messalina*, all colonials, and exceedingly rare.

Nero was succeeded in 68 A. D., by GALBA, a member of an ancient Roman family. Failing sufficiently to pay the Prætorians

FIRST BRONZE OF SERVIUS SULPICIUS GALBA.

for their services, these soon revolted, and a short reign of seven months was closed by the Emperor's murder as he was addressing the mutineers. His coins are very abundant.

The figure of *Roma*, in our illustration, is exceedingly bold and striking, and is probably the original of the figure of Britannia on English money, unless, indeed, we are to suppose a combination by the English mint-master of this coin and of that second brass of Hadrian's, which has on the reverse a female warrior seated on a rock, holding a spear, with a shield beside her, the word *Britannia* forming the legend round the field.

On the death of Galba, Marcus Salvius Otho, who claimed descent from the ancient Kings of Etruria, was proclaimed Emperor by the Italian troops. The German Legions, however, proclaimed their General, Aulus Vitellius, Emperor. Civil war ensued, when Otho, having received a crushing defeat, committed suicide after a reign of some ninety days. Of Otho, a few gold and silver coins exist, but as yet at least no bronze ones have been discovered.

Aulus Vitellius ascended the throne in 69 A. D. Devoid, as Emperor, of the energy and ability he had shown in a subordinate position, he gave himself up to the lowest and coarsest indulgences, and after a reign of eight months fell in a military revolt. His coins in Gold are rare, in Silver common, and in Bronze scarce. A few family coins exist, of his father, *Lucius Vitellius*, to whom the title of *Censor* is given—a fact unmentioned in history. The titles *Cæsar* and *Pater Patriæ* never occur on the coins of Vitellius.

Nero had appointed Titus Flavius Vespasianus to be commander of the troops fighting against the Jews. On the death of Otho, the Eastern legions, indignant that the Prætorians should have chosen a sovereign without consulting them, proclaimed Vespasian Emperor, an act concurred in by all the armies in the East, and, on the death of Vitellius, by Rome itself. Vespasian's reign lasted for ten years, and ended with his dying from natural

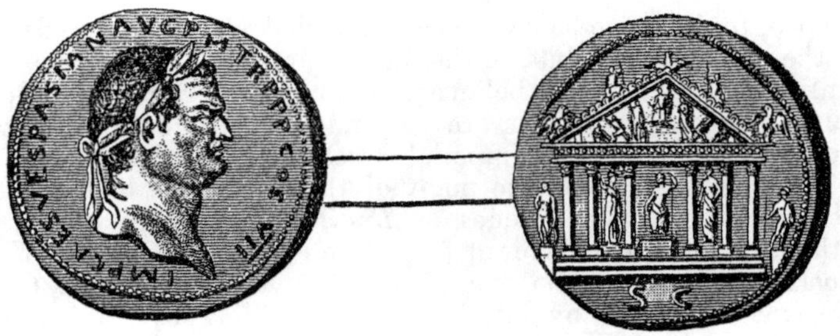

FIRST BRONZE OF JULIUS FLAVIUS VESPASIANUS.

causes, the first time since Augustus that a Roman Emperor had so died.

Vespasian's reign is chiefly famous for his wars with the Jews and the final overthrow of their power. This he commemorated by a very interesting and rather extensive series of coins, with reverses that are descriptive of the event. There are a few family coins of this reign, some of which are of the greatest rarity, such as of his wife *Flavia Domitilla*, who died before her husband became Emperor, and also of *Domitilla* their daughter, who died young. Those of *Titus* and *Domitian*, his two sons, are abundant.

On the death of Vespasian in 79 A. D., his eldest son, TITUS Flavius Sabinus Vespasianus, who had been associated with his father in the government in 71 A. D., was proclaimed Emperor. His early training and experience as a soldier qualified him for the chief command in Judea when his father was proclaimed Emperor. His successes, crowned by the capture and destruction of Jerusalem, 70 A. D., and the annihilation of the Jewish nation, were rewarded by a special triumph at Rome. An arch, which still survives, was erected in his honor, different incidents of his career being depicted on it. On many of his coins there are reverses like those of the *Judæa Capta* series of his father.

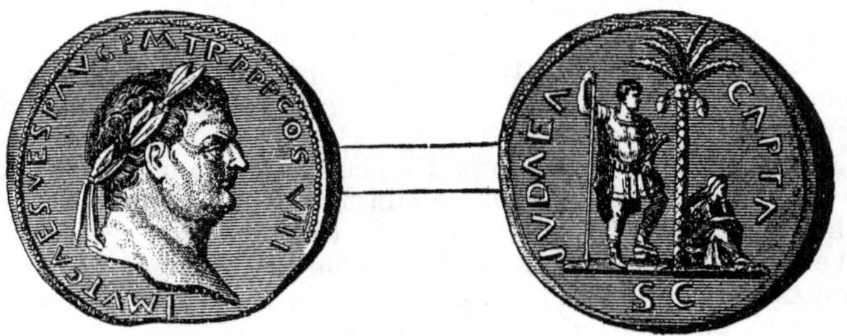

FIRST BRONZE OF TITUS FLAVIUS SABINUS VESPASIANUS.

Titus, for his great benevolence, was called "The love and delight of the human race," but, in the third year of his reign, died suddenly—poisoned, it was believed, by his younger brother, Domitian. The coins of Titus are very numerous, and in all metals, though the Colonial and Imperial Greek are somewhat rare.

Titus reissued in bronze many of the finer coins of his predecessors. These restored ones, or *Restituti*, as they are called, are rather rare, and much sought for. The legend of *T. Cæsar Vespa* proclaims the coin to be one of Titus'; but if it read *Ti. Cæsar Vesp.*, it is a reissue by Titus of a coin of *Tiberius*. A few coins of his daughter Julia, in all metals, have come down to us.

Titus was succeeded by his brother Titus Flavius Domitianus, the last of those commonly called the Twelve Cæsars, and in whom the Flavian and Cæsarian families ended. At first his reign promised to be a continuation of that of Titus, but, soured by great military losses in Germany, he vented his wrath at home, murdering or banishing almost every citizen of rank or standing. After a reign of sixteen years Domitian was assassinated by the sanction, if not order, of his wife Domitia, whom he had doomed to death.

The coins of Domitian are very common, and in the legend the name Domitian or its initial letter D, is always present; while Germ. or Germanicus frequently occurs in support of his fictitious German conquests, a fiction which he carried so far as to parody the *Judæa Capta* of Titus, by issuing some coins with the legend *Germania Capta* on them.

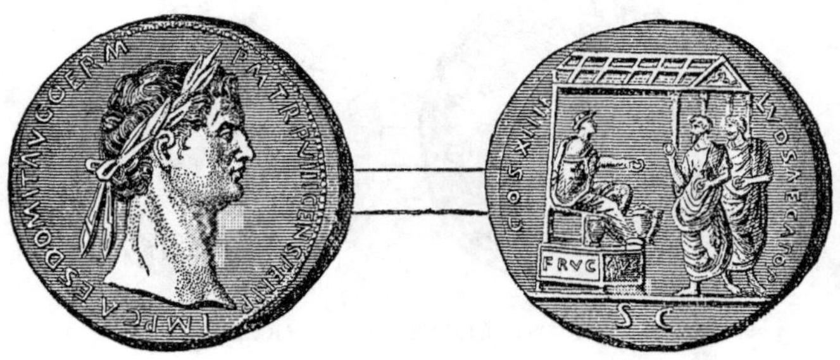

FIRST BRONZE OF TITUS FLAVIUS DOMITIANUS.

The reverse of our illustration records an incident of the Sæcular Games: the Emperor, seated on a throne whose pedestal bears the word Fruges—corn, is distributing bread in the form of ring-shaped loaves, to two citizens. Coins of his wife Domitia are very abundant.

CHAPTER VII.

In 96 A. D., Marcus Cocceius NERVA was chosen Emperor by the Senate, and during his short reign conducted public affairs with great wisdom and uprightness. Finding himself unable to keep the Prætorian Guards in check, he adopted Trajan, then commander of the German Legions, who became his successor in 98 A. D. On his accession, Nerva issued a coin or medal with the device of two hands joined and the legend *Concordia Exercitum*, a device that occurs on many of his coins with a great variety of details.

FIRST BRONZE OF NERVA.

Nerva's adopted son Marcus Ulpius Trajanitus Crinitus, a Spaniard by birth, become Emperor in 97 A. D. He personally led the legions that subdued Dacia, Armenia and Mesopotamia, adding those countries to the Roman territories. His foreign career was one of continuous conquest, and his domestic government one of benevolence and justice, contributing greatly to the improvement and beautifying of Rome. The many important events of Trajan's lengthened reign are recorded on his bronze coinage.

On the coins of Trajan a new title appears, *Optimus Princeps*, given to this Emperor by the Senate in acknowledgment of his virtuous character and equitable administration.

Trajan made a large reissue of the gold and silver coins of his predecessors, and though his own coins are very plentiful, the former are very scarce.

Trajan was succeeded in 117 A. D., by his adopted son and half cousin, Publius Ælius HADRIANUS, whose coin issues surpass in number, variety, and execution those of any other Emperor. Many perils threatened the Empire at this period, but by a judicious conciliating of some tribes and rigorous repressing of others he extricated Rome from her dangers, and received from the Senate the title of *Pater Patriæ.* To keep back the Picts who were pressing down on the Roman garrison in Britain, he built a great wall from the Solway to the Tyne, right across the whole country. In Turkey he founded what is still the second city of that Empire, and which continues to bear his name, while in many other localities abundant remains are found of the great energy of this distinguished ruler.

In 138 A. D., Hadrian adopted as his heir Titus Aurelius Fulvius Antoninus, a native of *Nemausus*, now *Nimes*, in Gaul, and who then assumed the names of T. Ælius Hadrianus Antoninus, and ascended the throne the same year. The private character of this monarch was worthy of all praise, while as a ruler he acted as the father of his people. "Happy the nation," it has been said, "that has no history," and the annals of Rome during the reign of A. are singularly free from the records of wars or revolts, and are occupied almost altogether with the accounts of domestic improvements. The title *Pius*, reminding us of Virgil's *Pius Æneas*, was conferred on Antoninus by the Senate because of his filial attachment to Hadrian.

FIRST BRONZE OF ANTONINUS.

When Hadrian adopted Antoninus as his successor, Antoninus adopted Marcus Aurius Verus as *his* heir. Hadrian, who had the highest estimate of the truthfulness of Verus, conferred on him the title of *Verissimus*, playing on his name *Verus.* In 101 A. D., Verus succeeded to the throne as Marcus Aurelius Antoninus, when his career, both in public and in private, proved him to be one of the most illustrious ornaments of our race. His coins are very numerous, and, from the fullness and variety of their legend, would almost enable us to construct a history of his reign.

Aurelius, having died at Vindebono, now Vienna, in 180 A D., was succeeded by his son Lucius Marcus Aurelius Commodus Antoninus, whose character and career were as infamous as his father's had been illustrious. In his fourteenth year Commodus received from the Senate the new title of *Princeps Juventutis*, and in his fifteenth was associated with his father in the government. The coins of this half monster, half madman, rank next to Trajan's for number, variety and beauty, and from their legends have been classified thus: those struck from the time when he was created Cæsar, 166 A. D., down to 180 A. D., and bearing the names of Lucius, Aurelius or Commodus; those struck between 180 A. D. and 191 A. D. having on them Marcus, Commodus, or Antoninus, and sometimes Marcus Aurelius Commodus Antoninus; and lastly, those struck between this period and his death, having the name Ælius added to the others.

FIRST BRONZE OF COMMODUS.

After a reign of twelve years, Commodus was strangled, and Publius Helvius PERTINAX raised to the throne. By attempting, however, to reform the military service, Pertinax incurred the enmity of the troops, and after a short reign of eighty-seven days was assassinated by a band of Prætorians. Owing to the short duration of his rule, the coins of Pertinax are very scarce. They bear the legend Imp. Cæs. P. Helv. Pert. Aug.

On the murder of Pertinax in 193 A. D., the army put up the throne for sale, when it was purchased by Marcus DIDIUS Severus JULIANUS. After, however, a reign of but sixty days, the Senate, alarmed by the approach to Rome of Lucius Septimius Severus, who claimed the throne and was supported by the legions of Gaul and Germany, ordered Julianus to be put to death, so that his coins are very scarce.

The purple was now conferred on CAIUS PESCENNIUS NIGER, commander of the army in the East, by the troops under him. The coins of this monarch are all colonials and of the highest degree of rarity. While the Asiatic Legions had proclaimed NIGER, Emperor, those of Britain proclaimed Decimus CLODIUS Septimius ALBINUS, and those of Gaul and Germany proclaimed SEVERUS. Severus promptly secured Rome and conciliated Clodius Albinus by making him *Cæsar*. He then marched against Niger and completely routed him in a battle on the banks of the Issus, 195 A. D. Turning then on Clodius, he finally defeated him at Lyons, 197

A. D., remaining thus, without a rival, in the possession of the throne. Coins of Clodius Albinus are exceedingly rare, those with Cæsar being alone considered Roman.

The career of Lucius Septimius SEVERUS was that of a soldier. He personally commanded the legions alike in their conflicts with the Parthians in Central Asia, and with the Picts and Scots or in the wilds of Britain. His coins are very numerous and record many notable events.

On the death of Severus at York in A. D. 211, his sons Marcus Aurelius Antoninus BASSIANUS, nick-named CARACALLA, and Publius Septimius GETA Cæsar conjointly occupied the throne. This joint sovereignty lasted for a year, when Caracalla murdered his brother. His subsequent career was one of frightful cruelty and vice, closing with his murder in 217 A. D., by a Prætorian.

The vacant throne was now occupied by Marcus Opelius Severus MACRINUS, by whose orders Caracalla had been assassinated, and who was proclaimed Emperor by the Prætorians. His reign was brief and unmarked by events of national importance. His coins are not common.

While Macrinus had been proclaimed Emperor at Rome, the Eastern legions had proclaimed their general Varius Avitus Bassianus, nephew of Julia Domna. In his youth this individual had become a priest of the Syro-Phœnician Sun-god El-gabal, whence his own popular name of ELAGABALUS. The rivals met at Antioch, when, Macrinus having been slain, Elagabalus became monarch, taking the names of Caracalla Marcus Aurelius Antoninus, claiming to be his son. His career was one of unspeakable debauchery, and lasted for less than four years, when he too fell by the Prætorians. His coins are moderately common and are often mistaken for those of Caracalla. A singular device on many of his coins is that of a conical-shaped stone ornamented with stars, or with stars in the field, the symbol of his deity El-gabal.

Elagabalus, having perished in a mutiny of his troops, was succeeded in 222 A. D. by his adopted son, known in history as SEVERUS ALEXANDER. Alexander paid great attention to the coinage, and the issues of his reign show that Rome had now reached the second stage of national life—that in which men, having ceased to do great deeds, erect memorials of qualities or principles that are no longer current in society. Personally one of the best of Roman Emperors, SEVERUS soon became hateful to the fierce Prætorians, and in a revolt headed by Maximinus, he and his mother, Julia Mamæa, perished, civil liberty at Rome perishing with them, the Empire changing into a military despotism.

Caius Julius Verus MAXIMINUS, who ascended the throne in 235 A. D., was by birth a Goth, and being a man more than eight feet in height, was possessed of immense physical strength. His reign lasted for but a couple of years ; his coins are pretty abundant, the legends on those issued at Rome being simply *Maximinus;* on the Latin colonials, Julius Maximinus; and on the Greek, Caius Jul Verus Maximinus.

Great anarchy now prevailed in the Roman Empire. Everywhere the legions elected their favorite general as Emperor, only after a few days or months possession of the titles, to replace the victim of their election by some other. The coins of such persons possess neither artistic nor historic merits, yet are much sought for because of their excessive rarity. We shall therefore simply mention the names of a few of the better known Emperors. The GORDIANS, father and son, both bearing the same legend, Imp. C. M. Ant. Gordianus Afr. Aug., and distinguishable only by the difference between the effigies, are much sought for. Coins exist of Decimus Cælius BALBINUS, and of Marcus Clodius PUPIENUS, both of whom were declared Emperors, and both perished within a year. Marcus Antonius Gordianus, commonly known as GORDIANUS III., ascended the throne in 238 A.D., as M. Ant. Gordianus, the absence of the *Africanus* from the legend sufficiently distinguishing his coins, which are very numerous, from those of his father or grandfather.

DENARIUS OF GORDIANUS III.

The legend on the reverse reads, *provincia mœsia superioris,* Col Vim An. IIII.

In 244 A. D., Gordianus was killed in a revolt and Marcus Julius PHILIPPUS, prefect of the Prætorians, ascended the throne. His reign lasted for five years. His coins and those of his wife, Marcia Otacilia Severa, are abundant. In 247 A. D., Philip associated with him in the government his eldest son, also Marcus Julius Philippus, whose coins are inscribed M. Jul. Philip Cæ.—M. Jul. Philippus nob. Cæs.—Imp. M. Jul. Philippus Aug. The coins of Caius Messius Quintus TRAJANUS DECIUS, who reigned in a military character 249–251 A. D., are very common and are inscribed Imp. C. M. Q. Trajanus Decius—Imp. Cæs. C. Mess. Q. Decius Traj. Aug.—while coins of his son Quintus Herennius Etruscus Messius Trajanus Decius, who had shared the throne with his father and perished with him, always bear the whole or part of his name, *Herennius.* Coins of his brother, Caius Valens Hostilianus Messius Quintus are scarce, his reign lasting but a few months. The coins of Caius Vilius Trebonianus Gallus, 251–254 A.D., are easily distinguished by their inscriptions, as are those of Volusianus. During the reign of Publius Licinius Valerianus, there were many issues of coins that are still abundant, while of his son, Publius Licinius Gallienus, and of his wife, Cornelia Salonina, we have also many, but most of them greatly debased. The reign of Gallienus was marked by a large number of restorations or memorial coins in honor of the early Emperors, inscribed *Divo Augusto, Divo Vespasiano, Divo Tito, Divo Nervæ, Divo Trajano, Hadriano, Pio,* (Antoninus Pius,) *Marco,* (Marcus Aurelius,) *Marco Antonino, Severo,* (Septimius Severus), *Alexandro,* (Severus Alexander), most of which have the word CONSECRATIO, to denote that these persons had been enrolled among the gods, on the reverse, and thus form what is known as the *Consecration* series.* These coins are made in billon, an alloy of a very little silver to a large amount of copper, largely used now-a-days in the coinage of Central Europe. The object of the alloy is to avoid the bulkiness of large copper coin, but it is easily counterfeited and soon acquires a dirty look and feel.

CONSECRATIO DENARIUS, OF MARINIANA, WIFE OF VALERIANUS AND MOTHER OF GALLIENUS.

GALLIENUS was succeeded by his son SALONINUS, of whom we have much billon or base silver money, but whose bronzes are very rare. On the murder of this monarch, the purple was assumed by Marcus Cassianus Latinius POSTUMUS, who issued many first bronzes, after which that coin disappeared from the Roman mintage. The reign of Postumus marks the commencement, 258 A. D., of that season of dreadful confusion and disorganization known as the period of the Thirty Tyrants. History has not preserved for us the names of all those persons, so we must take the figure as a round number.

* *Consecratio,* answering to the Greek Apotheosis, was the deification of an individual, and was frequently denoted by three different designs, a funeral pile, generally found on gold coins; an eagle or a peacock, generally found on silver or billon, and an altar with fire, generally found on brass.

BRONZE OF POSTUMUS, 258 A. D.

Of some of these, coins have come down to us, and of others so many counterfeits are in circulation, that the collector must exercise much care in dealing with them.

The Roman Empire was now apparently tumbling to pieces. The Huns swept across its provinces in the west; the Goths desolated Achaia, sacking Athens and Corinth; while the Persians, under Sapor, laid waste the Asiatic territory. The catastrophe was, however, delayed through the efforts of men like Marcus Aurelius Claudius, surnamed Gothicus from the great victory, 269 A.D. in which he drove back the Goths; of Lucius Claudius Domitius Aurelianus, one of the greatest of Roman Emperors, and to whom the title "Restorer of the Roman Empire" was given; of Marcus Aurelius Probus and of Marcus Aurelius Carus. When Caius Valerius Diocletianus ascended the throne, in 284 A. D., the danger seemed past. The consciousness that no one man could administer the affairs of so vast an Empire led Diocletian to divide the Government into *East*, which he kept in his own hands, and into *West*, which he assigned to Maximianus Herculius, whom he had assumed as colleague.

The floodgates of intrigue and revolt were now opened. A stream of civil dissension overspread the Empire till the strong hand of Flavius Galerius Valens Constantinus, son of Chlorus, adopted son of Maximianus Herculius, in 323 A. D., held the

BRONZE OF CONSTANTINE I., 323 A. D.

sceptre. Constantine I., or the Great, transferred the seat of Empire to *Byzantium*, which he named Constantinople, and declared Christianity to be the religion of the State. This change led to the presence of Christian symbols on the Imperial coinage. The coins of Constantine are exceedingly abundant, and distinguishable from those of his son Flavius Claudius Julius Constantinus, known as Constantine II., by the absence from them of the *Claudius*, always found on those of his son, on whose coins also appears the *labarum* or sacred banner, having on it the monogram of Christ.* In 361 A. D., Flavius Claudius JULIANUS I., known as Julian the Apostate, nephew of Constantine the Great, ascended the throne, and the Christian symbols disappear, to reappear, however, on the coinages of his successors.

In 395 A. D., Theodosius divided the Empire, bestowing Rome and the Western Provinces generally on his second son, HONORIUS. The coins of Honorius, whose capital was Ravenna, are not scarce, most of them having CONOB in the exergue. During this reign, the Roman authority was rapidly disappearing, Spain, Gaul and Pannonia, (the modern Austria), becoming occupied by invading German and Gothic tribes, driven from their homes by the Huns, some of these latter even crossing the Alps. At the head of his Visigoths, Alaric, who had previously swept Greece and plundered Athens, captured, in 410 A. D., Rome itself, when the Senate placed upon its throne PRISCUS ATTALUS, of whom a few coins remain. For fifty years after this, the history of Rome is but a record of court intrigues and conspiracies, of ecclesiastical dissensions, and of feeble and futile efforts to keep back the ever advancing power of the barbarians. Alaric and his Goths having shown the way to Rome, Attila and his Huns followed in 452 A. D., and a second capture of the city was averted only by the wise submissiveness of Pope Leo the 1st. In a few years, however, Genseric, King of the Vandals, who had crossed from Spain into Africa, recrossed the Mediterranean, captured Rome and so effectively destroyed its treasures as to lay a foundation for the word *Vandalism.*

Gaul, Britain, Spain, Northern Africa, the Mediterranean Islands, had now all been wrested from Rome and were being ruled or misruled by the fierce chiefs of fiercer tribes, when, in 475 A. D., ROMULUS AUGUSTUS, sneeringly called *Augustulus* by the people, who had been placed on the throne by his father Orestes, was deposed by Odoacer, King of the Heruli, and the Roman Western Empire ceased to exist.

THE GOTHIC KINGDOM.

With ODOACER, A. D. 476, begins the Gothic Kingdom of Italy, lasting for nearly a century. During this time we have the names of THEODORIC, who assumed the title of *King of Italy*, and ranks

*In the exergue of many coins, the word or letters *Cornob* may be found. As the name of the mint is generally on that part of the coin, these letters are supposed to stand for CO*nstantinopoli* R*omæ* N*ovæ* O*fficinæ* B : B being the Greek numeral for 2, denoting probably the second department or officer of the mint.

among the greatest of monarchs; of ATHALARICUS, 526 A. D., grandson of Theodoric, and of THEODOHATUS, 534 A. D., of whom we know very little. The coinages of these princes are known only by a few pieces of silver or third bronze, bearing simply the name of the monarch, and the title Rex. On the death of Theodohatus, the crown fell to WITIGES, who, after a brief career, was defeated and captured by Belisarius. With Baduela, or Baduila, his successor, 552 A. D., on whose coins, as on those of his predecessor, the head of Justinian appears, the Gothic Kingdom of Italy ended, and the Provinces of the West, emerging from their dependent condition, took form and shape as independent communities—the parents of the modern nations of Europe.

CHAPTER VIII.

THE EASTERN EMPIRE.

From the permanent division of the Roman Empire, on the death of Theodosius the Great in 395 A. D., is to be dated a new coin period. The symbols, devices and legends on the Roman Eastern coinage had hitherto been purely Heathen. But now Christian symbols,—such as the effigy of Christ, the Monogram, the Cross, the Virgin Mother, new titles, different letter characters, a different artistic style,—appear, to all of which the term *Byzantine* has been applied. This Byzantine period extended from the reign of Theodosius the Great, down to 1453 A. D., when Constantinople was captured by Mahommed the Second and the Eastern Empire swept away. The first section of this period extends down to ALEXIUS COMNENUS in 1081 A. D. Anastasius, (491 A. D.), greatly modified and improved the coinage, issuing in gold the *Solidus*, a modern name for the Roman *Aureus*, and worth about five dollars in gold, and the *Triens*, or the one-third of the Solidus, and in copper, pieces resembling the Roman Sestertius.

Dominus Noster ANASTASIUS, 490 A. D.

The As of the Roman Empire had gradually been debased in weight, till it was represented only by the third bronze. This again in the East had been brought down to the weight of ten grains, and known as the *noumia*, had yet become the standard of value. To the copper coinage of the East, the term *follis*, the name given by Dioclesian to a new piece he issued, was applied, stamped so as to declare how many *noumia* were contained in it. On these Byzantine coins, accordingly, we frequently find the whole field of the reverse covered by a large coarse letter, used as one of the Greek numerals, according to the following table :*

Units,	*Α*	*Β*	*Γ*	*Δ*	*Ε*	*Ϛ*	*Ζ*	*Η*	*Θ*
	1	2	3	4	5	6	7	8	9
Tens,	*Ι*	*Κ*	*Λ*	*Μ*	*Ν*	*Ξ*	*Ο*	*Π*	*Ϟ*
	10	20	30	40	50	60	70	80	90
Hundreds,	*Ρ*	*Σ*	*Τ*	*Υ*	*Φ*	*Χ*	*Ψ*	*Ω*	*ϡ*
	100	200	300	400	500	600	700	800	900

The letter M, therefore, is the numeral of value for forty, while K, also frequently met with, is that of ten—noumia. In the exergue, the letters CON, standing for Constantinople, frequently occur. By degrees Greek characters became employed, and were mixed up in a barbarous manner with Roman ones.

No history in the world presents us with such a record of crimes on the part of rulers and of sufferings on the part of people, as that of the Byzantine Empire. Ambition, intensified by religious fanaticism, led to a series of outrages against humanity that are without a parallel. While the Empire was thus torn by internal dissensions, it was little able to cope successfully with foreign assailants. In A.D. 636–641, the Caliph Omar, at the head of his Saracen hordes,

LEO III. WITH HIS SONS CONSTANTINE V., OR COPRONYMUS, AND LEO IV., 720 A. D.

* On Greek *regal* coins we frequently have the date expressed by combinations of the letters given above. There being, however, no universally recognized starting place, such as we have in the creation of the world, or the Birth of Christ, the dates denote the year of a certain epoch or period, according to the country and dynasty, such as the *Pontic* era, which dates from the accession of the Kings of Pontus and Bosphorus, and corresponds to our 301 B. C., the *Seleucidan* era dating from Seleucus, 312 B. C. Dates on the Ptolemy coins denote the year of the king's reign.

shattered the Asiatic power of the Empire, and commenced that series of attempts on Constantinople which was afterwards so successful. In 720 A.D., Leo III., a man of obscure birth, had become General of the Eastern Army. Having successfully conspired against Theodore III., whom he drove into a monastery, Leo ascended the throne and reigned for twenty-four years. From 857 to 867 A. D. the Byzantine sceptre was held by Michael III., son of Theophilus and Theodora. During the minority of her son,

MICHAEL AND HIS MOTHER THEODORA, 57 A. D.,
WITH BUST OF CHRIST.

Theodora had reigned, but on Michael's accession he consigned her to a convent, in which she died.

In 1081 A.D., Alexius Comnenus deposed Nicephorus. The reign of Alexius is memorable in Byzantine history, as it was the era in which those transactions began that led ultimately to the overthrow of the empire.

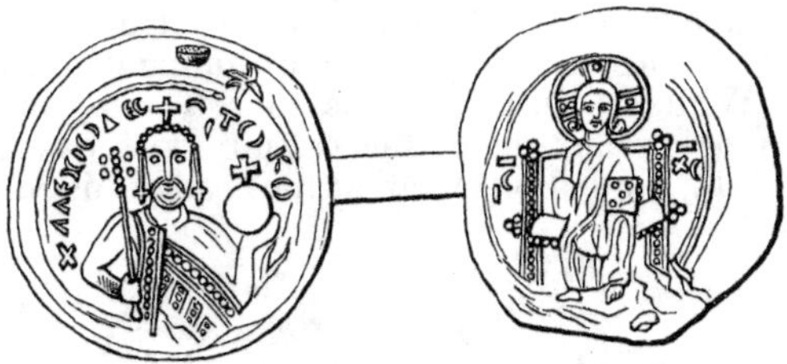

ALEXIUS COMNENUS, 1081 A. D., WITH FIGURE OF CHRIST. *

In 1081 A. D. came the Crusaders marching towards Jerusalem. Necessarily they took part in Byzantine politics, but did not at first meddle with the Empire. Soon, however, their hosts became mere mercenaries, and in 1203 A. D. assisted Alexius IV. in recovering the throne from his uncle, who had usurped it. Having thus learned their power, the Latin soldiers next year took

* Michael was afterwards murdered by Basilius I., whom he had associated with him in the empire.

possession of the throne themselves, and placing Baldwin, son of the Count of Flanders, on the throne of Constantinople, divided the territory among their four leading chiefs. The Byzantine court removed to Nicea and watched its opportunity. The varying fortunes of the Crusaders gave to the Byzantines an opportunity of recovering their capital. In 1207 A.D., Michael Palæologus, aided by the Genoese, recovered Constantinople, and the last chapter of Byzantine history began. The failure of the Crusaders to retain Jerusalem had been followed by a Turkish invasion of Europe. The hour of destiny, long delayed by the Western help given to the Byzantines, at last arrived. Offended by the insults offered to their Church, the Latin princes refused to help any longer. On May 29th, 1453 A. D., Constantine Palæologus being on the throne, Constantinople was captured by the Turks, and the last representative of the great Roman Empire passed away.

Mints of the Eastern Emperors.

Alexandria, - - - -	ΑΛΕ, ΑΛΕΞ, (St. Pierre.)
Antioch in Syria, (Theuopolis), -	ANT, THEVP, THEV.
Carthage, - - - - - -	CAR, KAR, KART.
Heracleia, - - - - -	H.
Catania, - - - - - -	CAT.
Tiberias, - - - - -	TIBERIAΔOC.
Constantinople, - - -	CON, CONS, CONST, KON.
Cyprus, - - - - - -	KVΠR.
Constantia in Cyprus, - -	KωN.
Cyzique, - - - - - -	CYZ, KYZ.
Cherson, - - - - - -	XEP, (St. Eugene.)
Milan, - - - - - - -	MD'PS.
Marseilles, - - - - -	MA.
Nicomedia, - - - - -	NIG, NIKO.
Nice, - - - - - -	ST. DEMETRIUS.
Ravenna, - - - - -	RA RAV RAVENNA.
Rome, - - - - - -	ROM ROMA.
Thessalonica, - - - -	TES, ΘEC.
Vienna, - - - - - -	VIENNA.
Sicily, - - - - - - -	SCL.

THE CRUSADERS.

The Crusades, planned with the view of securing to Christians the *right* of worshipping at the Holy Places in Palestine, soon became diverted into seeking the recovery of the whole territory from the Turks. As the Crusading armies began gradually to spread themselves throughout Syria and its adjacent districts, they established local sovereignties, in almost all of which money was struck. We have thus, coins of the Princes of Antioch, the series lasting from 1100 A. D., of the Counts of Edessa and of Tripoli, of the Kings of Jerusalem and of Cyprus, and of the Lords of Sidon and of Beyrout. To these may be added the coins of the western princes who assumed eastern titles, such as the Princes of Achaia, the Dukes of Athens, the Lords of Corfu, Ithaca, Cephalonia, and the like. On these coins there is generally some religious emblems, with the name of the place and of the prince in the legend on the reverse.

MODERN COINAGES.

CHAPTER IX.

FRANCE.

The coinages of modern Europe date from the break up of the Roman Empire, and especially from the setting up of a comparatively strong government in France. The conquests of the French monarchs soon included a large part of Europe. The great division of this territory that took place during the Carlovingian dynasty into the German Empire, Italy, and Spain, furnishes us with a natural order to be followed, the other European nations assuming importance at a date somewhat later. In treating, therefore, of modern coinages, we shall proceed, in the pages that follow, along the lines now indicated. Our readers, we trust, will keep ever in mind that our present custom of confining the devices and legends on coins* to the likeness, with name and titles of the sovereign, is of very recent origin, and is even yet not universal. During the Middle Ages a large part of European coin was medallic in its character, which, along with the frequent changes of territorial limits, has resulted in an endless variety of designs. In attempting any approach to system in our arrangement of modern coins, we must therefore adhere as closely as possible to historical lines.

While, then, the modern coinages of Europe commence on the overthrow of the Roman Empire, yet the numismatist will remember that there was a coinage in Gaul previous to that event. This native coinage was evidently suggested by the Staters of the Macedonian Philip, the coins of Northern Spain, and those of the Greek colony of Massilia or Marseilles. Roman influence, as resulting from commerce and war, was also felt and is shown. The metals employed were gold, silver, electrum, bronze and potin; the characters were Greek, Celtiberian, or Latin, and the designs

* The names of modern coins are much more varied than were those of antiquity. A few of these names are connected with the coins of former days; many are taken from the names of the issuers, as the *Edwards*, the *Williams*, the *Louis*, &c.; others from the locality or city; some from the devices they bear, while others are derived simply from their intrinsic value, or their proportion to the national standard.

were a blending of the mythology of the strangers with that of the natives.

In 510 A. D., Gaul was recognized by Anastasius as an independent kingdom under Childeric. The Franks (or *Freemen*, a name assumed by a confederation of German tribes), had not merely invaded Gaul, but had taken such instant and absolute possession of it, that the framework of society remained unbroken, and desolations like those of Italy were unknown. Among the great chieftains of that period were *Merovœus*, who had risen to such pre-eminence as to possess in 448 A. D. a national leadership which he transmitted to his children, thus founding the powerful *Merovingian* dynasty, whose representatives were Clovis, Childebert, Clotaire, Dagobert and others. During the continuance of this family several independent Royalties or Kingdoms were formed.

AQUITAINE, the South-eastern part of France, was, in 507, taken possession of by Clovis, and divided among his sons. In a few years all Aquitaine belonged to the kingdom of Austrasia. In 628 A. D., Dagobert was the sole possessor of all the lands that had belonged to the Merovingians. Two years after his accession, he gave one portion of these dominions to his half-brother Caribert. By a treaty in 630, Caribert gave to Dagobert certain estates, and thus arose the Merovingian Kingdom of Aquitaine, whose rulers were known as the Dukes of Gascony and Aquitaine, Counts of Fesenzac and Armagnac and the ancient Kings of Navarre. There are coins of all these rulers.

BURGUNDY.—The Kings of Burgundy were of the same race as the Ostrogoths in Italy and the Visigoths in Spain. Roman dignities at first were conferred upon them, so that they appear to have issued coins previous to 540 A. D., bearing the names and portraits of the Roman Emperors. Gradually, however, these were replaced by their own, and the powers of independent monarchs were thus quietly assumed.

NEUSTRIA, or western France, containing, therefore, Armorica or Brittany, became, about 574 A. D., an independent territory. Brittany had its local chiefs or Kings, down to about 830, when Louis Le Debonnaire succeeded in obtaining a nominal recognition. On the cession of Normandy to the Normans in 912, the name *Neustria* fell into disuse.

AUSTRASIA consisted of the Trans-Rhine portions of France, with the cities between the Rhine and the Meuse, Thuringia and Bavaria. In 546, Theodebert, grandson of Clovis, who had been reigning in Austrasia for about 20 years, abandoned the usual custom of placing the likenesses of the Roman Emperors on his coins, and placed there his own. It is said that this was done in retaliation against Justinian, who had assumed the surname of *Franciscus*, to indicate his sovereignty over the French. Before another century, however, Pepin V., son of Charles Martel, and founder of the *Carlovingian* dynasty, compelled Theodoric III. to appoint him Mayor of the Palace in each of the kingdoms of Neustria, Austrasia and Burgundy. The real power was thus in Pepin's hands In 752 A. D., Pepin's grandson, Pepin the Short, assumed the crown and was formally crowned king of the Franks. On Pepin's death, in 768 A. D., his sons Carloman and Charles, afterwards the Great, reigned jointly, the whole power falling to Charles on his brother's death. In 776, Charles was accepted by the Saxons as their sovereign. In 778 he successfully invaded Spain and in 800 A. D. was crowned at Rome by Leo III., as Carolus Augustus. This dynasty effected a great change in the coinage. *Silver* was used in place of *gold*, and devices national and christian replaced the names of moneyers. To bishops, monasteries and petty principalities was granted the right of issuing money, the church authorities using generally the device of a church building with the legend CHRISTIANA RELIGIO.

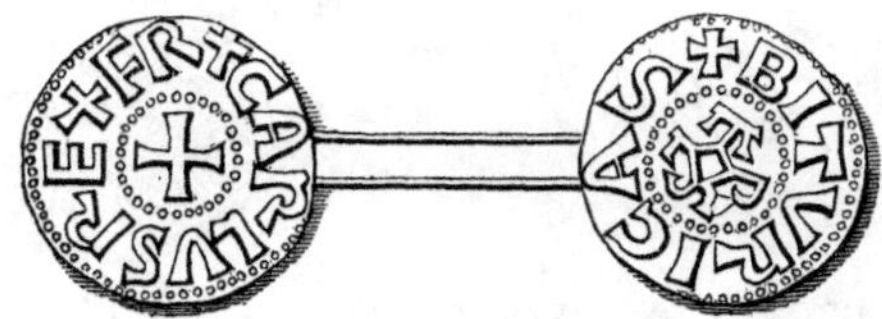

PENNY OF CHARLEMAGNE, ISSUED AT BITURIGAS, OR BOURGES.

The coins of Charlemagne bear simply a cross with the name CAROLUS REX, and on reverse, a cross with place of mintage. It is said that one of the Frankish customs on the election of a king, was to elevate him on a shield and to place in his hand, in place of a sceptre, a reed or lily in blossom. On some coins of these first two dynasties, therefore, the monarchs are represented with a *fleur de lis* in their hands, the flower that became eventually the armorial figure of France. The number of flowers on the shield was reduced by Charles VI. to *three*, a number since adhered to by the Bourbons. Charles died in 814 A. D., and was succeeded by his son, Louis I.—Le Debonnaire, 814–840 A. D. In 843 Louis gave to his eldest son, Lotharius I., the Imperial Crown, with Italy and the eastern French provinces; to his second son Louis the German, the German part of his dominions; and to Charles the Bald, who may be considered as the founder of the French dynasty, Neustria, Aquitaine and the Spanish mark or territory.

On the death of Louis V., in 987, Hugh Capet seized the throne and founded the third dynasty, surviving till 1328. During the early years of this *Capetian* line, the coinage remained unimproved, the barons issuing what they pleased. An immense amount of money was issued by the Abbey of St. Martin de Tour, giving rise to the *tournois*. Louis IX., (St. Louis,) 1250, A. D., made the *sou*, previously a coin of account, one of value ; the silver *sou*, worth about four silver pennies, he called the *gros*, while the *denier* was called the *little tournois*. He issued a few gold pieces, but made a free use of *billon* or black money in the form of the *Liard* or *Hardi*—ranking as three silver pennies, the *Maille* or half denier, and the *bourgeoise* or quarter.

In 1327, the House of Valois, a branch of the Capetian family, occupied the throne. The English armies now so overran the country, that Edward III. placed on his coins the title *King of France*. The gold pieces of Charles VII., with a crown on their reverses, introduced the silver *Ecu* or crown pieces into the coinage

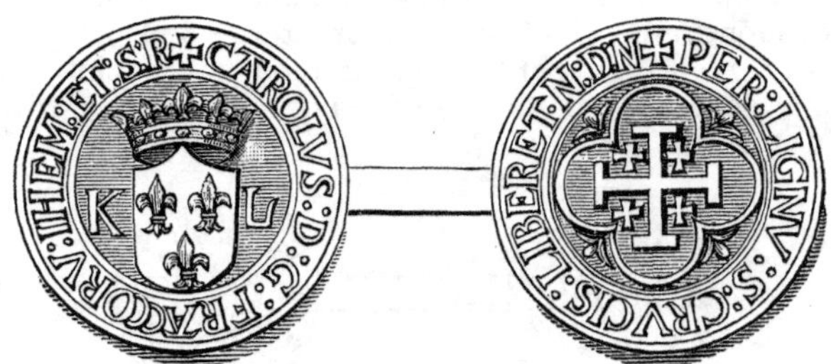

CROWN OF CHARLES VIII., A. D. 1483.

of Europe. The billon pieces bear the Arms of Anjou—three fleur de lis with SIT NOMEN D*omini* B*enedictum*, while the silver teston, (from TEST—proof or witness), or great head of Louis XII., (1498–1515), received its name from the king's portrait, identifying the coin as national money. Henry III. was assassinated in 1588, when Charles, Cardinal of Bourbon, was put forward as Charles X., by the League under the Duke of Guise. Coins of "The Pretender" were struck by the League for six years after his death. In 1593, however, Henry of Navarre, of the House of *Bourbon*, ascended the throne as Henry IV. of France. In

LOUIS D'OR OF LOUIS XV.

1614, on the coins of Louis XIII., who had been betrothed to Ann of Austria, daughter of Philip III., king of Spain, there appeared the legend CATALONIÆ PRINCEPS, the reverses sometimes showing six L's, so placed as to form a central triangle. The Louis d'or was issued in 1640, after which date no important change was made in the coinage until the Revolution of 1788.

CROWNS OF LOUIS XIV., 1643–1715 A. D., KING OF FRANCE AND NAVARRE, KING AND DUKE OF BEARN. (*The cow in the centre is the standard of Bearn.*)

In 1791 the coins bore the head of Louis XVI., with ROI DES FRANCAIS, and on the reverse Liberty writing the word CONSTITUTION on a tablet, with the year of Liberty below, or, a fasces and cap within branches, with LA NATION, LA LOI, LE ROI, with the year of our era. Some coins of 1793 have simply the tablet with REPUBLIQUE FRANCAIS and year of Liberty, and on reverse a wreath resting on a pair of scales, with LIBERTE, EGALITE. Others have Liberty with a Phrygian cap, with REPUBLIQUE FRANCAIS, and on reverse a wreath, with value. The money issued in France between 1791 and 1795 is called the *Constitutional* currency, be-

SIX LIVRES PIECE OF 1793.

cause issued under the Constitution proclaimed by Louis XVI. in 1791.

On the coins of Napoleon as Premier Consul or Emperor, there is his head with name and titles. After his fall in 1815, the head

CROWN OF LOUIS XVIII. DURING THE HUNDRED DAYS.

of Louis XVIII. is on the coins, with a crowned shield containing the arms of Anjou on the reverse. In 1831, on the acces-

REPUBLIC OF 1848. (HERCULES UNITING *Liberty* AND *Equality*.)

sion of Louis Philippe, the reverse bore simply the values, while in 1848 the Republican symbols again appear, to be replaced by the head of Napoleon as President of the Republic, and in 1852

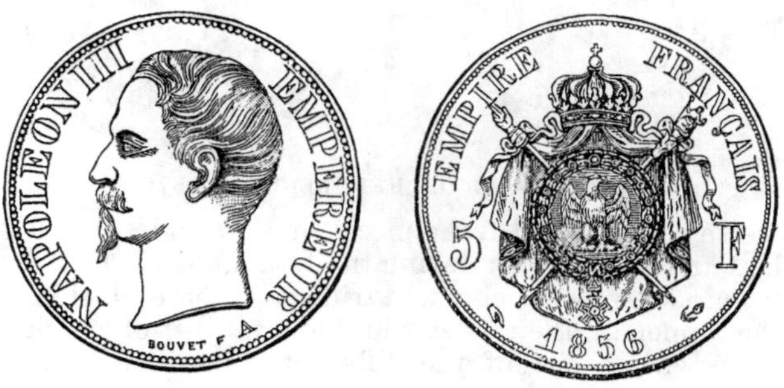

FIVE FRANC PIECE OF NAPOLEON III.

as Emperor.* On his overthrow, in 1870, the large head of Ceres was placed on the coins, with LIBERTE, EGALITE, FRATERNITE on

FIVE-FRANC PIECE OF 1871.

*A very valuable collection of coins was offered for sale in Paris, the other day, and among them was a five-franc piece with the effigy of Prince Louis Napoleon, president of the French Republic, and the date of 1851. The coin, much to the surprise of a bystander who was not in the secret, was run up to 113 francs. Curious to know why a coin which, from its recent date, could not, he imagined, be a rarity, fetched such a price, he asked the unsuccessful bidder why he had offered as much as 110 francs, and was met with the somewhat contemptuous reply, "Why, don't you see it is a piece with the lock of hair?" (*une piece a la meche.*) More and more puzzled he was obliged to ask for an explanation, and was told that one of the first decrees issued after the coup d'etat on the second of December, referred to the coining of new money, which was to be stamped with the effigy of the prince president. One of the five-franc pieces was brought to the Elysee for approval, but the late Emperor, having his attention taken by other things, forgot all about it for a few days. When he came to examine it, he noticed a lock of hair curled forward near the right temple, which displeased him, and he gave orders to have the mould altered. But, taking his silence for consent, the director of the mint had commenced the issue, and twenty-three five franc pieces could not be withdrawn from circulation. These are the coins which are now so highly prized by collectors.

TWO-FRANC OF REPUBLIC OF 1870.

the reverse*, as on the 5 franc pieces of 1797 and 1848. The letter A is the Paris mint mark: during the Commune of 1870, its mint's private markswere an anchor and trident one on each side of the A.

In the Appendix the reader will find a full list of the Sovereigns of France, with a list of the different coins issued by each of them.

The death of Charlemagne was followed by the existence, as semi-independent governments, of many feudal chiefs, each of whom was soon found issuing money in his own name. Of these our space allows us simply to mention a few. Within the kingdom of Neustria, for instance, lay the Dukedoms of France, Brittany, Normandy, Flanders and Champagne. There were Counts of Anjou, of Maine, Blois, Vendome, Artoise, Namur, Soissons, Valois, and others. The rulers, often bearing more than one title, issued money sometimes under one title and sometimes under another. The Principality of Sedan, founded in 1379, by Chas. V., became connected, in 1591, with the house of de La Tour D'Auvergne, when its coins tell of this union.

---

*It may interest our readers to have a list of the French mint marks :

A. Paris.
A. Q. Compeigne.
B. Rouen.
B. D. Bearn.
B. and an acorn—Boulogne.
C. St. Lo, near Caen.
D. Lyons.
E. Tours.
F. Angers.
G. Poitou.
G. and a lion—Geneva.
H. Rochelle.
I. Limoges.
K. Bordeaux.
L. L. Lille.
M. Toulouse. In 1803 V was added, but dropped in 1810.
M. with an inverted cup—Milan.
N. Montpellier.
O. St. Pourcain.
P. Dijon.
Q. Chalon sur Saone.
R. Villeneuve St. Andre les Avignon.
R. with crown and wolf—Rome.
R. and a fleur de lis—Londres in Gard.
S. Noyes.
T. St. Menehold.
V. Turin.
V. and an anchor—Venice.
X. Villefranche.
Y. Bourges.
Z. Dauphine.
&. Provence.
9. Rennes.
99. Nantes.
A.&M. Marseilles.
A. A. Metz.
B. B. Strasburg.
C. C. Besançon.
A. R. Arras.
Two Fish. Utrecht.

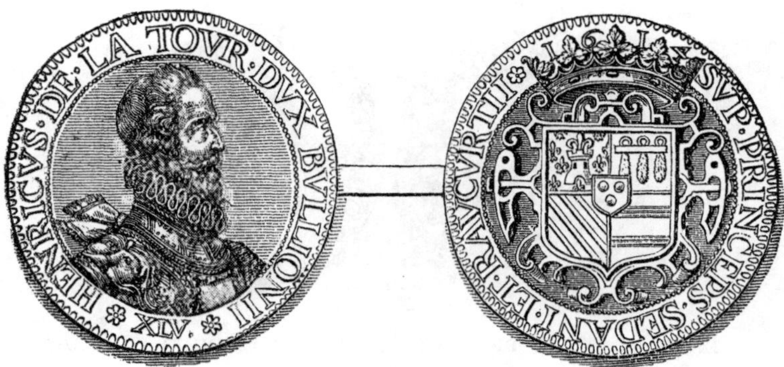

CROWN OF HENRY DE LA TOUR, VICOMTE TURRENNE, DUKE DE BOUILLON AND PRINCE OF SEDAN AND RAUCURT, 1614.

The Dukedom of Burgundy was founded in the Eleventh century, and terminated in 1477 A. D., when Maria, the last Duchess, married the Archduke Maximilian of Austria, carrying with her into that house her vast patrimony.

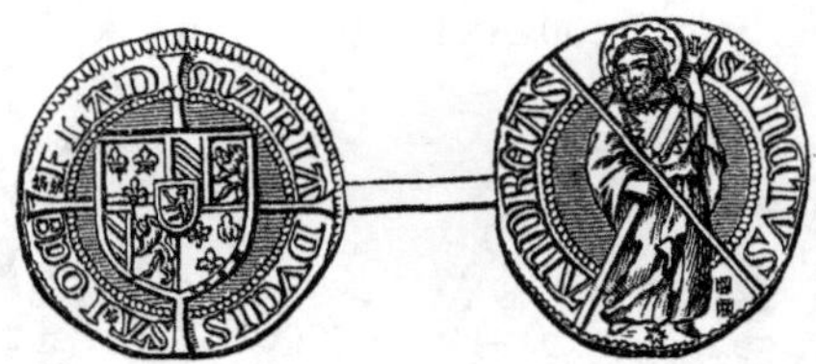

MARIA, DUCHESS OF BURGUNDY : *Rev.*, ST. ANDREW.

The Kingdom of Aquitaine embraced a large number of fiefs, among which was the famous Kingdom of Navarre, whose monarch Henry is better known as Henry IV. of France.

The Kingdom of Burgundy must be distinguished from the Duchy of the same name, this latter being a portion of Neustria. Among the celebrated territories of Burgundy were the County of Provence and the Principality of Orange. Within the County was Avignon, the seat of the Papacy from the year 1229 to 1348, though money was struck there, in the Pope's name, down to the year 1690.

The Seignory of *Dombes* formed part of Burgundy. At the commencement of the 14th century Dombes was acquired by the Duke of Bourbon. In 1560 it passed to the Duke of Montpensier, the sovereign line ending with the lady whose coin we engrave.

THALER OR FIVE SOL PIECE OF ANNA MARIA LOUISA, (MADEMOISELLE) PRINCESS OF DOMBES, 1673.

SWITZERLAND.

The present Switzerland was originally part of the dominions of the Kings of Burgundy. Under Charlemagne it formed part of his Empire, and in 1032 was given by Rudolph to the German Empire. As early as 1100 A. D. its bishops and semi-independent nobles and towns issued money. In 1315, under the lead of Uri and Unterwalden, the Forest Cantons threw off the German connection, and Schwyz, Uri, Unterwalden, Lucerne, Zurich, Glarus, Zug and Berne entered into a perpetual league, the foundation of the Swiss Confederation. In 1415 the league took Aargau, Thurgau and Ticino from Austria, adding these to the Con-

THALER OF THE MONASTERY OF ST. GALL, 1622.

CROWN OF ZURICH (CALLED TIGURUM BY THE ROMANS).

federacy. Freibourg and Soleure were next admitted. In 1510 Bazel, Schaffhausen and Appenzell were admitted. St. Gall,

MONEY OF THE CANTON OF ST. GALL.

Mullhausen and Bienne, and afterwards Geneva, Neufchatel, Valais

CROWN OF GENEVA.

and the Grisons were also admitted. In 1536 Berne wrested the Pays de Vaud from Savoy and became the leading State.

MONEY OF CANTON BERNE.

In 1798 these States were constituted by France into the *Helvetian Republic*, and the Cantonal issues being suppressed, coins

BASLE. HELVETIAN REPUBLIC.

were issued with the device of a soldier carrying a standard with legend, *Helvetische Republik.*

In 1815 the Confederacy was restored and the Cantonal issues resumed. In 1848 a general device was adopted of Liberty seated, with value and date on the reverse. Neufchatel, at first part of Burgundy, had been ceded in 1288 to the House of Chalons. In

FOUR FRANC OF LUCERNE.

1707 Frederick I. of Prussia, as representing that House, obtained the Duchy. In 1806 Napoleon bestowed it as a Grand Duchy on Berthier. In 1814 it was restored to Prussia, but in 1857 revolted, and while the title of Prince of Neufchatel is borne by the King of Prussia, the State now forms an integral part of the Swiss Confederation.

FIVE BATZEN OF AARGAU. TWENTY BATZEN LUCERNE.

CHAPTER X.

ITALY.

During the long interval between the reign of Honorius, 394 A. D., and the entrance of Victor Emmanuel into Rome in 1866, Italy was but a geographical expression. On the overthrow of that Gothic kingdom, 472–559 A. D., whose rulers had mainly made *Ravenna* their residence, JUSTINIAN conferred on Nares the title of *Exarch*, the term *Exarchate* being applied to the territory over which he ruled. The coinage of these Exarchs consists of a few pieces of small copper with the inscription FELIX RAVENNA.

Among the invaders of Italy were the Longobardi or Lombards, a tribe of the German people, and who had previously been masters of Pannonia. In 570 A. D., under their King Alboin, these took possession of Northern and Central Italy and soon reached an advanced degree of refinement. Their rulers sought to unite all the Italian tribes under one sceptre. This policy was hindered by the opposition of the papal power, aided by the Frankish kings, among whom was PEPIN, who had been anointed by Stephen II., Patriciate or Governor of Rome, and had thus, as well as from the dissensions among the Lombards themselves, a pretext for interfereing. In 773 A. D., Charlemagne crossed the Alps, and in the decisive battle of Pavia crushed the Lombard power. In 800 A. D. Charlemagne was crowned by the Pope as *Carolus Augustus*, Emperor of the Romans, when he issued a few silver coins with a rude bust, and on the reverse R. F., having previously issued from Milan, coins with a cross in place of the bust and on the reverse his monogram,—though before this date Pope Hadrian, 771-795 A. D., had already issued a silver penny on the model of the Roman Denarius.

On the division of the Roman Empire many petty sovereignties arose in Italy, and as among these there was no bond of union, the evils resulting became so intolerable that during the years 1856–66 State after State rose in revolt against their respective princes and connected themselves with Piedmont as ruled over by the House of Savoy. In 1866 Rome itself opened its gates, and Victor Emmanuel II. took possession as King of a United Italy.

We shall now describe the coins of some of the leading Italian States, as these existed previous to the late unification of that country.

SILVER FIVE LIRE OF VICTOR EMMANUEL II.

SAVOY.

In the year 1000 A. D., Rudolph of Burgundy bestowed Savoy and Maurienne on Berthold, making him Count of Savoy. The Bishops of Maurienne were already issuing money, but the earliest Savoy pieces are those of Humbert III., 1148 A. D. Other estates

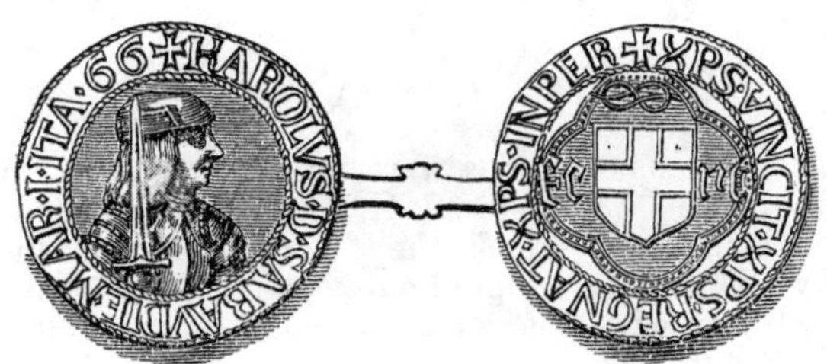

TESTON OF CHARLES I., DUKE OF SAVOY, 1470 A. D.

were gradually added, until, in 1417, the Principality of Piedmont was gained, and the family title became that of Duke of Savoy. In 1489 Charlotte of Lusignan, Queen of Cyprus, transferred all her crown rights to Charles, Duke of Savoy, whose descendants have since then claimed to be Kings of Cyprus and Jerusalem.

In 1713, Duke Victor Amadeus II. obtained Sicily, surrendering it, however, in 1720, to Austria, in exchange for Sardinia and the erection of his States into a kingdom.

In 1796 Savoy and Nice were annexed to France, while Piedmont was called the *Sub Alpine Republic.* On the fall of Napoleon, in 1814, Emmanuel IV. recovered his dominions, having Genoa added to them. The coins issued after this date will be found to have quartered on the shield, the Arms of Sardinia,

GOLD TWENTY LIRE OF CHARLES ALBERT.

Cypria and Jerusalem, Genoa and Savoy, with legend *Dux Sar, Janvae et Montisf. Princ. Ped. D.*

In 1860, Victor Emmanuel ceded Nice and Savoy to France, in exchange for the aid through which he ultimately became King of Italy, and now the coins for all the Peninsula bear his head with name and title.

MONACO.

With the coins of Savoy should be classed those of Monaco. To the Prince of this little territory Louis XIV. gave permission, in 1643, to issue gold and silver coin, and the next year these coins were current in France. Copper coins are still issued by its Prince.

GENOA.

Our earliest coins of Genoa were struck at Padua, in the Eleventh century. In 1138 Conrad II. conferred on the Genoese the right of a coinage, in which they were confirmed, in 1194, by Henry IV. They then adopted a device that is a speaking type a sort of gateway with the legend *Janva.* From 1339 the money

CROWN OF CONRAD II., KING OF THE ROMANS AND GOVERNOR OF THE GENOESE REPUBLIC, 1630.

bore the seal of the Republic. The name of Conrad is found on the coins of the Island of Chios, which had been ceded to the Genoese by the Emperor Michael Palæologus, and which remained a Republic till 1566. On the mediæval coins are religious figures and emblems, with the legend, DVX ET GVB REIP GENVA. In 1798 the Duchy of Genoa was constituted by Napoleon part of the *Ligurian Republic.* Coins were now issued, having the Goddess of Liberty crowned and seated, her arm resting on a shield bearing the arms of Genoa; on the reverse the fasces and cap between branches, and date.

NINETY-SIX LIRE OF GENOA.

In 1814 Genoa was given to Piedmont, retaining its liberty of issuing its own coinage, which bore the bust, with name and titles, of the Piedmontese King on the obverse, and on the reverse the crowned shield, with arms, with the legend, *Dux Sub Genvae et Montisf. Princ. Ped. &c.*

SILVER FIVE LIRE PIECES OF GENOA.

LOMBARDY.

The portion of Northern Italy, known as Lombardy, formed part of the territory assigned in 901 A. D. to the German Empire. A number of independent duchies, such as Mantua, Susa, Piedmont, and of free or republican cities, as Venice, Genoa, Milan, Pavia, soon arose, and, for a time a Lombard League maintained its independence. In 1540 Spain became master of the territory, but in 1706 was compelled to yield to Austria the portion lately known as Austrian-Lombardy. Coins were issued by the Austrian

COINS OF AUSTRIAN LOMBARDY.

Emperor under his titles of Duke of Burgundy and Count of Tyrol. In 1797 Napoleon proclaimed Lombardy to be a free State, under the name of the *Cisalpine Republic.* In 1805 it became Napoleon's Italian kingdom, issuing coins having Napoleon's head on the obverse, and on the reverse a French eagle,

TWO LIRE OF THE KINGDOM OF ITALY.

with a shield on its breast. On the lower values of these issues there is simply a large N, surmounted by the iron crown of Lombardy, said to be made out of the nails of the true cross, en-

TEN SOLDI OF THE KINGDOM OF ITALY.

closed in a wreath, and on the reverse the value and date with legend, *Napoleone Imperatore E. Re.* In 1814 Lombardy and Venice, hitherto governed by its own Doges, were given to Austria as the Lombardo-Venetian Kingdom, when coins were issued having the Austrian two-headed eagle surmounted by the imperial crown, those of low value having a ducal crown surmounted by the imperial one, with *Regno Lombardo Veneto*, and on reverse value and date.

In 1859 Lombardy was ceded to Piedmont, and since then its coinage has been the general one of Italy.

MILAN.

Milan was originally a Gallic city. Conquered by the Romans 222 B. C., it received the Roman franchise in 49 B. C. After 981 it was governed, in the names of the Emperors, by Dukes bearing the Roman name of the city—Mediolanum. Subsequently it came under the power of the Ghibellines, by whom it was made the master as well as capital of Lombardy. From 1545 to 1714, Milan was subject to France, Spain, or to Austria. In 1805, within its

CROWN OF THE DUKE OF MILAN AND MANTUA.

cathedral, Napoleon was crowned King of Italy, it being in succession the capital of the Cisalpine Republic, of the Italian Republic, and lastly of the Kingdom of Italy. In 1815 Milan was restored to Austria, but in 1859 was ceded to Piedmont.

On the coins of the Spanish monarchs the Milanese arms fill all the shield; on those of the Austrian they are frequently only on a shield of pretence.

VENICE.

The earliest inhabitants of Venetia were great traders, exchanging European products for those of the East. In 452 A. D. the Huns invaded the territory and drove the natives into those swamps on which Venice now stands. In 697 A. D., this settlement, already powerful through commerce and republican in government, gave to its chief magistrate the powers of a Dictator and the title of Doge or Dux—Duke.

PENNY OF DOGE ANDREAS DANDOLO, 1343 A. D.

In 829 A. D. the body of St. Mark was brought to Venice, which then placed itself under the Saint's protection. Venice soon became the mistress of the sea. In 1486 A. D., however, the Portuguese rounded the Cape of Good Hope and secured the Eastern trade, while maritime activity among the nations of Western Europe, consequent on the discovery of America, decided the downfall of Venice. On

DOGE FRANCISCO MORISINI, A. D. 1690.

the gold sequins and ducats or silver crowns of Venice there is generally a figure of the reigning Doge, and on the reverse some religious devices connected with St. Mark, or the national arms, a winged lion with or without a book, the ecclesiastical symbol of the Saint.

CROWN OF LUDOVICUS MANIN—THE LAST OF THE DOGES.

In 1797 Napoleon Buonaparte took possession of Venice and annexed it to Austria. In 1806, however, the territory of Venetia was joined to that of Napoleon's Kingdom of Italy, but on Napoleon's overthrow, in 1814, was transferred back to Austria, when it was joined to Lombardy as one of the Austrian crown lands. From this it was separated in 1859, remaining still subject to Austria, but in 1866 Venice was ceded to the present Italian Kingdom.

TUSCANY

May be regarded as the ancient *Etruria.* In the days of Charlemagne its chief city, Florence, was governed by a duke. In the Eleventh Century Florence was bequeathed to Pope Gregory VII. by the Countess Matilda,and soon became not only a free but a Republican city. In the beginning of the Thirteenth Century Florence, whose wealth and commercial influence throughout Europe was already unequalled, sided with the Guelphs, the friends of the Papacy, in their struggle against the Ghibellines, the friends of the Emperor. In 1252 Florence issued the famous golden *Florin*, weighing a drachm, having on the obverse a lily and the word *Florentia*, and on the reverse a figure of John the Baptist. In 1406 it became master of Pisa, long its great rival. At last, in 1528, Clement VII. formed a league with Charles V. of Germany, by which Florence was to become a Principality for the Pope's son, Alexander de Medici. In 1530, after a fearful seige, Florence fell, and was reduced to being simply the capital of the Grand Duchy of Tuscany.

MEDAL OF COSMO MEDICI, DUKE OF THE FLORENTINE REPUBLIC, 1569.

The singular device on the reverse of the above is copied from a piece of Augustus, whose faith in astrology had led him to issue a medal bearing the figure of Capricornus, the constellation of which the star of his destiny formed a part. By thus reproducing the device, Cosmo likened himself to Augustus, a comparison not inappropriate when the splendors and refinements of their respective administrations are considered. Since this loss of its independence,

LEOPOLD, OR TEN PAUL PIECE, AND HALF LEOPOLD OF TUSCANY.

the coins of Tuscany have generally borne on the obverse the bust, name and title of the sovereign, and on the reverse the Arms or a religious figure or design. In 1803 Tuscany was erected by Napoleon into a kingdom, under the name of Etruria, when the coinage bore a crowned shield with various inner shields bearing the arms of Spain and those of Anjou and Tuscany. In 1814 the Grand Duchy was restored to Ferdinand III., but in 1860, under the Garibaldian revolution, the State was annexed to Piedmont, the Provisional Government striking coins having on obverse a crowned shield bearing the Cross of Savoy, with Vittorio Emanuele Re Eletto, and on reverse value and date, with Governo Della Toscana.

LUCCA.

Lucca was a free republic so far back as 1370. Its early coinage bears a crowned shield enclosed by branches, with *Respublica Lucensis* and date, and on reverse St. Martin on horseback dividing his cloak with a beggar. In 1805 Napoleon erected Lucca into a Principality for his sister, in 1815 transferring it to Maria Lousia of Spain. Her son ceded it to Tuscany in 1847, and in 1860 it was annexed to Sardinia.

FIVE-FRANC PIECE OF LUCCA.

MODENA.

The city of this name is of great antiquity, being mentioned by Cicero and other Roman writers. In 960 A. D., to the House of Este was given the Marquisate of Modena, a title changed into a Dukedom in 1452 by the Emperor Frederick III. In 1796 it formed part of the Cisalpine Republic, but in 1814 was restored to the reigning family. In 1860 its inhabitants drove away their Ducal ruler, and joined themselves to Piedmont.

BOLOGNA

was founded by the ancient Etruscans, and is therefore an older city than Rome itself. In 189 B. C. the Romans made the city a Colony under the name of *Bononia*. Charlemagne made it a free city, and in 1112 Henry V. confirmed its independence. The success of the Guelphs—the Papal party—was fatal to the existence of the Bolognese Republic, which then became simply a city of the States of the Church. In 1796 Bologna was made the capital of the Cisalpine Republic, and in 1860, despite the opposition of the Vatican, it transferred itself to the rising power of Piedmont.

TWO PISTOLES OF BOLOGNA.

TEN PAULS OF BOLOGNA.

ROME.

The energy and perseverance of the early bishops of Rome in asserting the dignity and supremacy of their See, naturally led the citizens to regard them as their protectors. In 720 A. D., Pope Gregory III., having quarrelled with the Emperor Leo, declared Rome independent. Pepin and Charlemagne added to its terri-

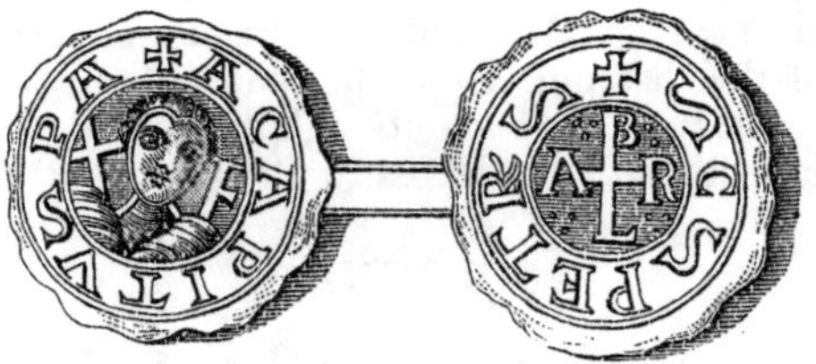

Coin of Agapitus, Pa*pa* (Pope) A. D., 946. (The monogram contains *Alberici*, the Pope's family name.)

tory. On the coins of this period we have generally on the one side, the legend Scvs (*Sanctus*) Petrus, and on the other side the name of the ruling Pope. This period lasted for nearly three centuries, during which additions were gradually made to the Papal territory. From 1100 to 1300 A. D., the coinage is that of the Roman people, having a figure of Peter, with ROMAN. PRINCIPE, and on reverse, SENAT. POPVL. Q. R. Sometimes the name of the civil governor is found, and on the reverse a female figure with ROMA CAPUT MUNDI. In 1470, Sextus IV. placed his profile likeness on the coins, an example since followed by his successors in the Papal See, down to the present day.

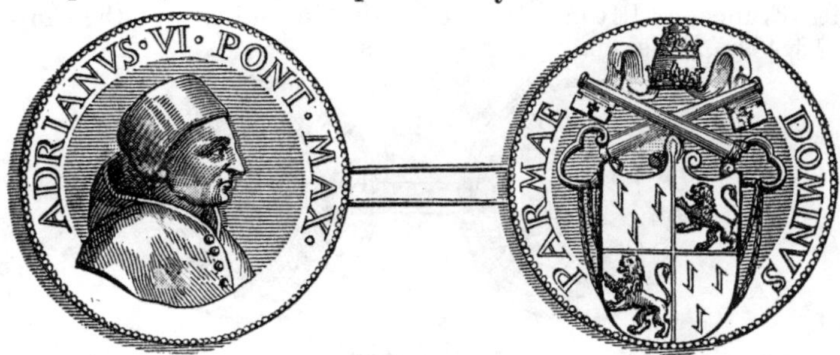

CROWN OF POPE ADRIAN VI., 1522 A. D.

The general device on Papal coins (those of the States of the Church) is a shield bearing the arms of the reigning Pope, surmounted by a tiara with insignia, and some religious or benevolent motto on the reverse. During the interregnum occasioned by the death of a Pope, the Cardinal Cammerling issues money which then always bears the legend SEDE VACANTE.

CROWN—SEDE VACANTE, 1667 A. D.

During all this period coins were issued by Episcopal authorities in various districts and also by many of the cities within the

Papal territory, but which still possessed a measure of municipal freedom—Mantua, Bologna, Ferrara, Aquileia and many others enjoying this liberty. The coins thus issued are of value and denomination like those of Rome, but bear the name of the issuing city.

In 1798, Napoleon formed the Papal States into the Roman Republic, issuing gold and silver crowns, and a copper coinage bearing the fasces and cap, with *Repubblica Romana*, and on the reverse the value within a wreath. In 1800, Pius VII. recovered his States and retained them till 1809, when they were incorporated with France, and Rome declared to be Second city of the Empire. In 1814 the Papal rule was re-established.

TWO LIRE, PIUS IX.

In 1848, Pius IX. fled to Gaeta, and the Second Republic, under Mazzini,was proclaimed, issuing a coinage--the 1 Bajocchi—(apparently *cast*) having *Bajocchi*, 1849, in 2 lines across the field, with 1, in a small wreath above it, and on the reverse the fasces and legend, while the 3 Bajocchi is remarkably fine—a large eagle enclosed in a wreath, and standing on the fasces with legend round Dio e Popolo, and on reverse 3 Bajocchi within a beaded circle, outside of which is Repubblica Romana, 1849.

In 1849 Pius was restored by the French troops, but in 1866 Rome set aside the temporal sovereignty of the Pope, and became the metropolis of the new kingdom of Italy.

NAPLES AND SICILY; or, THE KINGDOM OF THE TWO SICILIES.

After the overthrow of the Lombards, Arigisus II., Duke of Benevento and Salerno, sought to become independent of Charlemagne's authority. In 1077 Italy was invaded by the Normans, who formed the Kingdom of the Two Sicilies and the Dukedom of Calabria. Taking possession thus of Sicily, Salerno, Amalfi, Benevento, Capua, and all the Grecian and Arabian territories in Southern Italy, the Norman lords issued money on which they copied the Byzantine and Saracen devices—such as having on the obverse: Jesus Christ, the Conqueror of the

WORLD; and on the reverse: THERE IS BUT ONE GOD, AND HE IS ALONE WITHOUT A COMPANION.

The coins of Naples and Sicily thus constitute as many distinct series as there have been rulers. Commencing as early as the Ninth century then, we have the coins of the native Dukes;

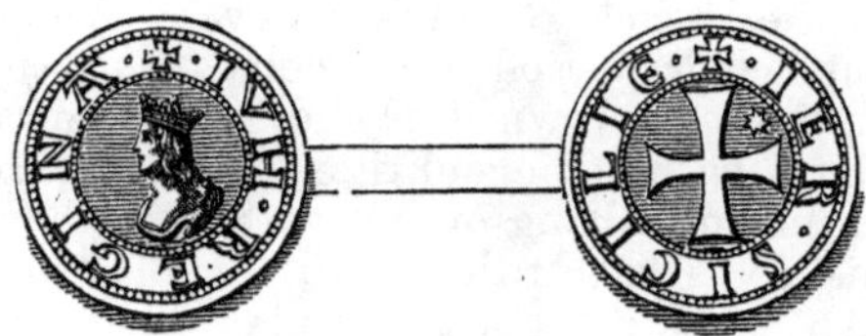

JOHANNA, QUEEN OF JERUSALEM AND SICILY, 1382 A. D.

then those of the Crusader Kings; then those of the Spanish rulers—House of Aragon,—the sons of that country always placing on their coins, through whatever line they came to the crown,

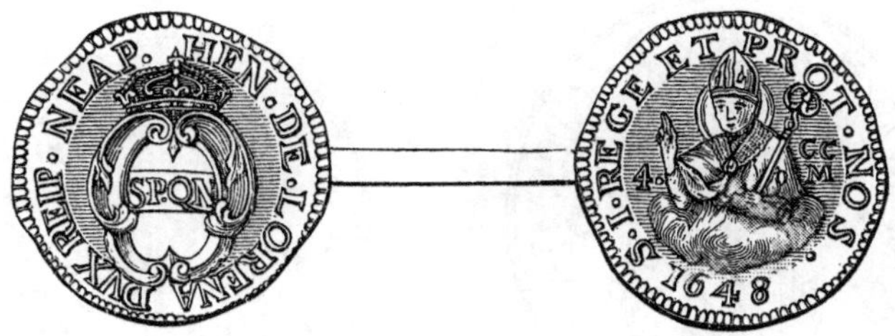

SILVER PIECE OF THE NEAPOLITAN REVOLUTIONISTS, UNDER HENRY OF LORRAINE, DUKE OF GUISE, 1648 A. D.

Hispaniarum Infans; then those of the German or Austrian rulers. From 1700 A. D. we have the coins of the Spanish Bourbon line, whose coins have either a bust or a crowned shield,

CARLIN OF CHARLES II. OF SPAIN, BUT V. OF NAPLES, 1692 A. D.

with D. G., HISP. NEAP. REX, or UTRIUSQUE SICILIÆ HIEROSOLYMÆ.

In 1713, Victor Amadæus II., of Savoy, became King of Sicily, but in 1718 exchanged the island for Sardinia, Sicily reverting to Charles VI. of Austria. In 1735, Charles VII., of Bourbon, became

King,—Sicily, thereafter, though politically separate from Naples, becoming a family appanage. In 1799, the French drove Ferdinand from Naples, which was declared to be the *Neapolitan* or *Parthenopian Republic.* The coinage now had the Goddess of Liberty with staff and cap, with the fasces and the legend *Republica Napolitana,* having on the reverse the value, and the year of the French Republic. Several changes took place during the Napoleonic period; the coins of *Joseph,* afterwards King of Spain, have a crowned shield with devices; those of *Murat* have a bust, with name and title. In 1814, Ferdinand was restored as Ferdinand I., King of the two Sicilies, having previously borne on his coins such titles as F. IV. of Naples, F. III., of Sicily, so that his titles are apt to perplex the student. In 1860, owing to the Garibaldian revolution, this monarchy was overthrown, and the Kingdom of the Two Sicilies annexed to Piedmont.

CROWNS OF FERDINAND IV.

DUCAT OF JOSEPH NAPOLEON, KING OF NAPLES, 1805-8.

CROWN OF FERDINAND, OF SICILY.

CHAPTER XI.

SPAIN.

Until the irruption of the Moors in 714, Spain existed as a compact and powerful kingdom, to which the Emperors of the East had conceded the privilege of a coinage. Hence its early gold triens. Of the coins of the Gotho-Iberian princes, a series exists coming down to the year 711, when the line terminated with Roderic, "the Last of the Goths," the Moorish power becoming masters of Spain. The coins of the Moorish rulers bear Cufic legends with the names of the monarchs or chiefs that issued them, from such places as Cordova, Saragossa, Seville, Toledo, Almeira, Valence, Granada and others. The Gothic natives, however, who had taken refuge in the mountains of Asturias and Leon, so stubbornly resisted the Moors, that about the year 1000 there existed the three Spanish monarchies of *Navarre*, *Aragon* and *Castile*, each issuing silver pennies, resembling those of the other countries of Europe. At last, in 1492, Ferdinand V. of Aragon, and his wife Isabella of Castile, took Granada, the last Moorish stronghold and became sovereigns of a United Spain.*

CROWN OF FERDINAND V., 1495 A. D.

Spanish coins consisted of the *gold* doubloon, its half, quarter or pistole, eighth or escudo, and sixteenth or gold dollar. Latterly the doubloon alone had been issued. The *silver* consisted of the dollar of twenty reals value, its half, quarter, eighth and sixteenth.

*Pope Alexander VI. conferred on Ferdinand, because of his fierce enmity against the Moors, the Jews and other opponents of the Holy See, the title of *Catholic*—one still borne by the monarchs of Spain.

Now we have the *dollar* and its half, the *peseta* of four reals, its half and the one real. Of the *real* there are three kinds: first, the Mexican, of which eight make a dollar; second, the real of new plate, (*de plata nueva*) of which ten make a dollar, and third, the *vellon*, used in Spain, of one hundred centimos, of which twenty make a dollar. The copper coinage consists of the two and the one *centos* of eight and four maravedi, (each worth three centimos) and the ochavos of two maravedis.

The Arms of United Spain consist of a lion rampant, the emblem of Leon, and of a castle, the emblem of Castile, on a shield or shields between two pillars, representing the pillars of Hercules, as Gibraltar and Ceuta were called. In 1513 Charles, Duke of Austria and of Burgundy, exercised sovereign power in Spain, his mother Johanna, queen regnant being insane, but her name always appearing along with his on the coinage.

DOUBLE REAL OF CHARLES AND JOHANNA, 1513 A. D.

In 1516 the thrones of Austria and Spain were united by Charles I., afterwards Charles V., Emperor of Germany. In

CROWN OR SEVILLE PIECE OF PHILIP V.

FOUR REALS, WITH THE ARMS OF ANJOU ON SHIELD OF PRETENCE.

1700 Charles II. died without issue, when the throne was claimed by Philip of Anjou, and by Charles, second son of Leopold of Austria. Philip stepped into occupancy,—the first of the Bourbons. Coins were now issued by the friends of Charles—now Charles III. of Austria, *the Pretender*, carrying the Austrian arms instead of the Spanish. Those of Philip have on the obverse a crowned shield, bearing the Spanish arms along with those of Anjou and legend PHILIPPUS V. D.G., and on reverse the Spanish arms, with HISPANIARUM REX. In 1808 Ferdinand VII. was proclaimed king, but the same year

CROWNS OF CHARLES IV., 1788–1808 A. D.

Napoleon bestowed the throne on his brother Joseph. From this date, down to 1812, we have coins of Joseph. During the same period,

CROWN OF JOSEPH NAPOLEON.

Pieces of Necessity were issued by Ferdinand. Ferdinand, restored in 1813, issued coins with his bust, name and date, having on the reverse a crowned shield with the arms of Spain and Anjou. The

CROWN OF FERDINAND VII, 1808–1833 A. D.

coins of Isabella II., 1834–68, are of the usual style—bust, name, title and date. During the Republic of 1870 the coins bore a fig-

TWO REALS OF ISABELLA II., 1833–1868 A. D.

FIVE PESETAS, OR DOLLAR OF THE REPUBLIC.

ure of Liberty reclining, with Espana for legend, and on the reverse the arms surmounted, not by a crown but a turret. Amadeus I., son of the King of Italy, succeeded, to be replaced, after an

FIVE PESETAS OF AMADEUS I.

interval, by the present monarch, Alonzo XII., son of the late Queen Isabella II.*

FIVE PESETAS OF ALONZO XII.

PORTUGAL.

About the year 1100, Alphonso VI., King of Castile, bestowed Portugal, as a dependent fief, on Henry of Burgundy. This dynasty possessed the throne for four hundred years—the most glorious period in Portuguese history.

---

*MONARCHS OF SPAIN FROM 1474 A. D.

Monarch	Year
Isabella of Castile, and Ferdinand V. of Aragon	1474
Johanna of Arragon, and Philip I, of Austria	1504
Charles I. of Castile and Arragon, afterwards the Emperor Charles V.	1516
Philip II., King of Castile, Arragon and Portugal	1556
Philip III., King of Castile, Arragon and Portugal	1598
Philip IV., King of Castile, Arragon and Portugal	1624
Charles II., King of Castile, Arragon and Portugal	1665
Philip V., of Anjou, King of Spain	1700
Louis, afterwards the second Philip V.	1724
Ferdinand VI	1746
Charles III	1759
Charles IV	1788
Ferdinand VII	1808
Joseph Napoleon	1808
Isabella II	1833
Amadeus I	1870
Alonzo XII	1874

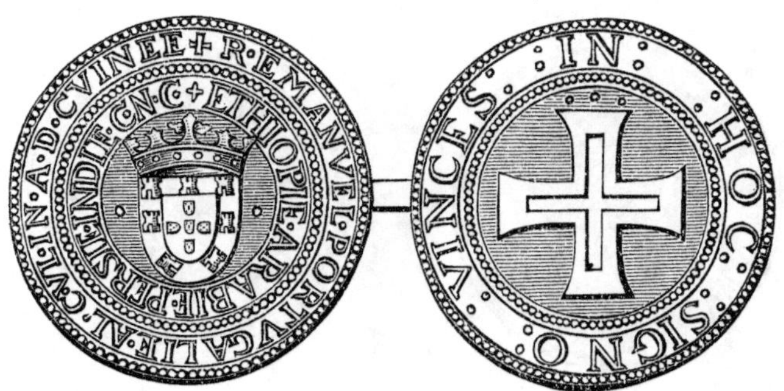

GOLD CRUSADO OF EMMANUEL, A. D. 1521—THE LEGEND READS: R*ex* EMANVEL PORTVGALIE AL*gaviorvm citra* VL*traque* IN A*frica* D*ominvs* CVINEE, ETHIOPIE, ARABIE, PERSIE, INDIE, *conqvistœ* N*avigationvm commercii.*

The last of the Burgundian family was Sebastian I., who perished in Africa in 1578. On his coins there is a crowned shield with the arms—five shields crosswise, bordered with seven castles—the arms of *Algarve*, with name and title, and on the reverse a large cross with IN HOC SIGNO VINCES. Philip II. of Spain now seized the throne, and for 60 years Portugal was subject to that country and involved in all its wars with the Netherlands. In 1640 the Portuguese revolted and placed the Duke of Braganza on

MOIDORE OF ALFONSUS VI., A. D. 1656.*

the throne, under the title of Joam (John) IV. The golden moidore, a four thousand rei or four dollar piece, was replaced in 1722 by the *joe* or piece of 12,800 reis.

*MONARCHS OF PORTUGAL.

Emanuel	1490	John V	1706
John III	1521	Joseph I	1750
Sebastian	1557	Don Pedro III	1777
Henry I	1578	Maria Frances Elizabeth	1786
Antony	1580	John VI	1816
Philip I., of Spain	1580	Maria II., of Braganza	1826
Philip II., of Spain	1598	Peter IV	1826
Philip III., of Spain	1621	Don Miguel	1828
John IV., of Braganza	1640	Maria II	1833
Alphonzo VI	1656	Louis I	
Don Pedro II	1683		

JOANNES V., A. D. 1706–1750.

In 1797 Queen Maria became imbecile, when her eldest son, John Maria, was appointed regent. In 1803 Joan substituted his own for his mother's name on the coinage, with the title of *P. Regens*, retaining this even after the queen's death in 1810.

JOAN MARIA, P. REGENS, A. D. 1808.

In 1807 John was defeated by Napoleon, and removed his whole court and capital to Rio Janeiro, in Brazil. In 1820, however, he returned to Lisbon, leaving his son Dom Pedro in charge. Brazil having shortly afterwards become independent, its name was taken off the Portuguese coinage.

500 REIS OF LOUIS I.

CHAPTER XII.

NETHERLANDS.

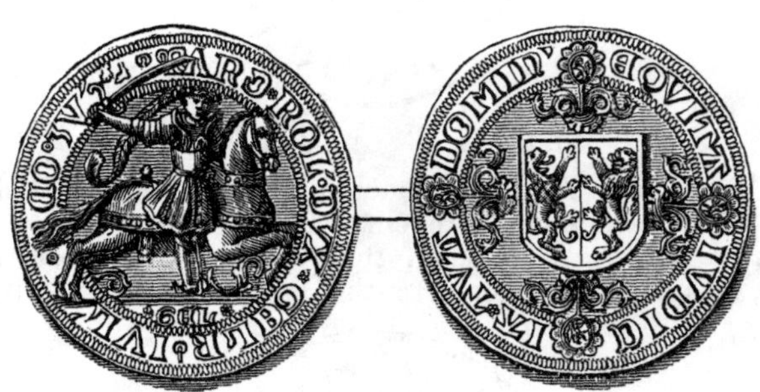

THALER OF CHARLES OF EGMOND, 1530.

The Belgæ were well known to the Roman armies. Toward the end of the Third century, the Franks, the Saxons and other tribes began to make inroads, so that by the Fifth century the Belgæ had disappeared. The Franks now held the soil, and Dagobert I., one of their princes, erected at *Utrecht*, a church which in 695 became a bishopric. Charlemagne's conquest of the territory led to the rise of a great number of petty Lordships or States, the chief being the Duchies of *Gueldres*, *Brabant*, *Luxemburg* and *Limburg*, the Marquisates of *Anvers* (Antwerp), the Counties of *Holland*, *Zealand*, *Zutphen*, *Flanders*, *Artois*, *Hainault* and *Namur*, and the Lordships of *Utrecht*, *Groningen*, *Overyssel*, *Friesland* and *Mechlin*, afterwards forming the provinces of the Netherlands. In 1384, the important county of Flanders, and with it the chief authority among the other States, passed to the Duke of Burgundy. In 1477, along with Burgundy, the Provinces passed to Austria. On the abdication of Charles V., in 1555, they passed to his son and successor on the Spanish throne, Philip II.

GOLD DUCAT OF THE BELGIC CONFEDERACY.

In that year came the revolt of *Holland*, *Zealand*, *Utrecht*, *Gueldresland*, *Overyssel*, *Groningen* and *Friesland* against Philip, ending in the independence of the United Provinces, with the Princes of Orange as hereditary Stadtholders, the other or Belgic Provinces remaining in connection with Spain. The coins from this period have generally on obverse, a man standing with drawn sword in one hand and arrows in the other, with date and legend, and on reverse a square tablet with legend.

THALERS OF THE NETHERLANDS.

In 1793 the French declared the Provinces to be the *Batavian Republic*, but in 1806 Napoleon made his brother Louis Napoleon, King of Holland, subsequently declaring the Kingdom to be a province of France. On the fall of Napoleon, the Northern and Southern Provinces were formed into the *Kingdom of the Netherlands*, to be divided in 1830, by the secession of Belgium, and its establishment as a separate kingdom.

CROWNS OF UTRECHT.

Holland or the Netherlands having had such a checquered history, its coinages are hopelessly complicated. Each province issued money in its own name of value and names sometimes like and sometimes unlike that of the other Provinces, while individual cities frequently struck money. Generally speaking, however, the name or crest of the issuing province is on the money, thus enabling us to identify its coins. On the earlier issues of *Utrecht* we find its Latinized name, CIVITAS TRAIECTEN, accompanied by various devices, while on those of last century we more frequently find STAD UTRECHT, and on reverse the crowned shield,

CROWN OF GUELDRES.

with or without lion supporters. On those of *Gueldres*, again, we have its arms, a crowned shield with two crowned lions rampant and fighting, with legend, IN DEO EST SPES NOSTRA, and on reverse, GELRIÆ. The arms of *Zealand* are a crowned shield with wavy

DOUBLE THALER AND SIX STIVERS OF ZEALAND.

lines to represent water, with a lion rampant rising from it, and

DOUBLE THALER AND SIX STIVERS OF WEST FRIESLAND.

the legend, LUCTOR ET EMERGO. The arms of *West Friesland* are a crowned shield with two lions running. *Holland* has a lion rampant within a circular fence with gateway, holding a liberty pole and hat.

TWO STIVERS OF HOLLAND.

During the short reign of Louis Napoleon, the coinage bore his head, name and title, with a crowned shield and date on the reverse. On the accession of William I., his head, name and title appear, the crowned shield on the reverse exhibiting the arms of the Kingdom, a crowned lion rampant, with sword and bundle of arrows.

TWO AND A HALF GULDEN OF WILLIAM III., NETHERLANDS.

BELGIUM.

On the division of the Belgian Provinces, at the revolt of the Netherlands, the southern or Celtic districts adhered to Spain. In 1598 Philip II. ceded these to Austria, when Belgium became

DUCAT OF BRABANT, 1584.

an independent kingdom. In 1621 it fell back into the hands of Spain, where it remained till 1713, when the peace of Utrecht terminated the war of the Spanish succession. It was then restored to Austria, and remained subject to her till 1797, when it was united to France. On the fall of Napoleon it was separated from France and joined to Holland to constitute the Kingdom of the Netherlands, only to separate in 1830 and become an independent monarchy under Leopold of Saxe Coburg, its present ruler.

The coinage of Belgium subsequent to 1598 is largely Austrian,

BRABANT. FLANDERS.

bearing the names and titles of the sovereigns, as Archdukes of Austria and Dukes of Burgundy, Lotharingia, Brabant, and Counts of Flanders. Toward the close of last century, while the bust, &c., was on the obverse, the reverse had simply AD USUM BELGII, AUSTR. In 1790, during a revolt against Austria, a gold and silver *Lion florin, half, and quarter* (known as the Lion series), were struck, having for their device a lion rampant, holding a sword or planting a liberty pole, with various Latin mottoes, such as AD USUM FŒDERATI BELGII.

SILVER LION OF BELGIUM.

No coins were issued by Belgium after its conquest by the French in 1794 till 1830, when the present series appeared with head and legend, LEOPOLD, PREMIER ROI DES BELGES, and on reverse, value and date within a wreath. On the copper coins a large ornamental L, surmounted by a crown, fills the obverse, and on the reverse a lion is seated holding a tablet with the inscription, CONSTITUTION BELGE, 1831, with legend, L'UNION FAIT LA FORCE. On the nickle pieces, of later date, the lion is rampant, without the tablets.

BELGIAN GOLD PIECE OF TWENTY-FIVE FRANCS.

LUXEMBURG.

About the Twelfth century, Luxemburg, an old German County, came into the hands of the Counts of Limburg, who then assumed the titles of Counts of L. Passing into the hands of Burgundy it became, in 1477, connected with Austria. In 1797 it was given to

France, and in 1814 raised to a Grand Duchy and given to Holland. In 1830 its territory was divided between Belgium and Holland, the title of Grand Duke of Luxemburg going to the King of Holland, while a separate coinage was still issued for the Duchy. On the obverse of these coins is the crowned shield, having a crowned lion rampant, called the Bohemian lion, from its *two tails*, the House of Luxemburg having given kings to Bohemia from 1310 to 1440 A. D.

CHAPTER XIII.

THE GERMAN EMPIRE.

By the treaty of Verdun in 843, Lothaire, son of Louis le Debonnaire, received all the eastern part of France, the Alps, and the French Rhine provinces and so formed the Kingdom of Lorraine. At the same time, all the German territories of Charlemagne, forming the Kingdom of Germany, were given to Louis the German. On the death of Lothaire, France took possession of Provence and Burgundy, while the remainder of his territory joined itself to the Kingdom of Germany, and thus laid the foundation of the first German Empire. In 953, Lorraine ceased to be a royalty, and became an Imperial province with two Duchies: *Moselle*, with the inner divisions of Lorraine, Luxemburg, the Palatinate of the Rhine, and the Bishoprics of Strasburg, Metz, Toul and Verdun, and *Lotharingia* or *Brabant*, with its divisions of Brabant Gueldres, and the Bishoprics of Cambrai, Liége and Cologne. At this time the Kingdom of Germany comprised Saxony, Thuringia, Suabia, Bavaria, Bohemia, Corinthia and Carniola. The rulers—spiritual and secular—in these two kingdoms being the Electors of the Empire.

On the death of Louis IV., in 912, the Electors of the Empire assembled at Worms, chose Conrad, Duke of Saxony, Franconia, and Hesse, to be Emperor. In his family the crown remained down to the death of Frederick Barbarossa, in 1190 A. D. After the election of Conrad, money was struck freely in all the States and principalities, the Emperors seeming to possess no right of issuing money except for their own domains. The name of a German Emperor, therefore, appearing on a coin issued by another prince, is simply to be regarded in the light of a date, or as a symbol of membership in that aristocratic confederation called the German Empire.

The German Empire continued as a bond of union among the sovereigns and princes of Central Europe until the wars of Napoleon. The frequent redistributions then of European territory enriched some of the members of the Empire at the cost of others, while the *Confederation of the Rhine* so weakened the Empire that at last it was formally dissolved in 1806. In 1814, however, it was reorganized by the Congress of Vienna, but died from natural causes in 1848.

THE SECOND GERMAN EMPIRE.

The great successes of Prussia in her war with France, in 1870, led to the occupation of Paris by the German armies. When in Paris, in April, the assembled princes and generals proclaimed the revival of the Empire, placing its crown on the head of Frederick William of Prussia. The Empire then formed has led to an extensive surrender of sovereign rights by States previously exercising them. Among other results, there is now but one coinage for all those petty States and Principalities that lie in Central Europe all having been merged in one great Empire.

In arranging the coin issues of the several States of the German Empire, it will be found impossible to form any such systematic series as is possible with those of some other countries. Territories changed masters, boundaries altered, titles appeared and disappeared so rapidly, that no one can keep the coins of different States from intermingling. Some knowledge of heraldry and of history will be needed in arranging these pieces, for on many of them the student will find on the one side simply certain initials, and on the other, perhaps, a coat of arms unlike, through the number of its quarterings, anything he ever saw before. On studying the devices in detail, however, he may have the satisfaction of tracing the coin to its issue.*

---

* List of the German Emperors, with the date of their accessions.

	A. D.
Adolphus, of Nassau	1292
Albert I., of Hapsburg	1298
............II., of Austria	1438
Alphonso X., King of Castile	1257
Arnulph	887
Charlemagne	800
Charles II.	875
Charles III	880
Charles IV., of Luxemburg	1347
Charles V	1519
Charles VI	1711
Charles VII., of Bavaria	1742
Conrad I	911
Conrad II	1024
Conrad III, of Hohenstauffen	1138
Conrad IV	1237
Ferdinand I	1558
Ferdinand II	1619
Ferdinand III	1637
Ferdinand I	1835
Francis I., of Lorraine	1745
Francis I., Emperor of Austria	1804
Francis II	1792
Frederick I., of Barbarossa	1152
Frederick II	1212
Frederick III	1300
Frederick IV	1440
Frederick William, of Prussia	1870
Henry I	918
Henry II	1002
Henry III	1039
Henry IV	1056
Henry V	1106
Henry VI., King of the Romans	1191
Henry VII., of Thuringia	1266
Henry VII., of Luxemburg	1308
Joseph I	1705
Joseph II	1765
Jossus, of Luxemburg	1410
Leopold I	1658
Leopold II	1790
Lothaire I	840
Lothaire II., Duke of Saxony	1125
Louis I., Le Debonnaire	814
Louis II	855
Louis III	899
Louis IV., of Bavaria	1314
Maria Theresa	1740
Matthias	1612
Maximilian I	1493
Maximilian II	1564
Otho I	911
Otho II	936
Otho III	973
Otho IV	983
Otho V., of Saxony	1208
Philip, Lord of Tuscany	1198
Robertus	1400
Rodolph I., of Hapsburg	1293
Rodolph II	1576
Rupert	1293
Sigismund, of Luxemburg	1410
Wenceslos, of Luxemburg	1378
William, of Holland	1250

SILVER MARK OF THE SECOND GERMAN EMPIRE.

PRUSSIA.

The inhabitants of the modern Prussia first appear in history about the Tenth Century, and were then known as the *Borussi.* From the Eleventh Century, the Prussians were subject to the Dukes of Poland until the Twelfth, when they secured their independence. About the Thirteenth Century, the Teutonic Knights attempted the conversion of the Borussi to Christianity, and after fifty years fighting had well nigh them all killed off, replacing them by German colonists. In the Fifteenth Century, Sigismund, King of Poland, took West Prussia from the Knights, while East Prussia was formed into a Duchy to be subject to Albert of Brandenburg, who had become Grand Master of the Order.*

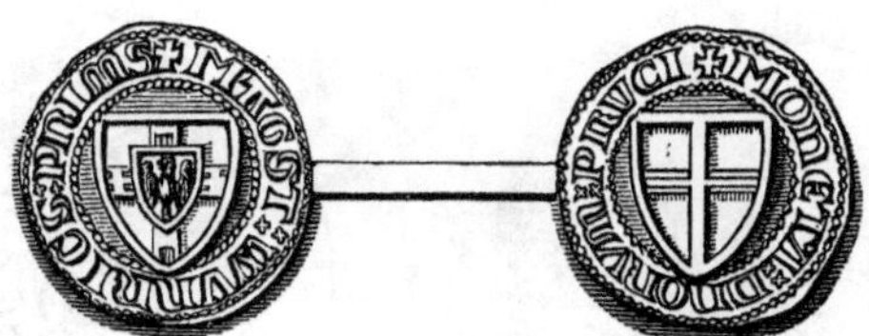

PENNY OF WUNRICS, GRAND MASTER OF THE KNIGHTS OF THE TEUTONIC ORDER, 1370, A. D.

In 1417, the Brandenburg lands were bestowed on Frederic I., who was at the same time raised to the Electorate. The Markgraf, Albert of Brandenburg, became, in 1525, Duke of Prussia. By the energies of the Electors of the Seventeenth century, Prussia

*During the Crusades, but specially at the siege of Acre, inhabitants of Lubeck and Bremen devoted themselves to nursing the wounded soldiers. For this conduct Frederick of Swabia formed them into the Teutonic Order of the Knights of St Mary of Jerusalem, only Germans of noble birth being admissible as members. In the Thirteenth century the Knights sought to Christianize the heathen tribes on the Southern shores of the Baltic, and thus became possessors of Prussia, Livonia, Courland, and other places. The Order was finally dissolved in 1809, by Napoleon, its estates passing to the sovereigns within whose territories they lay.

and Brandenburg so prospered that in 1701, the Electorate became a Kingdom, under Frederick III., who then became Frederick I., of the *royal* house of Prussia.

THALER OF WILLIAM III, ELECTOR OF BRANDENBURG, 1688–1713, A.D.

Of the coins of this earlier period our space forbids more than a general statement. On the obverse will be generally found a bust, with the name and titles, which will sometimes read—D. G. M. B. S. R. I., Arc. and El., meaning *Marchio Brandenburg Sacri Romani Imperii Archithesaurius et Elector;* on the reverse is a crowned shield with date, the legend reading Rex Borussiæ, or Borussorum Rex, with the Black Eagle, single headed

REVERSES OF PRUSSIAN THALERS OF LAST CENTURY. THE OBVERSES HAD SIMPLY THE KING'S BUST.

and crowned, having a sceptre in the right talon and an orb in the left one. Toward the close of the century the legend is in German, and reads, Koenig von Preussen, in which language it still appears.

In 1870 the German Empire was revived, and the Imperial

THALER OF FREDERICK WILLIAM III., OF PRUSSIA.

crown placed on the head of Frederick William IV. Since then the moneys of Prussia have been merged in the uniform coinage issued under the sanction of the new German Diet.*

GOLD TWENTY MARK PIECE OF PRUSSIA, 1872.

SAXONY.

So far back as the year 850, Saxony (*Sachsen*) was created a Dukedom, with Lubeck for its capital. In 912 its Duke, Henry "The Fowler," obtained the Imperial throne, and founded the Saxon line of German Emperors, lasting till 1024, A. D. In 1423 Saxony became an Electorate. In 1500, in the family of the then

*RULERS OF PRUSSIA.

Margraf Albert I	1134	Otho I	1170
Margraf Albert II	1206	Otho II	1184
Margraf Albert III	1470	Otho III	1221
Frederick I	1415	Otho IV	1282
Frederick II.	1440	Sigismund	1378
Henry I	1319	Waldemar	1309
Joachim I	1499	Wenceslos	1373
Joachim II	1535	Duke Frederick	1688
Joachim Frederick	1592	Duke William	1640
John I.	1221	Duke George William	1619
John II	1266	Duke John Sigismund	1616
John III	1476	King Frederick I	1701
John George	1571	King Frederick II	1740
John Sigismund	1698	King Frederick William I	1713
Jossus.	1388	King Frederick William II	1786
Louis I	1323	King Frederick William III	1797
Louis II	1352	King and Emperor Frederick William IV	1840

Elector, Frederick the Warlike, it was transferred to the younger branch of his children, as represented by Duke Maurice. The devices on the coinage of Saxony are for the most part of the usual

CROWN OF FREDERICK WILLIAM, DUKE OF SAXONY, 1594.

character—a bust, with name and titles, on the obverse, and on the reverse a crowned shield with arms or value and date.

John George I., 1611–1636, joined with Gustavus Adolphus and took part in the Thirty Years War. Subsequently joining Austria, he added largely to his estates, and raised the Electorate to its highest point. Succeeded by his son, John George II., his other

THALERS OF JOHN GEORGE I.

sons divided certain estates among themselves and founded cadet houses, all of which, however, ran out before 1750. In 1697, Duke Frederick Augustus became King of Poland. On his Polish coins he was now called Rex Poloniarum, a title that never

THALER OF JOHN GEORGE II, 1650–1680, A. D.

appeared on the Saxon coins. On their reverses are two shields bearing arms—the one of Saxony, the other of Poland and Lithu-

THALER OF THE SONS OF JOHN GEORGE I.

ania. In 1704 he was deposed from this rank, through the influence of Charles XII., of Sweden, yet continued issuing coins as King. After the overthrow of Charles at Pultowa in 1709, Frederick was restored to the throne, which remained in his family till the dismemberment of Poland, in 1795, by Russia, Prussia and Austria.

In 1711, Frederick issued a ducat, on the reverse of which are two altars, one holding the *imperial* vestment, sceptre, crown and orb ; the other the *regal* mantle, sword and crown. By this he showed his claim to the succession to the imperial throne. On

OBVERSE OF CROWN AND REVERSE OF $\frac{2}{3}$ PIECE OF FREDERICK I, 1694–1733, A. D.

some of the coins of last century we have on the reverse a shield with two fields, one containing the arms of Saxony, the other his personal arms, those of the House of Wettin—the cross swords—arms that appeared on coins of Saxony for the last time in 1807.

REVERSES OF THALERS OF SAXONY, WITH AND WITHOUT THE ARMS OF WETTIN.

In 1806, Frederick Augustus III. joined Napoleon, and was rewarded by the rank of King and the gift of the Polish Duchy of Warsaw. On the fall of Napoleon, however, though allowed to retain his new rank, he lost all his new territory.

In 1870 Saxony became part of the second German Empire.

SAXE-COBURG GOTHA.

The Principality of Coburg formerly comprised *Saxe-Saalfeld*, *Saxe-Meiningen*, *Saxe-Gotha* and *Saxe-Hildburghausen*. In 1826 Hildburghausen and Saalfeld were formed with Meiningen into the

Duchy of that name, while Coburg and Gotha were united in a Duchy, carrying the arms of Saxony. The coinages of these connected States is of no merit, and can easily be classified by means of the legends.

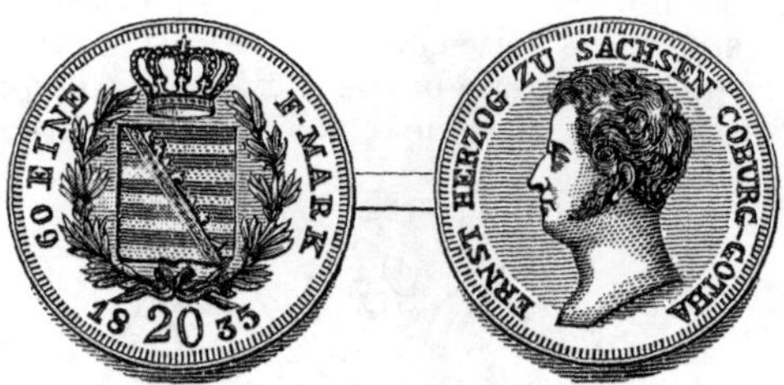

MARK PIECE OF SAXE-COBURG GOTHA.

SAXE WEIMAR-EISENACH.

When Frederick was deprived of his Electorate of Saxony, in 1547, he was made Duke of Weimar or Weimar-Eisenach. In this family the Dukedom remained till 1815, when, for his services against Napoleon, Duke Charles received an accession of territory and the rank of Grand Duke. The State now forms part of the German Empire. The device on the coins is the bust or crowned shield, with GROSHERZOGTHUM SACHSEN, and the Saxon arms on a shield of pretence.

HOHENZOLLERN.

The Hohenzollern family trace their pedigree back to the Ninth Century, when Count Thassilo built a castle near Hechingen, on the heights of Zollern. In 1105 the House divided into the Elder or Swabian line, and into the Younger or Franconian. In 1576 the Elder line divided into the two principalities of Hohenzollern Hechingen and Hohenzollern Sigmaringen. In 1415 the Younger or Franconian branch received from the Emperor the Electorate of Brandenburg, and now, as King of Prussia, occupies the throne of Germany. In 1842 the houses of the Elder line surrendered their States to Prussia, but retained the titles and receiving pensions. On the coinage we have the legends, HOHENZ. HECH. or HOHENZ. SIG., according to the State that issued them.

BAVARIA.

This territory was originally occupied by the Celtic *Boii*, from whom the old Latin name *Boiaria*, and its German name of Baiern or Bayren is derived. Charlemagne having added it to his territories, bestowed the Dukedom in 1180 on the Count of Wittlesbach, from whom its present ruler is descended. On coins issued during this period, we have shields with the Bavarian arms, religious figures and legends, while the titles of the Dukes often read as follows: *Dei Gratia, Utriusque, Bavariæ,* and *Palatinatus superioris Dux comes Palatinus Rheni sacri Romani Imperii Archidapifer* (cup-bearer) *Elector Landgravius Leuchtenbergæ.* In the case of some coins issued on the marriage of

BUST OF KING ON OBVERSE. DOUBLE THALER OF MAXIMILIAN JOSEPH.

Maximilian Joseph, in 1747, we have *added* to the above the words *Maria Anna Regia Princeps Poloniæ et Saxoniæ.*

From the Fifteenth to the Seventeenth centuries the limits of Bavaria were frequently changed, so that many petty States, Bishoprics and Free Cities, all of which issued money in their own names, were within its limits. In 1642 Bavaria became an Electorate, and in 1772 the *Rhenish Palatinate* was added to it.*

DOUBLE DUCAT OF CHARLES ALBERT, 1729–1745, A.D.

CAROLINE OF THE RHENISH PALATINATE.

*Under the Merovingians the *Comes Palatinus* was a high judicial officer of the King's *palatium* or palace. He was in fact the King's Law Adviser. Charlemagne conferred this title, with its natural authority, on powerful feudal Lords in frontier districts. Hence the territory subject to such persons was known as a Palatinate or county Palatine. Sometimes, therefore, the Rhenish Palatine formed part of Bavaria, when it is mentioned on the Bavarian money; sometimes it was an independent territory, and issued its own money.

In 1806, Napoleon erected Bavaria into a Kingdom, under Maximilian Joseph, its Duke, 1798–1825, a rank it still retains, though now part of the Second German Empire.

DOUBLE THALER OF BAVARIA.

BRUNSWICK.

In the days of Charlemagne, Brunswick formed part of Saxony. In 1235, along with Luneburg, it was made a Duchy under Duke Otho. In 1569, Henry, son of *Ernest the Confessor*, founded the house of *Brunswick-Wolfenbüttel*, or Brunswick, his younger brother William founding that of *Brunswick-Lüneburg*.

BELL THALER OF BRUNSWICK, 1643.

This Thaler was struck to commemorate the victory of Gustavus Adolphus of Sweden, and his ally, Duke George, of Brunswick, over the Imperialists at Duthlingen, and is a good specimen of the *medallic* coinage of the German and other European States.

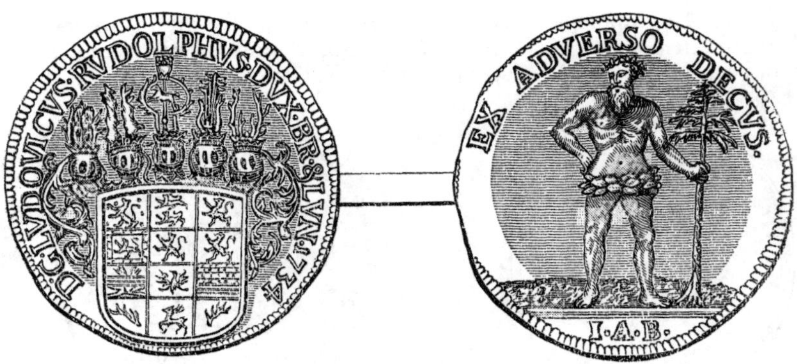

DOUBLE THALER OF LOUIS RUDOLPH, DUKE OF BR. AND LUN, 1734.

On the coins of Brunswick we have generally the customary bust, with name and titles. Sometimes there is the device of the wild man of the Hartz, a coarse savage with a cloth around his loins, and holding a pine tree in his hand; on the reverses will be the crowned shield or the values.

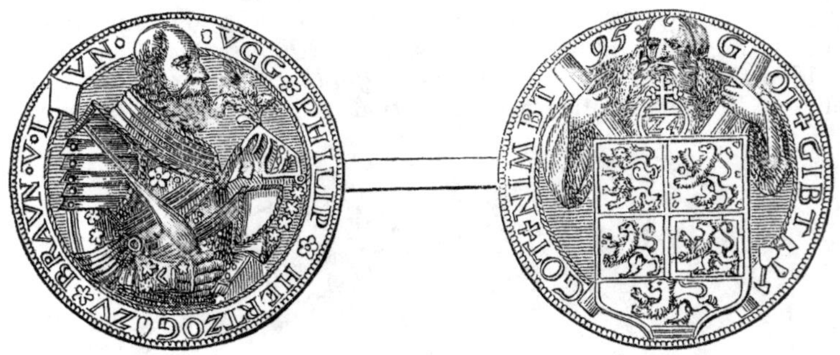

THALER OF PHILIP.

In 1806 Brunswick was seized by Napoleon, and used to make up his Kingdom of Westphalia. After the battle of Leipsic however, in 1813, it was restored to the son of the late Duke. In 1815, Duke Frederick William fell at Quatre Bras, when his heir, Charles Frederick, then a minor, was placed under the guardianship of the Prince Regent of England, so that on the coins issued between 1817 and 1823, the legend reads, *Georgius D. G. Princ. Regens*, and on the reverse, *Tutor nom. Caroli Ducis Bruns et Lun*, with the white horse of Hanover or the wild man of the Hartz.

Northeims is, or rather was, a small State within the limits of Brunswick.

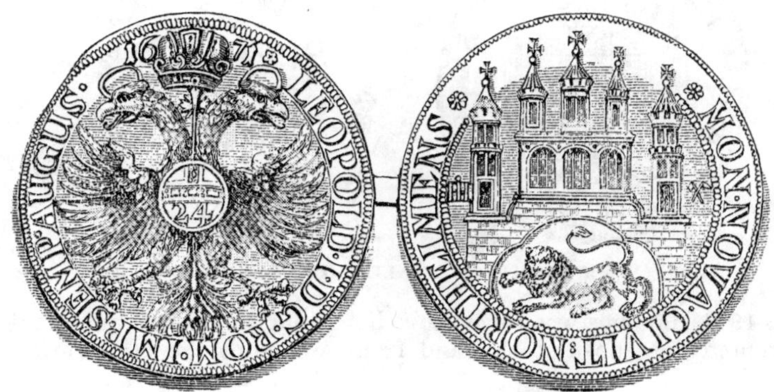

THALER OF NORTHEIMS, 1671.

HANOVER.

On the division of the House of Brunswick in 1569, the Duchies of Luneburg and Zell became the property of William. In 1692 Hanover became an Electorate, and in 1714, on the death of Queen Anne, Elector George Lewis, the nearest Protestant heir of that deceased sovereign, ascended the throne of England as George I., retaining his Lordship of Hanover.

TWO-THIRD PIECE OF BRUNSWICK, WITH HANOVERIAN REVERSE, 1764.

Pieces of various value were now issued, bearing either the bust and legend of the English sovereign, or the royal arms, along with some Hanoverian device, such as the horse running, the wild man of the Hartz, St. Andrew and his cross, having on them the Hanover value in thalers, Marien groschen, ducat, or pistole.

CONVENTION THALER OF 1788.

In 1814 Hanover was raised to a Kingdom, but as the Salic law prevented the Queen of England from assuming the Hanoverian

REVERSES OF COINS OF BRUNSWICK WITH ENGLISH ARMS.

crown, this passed in 1838 to Victoria's uncle, Ernest Augustus, Duke of Cumberland. On his death, in 1851, the throne was occupied by his son George, but the Kingdom has lately been absorbed by Prussia.

The coinages of Brunswick and Hanover seem to have been, to some extent, interchangeable, the titles of the sovereign on either being Dux Br et Luneb.

WESTPHALIA.

Westphalia, now a province of Prussia, derives its name from the *West-falen*, a Saxon tribe. Charlemagne, having subdued the Saxons, allowed their leader to remain *Duke of the Engern and West-falen*. In 1179 the electoral Archbishop of Cologne brought the district under his control, where it remained till 1802, when the larger part of it was given to the Hesse Darmstadt family. In 1807 Napoleon formed the Kingdom of Westphalia by taking portions from Hesse, Hanover, Brunswick and Upper Saxony, appointing his youngest brother Jerome, its monarch. On the battle of Leipsic in 1813, this kingdom ceased to exist, and the Duchy itself was united to Prussia. On the recent coins of Westphalia we have therefore a bust with king's name, HIERONYMUS NAPOLEON, and on reverse value and date.

THALER OF JEROME NAPOLEON OF WESTPHALIA.

WURTEMBERG.

Wurtemberg was under the control of *Counts* till 1495, when the Emperor Maximilian made it a *Dukedom.* On the peace of Lunéville in 1800, it was raised to an *Electorate.* In 1805 Napoleon conferred on its ruler the rank of *King*, adding largely to

DOUBLE THALER OF JOHN FREDERICK OF WURTEMBURG, 1623.

his dominions, a change confirmed by the Congress of Vienna. The State is now part of the German empire.

On recent coins of Wurtemburg we have the king's bust, with names and titles, such as DUX WURT or WIRT*emburg* ET TEC*ensis* (Teck) and the arms as usual on a crowned shield with supporters.

DOUBLE THALER OF CHARLES OF WURTEMBURG, 1869.

STUTTGART.

THALER OF STUTTGART, 1522 A. D.

Stuttgart is the capital of Wurtemburg, its history going back to the Twelfth century. In 1285 it was taken by the House of Hapsburg, and has since then been frequently the seat of war.

HESSE.

The territory of Hesse was occupied originally by the *Catti.* On their migration to Gaul the Saxons took possession, whence its name of *Saxon Hesse.* In 911 the Duke of Franconia and Hesse was elected Emperor of Germany. In the year 1300 the domains were portioned out among different branches of the ruling family, but in 1562 a final division was made into Hesse-Cassel (whose Landgraf was made an Elector in 1803), Hesse Darmstadt

(Grand Duchy in 1806), and Hesse Homburg (Landgraviate), each being so distinguished from the name of its capital.

The coinages of the three States are interchangeable, those since 1803 being distinguished only by the *titles* of the ruling prince. The arms of Hesse are a lion rampant, surmounted by a crown, the devices on the coins being generally a head or bust on the obverse, with name and titles, and on reverse the shield with arms or value and date.

BADEN.

In 1130 Herman II., the ruler of the Baden territory, assumed the title of *Markgraf.* In 1475 Baden was divided, according to the German custom, into *Baden-Baden* and *Baden-Dourlach.* In 1771 these were united by Duke Charles Frederick of Baden becoming Duke of Baden-Baden. In 1803 the Duchy was advanced to an Electorate. In 1806 the Elector received the title of Grand Duke (Grösherzog), the heir apparent being known as the Hereditary Grand Duke and the other sons and daughters as Margraves and Margravines. The coins are of the usual designs—busts, names and titles, with crowned shields with arms, value and dates.

THALER OF BADEN.

MECKLENBURG.

In the Twelfth century the Mecklenburg territory was made a dependency by Henry the Lion. In 1349 the Emperor Charles raised it to a Dukedom. In 1701, after several divisions and reunions, the State was divided into the Dukedoms of *Mecklenburg Schwerin* and of *Mecklenburg Strelitz.* In 1815 the Duke of Mecklenburg Schwerin was made a Grand Duke. Each of the Duchies has its own coinage, needing no description, as the name of the State always appears.

LIPPE.

The House of Lippe dates from 1129, though in 1013 it followed the usual German custom and divided its territory. The coins of Lippe bear a full-blown rose, filling up nearly all their field.

ANHALT.

The Principality of Anhalt consists of the Duchies of A. Bernburg, A. Dessau and A. Köthen. The independence of Anhalt dates from the 13th century, and the present threefold division goes as far back as the 17th century. The coins of Anhalt are easily recognized by their device of a bear with a ducal crown fastened on its collar, walking along a wall, while beneath it is an arched doorway.

OLDENBURG.

The present Oldenburg was in early times subject to Saxony, but in 1180 independent States were formed by the Counts of Oldenburg and Delmenhorst. The dynasty then founded has remained in possession of this territory till the present time, besides giving royal houses to other lands. In 1448, Christian of Oldenburg became King of Denmark, and founded the Danish house of Oldenburg. The Russian royal family is a branch of the Oldenburgs, as also was the late royal family of Sweden. On the coins of this Duchy the legend is generally OLDENBURG COURANT MÜNZE.

LORRAINE.

Lorraine was originally part of the German Empire, and dates from 855 A. D., when Lotharius II. obtained its lands. What is now called Rhenish Prussia was separated from it in the Tenth century, and in 1044 A. D., the remainder was divided into *Upper* and *Lower* Lorraine. In 1477 *Lower* Lorraine came into the hands of Austria, and now forms part of the Kingdom of Belgium, and the provinces of Brabant and Gelderland in Holland. In 1736, *Upper* Lorraine, which had previously been governed by its own dukes, was given to Stanilas, ex-King of Poland, but in 1766 was united to France as its province of Lorraine. As a result of the Franco-German war of 1870, Lorraine was ceded by France to Prussia, and its present coinage is now included within that of the German Empire.

METZ.

Metz, an old Roman town, became, on the death of Clovis, in 511 A. D., the capital of Austrasia and later, of Lorraine. In 985 it became a free Imperial city. By the treaty of Westphalia in 1648, it was ceded to France, but is now connected with Prussia. From 960 A. D. down to 1666, both the Bishop and City of Metz issued coins.

THALER OR LARGE CROWN OF METZ, 1632.

ORANGE.

The early home of the House of Orange is said to have been on the banks of the Rhone.

In 1178 A. D., Frederick I. granted the right of coining money to the Count of Orange. The earlier issues bear the name of Frederick on the obverse, and on the reverse the arms of Orange —a cornet or horn. During the sixteenth century the House of

THALER OF WILLIAM, PRINCE OF ORANGE, 1649.

Nassau succeeded that of Chalon, which was then in possession of the principality. In 1673 the King of France confiscated the estates of Nassau, restoring them, however, in 1678. They were again taken during the French War and, in 1702, given to the Prince of Conti, the title, Prince of Orange, passing to the descendants of the Prince of Nassau-Dietz.

NASSAU.

This Duchy is one of the southern States of Germany, and receives its name from the Castle of Nassau, the chief stronghold in the Twelfth century of the Counts of Laurenburg. A younger branch of this house, by marriage with the heiress of Gelders, founded the line of Nassau-Gelders, represented at present in the royal family of the Netherlands. This junior line, having also obtained the principality of Orange, is now known as the ruler of that principality. In 1806, Nassau was rendered a Duchy, but is now part of the German Empire. The coinage is of the usual monotonous style : a bust on the obverse, with name and titles of the sovereign, and on the reverse a crowned shield, with date and value.

THE HANSE TOWNS.

In the Thirteenth century, Hamburg, Lubeck and Bremen formed a mutual covenant or *Hansa* for trading purposes. The advantages of this League were so obvious that it soon included every commercial city in Holland and Livonia. By 1630, however, its general mission had been accomplished, and its power rapidly declined, so that it soon consisted only of the three first named cities and Dantzic. These formed free republics till 1810, when Napoleon added the first to France. In 1813, however, they joined with Frankfort-on-the-Main in forming what are now known as the Free Hanseatic Cities.

HAMBURG THALER OF 1553.

Of these cities *Hamburg* is the largest. So far back as the Twelfth century Hamburg was raised to the rank of a Free City by Otho IV. Its coinage is very easily recognized from its arms—a wall and gateway surmounted by three towers. On the old coins the fort was shown surrounded by water, referring to the Elbe.

As the city forms a member of the German Empire, the crowned double-headed eagle with the imperial orb on its breast, and holding sword and sceptre, with name and titles of the reigning Emperor is often found on the reverses.

GOLD DUCAT OF HAMBURG, 1840.

LUBECK.

Lubeck, one of the oldest North German towns, was declared, in 1226, a free city. As a member of the Empire, its coins bear the two-headed eagle, having on the breast the numeral of value, with Imperialis Civitas. On the reverses are the date, value, and name of the city.

DOUBLE THALER OF LUBECK.

BREMEN.

Bremen was erected, in the Eighth century, into a bishopric by Charlemagne, and has always been a city of importance. Its arms consist of a key diagonal-wise on a shield, surmounted by a coronet, with value in grotes, and on reverse the two-headed eagle having an orb on its breast sustaining the imperial crown, with the name and titles of the Emperor for legend. As Bremen was an

Episcopal city, we sometimes find on the reverses, in place of the eagle, a cross pattée with the legend CRUX CHRIS*ti* NOS SALVS, when the legend on the obverse will be MON*eta* N*ova* REIP*ublicæ* BR*emer*.

TWELVE GROTE OF BREMEN.

NUREMBERG.

Nuremberg was made a Free Imperial City by the Emperor Henry V. in 1219. In 1417 its inhabitants purchased their civic independence from the House of Hohenzollern. During the middle ages it held an important position as a trading and manufacturing city, but having joined the Confederation of the Rhine in 1806, was annexed to Bavaria. On its early coins is found the figure of its patron saint, St. Lawrence, with such legend as MONETA REIPUB. NURENBERGENSIS. Subsequently this device was replaced by the busts of the Emperors. Some of its gold coins—ducats—have on the obverse a lamb carrying a banner, bearing the word PAX. Such, with similar pieces from other countries, constitute a class of coins known as *Agnus* pieces.

FRANKFORT-ON-THE-MAIN.

Frankfort is the oldest of the free cities of Germany. In 1356 Charles IV. appointed it as the place in which the election of the Emperors of Germany should take place. Its coinage bears either the Emperor's bust, with name and title, or a view of the river Main, with Frankfort on the bank and a bridge crossing the river, and the crowned eagle on the reverse, with FREIE STADT FRANKFURT.

FRANKFORT THALER OF 1628.

COLOGNE.

This city was founded by the *Ubii* about 40 B. C., and about a hundred years later received, in honor of Agrippina, the wife of Claudius, the name of *Colonia* Agrippina, whence its modern name of Cologne. It entered the Hanse League in the Thirteenth century and contended with Lubeck for the first place. At first a bishopric, in the Eighth century Cologne was made an archbishopric. Some of the occupants of the See became distinguished as princes of the Empire, so that a struggle arose between them and the civic rulers, resulting in the removal of the archbishop's residence to Bonn. In 1801 the See was secularized, and in 1815 the whole territory was handed over to Prussia.

The coins of Cologne resemble, in general style, those of the other cities—the Emperor's bust, with name and titles, &c., or that of the archbishop, with such legends as AR*chiescopus* (or AR*chi* EPI*scopus*), Co*loniensis* PRIN*ceps* EL*ector*, and on the reverse a crowned shield, with date and legend, EP*iscopus* ET PRIN*ceps* DUX BUL*ensis* MAR*chio Franciæ Coloniensis*, &c., &c.

It is, however, both needless and impossible for us to attempt to describe the coinages of the other Episcopal or free cities. What we have said indicates their characteristics, each of course having the peculiarity of the name and rank of its ruler, and often some distinctive device. Those of *Salzburg*, for instance, are covered with ecclesiastical emblems and designs. *Stralsund* has for its arms a *broad arrow*. *Stolberg* has a stag with antlers, passing in front of a crowned pillar that is surmounted with the orb. *Augsburg* has a fir cone. *Danzic*, two crowned Maltese crosses in a shield. *Corveyland* (Corbei nova), *Paderborn*, *Hameln*, and so on all of which can easily be distinguished and classified by the collector.

TWENTY MARK OF STOLBERG, 1764.

CHAPTER XIV.

SCHLESWIG HOLSTEIN.

The arms of Schleswig are two lions running to the left. As connected with Denmark the coins of Schleswig have, on the obverse, the Danish arms, while on their reverses is found a crowned shield with the national arms, and on the *Scheidmunze*, or provincial currency of low values, the name of the State, value and date.

THALER OF SCHLESWIG HOLSTEIN, WITH DANISH ARMS, 1787.

In 1864, Schleswig, which had previously formed with Holstein one Principality, was formally taken possession of by Denmark. Prussia and Austria then attacked Denmark and took both States from it, finally quarrelling over the spoil.

DENMARK.

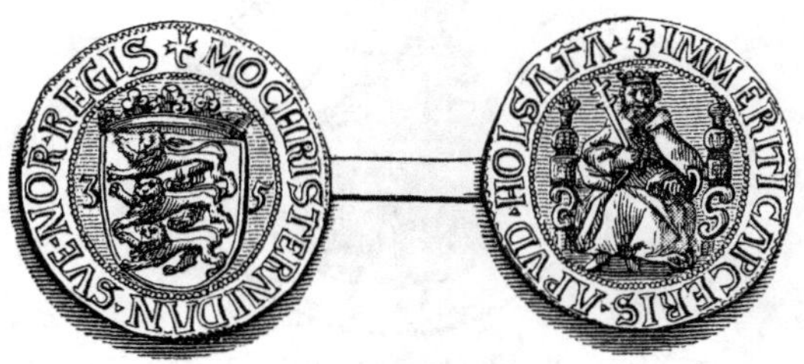

GROAT OF CHRISTIAN II., 1535.

The earliest known coins of Denmark are those struck in England and Ireland. Those of *Canute*, 1015 A. D., have his head with CNVT R., and on the reverse SIVORD I ROCI. In 1389 Margaret of Denmark added Sweden to her dominion, which, then, in 1448, when the House of Holstein, the present occupants of the throne, obtained supreme power, consisted of Denmark proper, Sweden and Norway. The coin system of Denmark is rather complex, there being distinct and contemporaneous issues for each of the three countries, Denmark retaining on her coins the arms of Sweden, though in 1528 that country, under Gustavus Wasa, secured its independence.

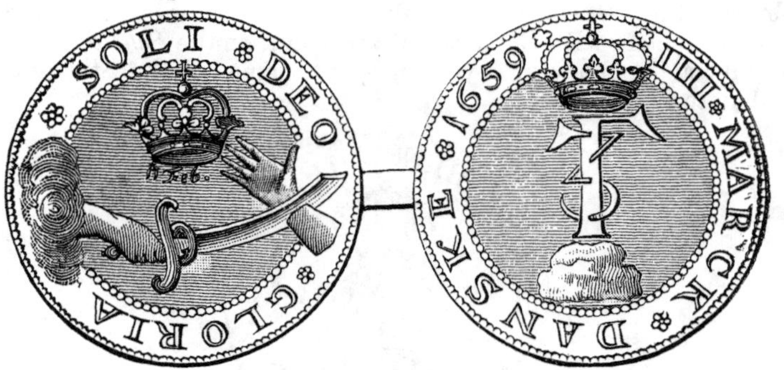

THALER OR FOUR MARK PIECE, 1659.

Struck to commemorate the suppression of a conspiracy against the crown.

SKILLING AND RIGSBANK DALER, OR RIGSDALER SPECIES.

This shield bears the arms of Denmark, Norway, Sweden, Schleswig, Gothen and Wenden. The shield resting on the cross carries the arms of Holstein, Stormarn and Ditmarsen, while the shield of pretence has those of Oldenburg and Delmenhorst.

The Danish coins have generally on the obverse the bust and name of the ruler, and on the reverse a crowned shield with the royal arms, three lions and nine hearts, or perhaps, as on recent issues, only value and date.

TWO RIGSDALER, 1868.

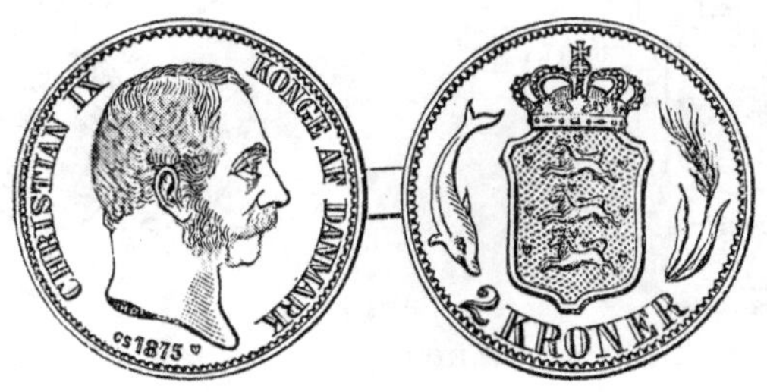

2 KRONER, 1875.

NORWAY.

Our earliest coins of Norway are those of Onlaf, 1066, having for legend Onlaf Rex Nor., the title being sometimes *Dux* rather than *Rex*. Toward the close of the Fourteenth century, Norway had been annexed to Denmark.

The Danish-Norwegian coins bore on the obverse the bust, name, and titles of the Danish king, and on the reverse the Nor-

THALER OF DUKE JOHN ADOLPHUS, HEIR OF NORWAY, DUKE OF SCHLESWIG HOLSTEIN, 1611.

wegian arms, a lion rampant, climbing a battle axe. In the exergue are two hammers crossed, the Norwegian M. M, with reference to the mines of Konigsberg. Up to 1818 the coins of Norway resemble those of Denmark ; since then they belong to the Swedish series.

DANISH THALER, STRUCK FOR NORWAY. NORWAY THALER, 1796.

SWEDEN.

COIN OF STEPHEN, ISSUED AT STOCKHOLM, 1512.

The arms of Sweden are three crowns, and as there is no gold coinage the *silver* money consists of the Rixsdaler or Government

RIXDALER OF SWEDEN.

dollar of 48 schillings. This dollar is worth 100 copper öre or aere, (*Lat.*, aerum). Lately this öre has been replaced by skillings of which there are two issues; the one, the government money, having a large crowned monogram of the King within branches, and on the reverse a large I on circular disk, with legend, SKILLING RIGSMONT. The other skilling is only half the value of this, and is called SKILLING BANCO.

On the coins of the *Wasa* family, 1528-1658, there is always a religious symbol, the obverse presenting, with bust, a legend, consisting of the king's name, and titles, D. G. SVEGOR*um* GOTHOR*um* VANDALOR*um* Rex, while the reverse is a crowned shield with arms.

During the wars of Charles XII., Sweden was greatly impoverished. As a measure of necessity, during 1715–1719, the Baron Goertz, the Prime Minister, issued a series of eleven dalers of copper to circulate at the value of silver. The reverses of these coins all bear "*I. Daler S. M.*" in three lines, and on the obverse of each there is a different design, as follows :

A Crown, 1715.
Pallas, 1716.
Publica fides, Wett och Wapin, 1717.
Saturn, 1718.
Flink och Fardig, 1718.
Jupiter, 1718.
Mars, 1718.
Mercurius, 1718.
Hoppel, 1719.
Phœbus, 1718.

The series was closed by one bearing the baron's own effigy, a circumstance that led, ultimately, to his being indicted and executed for treason.

SWEDISH DALER OF NECESSITY, 1718.

From 1736 until 1751, the arms of Hesse Cassel were on the coins, when the house of Holstein came to the throne, retaining it till 1810. Napoleon then appointed Bernadotte, one of his Marshals, Crown Prince, and in 1813 annexed Sweden to Norway. In 1818 Bernadotte ascended the throne as Charles XIV., his coins bearing his bust, and legend, SVERIGES NORR. G(*othland*) OCH (and) W*est-manland* Konung, with, on reverse, a crowned shield or two arrows *saltire*, with value and date.

RIXDALER OF OSCAR, 1844.

RIXDALER OF CHARLES XV.

RUSSIA.

In 981 A. D., the Byzantine Emperor, John Zimisces, having conquered the Russians, sealed a peace with them by giving his daughter in marriage to their Duke Vladomir. In 1328 the Tartars overthrew the rising civilization, but in 1462 their yoke was thrown off, and the modern Russian system began. During the earlier period of its history Russia consisted of many petty States, ruled over by the sons of the dominant Duke, each of whom issued money. In 1534 many of these States were brought together by Ivan, who then assumed the title of Tsar or Czar, while in 1721 Peter the Great assumed the title of Emperor. Russian money consists of the *gold* Imperial, with ten *silver* roubles, each of which is divided into 100 *copper* cents or copecks. From 1828 to 1837 *platinum* was used, but found to be unsuitable. The Russian

SIX ROUBLES. (*Platinum.*)

letters, so like and yet so unlike the Roman, render the coins very noticeable, while, at the same time, there is very little variety in the designs. On the obverses may be found the bust of the mon-

GOLD PIECE OF DEMETRIUS, 1580 A. D.

arch, and on the reverses, generally, the Russian two-headed eagle, each head crowned, with the Imperial crown above. On the eagle's breast is generally a shield, with figure of St. George and the dragon.

POLAND.

The name of Poland is found upon the earliest pages of European history. Specially famous for military prowess, it exhausted its energies on battlefields, and when torn by internal dissensions, became an easy prey to its allied adversaries, so that now it has ceased to exist. In 1573 Poland became an elective monarchy, and chose Henry of Valois for its ruler. Next year Henry abandoned his Polish crown on succeeding to the throne of France, as Henry III.

THIRTY GROS PIECE OF JOHN CASIMIR, 1665.

In 1772, the first partition of Poland took place at the hands of Russia, Austria and Prussia, these powers dividing among themselves nearly one-fourth of her territory, despite the protests of the people, the Diet and the King. The Polish coins of this date have on their obverse a head, with legend, STANILAUS AUGUSTUS D.G.REX. POL*oniæ* M*agnus* D*ux* LITU (*Lithuaniæ*), with a crowned shield on the reverse, having the arms of Poland and Lithuania. In 1793 the second partition, and in 1795 the last partition, or final division

THREE GROS PIECE OF SIGISMOND.

of Poland, was effected by the same powers. In 1807 Napoleon formed the *Duchy of Warsaw*, but in 1815, this, as the ***Kingdom*** *of Poland*, was given to Russia, by the bond of a personal union. On the Russian coins now issued the Czar was called *King of Poland.* In 1830 the Poles revolted and revived the Kingdom of Poland, declaring themselves independent, issuing the coins that bear on the obverse a crowned shield with the arms of Poland and Lithuania, and on the reverse, the value within branches, and the date below. The revolt was soon afterwards suppressed, and Poland declared to be an integral part of the Russian Empire.

FIVE ZLOTS OF THE KINGDOM OF POLAND, 1830.

In 1832 Russian silver one-and-a-half rouble pieces were issued. These correspond exactly in value to ten Polish zlotys. That these coins might circulate freely in both countries, their Russian value was stated in Russian, and their Polish value in Polish characters.

RUSSIAN-POLISH ONE-AND-A-HALF ROUBLE.

CHAPTER XV.

AUSTRIA.

Austria receives its name from its position in Europe—Ost-Reich—the East Country. This portion of his dominion was placed by Charlemagne under a *Mark-Graf*, or Lord of the Marches. Additions were made to the territory, so that in 1273 the House of Hapsburg (from Habsburg or Hawk's Castle on the Aar), its rulers, rose to the Imperial purple.

The Arms of Austria consist of a double-headed eagle, surmounted by the Imperial Crown, the eagle having on its breast a shield with arms, and holding a sword in the right talon and a sceptre in the left one. During the present century the sceptre has been replaced by the globe. On the obverse of Austrian coins is generally the Emperor's bust, with name and titles, and on the reverse the Austrian Eagle, with remainder of titles, or value and date. These titles are Emperor of Germany, Archduke of Austria, Duke of Burgundy, Count of the Tyrol, King of Hungary and of Bohemia, Count of Styria, &c., &c.

CROWN OF PHILIP III. OF AUSTRIA, KING OF CASTILE, 1621–1665 A. D.

Through Charles V., the Austrian monarchy became ruler over well nigh all Europe, and an immense variety of titles are found on the coins, according to the country for whose use such were specially issued.

In 1804 Francis II., Emperor of Germany, proclaimed himself hereditary Emperor of Austria, laying down, in 1806, his titles of

Emperor of Germany and King of the Romans. In 1815, Lombardy and Venice were added to Austria, and the names of these territories, with or without Galicia and Illyria, appeared

CROWN OF FRANCIS JOSEPH I., OF AUSTRIA.

on the Austrian coinage, while at the same time coins were issued for Lombardy and Venice, having the Austrian Eagle, with the values, dates and locality. In 1866, when Lombardy and Venice were annexed to Piedmont, this latter series ceased.

GOLD FOUR FLORIN OF AUSTRIA, 1871.

HUNGARY.

The Magyars, as the old Hungarians are called, are of Scythian origin, and entered their present home under the leadership of *Arpad*, about 890 A.D. About the year 1000, Arpad's descendant, St. Stephen, was crowned King of Hungary, his descend-

DUCAT OF ISABELLA, QUEEN OF HUNGARY, 1559.

ants retaining the throne till 1301. From this period the rulers were chosen from foreign houses till 1526, when, on the prostration of Hungary by the Turks, the Hapsburg family ascended the throne. Hungary never formed part of the Austrian Empire, but

THALER OF MARIA THERESA, A. D. 1742.

has always been connected with it by a personal union with its sovereign, retaining a large amount of independence. Hence, the coins struck for Hungary and Bohemia have on the obverse either the crowned shield, with arms, or the sovereign's bust, with name and Hungarian title, and on the reverse, religious emblems. During the struggle of Louis Kossuth in 1848, coins were issued by the Revolutionary Government, having on the obverse a crowned shield bearing the Hungarian Arms with legend, and on reverse the value in Hungarian and date. In 1867, a new arrangement was made between Austria and Hungary, securing the more perfect autonomy of the latter.

AUSTRO-HUNGARIAN FLORIN, 1869.

BOHEMIA.

The name *Bohemia* comes from the old Celtic tribe of the *Boii*, that having crossed from France into Italy was for several centuries at bitter war with Rome. On its final defeat by Scipio in 191 B. C., a portion of the tribe leaving Italy settled north of the Danube, hence the name of the territory *Boiohemium*—home of the Boii—contracted to *Böhmen*—*Bohemia.* In 937 A. D., Otho made Bohemia tributary to the German Empire, and in 1061 Henry VI. conferred the title of King of Bohemia on the Duke of Prague. In his family the throne remained till 1306 A. D. During this period, or from about the year 1200, Ottocar began the issue of *Bracteates,** cup-like coins of very thin silver, with the type on one

GROS OF THE CITY OF PRAGUE, ISSUED BY CHARLES I. OF LUXEMBURG, 1347.

side and the indent on the other, like the incused coins of Græcia Magna. From 1310 to 1437 Bohemia was ruled by kings of the

CROWN OF FERDINAND I. OF GERMANY, LAST INDEPENDENT KING OF BOHEMIA.

*These coins are now regarded as a feudal money, their one-sidedness proclaiming the dependent rank of their issuers, for the German Emperors at that same date were issuing solid money bearing a double impress. A large amount of it was issued at Strasburg.

House of Luxemburg. In 1440 this dynasty was expelled, and the throne made elective. In 1490 Ladislaus, its sovereign, was made King of Hungary. Under the reign of Ferdinand I., Bohemia was joined to Austria, and has remained so ever since.

With Bohemia is connected our familiar word *Dollar*, which is merely a corruption of *Thaler*, a name given to the silver pieces that, in 1517, were made from the mines in the Bohemian *Thals* or valleys.

RAGUSA.

Once an independent aristocratic Republic, like Venice, this State is now an Austrian dependency on the Adriatic. In 1358 Ragusa placed itself under the protection of Hungary, and afterwards under Turkey. In 1808 Napoleon abolished its Republican government, and incorporated it with the province of Dalmatia, when in 1814 it came into the possession of Austria. On its coins there is on the obverse a bust with legend *Rhacus Respubl*, and on the reverse a crowned shield, enclosed by crossed branches and religious motto.

TURKEY.

The coins of Turkey are devoid of interest. The Mahommedan religion forbids the making of any likeness of a natural object for any purpose, so that the coins bear simply Arabic inscriptions on either side. The monogram of the Sultan, called the Toghra, is very conspicuous on the obverse, while on the reverse is generally

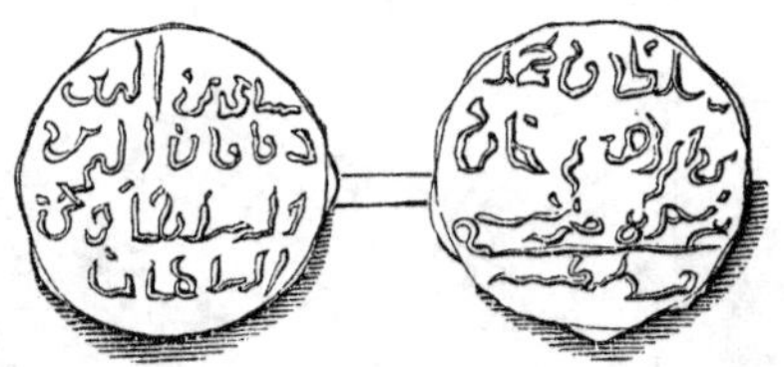

DUCAT OF MAHOMET IV., A. D. 1680.

the name of the mint, the Sultan's year of reign, and the date from the Hegira. The standard piece is the *piastre*, found with its multiples in gold and silver, and worth about 4 cents, while ten *paras* are worth one piastre. The Turkish *billon* dollar, oftentimes met with, is either a counterfeit, or was struck for Tripoli, whose coins resemble those of Turkey. The little flower beneath the Toghra is the State mint mark, guaranteeing the value of the coin.

Among the copper coins of low value issued by Turkey, chiefly for circulation in North Africa, is one that is easily recognized

PIASTRE OF MEHEMET ALI.

by a double triangle on the obverse, and on the reverse *Constantinople*, in coarsely designed Arabic, and the date of the Hegira in Roman letters. These coins seem to be cast by the yard, and broken off in lengths; they often perplex young collectors by the apparent anomaly of *Arabic* letters and *Roman* numerals.

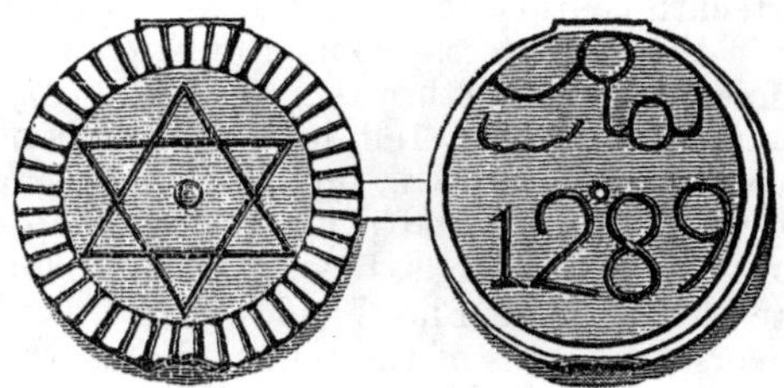

ROUMANIA.

Among the provinces of Eastern Europe subject to Turkey are the Danubian States of Moldavia and Wallachia. In 1859 these principalities formed a monarchical union, taking the name of Roumania, and calling their ruler Prince Hospodar. The coinage of Roumania is altogether modern, and has no interest, consisting chiefly in copper *Bani.*

GREECE.

In 1829 modern Greece, having successfully revolted from Turkey, adopted the monarchical form of government, and in 1833 called Otho of Bavaria to the throne. Greek money consists of *gold* pieces of 20 or 40 drachmè ; of *silver*, 5, 1, ½, and ¼ drachmè, each drachmè having 100 *copper* cents or lepta, of which there are 10 the diobolus, 5 or the obolus, with 2 and 1 lepta pieces. On these coins there is the bust, name and title of the King, and on the reverse, a crowned shield with the Greek arms ; on the copper coins the reverse bears the value within branches.

A few years ago Otho abdicated and was succeeded by Prince George of Denmark, whose coins are almost a counterpart of Otho's.

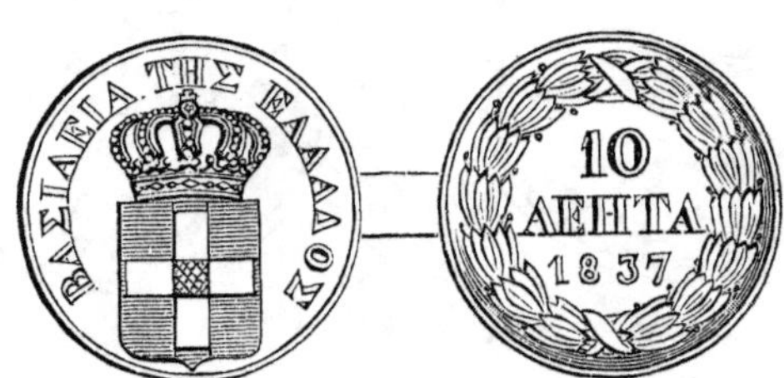

TEN LEPTA OF OTHO OF GREECE.

IONIAN ISLANDS.

In the Thirteenth century the Ionian Islands formed one of the principalities of the Crusaders. About the Fifteenth, they became subject to Venice, with whom they remained till 1797, when France took possession. In 1809 they fell into the hands of Britain, by whom they were formed, in 1815, into the Septinsular Republic. In 1819, copper coins—penny, halfpenny and farthing—were struck in England for the Ionian Islands, having on the obverse *Britannia* seated with an olive branch in her hand, with the word BRITANNIA, and on the reverse, the arms of the Ionian States, the winged lion holding arrows and a shield, with the Greek words *IONIKON ΚΡΑΤΟΣ* and date. In 1834 there was a coinage both of silver and of copper. On the obverse of the silver is a figure of Britannia, as before, but on the reverse an oak wreath encloses the numerals XXX, making the value equal to half a crown. The obverse of the copper called an *obolus*, was similar, but on the reverse has the winged lion of St. Mark as on old Venetian coins, with the inscription as before, and date.

In 1863 Great Britain ceded the islands to Greece, when its local, yet really British coinage, was replaced by the ordinary money of Greece.

CHAPTER XVI.

GREAT BRITAIN.

The coinage of Great Britain goes back to the very verge of prehistoric times. Cæsar, writing about the year 55 B. C., refers to the use by the Britons of some medium of exchange, but in terms so general as to leave it uncertain whether this were coined money or simply rings or plates of metal. Many coins indeed exist which are ascribed by zealous numismatists to the prehistoric period, but the coins themselves bear neither legend nor device by which they can be confidently assigned to Britain. They may, however, have been struck there by native workmen in rude imitation of Greek money. On one of these so-called British coins there are characters supposed to be the letters LEGO, considered to be an abbreviated form of *Legonax*, the name of one of Cæsar's assailants on his second invasion, in 54 B. C. On others are the letters C V N, C V N O, C V N O B E L I, with such other letters as C A M V, C A M V L, doubtless denoting *Camulodunum*, now Colchester in Essex, the capital of the territory ruled over by a native prince called Cunobeline, the Cymbeline of Shakspeare.

Shortly after Cunobeline's death, and the re-conquest of Britain, 54 A. D., all the native mintages were suppressed. During the Roman period of British history, from the Christian era to about the year 450 A. D., large quantities of coin, bearing Imperial devices, and known as *Colonials*, were struck. The number of molds for casting money, and the many dies for different rulers that have been found, show that counterfeiters must also have been all the time busy with their nefarious arts.

On the withdrawal of the Romans, the enfeebled British sought the aid of the Saxons to defend them against the assaults of the Northern tribes, the Picts and Scots. This led to the permanent occupancy of Britain by Saxon tribes, and the formation of those seven distinct kingdoms known in history as the *Heptarchy*, namely, *Kent, South Saxons, East Saxons, East Angles, West Saxons and Northumberland*, itself consisting of two principalities, *Deiva* and *Bernicia*. Of these kingdoms, many coins (silver) have come down to us. To the tiniest of these pieces, some of which were struck previous, and others subsequent to the conversion by St. Augustine, in 606 A. D., of the Saxons to Christianity, the term *Sceatta* or *Skeatta* is applied. Others are known as the

Penny, that coin whose weight, one two-hundred-and-fortieth of a pound, has furnished a name for that proportion of value which is characteristic of the modern coinage of Great Britain, the *Half-penny*, and the fourth part of the Penny—the *Fourth-ing* or *Farthing*. Brass or copper money known as *Stycas* were also used, each piece being equal in value to half a farthing. Such subdivision of values was needful when, as in the reign of Œthelstan, thirty pennies could purchase an ox, and twelve of them a sheep.

Of the coins of these Anglo-Saxon kingdoms, those of *Kent* are the most ancient, some of them being ascribed to Ethilbert, who reigned from 568 to 616 A. D. On some of these early coins not only the name of the king, but that also of the moneyer, may be found, while on a coin of Baldred, the last king of Kent, 823 A. D., we have for the first time the place of the mintage; the device being, on the obverse, a bust of the king, with the legend, BALDRED REX CANT., and on the reverse, DIORMOD MONETA, with DOVR CITS, a contraction for *Dorovernia civitas* or *Canterbury*, the place of mintage.

The kingdom of *Mercia* seems, from the number of its coins that have come down to us, to have been the most moneyed of all the States of the Heptarchy. The coins of Offa, 758–796 A. D., are the most artistic of the Anglo-Saxon series. Offa visited Rome two years before his death, and is supposed to have brought back with him some Italian artists. On these coins there occur the king's name, with his title, REX MERCIORUM, with that of the moneyer on the reverse, while the mint is left unnamed. A few coins of his queen, Cenetreth, have also been preserved. The coinage of Burgred, 855 A. D., was not only debased to the lowest point in its style of art, but also in its standard, the metal used being an exceedingly coarse alloy. This is supposed to have arisen from national poverty, caused by the inroads of the Danes, who, in 874 A. D., drove Burgred from his throne, when he fled to Rome, where he died.

No coins of the kingdom of the *East Angles* are known of an earlier date than 690 A. D. One of the famous kings of this territory was Eadmund, 855 A. D., whose coins bear the king's name and his title, REX AN. Murdered by the Danes in 870 A. D., Eadmund became subsequently known in the Church calendar as St. Eadmund, while Guthrum, a Dane, was then placed upon the throne by Alfred. Guthrum having embraced Christianity in 878 A. D., assumed the name of Ethelstan.

Northumberland is the only Anglo-Saxon kingdom that issued the mixed metal money known as *Stycas*, which seem to have fallen into disuse about 780 A. D., for none of later dates have been found. On some of the coins of Onlaf or Aulof, 937 A. D., we find the Saxon *Cunune*—the source of the German Kœnig and English King, in place of the Roman *Rex*.

Early in the ninth century, Ecgbeorht ascended the throne of the *West Saxon* kingdom, and soon made himself master of the whole of the Heptarchic States. To him, therefore, belongs properly the glory of being "the first sole monarch of England," though several of the kingdoms still retained a feudal independence. In 872 A. D., on the death of Æthelred, the throne became occupied by his brother Ælfred, known in history as Alfred the Great, whose career was remarkable for vicissitudes that surpass the dreams of the novelist, and the impress of whose mind is borne by the England of to-day. The necessities of Ælfred drove him to greatly debase the coinage, on which he is styled ÆLFRED or ÆLFRED REX, while the reverses have not only the moneyer's name, but frequently a monogram of the town in which the mint was situated, these towns being DORO—Dorovernia or Canterbury,—LONDINIA—London ; ORSNAFORDA—Oxford.

In 924 A. D., Œthelstan, Alfred's grandson, ascended the throne, and enacted that there should be but one kind of money for the whole realm. His design in this was to deprive noblemen and burghs, archbishops and abbeys alike of the privilege of issuing money. This law was steadily enforced till the reign of Edward I., when letters and other distinguishing marks were used to indicate by whom the current money had been coined. On Œthelstan's coins appear, the title not assumed by any of his predecessors, REX TOTIUS BRITANNIÆ—one, however, hardly justified by fact. Œthelstan had mints at more than twenty of the principal cities in the kingdom, showing the extent of his authority and the activity of his government in caring for the coinage of the realm. During the reign of Edgar, 960 A. D., the coin had become so reduced in value by clipping that a Penny would pass only for a Halfpenny. So seriously was social life affected by this dishonesty, that St. Dunstan* refused, on a certain Whitsunday, to celebrate mass until the moneyers found guilty of dishonesty had been punished in the usual manner by cutting off their right hands.

In 975 A. D., Eadmund the Martyr ascended the throne, placing on his coins the title REX ANGLORUM, having a rude, ill-drawn portrait on the obverse, and on the reverse the name of the moneyer and the place of the mint.

After a reign of four years, Edward was murdered by his step-

---

*St. Dunstan was of noble birth, and a man of extraordinary ability and accomplishments. As Abbot of Glastonbury he acquired the highest credit for personal sanctity and courage, having come off conqueror in a great contest with the Prince of Darkness. His public career was most checkered; one while he was high in favor at the court, domineering over king and people, and again fleeing to the Continent to save his life. He lived for two objects, the civil unification of Britain and the complete subjection of its church to that of Rome. Many great reforms were effected by him, not the least of which was the improvement of the coinage. In 960 A. D. he was made Archbishop of Canterbury, and died in 988 A. D.

mother Elfrida, that her son Æthelred might wear the crown. The character of the usurper was so weak, and his incompetency so flagrant, that the Danes swept the country as they pleased, extorting from the king, at different times, the sum, truly enormous for that period, of one hundred and sixty-seven thousand pounds. Still the coins of Æthelred are pretty numerous. On some of them the king is clothed in armor, and wears a helmet strengthened by ribs that give it the appearance of a spiked crown, the legend being ÆTHELRED REX ANGLO. On the reverse is our earliest example of a voided cross, with what are known as martlets in the angles, and with the name of the moneyer and of the mint around the edge. On another variety the king holds a sceptre, its first appearance on British coins. On one variety there is a hand on the reverse, with the Greek letters *A* and *Ω*, the only instance in which such characters are found on any of the Anglo-Saxon coins.

In the conflict between Æthelred's son, Edmund Ironside and Cnut (Canute) the Dane, son of Suein, fortune eventually favored Cnut, who became established in the kingdom in 1017 A. D. On his coins the title King of England is almost always to be found, though on a few very rare ones we find him styled REX DANORUM. Cnut had a larger number of mints than any of his predecessors, partly because of an increase of national wealth, and partly because certain burghers were willing to pay for that reputation which the presence of a mint within their towns would give them.

In 1042 A. D. the Saxon dynasty was restored, and Edward the Confessor obtained the throne. Edward soon introduced the French custom of moneyage or changing the device on the national currency, a custom bringing considerable profit to the crown. Hence, probably, the large number of types, amounting to nearly five hundred, of this monarch's coins. On some of these coins Edward is represented as wearing a large beard, an unusual feature on the coinage of this period. On others, for the first time in Anglo-Saxon coinage, the king is seated on a throne, crowned and holding the orb and sceptre, with the legend EADPARD *Rex Anglo*, the Saxon P being equivalent to the w of the Romans.

On the death of Edward, in 1066 A. D., Harold took possession of the vacant throne, claiming it as a gift made to him by Edward, in his dying hour. During his brief reign of nine months, Harold issued many coins bearing on the obverse his name and title, and on the reverse the name of the moneyer and of the place of mintage.

In 1066, the Saxon Harold fell at Hastings, in one of those decisive battles that give a new direction to human affairs. The Norman William, known as the Conqueror, then ascended the English throne, and a new period of European history commenced.

William's reign was not marked by any considerable change in the coinage. The Penny and its divisions remained as before, but the money of account was modified. The Saxon *Scilling* or *Shilling* —money of account—was now ordered to represent twelve Pennies. The value of the Danish *Mark*, also money of account, was fixed at one hundred and sixty Pennies. The coins of William resemble closely those of Harold. On the obverse is a bust crowned, either full faced or profile, with crosses of different designs on the reverses.

PENNY OF WILLIAM I., 1066–1087.—P. A. X. S. *type.*

In 1087 A. D. William Rufus ascended the throne. His coins are comparatively few, and so closely resemble those of his father, William the Conqueror, that we are often at a loss to distinguish between them.

On the death of Rufus, in 1100 A. D., his younger brother, Henry, seized the crown. Though called Beauclerk, from his scholarly tastes and attainments, the coinage does not seem to have had much attention paid it. Moneyage however, was abolished, and the severest punishments threatened against counterfeiters. The church also tried to protect the purity of the coinage by denouncing such persons as oppressors of the poor and disturbers of the state. Still, the practice went on. At length, in 1125, Henry inflicted on all the moneyers who had been guilty of debasing the coin—94 in number—the horrible punishments of the law, while to the honest moneyers was committed the task of recoining the whole money of the realm. There is considerable similarity among the coins of the first three Henrys. Those however that bear the greatest resemblance to the coins of the Williams are generally considered to belong to Henry the First.

PENNY OF HENRY I., 1130–1165—STRUCK IN SOUTHWARK.

On the death, in 1135 A. D., of Henry, leaving no son, the direct male line of the Normans became extinct. The throne was therefore seized by Stephen, son of a daughter of the Conqueror, to the prejudice of Maude or Matilda, Henry's daughter, an act that naturally led to war and turmoil during all Stephen's reign. Many of the barons, with or without the King's sanction, now issued money. The standard of value seems, however, to have been on the whole well maintained. On the obverse of Stephen's coins, which are very rare, is a bust, full-faced or profile, frequently facing the right, crowned, with sceptre or flag in the right hand, with legend. On the reverse is a cross, with name of moneyer and mint; oftentimes a number of ornaments take the place of these. The crown that Stephen wears is now fully developed into that *fleur-de-lis* pattern which continued to be depicted on the English coinage down to the reign of Henry the Seventh.

UNIQUE PENNY OF STEPHEN, WITH OBVERSE OF HIS BROTHER HENRY, BISHOP OF WINCHESTER.

In 1154 A. D. Stephen died when by arrangement, he was succeeded by Maude's son, Henry the Second. Henry was, perhaps, the most powerful sovereign of his time. From his father, Geoffroy Plantagenet Count of Anjou, he inherited the Principalities of Anjou, Tourraine and Maine; from his mother, Normandy ; through his wife, the County of Poitou and Dukedom of Aquitaine ; so that, in addition to the throne of England, he had immense territorial possessions in France. His early coins are exceedingly rude, but about 1180 A. D. he procured a French artist, Philip Aymary of Tours, under whose care considerable improvement was effected. The type of the *first* coinage is the usual one—a bust, full-faced, or profile, with fully defined *fleur-de-lis* crown, a sceptre in the right hand, generally resting on the shoulder, but sometimes held upright, with legend, and on the reverse a cross pattee, with small crosses in the angles. In 1180 the *second* issue took place, having on the reverse a *short double cross.* The dies of this issue are supposed to have been used during the reigns of Richard and of John, and to have been the used for the first coinage of Henry III.

In 1189 Richard the First—Cœur de Lion—succeeded his father. Though he reigned for ten years, not a single English coin bearing his name has come down to us. Either none were struck, or so many were melted down or exported to pay Richard's ransom that none now exist.

On Richard's death, in 1199, his brother John seized the throne. There exist a number of John's Irish coins, but none of his English issues have been preserved. John, having died in 1216 A. D., was succeeded by his son Henry the Third, who, so soon as his possession of the throne was secured, issued extensively Pennies, Halfpennies and Farthings. These resembled the coins of previous reigns, having the King's head, with a front face, with a *fleur-de-lis* crown; on the reverse is a short double cross,

PENNY OF HENRY III.—*First Issue.*

whose limbs were within the inner circle. The clipping, however, continued so mercilessly that in 1248 A. D. there was a great recoinage. The old money was called in and melted down. On this *second* coinage a new type was adopted, one that was retained more or less down to Henry the First. The double cross on the reverse was extended, with only three pellets in each quarter, to the outer edge of the circle containing the legend, so that any clipping would be obvious at once; while following the King's name on the obverse are either the Roman numerals III. or the word TERCI.

In 1257 A. D., the first coinage of English gold—the Ryal (or Royal)—took place; the King, though in great straits for money, issuing a gold Penny—that is, a coin of that size and style—ordering that it should be current for Twenty Pennies.

CHAPTER XVII.

In 1272 A. D., Edward the First succeeded his father, Henry, and sought to improve the coinage. Clipping and counterfeiting seem, however, to have been as prevalent as ever. The Jews, ever the victims of mediæval ignorance and prejudice, were assumed to be the chief actors in these dishonesties, and in 1290 A. D. were banished from the kingdom, never to return. At the same time, one-fifth part of all their movables was confiscated to the king by Parliament, a measure which was doubtless the real purpose of their banishment. The coins of Edward, and of his successors down to Henry the Seventh, all bear the king's bust, with a full-faced effigy wearing a crown fleurie—that is, one whose band has three fleur-de-lis projecting from it, and between these fleurs are other fleurs not rising so high. The effigy is merely a conventional king's head, and not a portrait. Owing to the absence of any numerals, the coins of the Edwards of the Saxon dynasty are

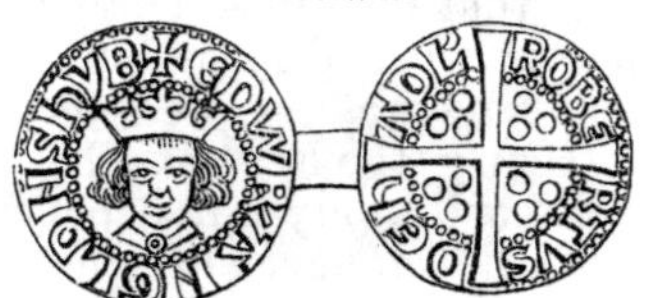

PENNY OF EDWARD I.

possibly intermingled, a similar absence of numerals having long caused great uncertainty about the coins of the Norman Edwards. As a general rule, however, we are warranted in thinking that all the coins having only EDW. on them belong to Edward the First; those having EDWARDVS, to Edward III, and all others to Edward II. The coins of this reign are the Penny, Halfpenny and Farthing.

To this reign belongs, it is thought, the issue of the first *Groat*, a word that combines the sounds of the French *gros* and of the English *great*. So few of these pieces were put into circulation that those we have are considered to have been merely patterns. The device consists of a full-faced effigy wearing the crown fleurie; the drapery round the neck is fastened with a rosette; while the legend reads EDWARDVS: DI: GRA: REX: ANGL:. On the reverse there is the long cross fleurie, with three pellets in the angles. Round the pellets are the words, "Londonia civi," while in an outer circle is the legend, DVX AQVT: DNS HBNIE: Duke of Aquitaine and Lord of Ireland.

Edward the First died in 1307 A. D., and was succeeded by his son, Edward the Second, whose weak character, making him dependent on favorites, repeatedly involved him in trouble with his nobles, and whose great invasion of Scotland was effectually checked at Bannockburn (1314 A. D.), by Robert the Bruce. His coins—Penny, Halfpenny and Farthing—differ from those of his father only in their legend, which reads EDWA, or EDWAR.

In one of the contests with the nobles, in which his wife joined their ranks, Edward the Second was taken prisoner, and put to death in 1326 A. D. by order of his queen, Isabel, sister of Charles the Fourth of France. His son, a lad of fifteen years, was at once proclaimed king as Edward the Third, the power during his minority being really in the hands of the queen-mother and her paramour. On attaining his majority, three years afterwards, Edward threw off this yoke, punished all who had been concerned in his father's death, and confined his mother as a prisoner to her own house for the remainder of her life. His Scottish wars, consequent on Baliol's recognition of him as king of that country, led only to great bloodshed, for the Scottish people would not brook a surrender of their independence. He also claimed to be king of France, upholding his claim by his most splendid victories at Cressy, in 1346 A. D., when his son, a lad of sixteen, took what is still the crest of the Prince of Wales, three ostrich feathers, with the motto, *Ich Dien*, from the helmet of the King of Bohemia, whom he had slain, and at Poitiers in 1356 A. D., when the French king was taken prisoner. The king's closing days were clouded. Losses in Scotland, losses in France, dissensions with his Parliament, opposition from the Black Prince (who died in 1376 A. D.), formed a sad contrast to the prosperity of his early years, so that he sank into the grave in 1377 A. D., having reigned fifty-one years.

The coinage of Edward was very varied. His first issue of *gold* consisted of Florins, having a device of the king crowned and robed and sitting under a canopy, with Halves and Quarters.

GOLD NOBLE OF EDWARD III., FOURTH ISSUE, 1347–1360.

On a second issue, one of Nobles and their Quarters, the king is represented armed and standing up in a ship; a third issue differs from the second only in having an E in place of L in the centre of the reverse, while a fourth issue, consisting of Nobles, halves and quarters, has AVTEM in the legend on the reverse. Our engraving is of a noble known to belong to the first period of the fourth issue, by the spelling TRANCIENS, and using IBA for IBAT. The words DEI GRATIA appear now for the first time on the coinage of England.

On his *silver* coins, consisting of Groats, Half-Groats, Pennies, Halfpennies and Farthings, the device is a bust of the king crowned, with full face; on the reverse of groats and half-groats there is an inner circle containing the place of mintage; the long cross with three pellets in the angles is on all the silver coins, while the king's name reads EDWARD or EDWARDVS.

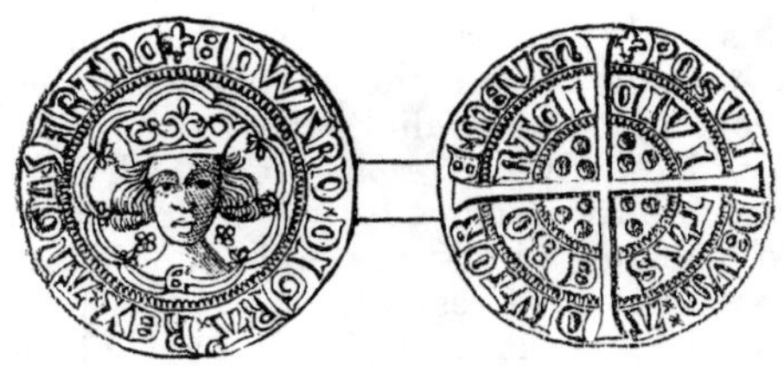

GROAT OF EDWARD III., 1327–1377 A. D.

In 1377 A. D. Richard the Second, son of the Black Prince, succeeded his grandfather. His reign is notable for the rise of the power of the House of Commons, by means of its right of taxation—a power that led to Wat Tyler's rebellion in 1380 A. D. During this reign every goldsmith was required to have his distinguishing mark, so that his work could be traced. Richard's coinage consisted of the *gold* Noble, with its Half and Quarter, with device of a ship like that of Edward III., and the *silver* Groat, Half-Groat, Penny, Halfpenny, and Farthing, having the king's bust, crowned, with full face; the name reads RICARD or RICARDUS, with the REX ANGL Z FRANCIE.

On the death of Richard, in 1399 A. D., his cousin Bolingbroke, Duke of Lancaster, usurped the crown as Henry the Fourth. The victories in 1402 A. D., of Henry Percy or Hotspur, over the Welsh and Scotch, did not prevent other revolts, and, after a troubled reign, Henry died in 1413 A. D., of epilepsy.

The first issue of Henry's *gold* coins consisted of Nobles, Halves and Quarters, with four fleur-de-lis on the shield of arms, the noble weighing 120 grains, and a second issue of nobles weighing only 108 grains, and quarters with, possibly, only *three* flowers.

The first issue of his *silver* coin consisted of Groat, Half-groat, Penny and Halfpenny, having the king's bust crowned, and full face. Of the second issue, there is no Halfpenny known. The first issue is called the *heavy* money, the Groat weighing 72 grains, and the second, the *light*, the Groat weighing only 60 grains. The coinages of the Henrys IV., V., VI. so closely resemble each other, that numismatists seldom attempt to distinguish between them. It is thought, however, that the light money, on which the crown is broad and flat, resembling that of Edward III., may belong to Henry VI., and that that on which it is high and large, resembling that of Richard III., may belong to Henry VII., before the recoinage of his fifth year. Among the coins of the Henrys are some having annulets between the pellets on one or two of the quarters on the reverses. Some of these were issued in London and others in Calais. They are generally regarded as a late issue of Henry V., or an early one of Henry VI. The first issue of Henry VI. (1422–1461 A. D.) is *heavy*, the second (1470 A. D.) is *light* money.

In 1461 A. D. Edward IV. ascended the throne to reign twenty-three years. His first issue of *gold*, made in 1464, consisted of the Noble of the usual device ; his second, made in 1465, consisted of the Noble or Real, with its halves and quarters. The Angel, with a device of Michael transfixing the dragon with his spear, and on the reverse a ship, and the Angelet or Half Angel. On the side of the vessel, on these coins, is a rose, badge of the House of York, while the sun in the center of the reverses is a memorial of the strange appearance of three suns in the heavens, called by astronomers a *parhelia*, which appeared just before the battle of Mortimer's Cross in 1465. Edward's *silver* coinage consisted of Groat, Half-Groat, Penny, Halfpenny and Farthing, all of the usual style.

GROAT OF EDWARD THE FOURTH, 1461, STRUCK AT YORK.

Edward's coins, previous to the fourth year of his reign, were *heavy* ; those issued subsequently were *light*.

Of Edward V., 1483 A. D., the reign was too brief to admit of any coinage, or the issues too few to admit of any being preserved, as no coins of any denomination have come down to us.

In the middle of June, 1483 A. D., the Duke of Gloucester took possession of the throne as Richard III. His coins are of same type as those of his predecessors. The *gold* consisted of the Angel and Angelet, and the *silver* of Groats struck in London or York, Half-Groats struck in London, Pennies and Halfpennies.

GROAT OF RICHARD THE THIRD.

Richard having perished in 1485, at Bosworth field, was succeeded by the Duke of Richmond as Henry VII. The first issue of *gold* consisted of the Noble or Rial, the Angel and the Angelet; the second consisted of the Sovereign and the Double Sovereign, a name taken from the device—that of the sovereign in his robes and on the throne. On the reverse of this coin is a double rose, emblem of the union of the houses of York and Lancaster in the monarch and his queen. The first issue of *silver*, 1485–9, consisting of Groat, Half-Groat, Penny and Halfpenny, has a device of the full face and open crown, resembling that of his predecessors.

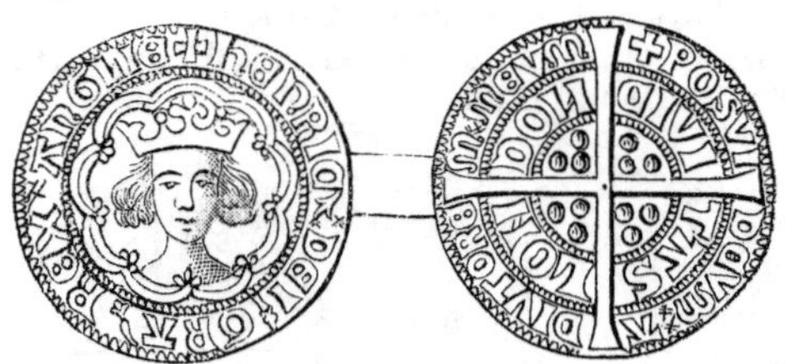

GROAT OF HENRY VII., FIRST COINAGE, YORK.

The *Second* issue of Groat, Half-Groat, Penny, Halfpenny and Farthing, with the front face, but high arched crown, with a reverse similar to that on the previous type, but with forked ends to the cross. The *Third*, issued in 1504, and consisting of Shillings, Groats, Half-Groats and Pennies, of superior workmanship and of types wholly different from anything hitherto used. This Shilling was the first coin of that value in England, and was declared to be equal to twelve Pennies. It presents us with the first true portrait on an

English silver coin. These Shillings are now extremely scarce. The Groats and Half-Groats of this coinage were of a similar

GROAT OF HENRY VII., SECOND COINAGE.

device, while the Pennies have the king seated on his throne, with orb and sceptre. They resemble the first coinage of Henry VIII.

SHILLING OR TESTOON OF HENRY VII., THIRD COINAGE.

In 1509 A. D., Henry VIII. ascended the throne to reign for nearly forty years. The first issue of *gold* (1527), consisted of Double Sovereign, Sovereign, Rose Noble, George Noble, Angel and Angelet. On the George Noble we have the now familiar device of St. George and the dragon, the reverse bearing a ship. The second issue (1544), consisted of the Sovereign-Angel, Angelet, Quarter Angel, Crown and Half-Crown. The device on the Crown consists of a double rose between the crowned initials of the king and his successive queens. On the Half-Crowns the letters are not crowned. The third issue (1545) consisted of the Sovereign, its half, the Crown and its half, with devices as before. For the first *silver* coinage (1509), consisting of Groat, Half-Groat, Penny, Halfpenny and Farthing, the dies of the third coinage of Henry VII. were used, the numerals VII. being changed into VIII.

GROAT OF HENRY VIII., TOURNAY COINAGE; HEAD OF HENRY VII.

In 1513, Henry captured Tournay, in France, when special coins were issued.

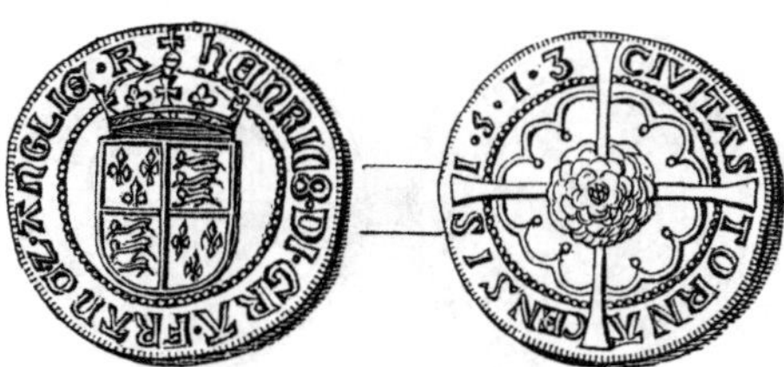

GROAT OF HENRY VIII., STRUCK ON THE CAPTURE OF TOURNAY IN 1513—FIRST APPEARANCE OF ARABIC NUMERALS ON ENGLISH COINS.

The second issue (1527) presents us with the side likeness of the king himself, encircled with his titles of King of England and France, variously abbreviated. The third coinage (1543) consisted of Testoon, Groat, Half-Groat, Penny and Halfpenny. Some of this issue is of fine silver, others of base metal. The device is a bust, full-faced, crowned, with beard and mustache; and, on reverse, a double rose, crowned sides.

The *fourth* coinage (1545) Shilling, Groat, Half-Groat and Penny, differ from the *third* only in its extremely debased character—being half silver and half alloy. The fifth coinage (1546) was the most debased that was ever current in Great Britain—one-third silver and two-thirds alloy. The devices resemble those of the earlier issues, but the members of this are known by the amount of alloy.

Edward VI., 1546, issued, in his first *gold* coinage, a Half-Sovereign, with device of the king crowned, and seated on the throne, holding the sceptre and orb; and a Crown and a Half-Crown, having the royal arms crowned. The second issue, 1549, consisted of the Treble Sovereign, having the king as before, but with a sword; the Sovereign, the Half, the Quarter or Crown, and the Half-Crown. The third issue, 1550, consisted of the Six-Angel piece, with Michael vanquishing the devil; Double-Sovereign, Sovereign, or Double-Royal, Angel and Angelet. On the fifth issue there is a half-length figure of the king in armor, crowned, and standing with sword in one hand and the orb in the other. The first issue of *silver*, consisting of Groat, Half-Groat, Penny and Halfpenny, had the king's profile to right. The second consisted of two kinds of testoons or shillings, the one being half silver and half alloy, the other, one part silver and three parts alloy. The type is the king's face in profile, with four varieties in the legend, one bearing MDXLIX, or MDL, the first English silver coins bearing date. Of the third coinage we have the Crown and Half with the king in armor on horseback; Shilling, Sixpence and Threepence, with bust of king, full-faced and crowned, with values; Penny and Halfpenny with king on throne, and Farthing with a portcullis.

PATTERN SHILLING OF EDWARD VI., 1547 (NEVER CURRENT).

In 1553 Edward was succeeded by his sister Mary, whose *gold* coins consisted of the Sovereign, having the queen crowned and seated on her throne; the Rial, the queen crowned and standing in a ship; the Angel and Angelet, with Michael and the dragon. Her *silver* consists of the Groat, Half-Groat and Penny.

GROAT OF QUEEN MARY, 1553.

In 1554, Mary married Philip of Spain, when an Angel and Angelet were issued, like those of 1553, but with Philip's name in the legend. On the first issue of *silver*, consisting of Groat, Half-groat and Penny, we have the queen's bust alone, with Philip's name in the legend; but on the second, consisting of Shilling and Sixpence, we have busts of Philip and Mary facing each other, with the Neapolitan and British arms on the reverse.

SHILLING OF PHILIP AND MARY, 1554.

Elizabeth succeeded her sister in 1558. Her first *gold* coins were the Sovereign, the queen crowned and seated on the throne; the Rial, the queen with high ruff standing in a ship; the Angel, Angelet and Quarter Angel, with device of Michael and dragon. During the same year she issued of *hammered* money, a Sovereign with bust in robes and high crown, and of *milled* money, with bust in mantle and a low crown of two arches, a Half-sovereign *hammered*, like the sovereign. This year she issued of *hammered* money, a Sovereign, Half-sovereign, Crown, Half-crown with bust to left, in robes and high arched crown; of *milled* money, a Sovereign, Half-sovereign, Crown and Half-crown, with small bust in mantle and low crown of two arches.

SHILLING OF ELIZABETH, 1582 (HAMMERED MONEY).

Elizabeth's *silver*, *hammered*, consists of the Shilling, Sixpence, Groat (or fourpence) Threepence, Twopence, Three halfpence, Penny, Three Farthings, Halfpenny. On all these except the Three-half penny, which has a portcullis, we have the queen's bust crowned, with long hair and ruff. Of the *milled* money we have the Crown, Half-crown, issued only in the years 1601–2, Shilling, Sixpence, Groat, Threepence, Twopence and Three Farthings, having a bust of the queen crowned, with sceptre and orb. As the coins of low value were of nearly equal size, to avoid mistakes a rose was placed behind the head of the alternate values; that is, on the Sixpence, the Threepence, the Three-halfpenny and the Three Farthing; the other coins—the Shilling, the Groat, Half-groat, Penny and Halfpenny are without it.

SIXPENCE OF ELIZABETH (MILLED MONEY).

The reader will notice the absence of any inner circle on this piece. This is characteristic of its mode of manufacture. In 1561 A. D., a Frenchman of name unknown employed a mill and screw for striking coins in place of the long used hammer and die, the result being much neater coins, sharper impressions, rounder forms, while various patterns could be struck on the edge. Milled money is known also by the absence of any inner circle between the legend and the device. This, however, did not lead to the discontinuance of the hammer, so that for some years both modes were employed.

In 1603 James VI. of Scotland succeeded Elizabeth as James I. of England. His first issue of *gold* consisted of Sovereign, Half and Quarter or Crown, having a bust of the king in armor, crowned, with legend, D. G. ANG. SCO. FRA., etc. During the same year he issued the Unit or Sovereign, Double Crown or half-sovereign, Crown and half, all similar to the coins of the first issue, but with the legend D. G. MAG. BRIT. FRA., etc. A Crown of this issue is known as the Thistle crown, from having a crowned thistle on the reverse. In 1605 the gold consisted of the Rose Rial or Sovereign, having the king in his robes and seated on the throne; the Spur Rial, with the king in armor; the Angel and Angelet with Michael and the dragon. In 1620, James issued a Rose Rial or thirty-shilling piece, having the king seated, with ruff and collar of the Garter; the Spur Rial, of fifteen shillings, with Scottish lion sitting crowned; the Angel, the Unit, the Double Crown and the Crown, with the king's bust in profile. Of the *silver* issued in 1603, the Crown and Half have the king on horseback; the Shilling, Sixpence, Fourpence and Penny have the king in profile, while the Halfpenny has a portcullis.

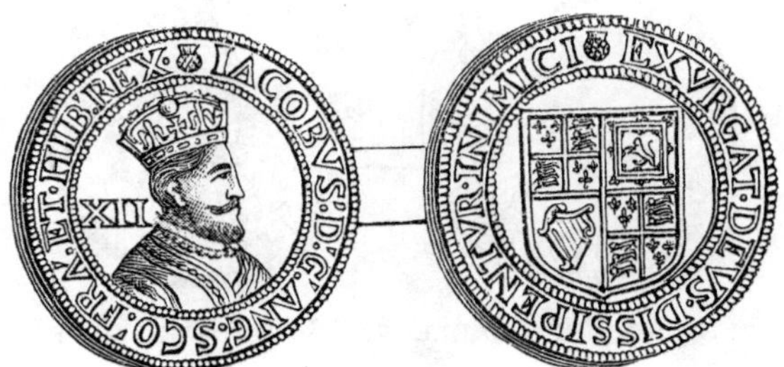

SHILLING OF JAMES I., 1603, FIRST COINAGE.

The silver of 1604 consists of the Crown and half as before, except that the Ang. Scot. of the legend is replaced by Mag. Brit. On the Shilling and Sixpence there is the bust with profile; the Half-Groat, Penny, and Halfpenny have a rose crowned.

Some of the Crowns, Half-crowns and Shillings have the Prince of Wales plume over the shield, indicating that they were made of silver from the Welsh mines, and as we know that these were not opened till 1621, we know at once a date before which, at least, these crowns were not issued.

This reign witnessed the issue of the first *copper* coins in Great Britain. The absence of small coins had led private persons to issue in great numbers what are now called *Tradesmen's tokens.* Partly to relieve this national want, and partly to obtain the profit of the issue, James, in 1613, issued *copper* farthings, to be current in England, Wales and Ireland. On the obverse is the crown over sceptres crosswise, with and without M. M., with legend JACO. D. G. MAG. BRIT., and on the reverse the Irish harp crowned with continuation of title FRA. ET HIB. REX.

Charles I. succeeded his father in 1625, when *gold* coins were issued from the mints of London, Oxford, Bristol and by Nicholas Briot, those of London consisting of the Unit or Broad, or Sovereign. The Half and Quarter are distinguished by the king wearing either a ruff and collar or a falling lace band. The Oxford pieces, the treble and single Unit and Half, have the king in armor, while Briot's coins—the Unit, Half and Angel—have the king's bust with the falling band.

A good-sized volume would hardly suffice for a detailed description of Charles' *silver* coinage; our space allows us to describe only a few pieces. Charles is the only English king that issued Twenty and Ten Shilling silver pieces; the device is of the king on horseback, with legend and dates, 1642-3-4. From the Tower mint come Crowns and Half-crowns with the king on

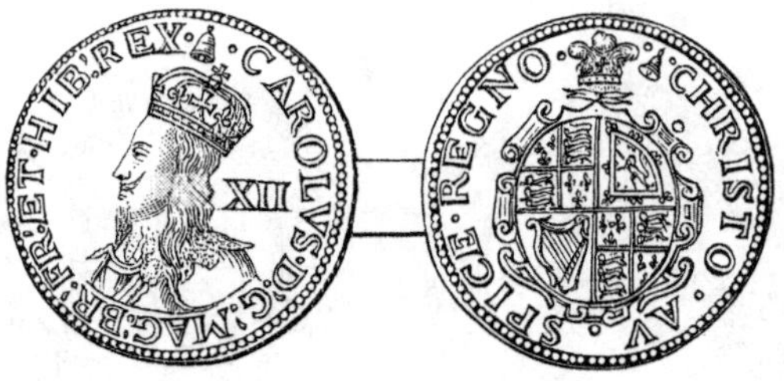

SHILLING OF CHARLES I., 1634, TOWER MINT.

horseback; Shillings and Sixpences with bust; Half-groat, Pennies and Halfpennies, with rose crowned on both sides or rose on one and thistle on the other. The Oxford mint also issued Crowns and Half-crowns; with the king on horseback, but the most desired of its series is that with a view of the city between the horse's legs.

THE OXFORD CROWN OF CHARLES I.

On the Shillings, Sixpences, Groats, Three-pennys, Half-groats and Pennies, we have simply the bust crowned and facing right or left. On the coins from Aberyswith, we have the Prince of Wales plume, to show that the metal came from the Welsh mines.

YORK HALF-CROWN OF CHARLES I.

During the great Rebellion, Charles was often unable to use his regular mints. He therefore issued pieces of irregular shapes, values and devices, according as his necessities required and which, because of their intrinsic worth, passed for money. Of these Obsidional or siege pieces, many survive, a full list being found in our Introduction.

HALF-CROWN SIEGE PIECE OF CHARLES I.

The *copper* Farthings of Charles' first issue resemble those of James; on the second issue, in 1635, the device is the crown with crossed sceptres, and legend CAROLUS D. G. MA. BRI., and on reverse a rose crowned with FRA ET HI REX. To prevent counterfeiting a small piece of brass was inserted in the centre.

CHAPTER XVIII.

On the execution of Charles, in 1649, the Parliament issued what is known as the money of the Commonwealth—Twenty, Ten and Five-shilling pieces in *gold;* with Crown, Half-crown, Shilling,

CROWN PIECE OF THE COMMONWEALTH.

Sixpence, Half-groat and Penny in *silver*, all of the same design ; the Halfpenny having on the reverse only the shield with the Irish harp.

During the Commonwealth, *copper* and *pewter* farthings appeared bearing the arms of the Commonwealth, but they never became very common, and it is uncertain whether they were issued by the government or by private parties.

In 1656 Cromwell prepared a *gold* Fifty shilling, Broad or Twenty-shilling, and a Half-broad or Ten-shilling piece ; as well

CROWN OF OLIVER CROMWELL, 1658.

as *silver* Crown, Half-crown, Shilling, Ninepenny and Sixpenny pieces, all of precisely the same design and legend; the coins are beautifully engraved, but never came into general use.

In 1660, Charles II. ascended the throne, issuing at once *gold* Broad or twenty-shilling pieces, Half-broad and Quarter, with a laureated bust in profile facing the left. Next year coins of similar denominations and design were issued, having the value in letters behind the head; both of these issues were *hammered* money, the restoration of the king being thus marked by a return to the old method. In 1662, there were issued Five-guinea, Two-guinea and Half-guinea pieces, with obverses like the earlier issues, but reverses have four C's interlinked in the center of a cross. This issue was of *milled* money. To denote that the metal came from the coast of Guinea in West Africa, the term guinea was now made use of, and an elephant or elephant and castle placed below the king's bust.

Silver Half-crown, Shilling, Sixpenny, Half-groat and Penny pieces were issued in 1660, all of one device.

SHILLING OF CHARLES II., 1660; HAMMERED MONEY.

A second and third issue of coins of similar denomination and devices were issued, with values in letters placed behind the king's head. These three issues were all of *hammered* money, but in 1662,

CROWN OF CHARLES II.

a Crown with a rose under the king's head, supposed to indicate that the metal came from the West of England mines, Half-Crown, Shilling and Sixpence, were issued of *milled* money. The design is a laureated bust to right with mantle over the shoulders; with interlinked C's in the angles of the crowned cross on the reverse, with an elephant and castle on some of the pieces and the Welsh plumes on others.

There might be said to have been another coinage, one of the smaller pieces, 4d., 3d., 2d., 1d., all of which have the numerals, but not the inner circle, and an M. M on their reverses. These are the last specimens of hammered money, and were probably struck, not for general circulation, but as Maunday money.*

In 1663, Shillings were issued, milled with straight lines, and resembling in device the Crown pieces; in 1670, the milling lines were placed obliquely. The first Sixpence was struck in 1674.

SIXPENCE OF CHARLES II.

Charles also issued a *copper* Halfpenny, having laureated bust in armor, with legend CAROLUS A CAROLO, and on reverse, Britannia seated holding spear and olive branch, with legend QVATVOR. MARIA. VINDICO., and in exergue BRITANNIA. The Farthing of same design had the date 1665. In 1672 he issued a Halfpenny and a Farthing of similar device, with BRITANNIA for legend on the reverse, and the date, 1672, in the exergue. In 1684 there was an issue of *tin* Farthings, similar in design to the above, with the legend on the edge, NVMMORVM FAMVLUS, 1684.

In 1685, James II. succeeded his brother, and soon issued *gold* Five, Two, One, and Half-guinea pieces, having the king's bust laureated and facing the left, with legend JACOBUS II., DEI. GRATIA; on the reverse four shields crosswise, each crowned, with elephant and castle on many of the coins. In 1686–7–8, James issued *silver* Crowns, Sixpences, Groats, and Two-pennies with Half-crowns, Shillings and Pennies in 1685–6–7–8. *Copper* money was

* Maunday money, so called from being given on Maunday Thursday (*mandatum*, Pilate's order for the crucifixion of our Lord), as royal bounty or alms to the poor. A small white leather bag containing as many sets of groats, three-pennies, two-pennies, and pennies, as there have been years in the sovereign's life. The custom is still observed, and the pieces so given are easily distinguished from ordinary currency by the absence of any milling on their edges.

not issued by James. In addition to such, in 1685, he issued a *tin* Farthing, having a laureated bust in armor; on the reverse is Britannia, and on the edge NVMMORVM FAMVLVS, with date. In 1687 he issued a *tin* Halfpenny, differing from the design on the Farthing only in the bust being draped.

HALF-CROWN AND THREE-PENNY OF JAMES II., 1686

In 1688 William and Mary occupied the English throne, and issued *gold* Five, Two, One, and Half-guinea pieces, with busts and names. *Silver* Crowns were issued in 1691, bearing the busts of the king and queen facing right, with a cross of shields on the reverse, with a monogram of W. and M. in the angles, and the arms of Nassau in the center. Half-Crowns were issued in 1689, having on the reverse a square shield, with the national arms quartered, and the date, 1689. Another of the same year has a shield of the same general design, yet different in detail. The reverse of the Half-crown resembles that of the Crown.

HALF-CROWN OF WILLIAM AND MARY, 1693.

The Shillings and Sixpences resemble the above design, while on the smaller money, the Maunday money, there are the Roman characters to indicate the value.

During this reign, *tin* Halfpennies were issued with busts and names, with Britannia on the reverse as before, with the date in exergue, 1689 or 1691. On Farthings of similar metal and design the dates are 1690–1 or 2. These were the last tin coins issued in England. In 1694, *copper* Halfpennies and Farthings of similar designs were issued.

In 1694 Queen Mary died, when William issued *gold* coins as before, the legend reading: GVLIELMVS III., and with reverses of shields crosswise with arms of Nassau in the centre. The *silver* Crowns resembled the gold Crowns; the Half-crowns, Shillings and Sixpences were similar, one Half-crown having the elephant and castle under the bust; another has the Welsh plume in each angle of the reverse; on some of the Shillings we have a rose in the angles, and on others roses and plumes, indicating a mixture of English and Welsh silver.

In 1696 all current hammered money was called in by the government, and to facilitate the isssue of the new money, mints were established in different parts of the country. The coins thus issued have, below the busts, the initial letter of the mint where they were struck as B*ristol*, C*hester*, E*xeter*, N*orwich*, Y*ork*. Those of London have no distinguishing letter.

SHILLING OF WILLIAM III.

Copper Halfpennies and Farthings were also issued, having bust of the King in armor with GVLIELMVS TERTIVS, and on the reverse, Britannia, with date 1695 to 1701 inclusive.

Ann succeeded to the throne in 1702, and issued *gold* Five, One and Half-guinea pieces, having bust of queen with ANNA DEI GRATIA, and on reverse four shields crosswise with rose in the center; from this four sceptres issue, each tipped with a harp, a thistle, a fleur-de-lis or an orb. The pieces of 1703 have *Vigo* under the bust, denoting metal taken from the Spanish galleons in Vigo Bay in 1702. After the union with Scotland in 1705, Ann issued Five, Two, One and Half-guinea pieces, with obverse as before, but on the reverse, the arms of England and Scotland are united on the 1st and 3d quarters, and the 2d is given to France.

The *silver* Crown, Half-crown, Shilling and Sixpence of 1702 and 1703 resemble the gold coins of those dates, the word *Vigo* being also found. Those issued after the Scottish union resemble the gold of the same dates.

SHILLING OF QUEEN ANN, 1705.

Ann issued a *copper* Farthing with bust on the obverse, and on reverse Britannia seated, with date 1714 in the exergue. The coin is handsomely engraved and is pretty common.

In 1714 the Elector of Brunswick Lunenburg succeeded Ann as George I. To the usual titles of the sovereign was now added that of F. D. for *Fidei Defensor*, a title conferred on Henry VIII. by Pope Leo X., and though since then always on the great seal, never hitherto placed on the coins. The fourth shield on the reverse was now filled with the arms of the king's German dominions, the two lions being the arms of Brunswick; the lion rampant that of Lunenburg; the horse that of Saxony; while the central crown is Charlemagne's—the symbol of the Elector's office as Arch-Treasurer of the Holy Roman Empire. The legend on the reverse in full is: BRUN*svicensis* ET L*unenburgensis* DVX S*acri* R*omani* IM*perii*, A*rchi*TH*esaurarius* ET EL*ector*, the angles being filled in with plumes or roses, with S.S.C. (South Sea Company), or with C. C. or W. C. C., to denote the Welsh Copper Company.

The *gold* coinage consisted of Five, Two, One-half and Quarter guinea pieces, having on the reverse the four shields crosswise, and the star of the Garter in the center. The Quarter guinea

HALF-CROWN OF GEORGE I, 1720.

was issued only in 1718. The *silver* Crown, Half-crown, Shilling and Sixpence resemble the coins of the gold issue. The Maunday money was issued as usual, having the large numeral of value crowned with the king's British title alone.

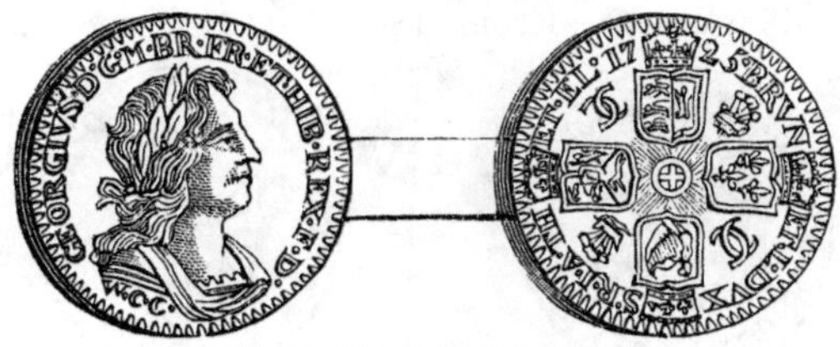

SHILLING OF GEORGE I.

The *copper* money consisted of Halfpennies and Farthings, having king's bust laureated and draped, with Britannia on reverse. The dates are from 1717 to 1724 inclusive. Those of 1717 and 1718 are thicker and smaller than those of later years.

In 1727 George II. issued *gold* Five, Two, One, and Half-guinea pieces, having king's bust with the *young head,* hair long and neck bare; on the reverse the shields are no longer arranged crosswise, but united as quarters of a single shield, as on the gold of William and Mary. In 1739 the bust has what is called the *old head,* in other respects the issue resembles that of 1727. The word LIMA is found on several pieces of this issue, signifying that the metal had been captured at Lima, in Peru.

The *silver* Crown, Half-crown, Shilling and Sixpence have the bust in armor with drapery over it, with the shields on the reverse crosswise. In 1743 the second issue of silver took place, with the old head design—in other respects resembling that of the first issue. Many of the coins of 1745–6 have Lima below the bust. The Maunday money is of the *young head* type alone. The *copper* coinage consisted of a young head Halfpenny and Farthing, from 1729 to 1739 inclusive, and an old head Halfpenny and Farthing from 1740 to 1754.

HALF-CROWN, WITH GROAT AND THREEPENNY OF GEORGE II.

In 1760 George III. succeeded his grandfather. His *gold* coins consist—1760–1786—of Guinea with bust, Half and Quarter, issued only and for the last time in 1762. From 1787 to 1800, a Guinea, Half, and One-third or Seven shilling piece were issued, with the arms on a shield of spade-ace pattern, and hence, commonly called the spade guinea. From 1801 to 1813 we have coins of

GUINEAS OF GEORGE III.

the same denominations—the Guinea being issued, however, only in 1813, the last issue of that value. These coins were issued for the troops embarking for France, and were not circulated in England. In 1817 a sovereign was issued having on the reverse St. George and the dragon, and a Half-sovereign with the arms on a shield.

In 1763, *silver* Shillings (called Northumberland shillings) were issued, having the king's bust, and on reverse, four crowned shields crosswise. In 1787 a Shilling and a Sixpence were issued, resembling the preceding, but with more drapery and armor, and a crown between the angles on the reverse; in 1798 another shilling, differing only in date from that of 1787. In 1801 the legislative union between Great Britain took effect, when the title King of France was quietly dropped from the list of those titles previously given to the

BANK OF ENGLAND DOLLAR, 1804.

English sovereign. Owing to the great scarcity of national money, while the Government was strangely unwilling to issue any from the mint, it yet authorized the Bank of England to issue a Five-shilling piece, or dollar—a name taken from the Spanish coinage, and the only one ever issued in England, followed during several years by Bank tokens of the values of Three Shillings and of Eighteenpence.

At last, in 1816, a great new coinage was issued. The Crowns in 1818–19–20, with the king's bust on the obverse and the figures of St. George and the dragon on the reverse. The Half crowns were issued in 1816–17, the obverse having the king's bust looking away from the spectator, with legend GEORGIUS III. DEI GRATIA, and on the reverse, a handsome armorial shield encircled by the collar of the Garter, with badge. In 1817–8–9 and 20, a new type was used showing less of the king's shoulder. Shillings and Sixpences of this type were also issued. Of the Maunday money, there were four varieties; 1st, that which resembles the Northumberland Shilling; 2d, that with bust resembling the Shilling of 1787, the numerals of value being in scrip and crowned, issued only in 1792; 3d, that with obverse like the last, but with Arabic numeral of value crowned; and 4th, that with the bust of 1816.

This reign was marked by an extensive and peculiar *copper* coinage. In 1770 a Halfpenny and Farthing were issued, having the king's bust in armor and the legend GEORGIUS III. REX, with Britannia on the reverse. In 1797 there was an issue of Two-penny and of One-penny pieces, the first of these values ever used in England, weighing respectively two and one ounce avoirdupois. These have a sunk centre and a raised rim on which is the legend with the king's bust on the obverse, and on the reverse Britannia seated. In 1799 there was a further issue of Twopennies, Pennies, Halfpennies, and Farthings of the previous design but without the raised rim; another issue of all except the Twopennies being made in 1805, of a somewhat similiar design but of lighter weight. In 1817 all the copper coin circulation was called in with the view to a recoinage.

In 1820 George IV. issued *gold* Two, One, and Half-sovereign pieces, having a head of the king with short curly hair, and on reverse St. George and the dragon, with date in the exergue. The Half Sovereign has on the reverse a shield like on the other coins, or a plain shield with rose, thistle and shamrock below it. In 1826 a Sovereign and Half-sovereign were issued having date below the bust. In 1821–2 *silver* Crowns were issued having the king's bust with bare neck and on reverse St. George and the dragon. In 1820–21–23, Half-crowns were issued, having on the reverse a crowned shield with rose below, thistle and shamrock on either side. A Shilling and a Sixpence of this design were issued in 1821. Others of this same year resemble the half-crown of 1823. In 1823–4, Half-crowns, Shillings and Sixpences were issued, having on reverse a plain square shield crowned. In 1825–26–28 and 29 there was an issue of a Half-crown with small bust and without

CROWN OF GEORGE IV., 1821.

drapery, and on reverse a square shield crowned. On the reverse of the Shillings of 1825–6–7 and 9 and the Sixpences of 1826–7–8 and 9, a crowned lion is standing on a crown. The Maunday

SHILLING OF GEORGE IV.

money has the head of the Crown of 1821, Pistrucci's, on the earlier pieces. The head of the Three-penny of 1822 is from the punch of the two-penny of the same date.

The *copper* coinage consists of a Farthing engraved by Pistrucci, and issued in 1821–2–3–5 and 6, having draped bust, and on reverse Britannia seated. In 1825–6 and 7, a Penny was issued with bare neck to the bust, and in exergue of reverse, a rose, thistle and shamrock. In 1826–7 Halfpennies, and in 1827 to 30 inclusive, Farthings of similar design were issued.

William IV. succeeded his brother in 1830, issuing a *gold* Sovereign, 1831 to 7 inclusive, with bust, and on reverse a square shield. He also issued a Half-sovereign of similar design for years 1834–7 inclusive. *Silver* Half-crowns were issued in 1831–4–5 and 6; Shillings and Sixpences of similar obverse, but the value in words across the centre of the reverse, the whole enclosed by branches. The Groats of 1836 and 7, have on the reverse Britannia seated. The Maunday money has crowned numerals and the *copper* Penny, Halfpenny and Farthing are all of the usual designs

In 1837 Victoria succeeded her uncle, and issued *gold* Sovereigns having bust, and on reverse, a square shield with rose, thistle

HALF-CROWN OF WILLIAM IV.

and shamrock below; the Half-sovereign has an ornamental shield, without the flowers. As the German dominions of the

GOLD FIVE-POUND PIECE OF VICTORIA.

late king passed to his brother, the arms of Hanover were now dropped from the English standard. On later coins, St. George

HALF-CROWN OF VICTORIA.

and the dragon appears on the reverse. A very beautiful Five-sovereign piece has also been struck, but has never come into circulation. The *silver* Crown and Half-crown have the queen's head filleted, with arms on plain shield within branches, rose, thistle and shamrock below. The issue of these pieces ceased in 1851.

In 1847, a very splendid Gothic Crown was prepared, but has never got into circulation.

GOTHIC CROWN OF VICTORIA

In 1848 a Florin, resembling the above Crown, was issued, but owing to the absence of the letters D. G., had to be recalled by the Government. Another was therefore prepared with those letters and is now in general use. The Shilling, Sixpence and Groat, resemble on the obverse those of William IV., while the Three-penny has on the reverse a large numeral of value, crowned. The Maunday money is like that of the previous sovereigns. Victoria's *copper* coinage consists of a copper Penny, Halfpenny and Farthing, with bust, the hair braided and the neck bare, with Britannia on the reverse. On the reverse of a Half-farthing, there is HALF-FARTHING in two lines across the field, with crown above and date below. The issue of these ceased in 1856. The current issue, struck in 1860, is of *bronze*, and consists of Penny, Halfpenny and Farthing, having laureated draped bust of the queen, and Britannia on reverse.

CHAPTER XIX.

COINS OF ENGLISH DEPENDENCIES.

ANGLO GALLIC.

Among the earliest foreign possessions of the English monarchs, were those French Provinces that through ancestral right, marriage or conquest, formed part of British territory. This sovereignty was exercised in part, by the establishing of local mints, whose names are frequently to be found on the coins of English sovereigns.

Perhaps the earliest of these is a Penny of Henry II. (1170 A. D.), struck in Aquitaine, and on which the king's title, HENRICVS REX, runs as a legend round the coin, while on the reverse is AQVI TANI E in three lines. On the coins of Richard I. sometimes his name and title run across the coins in two or even three lines, as *Dux Aqvitanie* or *Pictaviensis* (Poitou).

On the coins of Henry III. and Edward I. the lion of Aquitaine, with or without a crown, occupies the centre of the reverse. Edward II. also issued money for the Dukedom, for we read that in 1314 the French King closed Edward's mints. Edward III., having assumed, in 1339, the title King of France, placed that on his coins, omitting the lower one of Duke of Aquitaine. In 1360, however, he resumed the title of Duke, but in 1369 again employed the title of king, which thenceforth remained on the English coinage till 1801. Several succeeding monarchs also issued money for these French estates. Gradually, however, the French monarchy overran these districts until, at length, on the loss of Calais in 1558, the last vestige of England's early authority on continental Europe disappeared.

THE CHANNEL ISLANDS.

These are the only remains of the immense continental possessions of England. Among the peculiarities of these islands is a coinage distinct from that of the sovereign country, though of course, struck in London. On the obverse is a shield with three leopards or lions; the legend is STATE OF JERSEY, and the date 1813, while on the reverse, inclosed in a wreath, are the words THREE SHILLINGS TOKEN. On a *copper* coinage issued in 1844, is found the Queen's head, with inscription and date, and on reverse the arms of Jersey as before, with $\frac{1}{26}$ OF A SHILLING.

GUERNSEY has also its coins. On the obverse is a shield with the three leopards, and the word GUERNSEY below it; and on the reverse, the value, TWO, FOUR, SIX or EIGHT DOUBLES, with date. On the high values, the word Guernsey is *above* the shield, and the lower part of this is placed in a wreath.

ISLE OF MAN.

In 1786, the British government purchased the Isle of Man from the duke of Athol. As the island had a peculiar history and constitution, Pence and Half-pence were at once struck for its local currency. On the obverse is the king's bust, with the legend GEORGIUS III. DEI GRATIA, 1786, and on the reverse the arms of Man, three legs in armor joined at the thigh, with the legend on a broad band or border, QUOCUMQVE JECERIS STABIT.

Similar coins were struck in succeeding reigns till 1839, when the separate coinage was abolished.

IRELAND.

Previous to the conquest of Ireland by the Danes and by the Finns, as the Northmen are popularly called, the national money consisted of gold, silver and brass rings of a high degree of purity and of carefully graduated weights, reminding one of the animal weights found in Babylon. The earliest known coins are those of the Danish period, 850–1200 A.D. These coins, issued from mints

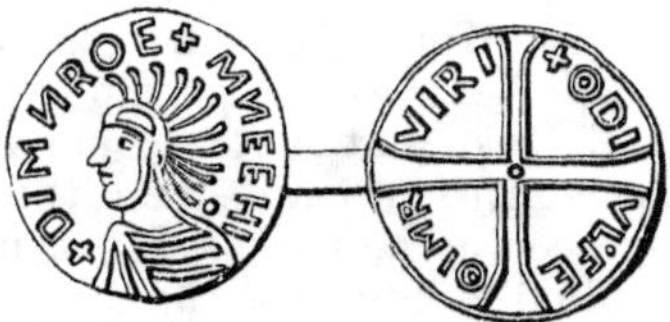

EARLY IRISH COIN OF DONALD, KING OF MONAGHAN, 850 A. D.

at Dublin, Limerick and Waterford, seem to be rude copies of Anglo-Saxon pieces, having, like the early Danish money, merely strokes, ||||||||'s, to represent letters. During this period certain native princes are supposed to have issued a few bracteate and other coins that are evidently copied in their style from those of the Danes. The authority of the Anglo-Saxon and Danish rulers of England was already so powerful in the eastern portion of the island known as the Pale, that there are coins of Ethelred, Edred, Edgar and of Canute, 886–1035 A. D., struck in Dublin.

In 1185, during the Norman period, John, then Lord of Ireland, issued for use in Ireland, Halfpennies and Farthings having the short double cross with an annulet in each angle on the reverse. Those struck then are called, from the full face design, full moon pieces. The legend is IOHANNES DOM (inus), and on the reverse TOMAS ON DW (Thomas of Dublin).

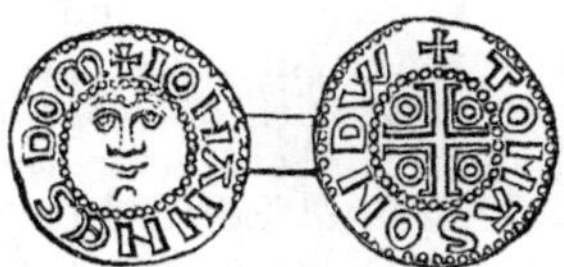

IRISH HALFPENNY OF JOHN, 1185 A. D.

After his accession to the English throne, John issued Pennies for Ireland of a wholly different design. The triangle, thought by some to reappear in the Irish triangular harp, is probably the symbol of the Trinity. It is so employed in church architecture, and as is known the conversion of Ireland from paganism to Christianity is connected with St. Patrick's advocacy of that mystery of the Christian faith, and his use of the trefoil as a natural analogue. The legend on the reverse is ROBERT ON DIVE. Halfpennies and Farthings were also issued.

IRISH PENNY OF KING JOHN.

In 1248, Henry III. issued his *second* coinage of the long double cross with the three pellets in the angles on the reverse. His Irish Pennies, with the king's head in the triangle, belong, from their obverses, to this period. On the coins of his successors, the first three Edwards, the title DNS. HYB.—*Dominus Hiberniæ*—first appears, while the triangle was inverted. Our readers will remember that on the coins of Edward I. we have simply EDW., on those of the II., EDWA. or EDWAR., and on those of the III., EDWARDVS.

IRISH PENNY OF EDWARD I.

On the Groat of Henry VI. there is on the obverse a large crown surrounded by a tressure, and on the reverse a long cross with pellets, and CIVITAS DVBLINIE. On a Groat of Edward IV. there are rays proceeding from a rose, to an outer circle in which is CIVITAS DVBLINIE divided into four sections by roses, the badge of the house of York, and by suns, the king's own crest. On another, there are the Irish arms, "three crowns impale," that is, one above the other, with a sword or spear passing upward through them, and on the reverse the British arms on a shield, with legend *Rex Hibernie,* Edward being the first to assume this title. Another has the large crown of Henry VI. Pennies and Halfpennies were also issued. The Groat of Richard III., and that of Henry VII. resemble the second one of Edward IV. Of Edward VI. there are no coins. The Sixpence of Henry VIII., base metal, issued in 1541, has the English arms on a crowned shield with *Henric* 8, *D. G., Angl. Franc,* and on reverse, *Et Hibernie Rex,* 38. The device on the reverse is the Irish harp facing left crowned, with H. R. on either side, also crowned. Heny's marital relations can be followed by his Irish Groats, which were apparently issued on each new marriage, and bear beside the harp the initial of the new queen. On a 6d., 3d., 1½d., and ¾d., issued in 1544, minted in Dublin, there is a full face of the king, and on the reverse the English shield. In 1553, Mary issued a Shilling, Groat, Half and Penny, with her bust, and on the reverse a crowned harp. Next year Shillings, Groats and Sixpences, base, with busts of Philip and Mary facing each other, were issued; the Groats resemble the Shillings, but have the date above the heads. In 1558, Elizabeth issued various base silver pieces, and also a *copper* Penny and Halfpenny, the first Irish copper coinage, differing from the device on the silver only in having a shield between the letters E R, and the harp between the years of the date 16—01 or 16—02. In 1602, James I. issued several base silver pieces with his bust on them, and in 1613, two varieties of a copper farthing, having a crown with sceptres crosswise, and legend *Jaco D. G., Mag. Brit.,* and on reverse *Fra et Hib. Rex,* with crowned harp. While these coins were of equal intrinsic value, and to be used both in England and in Ireland, that possibly for England has a rose for M. M. above the crown, while that for Ireland has a trefoil for M. M. on the reverse, the crown and harp being smaller and of different design from that on the other. In 1625, Charles I. issued copper Farthings resembling those of James in design, with the legend *Caro* or *Carolus D. G. Mag. Bri.* or *Brit.,* and on reverse *Fra et Hib. Rex.* During Charles' Irish troubles, what are known as the St. Patrick's pence were coined.* On the Halfpenny is a harper with legend *Floreat Rex;*

* The history of these pieces is very obscure; that they circulated in Ireland as halfpence and farthings, and were in common use as such till a century ago, shows that a very large amount must have been issued. Their device on both sides being ecclesiastical, shows that they either sprung from an ecclesiastical source or appealed to some ecclesiastical sentiment.

on reverse St. Patrick, mitred, and with crosier, holding out the trefoil, with the arms of Dublin at his side, with legend *Ecce Grex.* On the Farthing is a similar obverse, but on reverse the saint, holding a double or metropolitan cross, is driving venomous animals before him; a cathedral is in the background, and the legend *Qviescat Plebs.* The Ormond money was coined in 1643, and is obsidional. Charles II. issued, in 1660, a copper Farthing having legend *Carolvs II., D. G. M. B.*, and on reverse a crowned harp, with *Fra et Hib. Rex.*, and in 1680, a Halfpenny with bust of king facing left, legend *Carolvs II. Dei Gratia*, and on reverse a crowned harp, dividing the date 1680; legend *Mag. Br. Fra. et Hib. Rex.* James II. issued a copper Halfpenny in 1686, with his bust facing left, with reverse like that of Charles II., the crown and harp being somewhat larger. In 1689 came his Gun money, coined in Ireland from old metal,

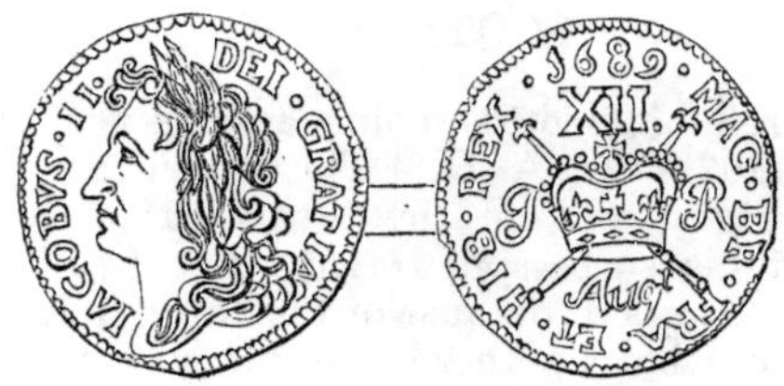

SHILLING OF JAMES II. GUN MONEY.

and consisting of *Crowns*, having the king on horseback with drawn sword, legend *Jac. II. Dei Gra. Mag. Bri. Fra. et Hib. Rex.* On the reverse are the national arms on four crowned shields placed crosswise, with a crown in the center; legend *Christo victore triumpho*, and in the angles of the shields *Ano Dom* 1690. The Half-crowns, Shillings and Sixpences have laureated bust facing left, with legend *Jacobvs II. Dei Gratia*, and on reverse, crown and sceptres crossed with I. R. with the value, XXX, XII, VI, in the upper angle, and the month of issue in the lower one, with legend *Mag. Br. Fra. et. Hib. Rex* 1689. White metal Penny and Halfpenny pieces in 1689. In 1690 a Five shilling piece in the same metal, and copper Halfpennies resembling those of 1686, but with date *above* the crown, and with date divided by the upper part of the crown, and also by the lower part of the harp. After James' flight from Ireland some of his followers issued from

They therefore have no connection with the royal mint, and were probably struck for use in the Irish rebellion of 1640, by or for the Catholic party. Now remembering that on the silver piece there are on a shield the arms of the city of Dublin, and that on the copper piece there is a figure of a cathedral, and that the famous St. Patrick's Cathedral is in Dublin, it is more than probable that these coins owe their origin to Dublin. In 1681, a man named Newby arrived in New Jersey from Dublin, bringing so many of these with him as to justify an Act of the Jersey Legislature in sanctioning their use as a New Jersey currency, a fact that strengthens the theory of their Dublin mintage.

Limerick, Halfpenny pieces with obverse as on the Gun money, and reverse a seated woman resting on a harp and holding up a cross, with legend *Hibernia* 1791.* In 1692 William and Mary issued a copper Halfpenny and Farthing with their busts in profile, with crowned harp on reverse dividing the date.

Anne issued no Irish money. The well known Wood Pennies and Halfpennies of 1722-3-4 were the only issues of George I. George II. issued a Halfpenny and a Farthing in 1736, having simply *Georgius II. Rex*, with, on the reverse *Hibernia*, above a crowned harp, and date below. George III. issued a Halfpenny in 1766: bust to left, and a Penny, Halfpenny and a Farthing in 1805, with bust clothed, while in 1822 George IV. issued a Penny and a Halfpenny and a pattern Farthing, and thus closed the series of Irish money.

SCOTLAND.

The earliest reliable Scottish coins are the very few ascribed to Alexander I., 1107-1124, A. D. These have a rude profile with sceptre, facing right, and on the reverse a cross with pellets in the angles. Of his successor, David, that "sair sanct for the crown," as he was styled because of his large donations of crown property to the Church, there are many coins, all of which resemble those of Alexander—the name being generally spelt DAVIT. We have no coins of the next monarch, Malcolm IV., but of William the Lion, 1166-1213, there are: 1st. Those with King's head to right, with short single cross; 2d. Those with

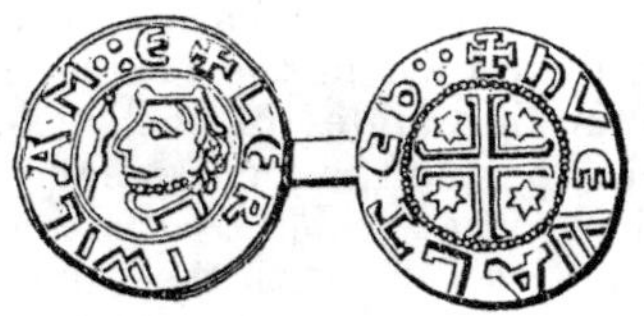

PENNY OF WILLIAM.

same head, but short double cross; and 3d. Those with head to left, all coined at *Berewic* (Herwick), *Edenbv* (Edinburgh), *Pert* (Perth), or *Rocesbu* (Roxburgh).

The coins of Alexander II. 1213-1249, are exceedingly rare, and were all minted at Roxburgh. Of those of Alexander III. 1249-1286, there were several issues. In 1250 it was ordered that the cross on the reverse should pass through the circle, making

* The Gun money of James II. was issued at the following dates: Sixpences 1689, July, Aug., Sep., 7ber, Nov., Dec., and 1690, Jan. and Feb. Shillings 1689, July, Aug., Sep., Oct., Nov., Dec., 8bor, 9ber, 10ber, 1690, Jan., Feb., Mar., Ap., May,, June and Sep., with large and small for Mar., and Ap. Half-crowns 1689, July to Aug., 1690, inclusive, and one for Oct., with large and small for Mar., Ap. and May.

what is called the *long* cross.* We have thus on some coins a long double cross, and on others a long single one, with a six-pointed mullet or star with open center in each angle. On the obverse is a crowned head with sceptre, facing left. On the Pennies and Halfpennies the legend is *Alexander Dei Gra.*, with continuation on the reverse, *Rex Scotorum.* The Farthings all belong to the single cross issue, and bear merely *Alexander Rex Scotorum.* Margaret, the Maid of Norway, Alexander's successor, having died before her accession, the period of confusion that followed the king's death ended in the placing, by Edward I. of England, of John Baliol on the Scottish throne. On Baliol's coins—Pennies, Halfpennies, and possibly Farthings, there is a bust with sceptre, and with the legend *Johannes Dei G. Rex Scotorum.* In 1306 Robert the Bruce occupied the throne, and issued Pennies, Halfpennies and Farthings, with a profile likeness and *Rex Scotorum.*

David II., 1329-1370, issued Pennies, Halfpennies and Farthings, and added the Groat and the Half-groat to the money of Scotland. These have on the reverse an inner circle with place of mintage and an outer circle with legend such as *Dns Protector meorum.* David

GROAT OF DAVID II.

issued the first Scottish *gold* money. His coins are numerous and very varied. Having been captured by Edward, the payment of the heavy ransom of 100,000 marks greatly impoverished his country and led to a depreciation of Scottish money. Robert II., 1370-1390, issued Groats, Half-groats, Pennies and Halfpennies. Art must have been at a low ebb at this period in Scotland, for the likeness on the coins which stands for Robert, also represents David. The coins of Robert III., 1390-1406, with a full face on the obverse, are easily recognized by the *pellets*, in place of the *mullets* in the angles of the cross on the reverse, a change again copied from the coins of England. Robert was the first to issue *billon* coins, and did so from Inverness. James I. issued Groats small in size, Pennies and Halfpennies, all having *pellets* in the

* A similar device was employed in England, by Henry III., in 1249.

angles of the cross. On James' assassination, in 1437, James II., a minor, was declared king. In his *first* issue of Groats, Half-groats and Pennies, made previous to 1451, there is in the angles of the cross a fleur-de-lis alternating with a sceptre. On the *second* issue, the king has no sceptre, and his neck is bare, with crowns in the angles on the reverse, an issue consisting of Half-groats and Pennies. And on the *third* issue, the king's neck is clothed. The Groats of this reign are as large as an English Shilling.

In 1460 James III. ascended the throne, and issued silver coins; *first*, having pellets in the angles of the cross ; *second*, having one large six-pointed mullet alternating with three pellets, with an annulet in their center ; *third*, havinga small mulet and pellets without the annulet and known as the Borage Groat ; *fourth*, having mullet of five points and pellets ; *fifth*, with crowns and pellets alternating, and *sixth*, with crowns and fleur-de-lis opposite, and pellets between, with legend *Dns Protor mevm et mevor*. James' *billon* groats have on the obverse the Scottish lion on a shield, and on the reverse an open cross with small St. Andrews cross in the centre, and crowns in the angles. His billon Farthings have the king's head crowned, and on the reverse a cross with pellets and *villa Edinbvrgi*.

Of James IV, 1488–1513 we have, *first*, coins with a full face and an open crown, and *second*, those with a three-quarter face and an arched crown. The billon Pennies, Halfpennies and Farthings resemble those of the previous reign.

On the death of James at Flodden, his son, James V. was declared king. His *first* issue has the three-quarter face, with open crown, thistles and mullets in the reverse ; the *second*, known as the Douglas Groat, of very fine workmanship, has a single arched crown, and the *third* has a double arched crown. On the reverses of the latter two are the national arms, the lion rampant. James' billon Groats or Placks have a large thistle crowned with I. 5, on either side, and a St. Andrews cross with two fleur-de-lis on the reverse. His gold pieces are known as *Bonnet* pieces from the small cap on the king's head.

The coins of Mary, Queen of Scots, are very numerous, and may be classified thus : 1st. Those issued previous to her marriage with the French Dauphin ; in 1553, Testoons and half-testoons, with the queen's bust, and on the reverse the arms of Scotland and of France. *Marks* were also issued. 2d. Those issued during her married state. 3d. Those during her widowhood. 4th. Those during her marriage with Darnley ; and 5th, those subsequent to his murder. In 1565 the first Scottish issue of silver Crowns, or Mary Ryalls, took place. These weighed one ounce, and passed for 30 shillings Scots. Smaller pieces of xx and x shillings value were also issued. These xxx shillings are commonly called Cruickston dollars, the palm tree on the reverse suggesting to the popular mind a yew tree at Cruickston Castle, the seat of Lord Darnley. Owing to the poverty of the crown, the issue of silver Groats and Pennies was replaced by one of *billon*, or rather of copper, washed with silver. The Two-penny piece was now called a *Bodle*, a corruption of Lord Bothwell's name, by whom it was prepared.

James VI., having succeeded his mother in 1571, revived the issue of Marks and Half-marks. His *First* issue was that of the Sword Dollar and its Half, with the national arms on the obverse, and on the reverse an erect sword crowned, with value and date. This is called the James Riall. *Second*, the Noble and its Half, having the arms as before, but on the reverse a cross, with crowns and thistles in the angles. *Third*, in 1578, the Thistle Dollar, from the large thistle crowned, its motto, "*Nemo me impune lacesset*," now appearing for the first time. *Fourth*, in 1582, the XL, XXX, XX and X Penny pieces, having the king in

THE CRUICKSTON DOLLAR.

armor and crowned, and on the reverse the arms. In 1589 the value of the XL Penny piece was raised to L, and in 1601, when the last Scottish crown was issued, it was raised to LX, as being worth sixty shillings Scots. *Fifth*, the Balance Mark, so called from the pair of scales and sword point on the reverse. *Sixth*, the Bare-headed Mark, having the king in armor and with head uncovered on the obverse, and on the reverse a three-headed thistle crowned; and, *Seventh*, the Thistle Mark, from the large single thistle crowned with arms on the reverse. James' billon money was extensive, and very much resembled that of his mother. For the first time a pure *copper* coinage was now issued, consisting of a Penny piece, with the bare-headed bust of the king and three thistle heads on the reverse. The billon Penny has I. R. under a crown, with legend, *Jacobus*, *D. G. R.*, *Scoto*, and on the reverse the arms, with one dot behind the lion, and place of mintage, while on the billon bodle, or *Turner*, as it was now called, a corruption of the French *Tournois*, are two dots with legend, *Vincit veritas.*

On the death of Elizabeth, in 1603, James VI. succeeded to the throne of England under the title of James I. The coins henceforth struck for use in Scotland resemble in design those of England, except that in the shield on the reverses, the arms of Scotland—the lion rampant—occupy the first and third quarters, while on those of England they appear only in the second quarter. The *gold* pieces of James consist of the Sceptre, the Double Crown, the Crown, the Thistle Crown and the Half-Crown. On the *silver* Crown and Half-crown pieces there is also a thistle in place of a rose

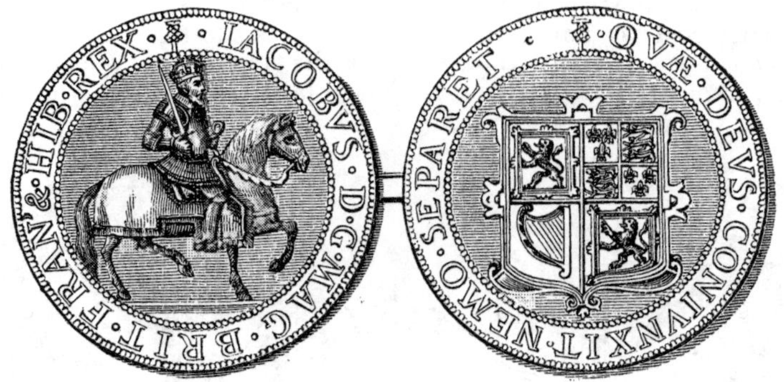

CROWN OF JAMES I.

on the trappings of the horse. The copper *Hardhead* has the three-headed thistle with *Jacobus D. G. Mag. Brit.*, and on the reverse the lion rampant.

The *gold* of Charles I. consisted of the Quarter, the Unit, its Half, Quarter and Half-quarter. On the *silver* Shillings and Sixpence, there is the value in numerals behind the head. Half-marks were issued resembling the English shillings, also Forty and Twenty-penny pieces, and a Two-shilling piece with the arms on the reverse, Scotch value.

FORTY-PENNY PIECES (SCOTS), CHARLES I.

The copper *Bodle* has a large C. R. crowned, with *Car D. G. Scot Ang. Fr. et Hib. R.*, and on the reverse a large thistle with *Nemo Me*, etc.

Charles II. issued a Four, a Two, a One and a Half-mark piece, having the king's bust in armor to left, and on the reverse four shields arranged crosswise, with crowned interlinked C's in the angles, with legend *Mag. Bri. Fra. et Hib. Rex.* 1672. There was also a Dollar, Half, Quarter and Eighth, with bust to right, and legend *Sco. Ang. Fr. et Hib. Rex.* 1676, with thistles in the angles on the reverse. The Sixteenth of the dollar was issued in 1681, having on the reverse a St. Andrew's cross, crowned with national emblems in the angles. On that of Charles II., in place of the C. R. there is the sword and sceptre crossed, and on the reverse the date. On the *copper Bawbee*, the King's head with legend, and on the reverse the crowned thistle with date.

In 1687 James II. issued a Forty-shilling piece, with British shield crowned on the reverse, and a Ten-shilling piece, with St. Andrew's cross on the reverse, the value being expressed beneath the bust.

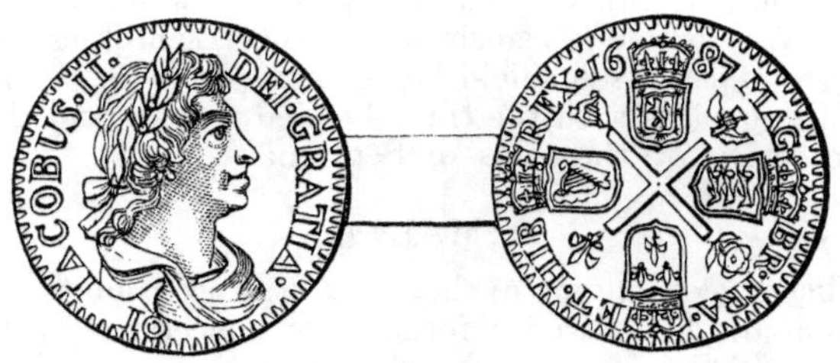

TEN SHILLING (SCOTS) PIECE OF JAMES II.

In 1689 and 1691, William and Mary issued pieces of Sixty, Forty, Twenty and Ten shillings value, bearing both their busts, facing left, and on reverse the British shield, with the Arms

FORTY SHILLING (SCOTS) OF WILLIAM AND MARY.

of Nassau in the centre, and a Five-shilling piece with a monogram of W. and M. on the reverse. The copper *Bawbee* has both busts with the large crowned thistle on the reverse, the *Half-bawbee* has the crowned monogram of W. and M., with reverse as before. After Mary's death, William issued pieces of similar value and design, but bearing only his own bust, his Five-shilling piece

TEN-SHILLING (SCOTS) PIECE OF WILLIAM III.

having on the reverse a three-headed thistle crowned. William's copper *Bawbee*, of 1695, has his own head, the *Half*, in place of the monogram, having the sword and sceptre crosswise, crowned.

In 1705, Ann issued a Ten-shilling piece resembling that of her predecessor, the Nassau shield being removed from the arms, and a Five-shilling piece with the three-headed thistle, and thus terminated the series of the coins of Scotland.

MALTA.

Malta has ever been one of the great strategic points of the Mediterranean, and has passed in former ages successively through the hands of the Phœnicians, Greeks, Carthagenians and of the Romans, by whom it was placed under the rule of the Prætor of Sicily. On the division of the Empire in 395 A. D., Malta fell to the Eastern section, to which it was attached till about the Ninth century. In 870 the Arabs drove out the Greeks, and in 1090 were themselves expelled by Count Roger of Sicily, who gave the inhabitants a comparatively free and popular government. During the Crusades, Malta became subject to the houses of Anjou and Castile.

In 1530 Charles V. granted Malta, along with Gozo and Tripoli, in perpetual sovereignty, to the Knights of St. John of Jerusalem, who had been driven by the Turks out of Rhodes, where they had issued money. Thə coins now bore the name and effigy of the Grand Master of the Order, with legend *Frater*, (*name*) *Magnus Magister Hospitalis*, &c., &o. The arms are on a shield that covers the head and body of an eagle; the value is in *Scudos* of twelve *tarins* each. In 1798 Malta was captured by the French, and the order of St. John dissolved. Soon after, however, it was taken by the British, in whose hands it still remains. In 1827, and again in 1835 and in 1844, there were coined for Malta copper pieces, in value one-third of a farthing, the device being a reduced copy of the English penny of those years.

AMERICA.

CHAPTER XX.

DOMINION OF CANADA.

From the early occupancy of Canada by France, a French coinage in that country was to be expected. In 1670 Louis the Fourteenth issued a silver piece of five sou value, having on the obverse a bust of the king with old head, laureated, surmounted by a small figure of the sun, with the legend LVD. XIII D. G. FR. ET. NAV. REX; on the reverse, the royal arms crowned, and the legend GLORIAM REGNI. TVI. DICENT. 1670. There is also a copper DOUBLE or two-denier piece, having on the obverse a large Roman L crowned dividing the date, 1670; with the letter A (Paris mint mark) below it, the legend being LVDOVICVS. XIII. D. GR. FRAN. ET. NAV. REX. On the obverse is the inscription, in four lines across the field, DOVBLI DE. L AMERIQUE. FRANCOISE, with the mint mark A in the exergue, and on either side of it a fleur-de-lis.

On the conquest of Canada (which then consisted of little else than the present Lower Canada), by the British in 1760, French money, of course, was in circulation in the form of the Sou, the Livre or Franc, and the Escu or Crown. In 1790, a British colony or settlement at a place called Kentucky issued in silver and in copper a coin that is often supposed to be connected with the United States Kentucky, but which is really a local token of Canada.

As we have nothing to do with the tokens of Canada, we omit all description of the

NOVA SCOTIA

tokens of 1814, and mention only its provincial coinage of Pence and Halfpence in 1823 and 1824, with the head of George IV. and legend, PROVINCE OF NOVA SCOTIA, having on the reverse a large thistle with legend, HALF-PENNY TOKEN 1823. Some of these coins bear the date 1832, the old ones with dates changed, being used under William IV. In 1840 we have the head of Victoria on coins otherwise mere duplicates of those of 1823, while coins of 1843 and 1856 were struck from very much superior dies. In 1856 the elaborate Mayflower Penny and Halfpenny were issued, having VICTORIA D : G : BRITANNIAR: REG : F :

D. with coroneted head and date, and on the reverse a large bunch of flowers with, PROVINCE OF NOVA SCOTIA and PENNY or HALFPENNY TOKEN. In 1861, 1862 and 1864, thin bronze Cent and Half-cent pieces were issued having laureated bust and legend as before and on reverse a wreath of flowers, surmounted by ONE CENT, and in exergue, NOVA SCOTIA inclosing a Crown with date below it.

Coins of a Cent value appeared in

PRINCE EDWARD ISLAND

having the name PRINCE EDWARD ISLAND round the obverse, and the date 1855 and 1857, while on the reverse are the words SELF-GOVERNMENT AND FREE TRADE, in five lines. In 1871 there was issued a Cent, having on obverse the Queen's head with diadem, and in a circle round the device the words, VICTORIA QUEEN. On the obverse we find a large and a small tree with PARVA SUBINGENTI below them, and in outer circle PRINCE EDWARD ISLAND ONE CENT.

In 1843

NEW BRUNSWICK

issued her beautiful Frigate Pence and Halfpence, with diademed Queen's head with inscription and date, and on the reverse a Frigate at anchor with sails furled, and inscription: NEW BRUNSWICK, ONE PENNY TOKEN. In 1854 a better shaped head with the hair fastened by a ribbon, and Frigate as before, with the words, on the reverse, ONE PENNY CURRENCY. Silver 5, 10 and 20 Cents and bronze Cents and Half-cents were issued in 1861–64 from dies that were used in the same year for NOVA SCOTIA, the name on the obverse being changed.

NEWFOUNDLAND

was the most ambitious of these maritime provinces. Not issuing any separate coinage till 1865, it then issued a Two dollar *gold* piece,

GOLD TWO DOLLAR PIECE OF NEWFOUNDLAND.

the only Canadian gold, a 20, 10 and 5 Cent *silver* and a 1 Cent *copper* piece. In 1870, a 50, and 20 cent silver, having queen's head laureated, with NEWFOUNDLAND below and on reverse value and date inclosed in a circle, and in 1870 a *copper* cent were issued.

The coinage of

CANADA

itself, whether Upper or Lower, is very scanty, the wante of the country having been met till lately by an immenss issue of private tokens. The coins having CANADA with the date, 1830, 1841, 1842 and 1844, with HALFPENNY on the reverse, were all private ventures. So was the CANADA HALFPENNY TOKEN with the Ship on the reverse. The first *government* issue, was the coin having the head of George IV. with legend PROVINCE OF UPPER CANADA, and on reverse Britannia seated, with HALFPENNY TOKEN and date 1832, the obversebeing from the die of the Nova Scotia copper of same date. In 1858, were issued, a silver 20, 10 and 5 cent piece, and a bronze Cent with a large head wreathed, having in outer circle, VICTORIA DEI GRATIA REGINA CANADA, and on the obverse, a wavy wreath of maple leaves, inclosing the words ONE CENT 1858.

CANADIAN SILVER TWENTY CENT PIECE.

Canada has added a 25 and a 50 cent piece in silver to her coinage, but the copper is still confined to the cent.

UNITED STATES.

No coins in the world are so rare and costly when in good condition as those of the American series. Of many of the pieces the issue was extremely small, and as when issued they were at once used in business transactions, they speedily became worn and defaced. The poverty of the colonists, moreover, and their deficiency in art tastes, account for the absence in those days of collectors, so that specimens in fine condition of the early coins of America are very rare. As the circle of collectors enlarges, the demand for these coins will necessarily increase, while perhaps, the total supply is already in the market.

The earliest medium of exchange that we find in use between the European colonists on these shores and the Indian natives, was wampum, or strings of shells, ground down to about the size of a grain of corn. These were used by the Indians for ornament and for barter, so that for trading purposes the settlers also required to deal in them.

By 1652 colonial life had so advanced that a metallic currency was demanded. In that year the General Court of Massachusetts issued at Boston some silver pieces, having stamped on them on the one side the letters N. E. (New England), and on the other the values, XIId., VId. and IIId. respectively. Of the Three-penny pieces only *two*, that are known to be genuine, can now be

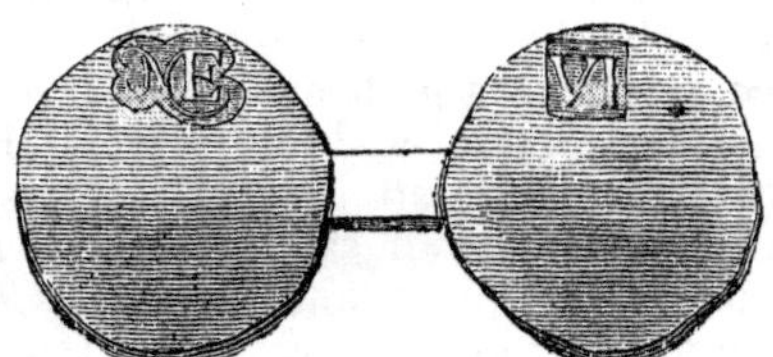

NEW ENGLAND SIXPENCE.

traced. These pieces have no date, and, despite their rude execution, possess considerable interest as being the earliest American coinage. The absence of any design gave such offense, however, that another series was issued in October, 1652. The design on these coins is an *Oak* tree with scraggy branches, inclosed in a circle of dots, the outer edge having a similar ring, and between the rings the words, MASATHUSETS, IN, and continued on the reverse, NEW ENGLAND. AN : DOM. ∴· the date, 1652, being in the centre, with the numerals of value immediately below, XII., VI. or III. In 1662, Penny and Twopenny pieces of this oak tree design were issued. A second series of this tree money bears a *Pine* tree, but in other respects resembles its companion.

PINE TREE SHILLING.

This tree money, once known as Boston or Bay shillings, was issued at different intervals for nearly thirty years, yet the original date, 1652, was retained on every piece. No genuine Penny pieces of either type are now known; the genuine having been struck on a die, all that are *cast* must be counterfeits.

In 1685, the Boston mint was closed by order of Charles II. No more issues of Massachusetts money were then made until 1766, when the colonists, in expression of their gratitude to William Pitt for his exertions in obtaining the repeal of the Stamp Act, issued a medalet or token, which soon became used as current money. On the obverse is a bust of Pitt, with wig and queue, with the legend, "THE RESTORER OF COMMERCE, 1776;" and below the bust, the words NO STAMPS. On the reverse is a ship sailing to the right, with the word AMERICA on the field behind it, with the legend, THANKS TO THE FRIENDS OF LIBERTY AND TRADE.

In 1787, Massachusetts, in order to lessen the drain on the resources of the Federal Government, issued a copper Cent and Half-cent. The device is that of an Indian chief with his bow and arrow, a star to left of his face, with the legend, COMMONWEALTH; on the reverse is an American eagle, having in its right talon a bundle of arrows, and in the left an olive branch, on the breast is a shield, bearing the word CENT. The legend is MASSACHUSETTS, and in the exergue is the date, 1787 or 1788. Of the Cent of 1787 there are three marked varieties; on the 1st the eagle holds arrows in the right talon, and an olive branch in the left; on the 2d, a long tapering branch of olive in the right, and arrows in the left, and on the 3d, a wide branching olive in the

MASSACHUSETTS CENT.

right, and arrows in the left. The Half-cent, for each year, bears the same general device, with the words HALF CENT on the shield, but has many varieties.

In 1788, the Federal Government prohibited any further State coinage, and so, for the second time, the mint of Massachusetts was closed.

The New England issues of coin were, however, not confined to Massachusetts. Other of the colonies having their State rights, availed themselves of these in issues of money. In 1785, CONNECTICUT issued a copper Cent having a bust, passing for Washington, with the legend AUCTORI CONNEC, and on the reverse, the Goddess of Liberty, with the legend IND. ET LIB, the date 1785 being in the exergue. Of this issue there were eight distinct types, distinguishable from each other by differences in the punctuation, before, between, and after the legend on the obverse, by the bust facing right or left, draped or in armor, or by the head being laureated or filleted. In 1786 there was another issue of as many types with the same general device. The edges of the planchet having been carefully milled, the pieces of this date are generally found in a better condition than those of 1785. In 1787 another issue took place, and one that, judging from the frequency with which coins of this date are found, must have been very extensive.

CONNECTICUT CENT.

The differences of the punctuation may denote different die cutters, or the different purchasers of the coin from the mint. Of this issue nearly fifty distinct types are known, making more than a hundred varieties. Some of these types are extremely rare, especially such as have any peculiarity in either of the legends; for sometimes we read AUCION, AUTOPI, AUCTOBE, AUCTOBI, in place of AUCTORI; very frequently obverse dies are found with a variety of reverses, and again reverses with a variety of obverses. Such pieces are known as mules.

Though the General Congress prohibited in 1787 any further State coinage, yet we have Connecticut Cents of 1788. As their

VERMONT CENT, 1786.

number is comparatively small, it is supposed that the mint remained in operation long enough to work off the stock of metal on hand. There are some fifteen or twenty types of this issue, differing as before in the style of the effigy, punctuation, etc.*

VERMONT has also an honorable place on the list of States possessing a local coinage, having had such a coinage even before she was formally recognized as a State by Congress. In 1785 there appeared under State sanction a Cent with a device both poetical and patriotic. On the obverse the All-seeing Eye with radiating lines, *thirteen* of which have shot out further and are more conspicuous than the rest, between each of which is a six-pointed star, while the legend reads QUARTA DECIMA STELLA, with reference to Vermont's claim to be the fourteenth star in the Union.

VERMONT CENT, 1788.

On the reverse is the sun radiated, but only partly visible as he rises over mountains that slope to the right, and are crowned by eight

* Among the unauthorized pieces whose history is somewhat uncertain, but which we think may belong to Connecticut, is one having a large bust, with the legend AUCTORI PLEBIS, with the Goddess of Liberty seated on the reverse, with the legend INDE. ET LIBER and the date 1787; a coin rather rare, consisting of but one type, with a few varieties. There is also one known as the Granby Copper, issued in 1737. In that year a Mr. Highley, of Granby, issued a coin having on the obverse a deer standing inside a circle, with the legend, ☞ WALUE. ME. AS. YOU. PLEASE., with the letters III. in the exergue. On the

GRANBY COPPER.

reverse, are three sledge hammers crowned with the legend ☞ I. AM. GOOD. COPPER., with 1737 in the exergue. Another issue of this piece is equal in size to half a cent, with the legend on the obverse ☞ THE. VALUE. OF. THREE. PENCE., with the word CONNECTICUT above on the reverse. On another piece with a similar obverse, the reverse bears the head of an ox, with the legend ☞ I. CUT. MY. WAY. THROUGH. On some pieces of this type the date 1737 is omitted. An issue of the first mentioned type seems to have been made as late as 1739. These pieces were, of course, only private tokens. Their issue was limited; specimens are only occasionally met, while the metal was poorly alloyed, so that those in good condition are extremely rare.

trees. Below the mountains is a plough, in the exergue, the date. The legend is VERMONTS RES. PUBLICA or VERMONTIS RES. PUBLICA. Next year the legend reads VERMONTENSIUM RES. PUBLICA. The number of trees varying from seven to nine. A second design appeared this year, having bust of Washington in armor with VERMON AUCTORI, and on the reverse Liberty seated, with INDE ET LIB. and dates 1786–7–8. From its peculiarly large head an issue of 1786 is known as the "baby head" variety, and specimens in good condition are rare.*

NEW JERSEY, or, as it was first called, *Nova Caesarea*, in honor of its first governor, Lord Jersey, whose title came from the English Channel Islands, (called by the Romans *Cæsarea*), does not seem to have had any local mint until 1786. On the coins then issued the device on the obverse is a plough surmounted by a horse's head, with the legend NOVA CÆSAREA and in the exergue the dates 1786 or 7. On the reverse is a heart-shaped shield, with bars or stripes in the upper part running across the shield, and in the lower part running lengthways, with the legend E PLURIBUS UNUM. Of

NEW JERSEY CENT.

this issue there are a dozen varieties, with a large number of variations, differing on such points as the length of the plough's handle, long or short, equal or unequal, round or square, the beam straight or curved, the horse's head raised or not, the shield broad or narrow, the ploughshare large or small, the coulter present or absent. On one issue of 1787 the legend reads E PLURIBS. 1788, the year so fatal to local issues, saw the last of the New Jersey cents. This issue resembles those previously issued, but must have been very limited, as only some ten varieties are known, on one of which the horse and plough face the left; one or two being called the dog or fox cent from a very small figure of such an animal, a mint mark we suppose, preceding the legend on the reverse.†

* Connected with these genuine Vermont pieces are those having a bust of George III. with legend GEORGIUS III. REX, with Britannia seated on the reverse and the legend *Vermon Auctori*, and those having the king's bust with the legend on the reverse of IMMUNE COLUMBIA, some of which, however, were State money.

† In 1787 some one issued a piece, bearing on the obverse a figure of Justice, seated on a globe, holding a pair of scales in the left hand and a flag in the right, with a wonderful life

Among the genuine native issues we must include what is known as the *Annapolis* money of MARYLAND. Of these pieces the Shilling has on its obverse for device a wreath inclosing two hands clasped, with the name of the issuer, J. CHALMERS, ANNAPOLIS. On the reverse are the figures of two birds pecking at a plant growing out of water, (canvas-back ducks?) with value and date 1783. The obverse of the sixpence is similar to that of the shilling, but on the reverse is an ornamental cross, with SIXPENCE and date 1783, while the Three-penny piece with obverse as before, but without wreath, has on the reverse a laurel branch surmounted by a wreath, with value.

In 1659 Lord Baltimore, proprietor and Governor of Maryland, issued silver Shillings and Sixpences for that colony. These pieces are now all rare, while a silver Groat and a copper Penny

BALTIMORE SHILLING, 1659.

may be called unique. On the obverse is a profile bust of Lord Baltimore facing the left, with the mint mark over his head and a cross patee, and the legend CÆCILIUS, DNS. TERRÆ-MARIÆ &ct. On the reverse, are the arms of the Palatinate surmounted by a crown with Roman letters of value at the side, and the legend CRESCITE: ET: MULTIPLICAMINI:

Another Colonial piece of the utmost rarity is that known as the CAROLINA halfpenny, having the device of an elepnant with a legend across the reverse of the coin of "GOD PRESERVE CAROLINA & THE LORDS PROPRIETORS," the date 1694 being below it. The history of this piece is unknown. The device of the elephant is found on a token known as the London halfpenny, and issued in London during the reign of Charles the Second, bearing on its reverse the civic arms. Such a device would very naturally be adopted by some of the East or West Indian trading companies of that date, and thus become a kind of symbol of foreign trade. Another specimen of this elephant halfpenny, bearing the same date 1694, has for legend the words, "God preserve New England." The device of

---

in the attitude, the legend being IMMUNIS COLUMBIA with the date. On the reverse is the Jersey shield and legend. This may have been a currency, but from its rarity and the fine condition in which it is generally found, it was more probably only a pattern. The similarity between the style and condition of the lettering on many New Jersey cents and that on some of Vermont and Connecticut, would indicate that the same die-sinker worked for the three States.

an elephant appears, we may observe, on the coins issued till lately by the British Government for use in Ceylon.

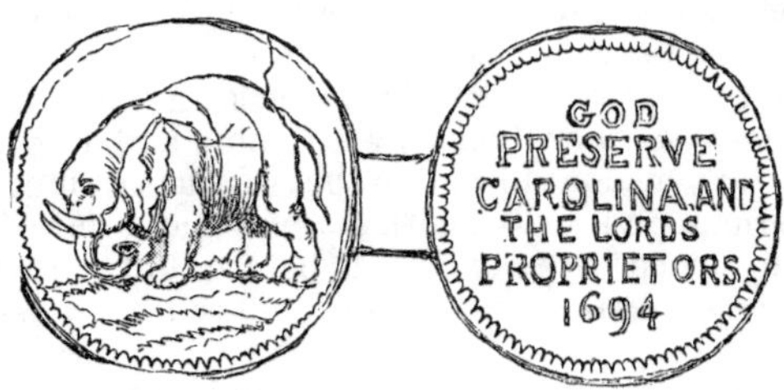

CAROLINA CENT.

In 1722, William Wood, the author of the Irish Wood Halfpence of the same date, issued under a Royal Patent, for use in the Colonies, Two-Penny, Penny, and Halfpenny pieces. These pieces are known from their device as the ROSA AMERICANA series. On the obverse is a well-cut head of George the First, the counterpart of that on the Irish pennies, with the legend: GEORGIUS D: G: MAG: BRI: FRA: ET I H:B: REX, and on the

ROSA AMERICANA TWO-PENNY, 1733.

reverse a full-blown rose in the centre. Above it are the words ROSA AMERICANA, 1722 (though two varieties are without a date), and on a ribbon below it, are the words, UTILE DULCI. On the obverse of the Penny and of the Halfpenny the legend is *Georgius. Dei. Gratia. Rex*, with the reverse as before. In 1723, the rose was surmounted by a crown, and, the date being changed, in other respects the issue resembled that of the preceding year. In 1733, there was another but very small issue of the Two-Penny piece, the head being that of George the Second, and the rose having leaves and a bud. Only some three or four specimens of this are known ; probably only a few patterns were struck.

Another of the foreign struck pieces is the VIRGINIA Halfpenny, which bears on the obverse a bust of George the Third, facing the right with the legend GEORGIUS III. REX. On the reverse are the arms of Great Britain, quartered, surrounded by the crown, which divides the date, 17—73, while the legend reads

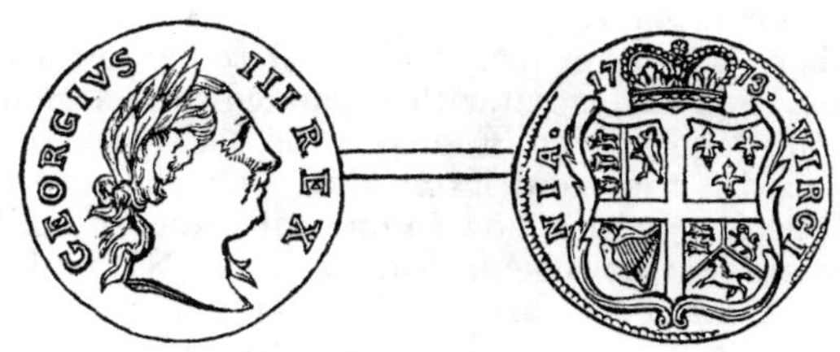

VIRGINIA HALFPENNY, 1773.

Virginia. Of this piece there are large and small planchets and a number of varieties. In 1774, a silver issue was made with the Virginia arms crowned.

It is not believed that any coins were ever issued by authority of the Legislature of NEW YORK, or that even any legal mints everexisted in the State. A number of copper coins do indeed exist called New York pieces, but all of these were struck in England and sent to this country as a trading speculation. The earliest of these pieces has on the obverse a bust of Washington in army dress, with the legend NON VI VIRTUTE VICI ; on the reverse is Liberty seated and holding a pair of scales with a staff surmounted by a liberty cap,lying on her right arm. The legend is NEO EBORA CENSIS, and the date 1786. We have also a coin bearing on the obverse a design, legend and date, the exact counterpart of the New Jersey IMMUNIS COLUMBIA piece, while on the reverse is a large eagle upright, with arrows in one talon and a laurel branch in the other, and the legend E PLURIBUS UNUM.

In 1786 there appeared the Excelsior cent, having on the obverse the New York arms, an oval shield with device of the rising sun, the shield surmounted by an eagle with open wings and supported by Justice and Liberty, with the word EXCELSIOR in the exergue. On the reverse is a roughly designed eagle, holding an olive branch in the left talon and arrows in the right; on the breast is a shield, while the head is surrounded by thirteen stars with the legend E PLURIBUS UNUM, and in the exergue 1786. Another issue of this coin, having a similar obverse, but the reverse altered in a few particulars, eleven stars in place of thirteen surrounding the head, arrows in the left and olive in the right instead of the reverse, and bearing the date 1787—was issued the next year. Of the same date is another piece with a bust in armor on the obverse, and the legend NOVA EBORAC, and on the reverse, Liberty, bearing a most suspicious resemblance to the Britannia on old English money, with the legend VIRT. ET LIB. date 1787. Of this piece, two types with several varieties are known. There is another piece of this date having a fine device. On the obverse is an eagle with expanded wings standing on a rock, with the legend NEO EBORACENSIS, 1787, while round the base of the field is the word EXCELSIOR. On the reverse is an Indian chief, standing with a bow in one hand and an uplifted tomahawk in the other; the legend reading LIBER NATUS LIBERTATEM DEFENDO. A variety of this coin has on the obverse a small oval shield with the sun rising; this is surmounted by a small eagle with expanded wings, and is supported by the figures of Justice and Mercy; at the base is the date 1787, and below this the word EXCELSIOR. There is, however, beyond the agreement in design with the preceding piece, nothing special about this coin to connect it with New York.

Among the other tokens or local cents connected with New York, are those having on the obverse the device of a ship in full sail, and with TALBOT ALLUM AND LEE, NEW YORK, and in the exergue ONE CENT. On the reverse is an erect figure of Liberty, standing beside a wool bale and holding a staff with liberty cap. The legend being LIBERTY AND COMMERCE, and the date 1794, while on the edge we read, PAYABLE AT THE STORE OF. This was plainly what we now call a store card or tradesman's token, an advertisement from its legends, a coin from its intrinsic value. A second issue, with some variation in the design, was made the next year.

MISCELLANEOUS.

Toward the close of the Colonial perio da large amount of copper tokens of thin planchets and light weight was in circulation, with a great variety of legends and devices, some interesting, not a few very stupid. Many of these were imported from England by traders of doubtful honesty, while not a few were of home manufacture, and struck, it is feared, mainly in Philadelphia. On the obverse of one of these is a laureated bust facing the right, with the legend GEORGIUS TRIUMPHO. On the reverse is Liberty holding a staff in her left hand, a laural branch in her right, while in front of her is a grate or paling of thirteen bars, with the legend, VOCE POPOLI, and the date 1783.

In 1783 there also appeared a copper piece, having on the obverse, in the center, the All-seeing Eye, with radiating beams, among which are thirteen stars, the legend being NOVA CONSTELLATIO. On the reverse is a wreath inclosing the letters U. S. in Roman characters, with the legend LIBERTAS —JUSTITIA, and the date 1783. The three types of this issue have different punctuations: In the first type CONSTELATIO is spelled with only one L; the rays have blunt ends, while on the others these

GOLD IMMUNSE COLUMBIA.—*Costellatio Series*

are pointed. There was another issue of these pieces in 1785, with similar devices. The legend on the obverse, however, has now CONSTELLATIO, while on the reverse the U. S. is in scrip, and the legend reading LIBERTAS ET JUSTITIA, 1785. Of this also there are

NOVA CONSTELLATIO, 1785.

three types, differing as before by the spelling in CONSTELLATIO, and by the punctuation. The ends of the second type of this year's issue are blunt, those of the others pointed. There was also an issue of this piece in 1786, having the U. S. in Roman characters, while the legend reads LIBERTAS ET JUSTITIA.

KENTUCKY CENT, 1791.

What is called the Kentucky Cent is a very pretty and tasteful piece, struck at Lancaster, in England, in 1791. On the obverse are fifteen stars, forming a triangle, each star bearing the initial letter of one of the States, Kentucky, whence its name, being at the apex. On the reverse is a hand holding an open scroll on which we read, OUR CAUSE IS JUST, while the legend is, UNANIMITY IS THE STRENGTH OF SOCIETY. Round the edge of the coin we read, Payable in Lancaster, London or Bristol. Some were struck on a thin and some on a thick planchet.

Akin in some respects to this Kentucky piece is the Confederatio Copper. On the obverse, a circle of rays whose center is occupied by thirteen stars, the legend being CONFEDERATIO, and the date 1785. On the reverse is the figure of an Indian standing beside an altar, with bow and arrow in his hands, and his foot on a crown, with the legend, INIMICA TYRANNIS AMERICANA.

Another of these imported coins bears on the obverse a female figure seated, with her left hand resting on a harp, the legend being, NORTH AMERICAN TOKEN, and the date in the exergue, 1781. On the reverse is a brig sailing to the right, with the legend, COMMERCE.

To this same period and to the same origin we must ascribe the Washington Cents. On the first of these, known as the *Small-head* Washington, we have a bust of Washington in military dress, facing the left, with the legend, WASHINGTON AND INDEPENDENCE, and in the exergue, 1783. On the reverse is Liberty seated, holding in her right an olive branch, and in her left a liberty pole with cap, the legend being, UNITED STATES, the exergue blank, but the letters T. W. I. in one corner and K. S. in the other. On the second type, the *Double-headed* Washington, we have Washington as before, with simply the word WASHINGTON, and in the exergue an oblong star of eight points. The reverse is the same as the obverse, with the legend, ONE CENT. The third type, called the *Unity* Cent, has on the obverse the bust of Washington laureated, facing the left, with WASHINGTON AND INDEPENDENCE, and date 1783, the reverse consisting of a laurel wreath inclosing the words, ONE CENT, while the legend

LOUISIANA CENT.

is, UNITY STATES OF AMERICA, and in the exergue, 1-100. The fourth of this series, known as the *Large-head* Washington, has Washington, legend and date as before, its reverse being a copy of that on the first type.

In the beginning of last century copper coins were struck in Paris for the use of the French Colonies generally. As at that time Louisiana belonged to France, certain of these pieces are known among collectors as *Louisiana Cents.* Of those issued—1721 and 1722—the obverse presents two L's saltire wise, sur mounted with a crown, with the Anjou legend, *Sit Nomen Domini Benedictum,* and on the reverse, *Colonies Françoise,* 1722. Another issue was made in 1767. These coins are found with and without a counterstamp.

LOUISIANA CENT.

CHAPTER XXI.

FEDERAL CURRENCY.

Although the Declaration of Independence had been adopted in 1776, it was not until several years afterwards that a Federal coinage was issued. Up to that period the Colonies had either minted on their own account, or private individuals had struck or imported copper coins for currency. In 1787 the Government

FRANKLIN PENNY, 1787.

issued the FIRST UNITED STATES CENT—now called the *Franklin penny*, because one of his terse sayings was inscribed upon it. On the obverse is a sun-dial in the centre, shone upon by the sun, with the word FUGIO on the right, and 1787 in the left, and in the exergue MIND YOUR BUSINESS. On the reverse is a circle formed of thirteen rings, representing the original number of the States; the small circles on one type, plain, and on another, each bears the name of one of the States. The large circle incloses a smaller one, on which are inscribed the words UNITED STATES; on one variety—there are seven—the order is reversed, and the words read, STATES UNITED, while in the centre is the legend, WE ARE ONE.

With the issue of this solitary but interesting piece, the Federal mint contented itself from 1787 to 1791, when the present mint was established and at once proceeded to prepare dies for new issues. In 1791, there appeared three pattern pieces, now called the Eagle cents. On the obverse of the first is a bust of Washington, facing to the left, with the legend, WASHINGTON PRESIDENT, with the date, 1791, in the exergue. The reverse resembles that of the Massachusetts cent, an eagle with expanded wings, the body nearly covered with a heart-shaped shield, the right talon holding a laurel branch, the left a bundle of arrows, and on a scroll, held by the beak, are the words UNUM E PLURIBUS, with the legend, One Cent. On the edge we read, United States of America. This is now known as the *Large* eagle cent. On the second of these pieces we have a similar obverse, without the date, however; on the reverse is an eagle, with upraised wings, that rise above its head and are connected by a cloud-wreath, between which and the eagle are eight stars; on the eagle's breast is a shield with stripes, crossways at the top; the date in the exergue and legend as before. This is known as the *Small* eagle cent. The third has an obverse similar to that on the large eagle cent, while on the reverse the eagle's wings are upraised, but are only level with the head; the clouds are wanting; the stars are six in place of eight in number, and the legend above is cent, in place of one cent. There was a small experimental issue of these pieces, which are now much sought for by collectors, but Washington so determinedly opposed the placing of his effigy on the national coinage that the device was rejected, and the dies themselves, it is said, were broken.

In 1792 another piece was issued having on the obverse a bust of Washington, with the legend, G. Washington, President I., and the date in the exergue. On the reverse is an eagle with upraised wings, between the tips are fifteen stars; on the breast a shield, as before, the legend being United States of America. Washington, it is said, was much pleased with this service, but his fatal objection to it was the numeral after the word President. On another piece of the same date we have a naked bust of Washington, filleted, facing right, with date below, and a reverse copied from the third pattern of 1791.

There is yet one other pattern piece of this year that is sometimes met; the obverse is apparently a copy of that of the Cent or *second* pattern piece of 1791, while the reverse is a copy of that on the large eagle or *first* pattern of that date, with one star resting on the head of the eagle and a row of twelve stars connecting the wings in place of the legend Cent.

GOLD COINAGE.

Eagle.—Of the gold coinage of the United States there is considerable variety. The first piece struck was an Eagle or Ten dollar gold piece, in 1795, having on the obverse a female head with large liberty cap. The legend is Liberty. Round the edge of the field are five six-pointed stars to the right, and ten to the left. On the reverse is an eagle with expanded wings, holding a wreath in its beak and a long olive branch in its talons, the legend being United States of America.

In 1796 the Eagle had sixteen stars to mark the admission of Tennessee into the Union. In 1797, the obverse being unchanged, the eagle on the reverse has a large shield on its breast, the wings are uplifted and their tips connected by a wreath of clouds with thirteen stars ; a scroll across the eagle's neck has E PLURIBUS UNUM, while the legend round the edge of the field is UNITED STATES OF AMERICA. From 1798 to 1804, inclusive, the stars on the obverse were reduced to thirteen. No Eagles, properly so called, were issued after this date. In 1838, however, a piece of equal value, but called a Ten Dollar piece, was issued, having on the obverse Liberty facing left, having her hair tied up into a knot, and on a band the word LIBERTY, with thirteen stars round the field, and date in the exergue ; and on reverse an eagle with shield and uplifted wings. The legend is UNITED STATES OF AMERICA, and below the eagle we read, TEN D. In 1839-40, 1, 2, 3, 4, 5, 6, 7 and 8 similar pieces were issued. In 1849 a Double Eagle or Twenty Dollar piece was issued, and continued to be issued down to 1857.

TWENTY DOLLAR PIECE.

HALF-EAGLE.—The Half-eagles of 1795 to 1804, inclusive, resembled the Eagles of those years, the device of 1804 remaining in use

HALF EAGLE OF 1795.

during 1805, 6, and 7. In 1808 we have the Matron head, facing left, wearing a loose cap with LIBERTY on its band, with date below aud thirteen stars round the edge of the field. On the reverse is an eagle, shield, and uplifted wings, connected by a scroll having E PLURIBUS UNUM and 5 D. in the exergue. This device appears on the Halves of 1809 to 15 inclusive. During 1816 and 17 there was no gold coinage. The old device was then resumed, and is found on the Halves of 1818 to 1833 inclusive.

On the Half of 1834 the scroll with its legend, E. Pluribus Unum, is omitted, the device being otherwise unchanged from the preceding years, and so remained for 1835-6, and 7—the last year of the Half Eagle. In 1838 "Five Dollar" pieces were issued, with device similar to that on the Ten dollar pieces of this year, and so again from 1839 to 1857 inclusive.

Quarter-Eagle.—The first Quarter Eagle was issued in 1796, and in device and legend resembled the other gold coins of the same year. Toward the close of the year another device was employed, the stars being left off the obverse, and on the reverse the eagle is entirely changed, its wings are expanded, on the breast is a shield, the wings are uplifted and their tips connected with a wreath of clouds, below which are sixteen stars, while a scroll in the beak of the eagle has the words, E Pluribus Unum. In 1797–8 and 9 the device was unchanged. In 1800–1 and 2 no Quarter-Eagles were issued. In 1803–4–5–6 and 7 the Quarter re-appeared, with device as before. In 1808 its device resembled that on the Half-Eagle of this year, when it was dropped till 1821. During 1822–3 it was absent, but was present from 1824 to 1827. In 1828 it was again wanting, re-appearing again in 1829–30–31–32 and 33. In 1834–5–6–7 it bore the device of the Half-Eagle of this year, again in 1838 changing to become like the Eagle of the same date. There was no change in 1839–40 or 41, (except that in this year the letter C appears on the reverse, indicating that the issue was intended for California), nor in 1842–3–4–5–6–7–8–9–50–51–2–3–4–5–6–7.

QUARTER-EAGLE, 1870.

Three-Dollar Piece.—In 1854 a Three-Dollar piece was issued, having a female head to represent an Indian princess, with

THREE-DOLLAR PIECE.

upright wreath of feathers, on whose band is the word Liberty, while round the field we read, United States of America. On the reverse is a tobacco wreath, inclosing value and date. Similar coins were issued in 1855–6 and 7.

ONE DOLLAR.—In 1849 a One-Dollar piece was issued, having an obverse like the other coins of the date, but on the reverse a

ONE DOLLAR.

wreath enclosing, 1 DOLLAR, 1849. So also in 1850–1 and 2. In 1853 the dollar was wanting, but re-appeared in 1854 with an obverse re-

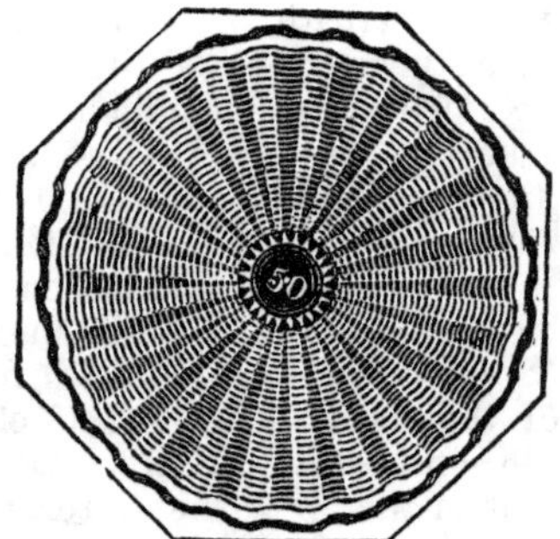

CALIFORNIAN FIFTY-DOLLAR PIECE ISSUED IN 1851 BY THE ASSAY OFFICE IN SAN FRANCISCO.

sembling that of the Three-Dollar piece of the same year, a device it continued to bear down to the present.

SILVER COINAGE.

SILVER DOLLAR OF 1794.

DOLLAR.—In 1794 a Silver Dollar was issued having on the obverse a female head facing right with flowing hair; the date is in the exergue, seven stars are on the one side and eight on the other of the word *Liberty*. On the reverse, an eagle as if about to fly is standing within a wreath, while the words UNITED STATES OF AMERICA are round the border of the field. On the edge of the coin are the words ONE, DOLLAR, OR, UNIT, HUNDRED, CENTS. In 1795, the Dollar was of last year's type till near the close of the year, when Liberty's bust was made larger and draped, and the hair tied by a ribbon or fillet at the back of the head. On the reverse the eagle is smaller and is standing on a cloud. The Dollar of 1796 bears

SILVER DOLLAR OF 1795, (2d TYPE,)—AND OF 1796.

the same device. In 1797 the device is unchanged, but on some dollars there are fifteen stars, the effigy facing seven; on others there are sixteen, the effigy facing on some six and on others seven.

SILVER DOLLAR OF 1798.

In 1798, the obverse is unchanged, except that there are only thirteen stars, six in front of the effigy. On the first issue, the reverse still bears the small eagle, but on a second issue later in the year the device resembles that on the second type of the gold quarter eagle of 1796.

The dollar of 1799 has always 13 stars on the reverse, resembling that of 1798, having however, on one type eight stars in front of the effigy and seven behind, and on another seven in front and six behind. In 1800–1–2–3–4–5 dollars were issued resembling that of 1799, and then none were struck till 1836, when the beautiful Gobiecht pattern was prepared, having Liberty seated beside a shield, and holding a spear and cap, with date, and on the reverse an eagle flying across a field studded with twenty-six large and six small stars, and legend "UNITED STATES OF AMERICA, ONE DOLLAR."*

In 1837 there were no dollars issued; but in 1838, Gobrecht's device was adopted, differing from the pattern of 1836 only in, having thirteen stars round the edge of the field of the obverse while the field of the reverse is without stars. It is said that only eighteen of this design were issued. The dollar of 1839 resembled that of the previous year, while on that of 1840 there is a new device. The obverse is as before, Liberty seated, facing right,

SILVER DOLLAR OF 1840.

but the reverse is an eagle about to fly, with expanded wings, and holding in its talons arrows and laurel branch, with legend UNITED STATES OF AMERICA, ONE DOL. From this date down to 1873 the dollar was regularly issued, and always of the one device.

TRADE DOLLAR.—In 1873 there was issued what is known as the Trade Dollar, a piece somewhat heavier than the ordinary coin, and having a device somewhat different. It is intended chiefly for cirulation abroad, and has been issued every year since.

*On one variety, *Gobrecht* is engraved on the base of Liberty; on another, extremely rare, it is on the field, between Liberty and the date.

TRADE DOLLAR OF 1873.

HALF-DOLLAR.—The first Half-dollar was issued in 1794 and resembled in device the dollar of that year. The Half-dollar of 1795 bears the same device as that of 1794. In 1796 and 7 it resembled the Dollars of these years respectively. There was then

SILVER HALF-DOLLAR OF 1794.

no Half issued till 1801–2-3-4-5-6 and 7, when it resembled the Dollars of these years respectively. Toward the close of this year

HALF-DOLLAR OF 1803.

there (1807), was a complete change of the design; Liberty faced left, wears a loose cap with LIBERTY on the band, having seven stars in front of the effigy and six behind, with date in the exergue. On the reverse an eagle preparing to fly and holding arrows and olive branch in its talons, over its head a scroll with the words E. PLURIBUS UNUM, while around the edge of the field we read UNITED STATES OF AMERICA, and below the eagle 50 CENTS, a device continued each year down to 1815 inclusive. In 1816 there was no silvrr coinage, but in 1817 the Half-dollar was resumed and continued to be issued regularly down to the year 1836 inclusive, without any change except that in 1826 the stars were small and in 1827 were large. In 1834 there were large and small dates. In 1837 the scroll

SILVER HALF-DOLLAR OF 1837-8-9.

with its legend was removed from the reverse and 50 CENTS took the place of 50 C, while the edge was milled. On a late issue of 1839 and during the whole of 1840 Liberty is seated, with date below and six stars in front of the effigy and seven behind. The reverse is as before with HALF DOL. substituted for 50 CENTS. This

HALF-DOLLAR OF 1840.

device was continued down to 1852 inclusive. In 1853 a barbed arrow was placed on each side of the date on the obverse and the background of the reverse was covered with rays. In 1854 the rays were wanting, and in 1856 the barbed arrows were removed. In 1866-7 a scroll was placed on the reverse bearing *In God we Trust.* In 1873 on a second issue, and in 1874, an arrow head was placed on each side of the date in the exergue. In 1875 and 1876 the arrow-head was absent.

SILVER QUARTER-DOLLAR OF 1796.

QUARTER-DOLLAR.—The first Quarter-dollar was issued in 1796, with device resembling the dollar of the same year. The next issue of the Quarter took place in 1804, again resembling the dollar of its year, the same device being used on the issues of 1805–6–7. There were then no Quarters issued until 1815, when a new is-

SILVER DOLLAR OF 1815.

sue resembled the Half-dollar of same year. In 1816 there was no coinage. In 1817 the Quarter was absent, but in 1818 it re-ap-

SILVER QUARTER-DOLLAR OF 1831.

peared with device of 1815, which it retained each year till 1825 inclusive. In 1826 there was no Quarter issued. Re-appearing in

1827 and 1828, it was again wanting in 1829 and 1830. In 1831 the size was reduced, the scroll left off, the edge raised, and remained so down to 1839 inclusive. In 1840 Liberty was seated, with the date below, while on the reverse QUAR. DOL. took the

SILVER QUARTER DOLLAR OF 1840 TO 1852.

place of 25 c. This continued for each year down to 1853, when the background of the eagle was filled in with rays, and on a later issue of same year an arrow was placed on each side of the date on the obverse, a device retained during 1855 and 1856, then dropped to re-appear in 1874 alone. In 1854 the rays were dropped, and in

SILVER QUARTER DOLLAR OF 1853.

1867 a scroll appeared, with the words, *In God we trust*, since which time the Quarter has been issued each year with the same device. In 1873 arrow heads were placed beside the date.

THE DIME.—The first Dime or Ten-cent piece was issued in 1796 and resembled the Dollar of that year. In 1797 there was a

SILVER DIME OF 1796.

complete change on the reverse, as our illustration shows, and on the obverse in place of the fifteen stars that had appeared on the Dime of the previous year, only thirteen, with reference to the "Old Thirteen" were placed on the obverse. In 1799 there were no Dimes issued. In 1801–2–3–4–5 the early device was resumed, with

SILVER DIME OF 1797–8.

thirteen stars in place of sixteen on the reverse. In 1806–7–8 there were no Dimes. In 1809 the device resembled that of the Half-

SILVER DIME OF 1809–1814.

Dollar of this year, and remained so in use each year down to 1814. Then no Dimes were issued until 1820, when one appeared

SILVER DIME OF 1837.

with the old device, which was continued on the Dimes of 1821 to 1836 inclusive, excepting 1826, in which there was no Dime

SILVER DIME OF 1838–1876.

issued. In 1837 the device was unchanged, but on a *second* issue, as our illustration shows, both obverse and reverse were changed, while the stars reappear on the obverse of that of 1838,* though in all other respects the device is similar, the Dime of every year since bearing it unchanged. In 1853 the device was unchanged, but on a *second* issue an arrow-head was placed on either side of the date, and retained during 1854 and 1855, but removed in 1856, since which time the Dime has been issued every year with device unchanged, except in 1873–4, when the arrows reappeared.

SILVER HALF-DIME, 1794–5.

Half-Dime.—The first Half-Dime was issued in 1794, and resembled the dollar of the same year, that of 1795 being similar. In 1796 the fillet-head of Liberty is used, and the Half-Dime resem-

SILVER HALF-DIME, 1796.

bles the dollar. In 1797 the same device is used, but there are now eight stars facing the effigy, and seven behind it. In 1798 and 1799 there were on Half-Dimes. In 1800 the stars were reduced to thirteen, six facing the effigy and seven behind it; and so, also, on the Half-Dimes of 1801–2 and 3. In 1804 no Half-Dime was issued, and that of 1805 bore the old device. The Half-Dime was then discontinued until 1829, when a new device appeared,

SILVER HALF-DIME OF 1829.

used every year down to 1836 inclusive. In 1837 the Half-Dime appeared at first with the device unchanged, but, on a *second* issue it resembled the Dime of this year, having Liberty seated, without stars. In 1838 thirteen stars are placed round the edge of the

* The New Orleans mint retained the starless obverse on the Dime of 1838.

obverse, a device that has since been used every year to the present. On a *second* issue in 1853, an arrow was placed on each

SILVER HALF-DIME, 1838-1876

side of the date, and retained during 1854 and 1855, absent in 1856, but reappearing in 1873, when the issue ceased.

THREE CENT PIECE.—In 1851, the first Three Cent piece was issued, having on the obverse a large star, with UNITED STATES OF AMERICA, and date, and on the reverse a large C, with the numerals III in the center and thirteen stars around the edge of the field.

SILVER THREE-CENT PIECE, 1851.

In 1853 arrows were placed *below*, and an olive branch placed *above* the numerals inside the C, and were on each year's

SILVER THREE-CENT PIECE, 1853.

issue down to 1873, when the further issue of the piece was stopped, after only a few of that year had got into circulation.

PATTERN OBVERSE SILVER TWENTY CENT PIECE.

TWENTY CENT PIECE.—In 1873 a Twenty Cent piece, without milled edge, was issued with the old device of Liberty on the obverse, but on the reverse a very high-shouldered eagle resembling that on the Trade Dollar. The legend reads UNITED STATES OF AMERICA, with TWENTY CENTS in the exergue. This coin has been issued chiefly for use in the Pacific States, and has appeared in 1873–4–5–6.

COPPER COINAGE.

CENT.—In 1793 appeared the first of our national copper Cents. This Cent was issued in three distinct forms; first, as the *Chain* Cent, having on the obverse a circle composed of fifteen links forming a chain inclosing the word ONE CENT $\frac{1}{100}$, with the legend UNITED STATES OF AMERICA; on the reverse is a head of Liberty facing right, with the hair unbound and streaming, the legend being

CHAIN CENT OF 1793.

LIBERTY, and in the exergue the date 1793. Of this form there are four types, on one of which the legend reads AMERI, with several varieties. The second form is known as the *Wreath* Cent, having on the obverse, in place of the chain, a wreath with many berries inclosing the words ONE CENT. The stems of the wreath are tied with ribbon, and between their ends we read $\frac{1}{100}$, with legend as before. On the

LIBERTY CAP CENT OF 1793.

reverse is head of Liberty with hair unbound and flowing loosely, and in the exergue a twig with leaves. Of this Cent there are two types—a small head with many varieties and a large head with only a few. The third form is the *Liberty Cap* Cent, having, as before, a wreath inclosing the words ONE CENT; but now, thrown over the left shoulder of Liberty is a pole surmounted by a Liberty cap. In 1794 and 1795 this was the device used. It also appeared in 1796, but on a second issue was replaced by the *Fillet-head.* From this the cap and pole were dropped, the hair tied at the back of the head by a ribbon, while the bust was draped. Of this pattern are the Cents of the years 1797 to 1808, inclusive. In the latter part of this year, however, a very matronly head of Liberty, with her forehead encircled by a band bearing the word LIBERTY, was placed on the coins, while thirteen stars took the place of the legend and the date in the exergue.

On the reverse of this Cent, the wreath has become a circular garland inclosing the words ONE CENT. This device was used from 1808 to 1838 with the following variations. In 1815 there were no Cents issued. Of the Cent of 1817, there were two issues, one having thirteen and the other fifteen stars on the obverse. In 1819 and in 1825 the date appeared in both large and small issues. In 1826, the hair of Liberty, which had resembled a loose cap, was made up into a double knot, according to the fashion of that day. Of the Cent of 1839, there were four varieties, one having the head of 1838, the hair being tied with twine; for another, beads were used; on the third, the head is somewhat small, while on the fourth and last, the hair has a peculiar arrangement, the dot under the ONE, and the line under the CENT being both absent. In 1840 and 1844 the dates are in large and small figures. Of 1843 there are three varieties: 1st, resembling that of 1842, but with date 1843; 2d, with obverse of '42, and reverse of '44, and 3d, with devices of the Cent of 1844. Of 1855, we have the dates in straight and in slanting figures, and in 1857 the last of the large Cents was issued with the dates in large and small type.

NICKEL CENT OF 1856.

In 1856, there was issued a small nickel Cent, having on the obverse an eagle flying across the field, the legend being UNITED STATES OF AMERICA, and in the exergue the date of 1856, while on the reverse are the words ONE CENT inclosed by a tobacco wreath. This device was retained for 1857 and '58, but was changed in 1859 for the head of an Indian wearing a coronet of feathers, LIBERTY being printed round their base, with the legend as before, and date to suit, while on the reverse the wreath is oak. In 1860, there was another change, the obverse remaining as before, but on the

NICKEL CENTS—1858 AND 1860.

reverse there was an oak wreath with arrows at the base, and a small shield at the top, with the words ONE CENT enclosed. In 1864 the *metal* was changed from nickel to bronze. Since then the device has remained unchanged to the present.

HALF-CENT.—The first Half-cent was issued in 1793, and resembled the Liberty Cap cent of that year, except that Liberty faces left. In 1794, 5, 6 and 7, a similar device was employed—Liberty facing right. In 1798, no Half-cents were issued, and of 1799 none are known. In 1800 the fillet-head is employed. In 1801 there was no Half-cent, but in 1802–3–4–5–6–7–9, there were Half-cents of the old device. In 1809 the Half-cent had the matron head of Liberty, as on the cent of the previous year, a device retained for 1809, 1810, and 1811. There was now no issue of Half-cents till 1825, when the same old device re-appears, as also on that of 1826. In 1827 there was no Half-cent, but in 1828 it appeared, having thirteen stars on one issue and only twelve on another. In 1829 the Half-cent appeared, but not in 1830. It did so, however, in 1831–2 3–4–5 and 6. It is then absent until 1840, when it appeared with the *Knotted-head*, the hair being tied on a double knot on the back of the head—a design it retained each year down to 1857—when the issue of Half-cents was discontinued.

TWO CENT.—In 1864, there appeared a very pretty TWO-CENT piece in bronze, having on the obverse a large 2 with CENTS below it, inclosed in a wheat wreath, with the legend UNITED STATES OF AMERICA; on the reverse is a large shield with crossed arrows behind, and above, a scroll with legend IN GOD WE TRUST, with date 1864 in exergue. These pieces were issued regularly till April 1873, when they were discontinued by Act of Congress.

WHITE METAL.—In 1865, there was issued a THREE-CENT PIECE in a white metal composition, having large numerals III, inclosed by an olive wreath on the obverse and a female head with bandeau bearing the word LIBERTY on the reverse with legend UNITED STATES OF AMERICA and date 1865. Since that date this piece has been issued regularly down to the present year.

Five Cent.—In 1866, a *Five-cent* nickel piece was issued having on the obverse a large 5 surrounded by a circle of thirteen stars and separated from each other by rays, with the legend United States of America, and in the exergue the word cents. On the reverse is a shield, with olive branches overhanging, and the legend In God we Trust, with the date 1866 in the exergue. In 1867, the rays were omitted from the obverse, and since then, these pieces have been issued unchanged down to the present year.

CHAPTER XXII.

MEXICO.

The coined money circulating through Spanish America, down to about 1820, consisted of pieces coined either in Mexico or in Spain itself. From 1690 to 1770, flat, irregularly-shaped pieces of hammered silver, roughly stamped with the arms of Spain, and

MEXICAN GLOBE DOLLAR OF CHARLES III.

of all values, from the doubloon down, and known as Cob money, were in circulation. The date on these pieces is always defective, the numeral of the 1000 being always omitted—1750, for instance, reading as only 750, and so on. Toward the close of last century the *Globe* dollars of Charles III.—the two globes repre-

MEXICAN PILLAR DOLLAR, 1807.

senting the old and the new worlds as subject to Spain—and the *Pillar* dollars of Charles IV., were common. In the beginning of this century Ferdinand VII. issued at Caraccas his well-

CARACCAS 2 REAL PIECE, FERDINAND VII., 1821.

known pieces of four and two Reals. He also issued thin copper coins having a lion and a shield, with cross crowned, and ANO DE 1818. CARACAS, and on reverse his monogram. In 1810 Hidalgo, a Mexican priest, commenced that revolutionary struggle which lasted till 1821, when national independence was se-

DOLLARS OF ITURBIDE.

cured. During all this period the royalist mints kept issuing dollars bearing a bust of Ferdinand VII. and the Spanish arms, while the Republican leaders also kept issuing money, each party restamping the coins issued by the other. We have thus dollars of the *Zacatecas* mint down to 1821, with the Spanish arms—the crowned shield between pillars. On the obverse of one of 1811 there is a rude impression of a volcano and the letters L. V. O. beneath it. In 1812 the Republican General *Vargas* restruck the obverse of dollars with his own name, placing the date across the field, and on the reverse effaced the royalist inscription by the legend R. CAXA DE SOMBRERETE, his headquarters. In 1813 the Republican leader *Morelos* issued a cast dollar, half and quarter, having on the obverse a bow and arrow within branches, and below the word SUD, denoting the Army of the South; while on the reverse are the value and date within a wreath.

In 1821 we have the coinage of Iturbide—AUGUSTUS I. On the medal money is a military bust, and on reverse are two wolves climbing a tree. On his ordinary money the bust is bare, and on reverse a small crowned eagle erect on a cactus; and on a variety a larger eagle stooping to fly.

CROOK-NECK QUARTER DOLLAR OF MEXICO, 1824.

In 1823 this monarchy was replaced by a Republic, when the mints of *Mexico*, *Durango* and *Guanaxato* issued dollars having

MEXICAN DOLLAR OF 1844.

on the obverse a liberty cap and rays, and on reverse a large *crook-necked* eagle with snake. From 1824 the eagle was small, *straight-necked*, and stood upright, a Liberty cap resting on rays being on the reverse.

During 1864–5–6 and 7 the bust of *Maximilian* was on the coins, with his arms on the reverse, the 10, 5 and copper 1 cent pieces bearing

DOLLAR OF THE EMPEROR MAXIMILIAN.

a crowned eagle. Republican dollars were, however, also issued in 1866 and 1867, having the liberty cap and rays with uncrowned eagle. On the overthrow of the Empire, the new Republic adopted the device on the present coins.

MEXICAN DOLLAR (OR PESO) OF 1869.

On Mexican dollars with the liberty cap, the legend consists of the *value*, *place of mintage*, *year of issue*, *mint master's initials* and *degree of fineness.* The following are the principal mint marks: $\mathring{M}$ or M^o, E^o, M^o, or GC. for *Mexico.* Z^s for *Zacatecas*, 1810. G^o for *Guanaxato*, 1812. D^o for *Durango*, 1811. P^i for *San Luis Potosi*, 1829. C^A for *Chihuahua*, 1811–14; 1822. G^A for *Guadalaxara*, 1814. ME. for *Ilalpan.* G.C. for *Guadalupe Y Callao*, 1844. C. for *Culican*, in Sinaloa, 1846.

Copper coins have been issued at Jalisco having bow and quiver, with an unfurled flag, and legend *Estado Libre de Jalisco*, 1829, and on reverse Liberty seated, holding pole and cap, with *un quarto.* At Sonora, with Liberty seated, holding pole and cap with a cornucopia at her feet, with *una quartilla de real* 1859, and on the reverse the Mexican eagle with *Est*^{a} *Lib*^{l} *Y Sob*^{o} *de Sonora*. At Sinora, with small head of Liberty between branches. At Chihuahua, with figure of Indian chief, with bow and arrow, etc.

CENTRAL AMERICA

Embraces the States of Guatemala, San Salvador, Honduras, Nicaragua and Costa Rica. On the *gold* coins bearing the names of these States and circulating throughout the confederacy, the device is that of the sun in the sky, shining above a row of mountain peaks, with the legend REPUBLICA DEL CENTRO DE AMERICA. On the reverse, a tree, with value, and legend LIBRE CRESCA FECUNDO. On the *silver* and *copper* coins, the sun is represented as just rising

DOLLAR OF CENTRAL AMERICA.

from behind the mountains, but in other respects the devices are similar. Those of Costa Rica, 1865, have its arms on a plain shield resting against a trophy of spears.

UNITED STATES OF COLOMBIA,

Is the present title of what has been *Colombia*, and then consisted of New Grenada, Venezuela and Ecuador, but now embraces the States of Panama, Bolivar, Canca, Antioquia, Cundinamarca, Boyaca, Santander and Magdalena. In 1819, New Granada (*Nueva Granada*) issued a dollar, having an Indian head, with crown of feathers, and on the reverse a pomegranate (the arms of Granada in Spain). The same device is on the coins of Cundinamarca, is-

DOLLAR OF CUNDINAMARCA.

sued in 1820-1. In 1827, the Republic of Colombia made use of the female bust of Liberty ; and on reverse, the fasces, crossed by bow and arrow *saltire*, between two cornucopias.

DOLLAR OR EIGHT REALS OF COLOMBIA.

In 1837, the dollar of the REPUBLICA DE LA NUEVA GRANADA, bore a pointed shield with the arms in three fields ; that of

DOLLAR OF NEW GRANADA.

DOLLAR OF NEW GRANADA.

1839, a cornucopia, above which is a condor flying. On that of 1848, the shield rested on four flags, surmounted by the condor.

VENEZUELA

Is the diminutive of *Venezia*—Venice, and was the name given in 1499 to an Indian village, built like the British cranoges on piles set in the water. During the war of Independence, Venezuela formed part of the Republic of Colombia. In 1815 the republican leaders issued from *Caracas* a *cob*-like peseta of two reals. In 1821 there was the same from Ferd. VII., having the Spanish arms, with F. 7, and on reverse two pillars, with the inscription 2 (*Reals*) PLV—SVL—TRA. B. 1821—S, while below is *Caracas*. The Republican money of 1824 has only part of this inscription, 2—U—SVL—TR—24. In 1843 one, one-half and quarter copper centavos were issued, having a female bust of Liberty, and on reverse value and date. In 1852, a copper centavo and half-centavo were issued, having large head of Liberty and REPUBLICA DE VENEZUELA, with, on reverse, value and date, between branches.

ECUADOR,

Under the name of Quito, was formerly part of Venezuela, and as such included in the Republic of Colombia. On the break up of that union, in 1831, Quito became independent, taking the name of *Ecuador*, its territory lying on both sides of the equatorial line. The coinage is very limited, the money of the surrounding States circulating freely. On the gold coins is a female bust of Liberty, and on reverse two mountain peaks with a condor on each, the sun above. On the silver coins of 1836 there are a fasces crossed by bow and arrow, between two cornucopias, with reverse like that on the gold. On a doubloon of 1847 there is a bust of Bolivar. The coins of Ecuador are a *gold* Condor,

GOLD DOUBLOON OF ECUADOR, FORMERLY CHILI.

or Ten Dollar piece, with its half, the Escudo; *silver* Peso, and *copper* Centavo and half.

PERU

Commenced its revolt against Spain in 1821, and issued its own first dollar in 1822. Spain, however, did not acknowledge its independence till 1824, and continued issuing money for Peru until that year, so that for this period we have two sets of coins, often restamped, confusing the collector.

On the Peruvian dollar of 1822, the obverse bears the arms, with *Peru Libre*, and on the reverse there is a column and scroll

DOLLAR OF PERU, 1822.

supported by Virtue and Liberty. In 1825 the obverse had Liberty standing, in her right hand sometimes a staff and cap, and sometimes a spear, with her left hand resting on a shield, and reverse, the arms on a shield, with *Repub Peruana.* In 1836 the Republic divided into North and South Peru. The dollar for North Peru retained the last-mentioned device, but bore the words,

PERUVIAN DOLLAR OF 1825.

Est Nor-Peruana, with for M. M., a monogram of Lima. In 1837 South Peru issued from Cuzco a dollar having a sun and stars, with *Repub Sud Peruana,* and on reverse a castle and volcano,

DOLLAR OF SOUTH PERU, 1837.

with ship and cornucopia. On the dollar of 1864, Liberty, holding pole and cap, is seated beside an altar, with reverse, arms on a shield. One and two centavo pieces of nickle have sun and rays on obverse, with *Republica Peruana,* and on reverse, two cornucopias inclosing value. The general coinage consists of the *gold* Sol of Twenty Dollars value, and its divisions, Medio Sol, Doblin, Escudo, and Medio Escudo; *silver* Dollar, Half, Peseta, Dinero and Medio Dinero; *copper* Centavo and Half.

BOLIVIA, OR UPPER PERU,

Effected its independence in 1824, through the labors of *El Libertador*, General Simon Bolivar, from whom it takes its name. On its coins of 1827 is a military bust of Bolivar, with his name below, and on reverse, two lamas lying under a tree, with six stars above. On those of 1842 the bust is laureated and bare, and with-

DOLLAR OF BOLIVIA.

out name In 1850 the bust is that of General Belzu, with reverse, Hercules treading down a dragon. In 1858 the dollar had a legend within a wreath, and on reverse the arms of the Republic. In 1865 the bust of General Melgarejo was placed on the coinage, while the present issue resembles that of 1858. The M. M. is P. T. S. I. (Potosi,).

CHILI

Began its struggle for liberty in 1810. The Republican dollar of *Santiago* (M. M. S̊.), bears a volcano in action, and in wreath above, UN PESO, with reverse, a high column surmounted by globe

DOLLAR OF CHILI.

and star, with date, 1817, in exergue. In 1834 the device was changed on the reverse to a condor with broken chain, and on obverse, a star on a shield, surmounted by a plume and inclosed in

CHILIAN DOLLAR, 1848.

branches, with REPUBLICA DE CHILE. In 1853 the condor supported an oval shield, while the half dollars of 1856 represent the condor flying with a broken chain. The copper centavo and half-centavo have a large star on obverse, with value inclosed by branches on reverse. In 1875 the device was again changed.

DOLLAR OF 1875.

LA PLATA, OR THE ARGENTINE CONFEDERACY,[1]

As it is now called (the former being the Spanish and the latter a Latinized word for *silver*), was formed in 1810 by the union of provinces that had been subject to the Spanish Viceroy of Peru. On a dollar of 1813 the device is that of the sun, with legend, PROVINCIAS DEL RIO DE LA PLATA, and on reverse, the arms of the Confederacy, two hands supporting a Liberty pole and cap. The chief mint is at *Rioja*; M.M.: R. A., or R. In 1822 Buenos Ayres issued a copper *decimo*, having the arms between branches crossed,

REVERSE OF DOLLAR AND OBVERSE OF DINERO OF LA PLATA, 1832.

and on reverse, BUENOS AYRES, 1822, UN DECIMO; and in 1827, a ten decimo piece, having a phœnix in a ring, and on reverse, BANCO

ARGENTINE CONFEDERACY.

NACIONAL, BUENOS AYRES, 1827. The Dollar of 1838 has a bust of General Rosas on the obverse, or the Arms of the Confederacy, with the mountain of Potosi on the reverse, as in our illustration.

URUGUAY, OR BANDA ORIENTAL,

once formed part of Buenos Ayres, but in 1825 seceded. On the dollar are the arms (scales, a castle, a horse, and a cow, in quarters), surmounted by the rising sun, and inclosed by oak branches with REPUBLICA ORIENTAL DEL URUGUAY and date in exergue, and on reverse nine stars in a ring inclosing value, and SITIO DE MONTEVIDEO. A copper twenty centesimas was issued in 1854, and a forty and a twenty centesimas in 1857.

HONDURAS.

Honduras is the middle state of Central America. Formerly it was subject to Spain, but is now an independent Republic, having its own coinage. The nickel coins consist of 1, $\frac{1}{2}$, $\frac{1}{4}$ and $\frac{1}{8}$ reals. The copper peso of 1862, Provincial Government, has the sea, two turrets connected by an arch, liberty cap; on reverse a mountain with feathered crown above and cornucopias at the side. Those of 1871 have on the obverse the legend DIOS UNION LIBERTAD, 15 DE SEPT. 1821. In the centre are two branches that enclose a tree whose stem divides the value, while above the tree are eleven stars; on the reverse are two inverted cornucopias, forming with the flags a trophy and oval centre; outside of this are the words REPUBLICA DE HONDURAS round a small pyramid, below which is the date, 1871, while a coronet of feathers surmounts the whole design.

PARAGUAY,

under the leadership of Dr. Francia, threw off the Spanish yoke in 1814, and formed one of the original Argentine Republic provinces. On its coins are the arms—a lion guarding, or supporting, a Liberty pole with cap.

BRAZIL

was taken possession of by the Portuguese in 1500. In 1806, on the entrance of the French troops into Portugal, the Regent John removed his court from Lisbon to Rio de Janeiro. On his

PORTUGUESE DOLLAR, RESTAMPED BY BRAZIL, 1820.

return to Europe in 1821, Brazil, under the leadership of John's son, *Dom Pedro*, revolted, and in 1822 became independent. Previous to 1833 the silver coinage consisted of Spanish-American dollars, restamped with the Brazilian arms. On the present coinage are the arms—the belted globe surmounted by a crown and inclosed by branches, with value and date on reverse.

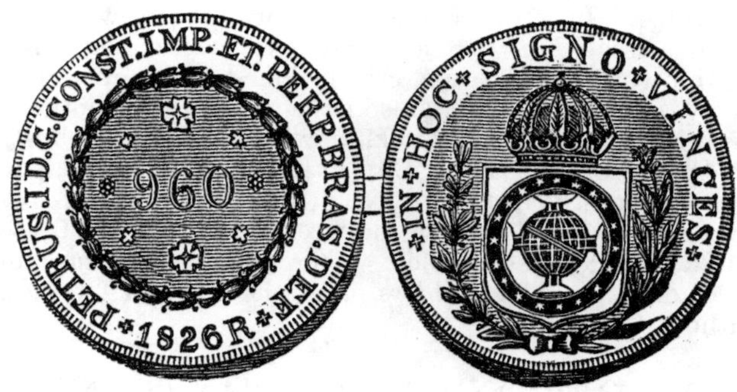

THREE PATAC, OR 960 REIS OF BRAZIL, 1826.

CAYENNE

is the name given to that whole district of French Guiana, within which is the famous penal colony of France. During the last century, coins were struck in billon, washed in gold and silver, by Louis XV. and Louis XVI., in Paris, for use in the French colonies. On those for Cayenne the legend is COLONIE DE CAYENNE, the coins themselves, in other respects, resembling those in use in the Island of Reunion.

DEMERARA AND ESSEQUIBO.

For these two divisions of British Guiana there were issued in 1809, a silver Three-shilling or Guilder token, having on the obverse a bust of George III., with legend GEORGIUS III. DEI

THREE-SHILLING, OR GUILDER OF DEMERARA.

GRATIA, and on the reverse a wreath inclosing a large 3 surmounted by a crown, while on a broad band or border are the words, COLONIES OF ESSEQUEBO AND DEMERARY TOKEN, 1809, with copper coins of same device, but of 2, 1, ½ and ¼ stiver (or penny), value. In 1813 a copper stiver was issued, with the head of previous issue, but with a different reverse, an oak wreath inclosing the words ONE STIVER, crowned, and no inner circle to the legend; ½ and ¼ stivers were also issued. In 1816 another silver Three-shilling token was struck, having the King's bust, with legend, GEORGIUS III., D. G. BRITANNIARUM REX, with a reverse like that of the stiver of 1813, except that instead of ONE STIVER, we have a large 3 inclosed by the wreath, with legend, COLONY OF DEMERARA AND ESSEQUEBO. There were also issues, in 1831 and 1833, of 3, 2 and 1 guilders, with the ½, ¼ and ⅛ values, with and without the crown.

ATLANTIC AND WEST INDIAN ISLANDS.

BRITISH POSSESSIONS—BERMUDA.

The earliest of the coins of these islands is that known as the Sommer Island piece, struck in England *previous to* 1616. Of this coin only 2 pieces, one the size of an English penny, and the other of a halfpenny, are known. On the obverse is a hog and above it the numerals XII. with the legend SOMMER * ISLANDS *, while on the reverse is a full-rigged ship under sail with a flag from each of her four masts. The smaller piece has the same device, but with the numerals VI. These pieces were struck for use in the Bermudas, called at first the Sommer Islands, because colonized about

SOMMER ISLAND PENNY.

1609 from Virginia by Sir George Sommers, who afterwards died there. In 1793 a halfpenny was struck in England for Bermuda, having the head of George III. facing the right, and on the reverse a ship in full sail going to the left, with the legend BERMUDA and the date 1793 in the exergue.

For the BAHAMAS, a halfpenny was struck in 1806, having a

small head of George III. with date 1806, and on the reverse a ship in full sail—two small vessels in the offing, with the legend BAHAMA, and in the exergue, EXPULSIS PIRATIS RESTITUTA COMMERCIA, a device copied from that great seal of the island which had been adopted in 1717, when the Crown resumed the government of the islands, and appointed a Captain Rogers as Governor.

In 1788, there were issued penny and halfpenny pieces for BARBADOES, with obverse, a negro's head with coronet of Prince of Wales, and under the neck, the words I SERVE ; on the reverse a pine apple with legend, BARBADOES PENNY, and date 1788.

In 1792 another penny and halfpenny were struck, with obverse like the last, but on the reverse King George as Neptune seated in a car and driving two sea horses, with legend and date, being a copy of the great seal of the island.

For ANTIGUA, farthings have been issued having a palm tree for the device.

In 1838-9-40 large numbers of English threepennies, two-pennies and three halfpenny silver pieces were exported to JAMAICA and the colonies generally, for currency.

In 1869 a nickle penny and halfpenny were struck in England for this island, having on the obverse the Queen's head, with a diadem surrounded by a circle of beads, outside of which are the words VICTORIA QUEEN, with date. On the reverse is a shield, 5 pineapples on a cross, an alligator surmounting it, and below a badge with legend INDUS UTERQUE SERVIET UNI. Outside a circle of beads are the words, JAMAICA HALF-PENNY.

DUTCH WEST INDIA ISLANDS.

SURINAM and CURACAO in the West Indies, belong to the Netherlands.

REAL OF CURACAO.

FRENCH WEST INDIA ISLANDS.

For Martinique and Guadaloupe, small coins of silver and of gold-washed billon were struck in France during parts of last century.

On the obverse is a bust of Louis XV. or of Louis XVI. laureated, and on the reverse, the locality for which issued.

TWELVE-SOU PIECE OF THE WINDWARD ISLES.

DANISH WEST INDIA ISLANDS.

To Denmark belong the islands of St. Croix, St. Thomas and St. John. For these there was issued, in 1763 and 1767, a colonial coinage of silver and copper, having usually the royal monogram on the obverse and a ship of war on the reverse, with legend Dansk Amerikansk Mynt. The more recent issues have the Danish arms on a shield crowned, with name and title of the sovereign, and on reverse the value within branches, with legend Dansk Vestindisk Mont.

SKILLING PIECES OF DANISH WEST INDIES.

HAYTI.

Hayti, or St. Domingo, revolted from French rule in 1791, finally securing its independence in 1803, when Dessalines became Emperor. His death, in 1806, was followed by a monarchy in the southern part of the island under Henry I., and by a republic in the northern part under Petion, a rival of Henry's. Petion's coins have his head and on reverse tree and arms. In 1820 J. P. Boyer, Petion's successor, effected a union of the Spanish and French portions of the island, but in 1843 was compelled to flee the island. On his coins also is a tree with warlike implements and year of the Republic, and on reverse a snake. In 1840–6 the copper coins have the fasces and liberty cap with legend, value and date, and on reverse, value with year of Republic. In 1843 Eastern or Spanish Hayti broke off from this union and formed itself into the Dominican Republic, issuing brass one-fourth pieces of 1844 and 1848, under the protection of Spain. Western or French Hayti remained Republican until 1849, when General Soulouque became Emperor as Faustin

COINS OF HAYTI.

I., issuing coins with his crowned bust, legend and date, and on reverse arms with legend and value. In 1859 Soulouque abdicated and again a Republic was proclaimed with Geffrard for President. The present coins bear Geffrard's head, with name, title and date, and on the reverse a tree with arms and value.

CHAPTER XXIII.

ASIA.

PERSIA.

Persia, called by the natives Iran, is substantially the ancient Media. During the period of the Sassanidæ, or Second Persian Empire, 226-620, A.D., this Power was at its height. On its conquest by the Saracens, its native coinage was replaced by one with Cufic inscriptions. The history of Persia from that period down to the present day is the most extraordinary record the world possesses of successive revolutions or invasions. During this period the Persian arms, a sun shining over the back of a lion armed with a sword, has been placed on its copper coins, with an extract from the Koran on the reverse. Gold and silver coins still have such extracts on both sides.

Persian coins are the *gold* Toman and Half-Toman; the *silver*, Sahib-Koran and its half, the Penebad, and the *copper* shahee and its half. The proportion of values is somewhat decimal: Ten Shahees, one Penebad; Two Penebads or Twenty Sahib-Korans, one Toman.

INDIA.

The coinages of the native States of India resemble those of other Eastern powers in their neglect of artistic devices. So far as the Mussulman Powers are concerned, their Koran forbids any likenesses ; on their coins, therefore we have only inscriptions of the name and era of the ruling prince. Not until we come to the period of the East India Company which so long controlled India, do we come to a coinage that is of general interest. This famous Company was founded in 1600 by Charter from Queen Elizabeth, for the purposes merely of trade. By that deed a monopoly of the traffic of the whole East was obtained. In 1612, it obtained from native princes leave to establish agencies or factories at several points. In 1662, Charles II. virtually conferred on it a sovereignty in India, by empowering it to make peace or war with the native princes. In 1677, Charles permitted the Company to coin money at Bombay, provided such did not interfere with the coinage of Great Britian. At a later date a mint was set up at Madras, and at a still later date at Calcutta. In the mints of the native princes the dies were twice the diameter of the coin, so that only a portion of the inscription could be presented.

The coins in ordinary currency have all, therefore, imperfect legends. When native coins are found with complete legends it is because such have been struck, not for currency, but for some festive occasion.

If the early French and English sovereigns sought to enrich themselves by their custom of changing the devices on their coins, the Indian rulers secured the same result by declaring that the rupee, one year after its date, was depreciated three per cent., and five per cent. by the second year, a system that led to a frequent recoinage, with proportional profit to the government. This was, however, so burdensome that in 1773 the government ordered that coins, no matter at what period they might be issued, should be always of par value, unless reduced in weight. In 1790 new machinery was employed at the mints and the size of the die so reduced that the whole device could appear on the money.

The earliest of what may be called the East Indian Company series, are silver crowns, half-crowns, shillings and sixpences, issued in 1601 by Elizabeth, expressly for the use of the Company.

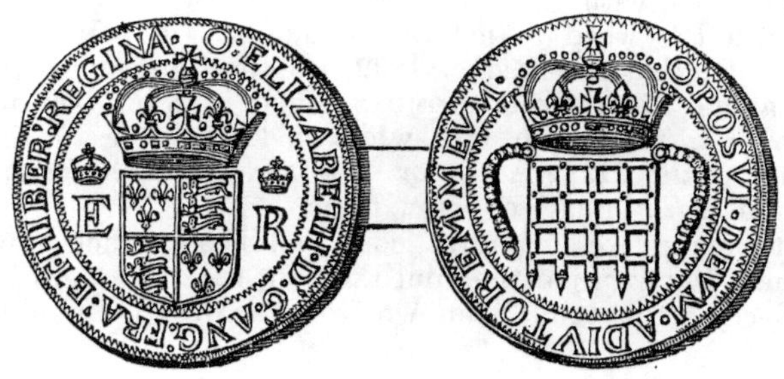

ELIZABETH'S EAST INDIA HALF-CROWN.

This is commonly called Elizabeth's *Portcullis* money, because having the royal arms on the obverse with *E. R.* crowned on either side, and on the reverse a large Portcullis crowned. (The Portcullis was the badge of the Beaufort family because of their descent from the Tudors.)

In 1671, the India Company established, on their own responsibility, a mint at Bombay, formerly a Portuguese settlement, but which had been given to Charles II., on his marriage, in 1662, with the Portuguese Princess Royal. This money was for use only in India, and therefore consisted of *Rupees* and *Fanams*. In 1677 this mint secured the royal sanction, and its money, while bearing the company's arms on the obverse, by the words MON BOMBAY ANGLIC REGIMS 1687, sufficiently acknowledged the supremacy of the crown. Copper money of somewhat similar devices was struck in the same reign, in the brief one of James II., and also in that of George II., bearing date 1728. The Bombay Rupee was marked with Persian characters and was at first very imperfect in its impression and differs but slightly from that for Madras.

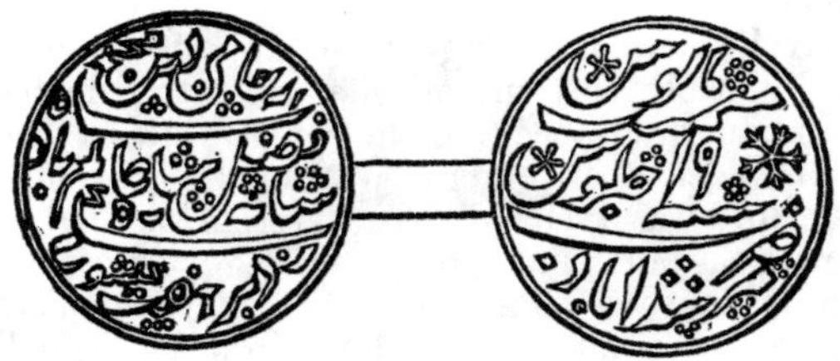

BOMBAY RUPEE.

Up to 1791 the copper coinage for this Presidency had been struck in England, but after that date it was manufactured at Bombay. The earliest of these issues is the *Half-Anna* or 4 pie piece, having on the obverse a large heart surmounted by the numeral of value, with the date 1791, and on the reverse a pair of scales with the word in native characters, *Adil*—Just weight or Justice. On that struck since 1832, are the Company's arms, with legend above, East India Company, and in scroll beneath, Aup. Reg. et Sen. Ang. with date, while on the reverse are the scales with the value, Half-Anna or Pie in English characters above them, and *Adil*, in native, below them.

As at Bombay, so at Madras, coin had been struck previous to the formal legalizing of the mint there in 1743. A very beautiful gold piece of this mint is known from the design upon it, as the

QUARTER PAGODA (GOLD) STRUCK AT MADRAS.—GEORGE III.

Pagoda. On the reverse is a representation of Vishnu the Destroyer, one of the great deities of Hindoo mythology. In 1808 this design appeared in silver, but in 1820 the ordinary Madras Rupee was issued, but replaced in 1835 by the Company's Rupee. Previous to 1807, the copper coinage of Madras had been struck in England, having an obverse like that of the Bombay Half-Anna, with date 1794, and on the reverse the Company's arms, with the legend, Auspicio Regis et Senatus Angliæ on a broad band edging the piece, and with the figures 48 below the arms, and referring to One Rupee in the band, while on a narrow scroll beneath the arms are the words United East India Company.

MADRAS RUPEE.

In 1803 Cash pieces were struck, having on the obverse the arms, the legend, East India Company and the date, and on the reverse, a Persian inscription with the value, xx, x, or v, cash in the exergue. The small I Cash has simply the Company's crest. The lion rampant, with the value, on the reverse.

In 1766 a mint was established at Calcutta for Bengal. The gold mohurs issued here resembled the silver rupee, having the same design and legend. The copper Pice was

GOLD MOHUR OF BENGAL.

struck in England up to 1792, after which date it was issued from Calcutta. At first this had simply a date on one side and a shield on the other, but after 1795 it bore native legends with date. Later in the century, the Half-Anna was issued having the Company's arms on the obverse, with AUSP. REGIS ET SEN. ANGLIÆ on a waved scroll below, with date 1825, and on the reverse a wreath inclosing words HALF-ANNA, with legend EAST INDIA COMPANY. In 1833 a Four Pie piece was issued with obverse like the last, with wreath on the reverse inclosing large numeral 4. After 1835 nothing was issued but the Half-Anna and the one Pie.

In 1845, however, the denomination was changed from Annas to Cents and in that year there was an issue of Cents, Halves and Quarters, having on the reverse a large head with diadem with VICTORIA QUEEN, and on the obverse simply a wreath enclosing ONE CENT, and having outside EAST INDIA COMPANY, with date.

SILVER HALF RUPEE OF INDIA.

In 1858 the British Government abolished the great Company that for more than two hundred years had monopolized the traffic of the East. Since then, all the money issued for circulation in India has born, the crowned bust of Queen Victoria.

RECENT COPPER COINAGE OF INDIA.

There is a large amount of copper coin current in the East issued at different times by the East India Company for their possessions outside of India, all however of the same general type ; the Annas for the one side, and on the other some device with native inscriptions. Those of Bombay, for instance, were also used at SUMATRA, while there were also pieces struck in 1804 with the legend ISLAND OF SUMATRA on them; those for the PRINCE OF WALES ISLAND, have the arms with date 1810 in the exergue, and on the other side different kinds of wreaths inclosing the words *Pulo Penang* in native characters.

CEYLON.

The modern coinage of CEYLON has always been struck by the British Government, the distinctive device being an elephant, alike on the silver and on the copper money. On the coin of 1815 the bust of George III. was placed on the obverse, the elephant remaining as before on the reverse; while on the silver coinage of 1821 there is the bust of George IV. In 1828 and in 1837 there was struck in England, a copper half farthing for Ceylon. There has recently been issued for Ceylon a very handsome series of coins, copper and silver, of the style here given.

COPPER FIVE CENTS OF CEYLON.

STRAITS SETTLEMENT.

In 1862, there was issued a cent having obverse like the East India Company's cent of 1845, with reverse a wreath and words, ONE CENT, INDIA, STRAITS, 1862, in five lines. A later issue has the Queen's head, with coronet, and on reverse a large I, inside a beaded circle, round which are the words, STRAITS SETTLEMENT, ONE CENT, 1874. Goa belongs to Portugal, and Pondicherry to France, for which rupees and fanams were issued by Louis XV. and Louis XVI.

EAST INDIA ISLANDS.

To the Kingdom of the Netherlands belong the islands of Java, Sumatra, Borneo, Celebes, the Spice Islands and New

Guinea. For these, as grouped together under the name of NEDERLANDISCHE INDIE, or for the Colonial settlements among them, coins have been issued. On those of early dates, gold and silver rupees, with their halves and quarters, issued by the Dutch East India Company, we have Oriental inscriptions, but with dates in Arabic numerals. The copper coins of this series bear the arms of Utrecht or of Guelders. From 1811 to 1816 these islands were in the hands of the British, and the coins were issued by the East India Company. (See East India series.) In 1816 they were restored to the Dutch, when the modern Dutch series begins, having on the obverse the king's head, or NEDERL. INDIE, with date across the field, with arms on the reverse. The latest issue have the Royal arms crowned, with date and value, and on the reverse, inscriptions in two Eastern languages.

PHILIPPINE ISLANDS.

In 1521 Magellan discovered these islands, which lie to the north of Borneo, losing his life soon afterwards in a struggle with the natives. Some years ago they received their present name in honor of Philip II. of Spain. In 1581, Manila was founded, and has since then continued to be the capital of the Spanish colonies and settlements throughout the islands.

FOUR PIASTRES OF PHILIPPINE ISLANDS.

BORNEO.

One of the most important settlements on Borneo is that of Sarawak, where, in 1841, Sir James Brooke established himself as Rajah, and has marked his supremacy by an issue of copper cents. On the obverse is an excellent likeness, with BROOKE RAJAH, and on the reverse the words ONE CENT, encircled in a wreath, between which and the edge of the coin we read SARAWAK and the date. Sarawak is at present governed by the nephew of its founder, and in his name also coins are issued.

SIAM.

The money of Siam is bullet-shaped, and is formed by bringing together the ends of oval pieces of silver. Each piece bears a minute stamp declaring its value. The manufacture of this money shows wonderful skill on the part of its workers, for, while it consists of seven pieces—the Sibat, Songbat, Tical Bat, Song Salung, Salung, Fung Sung Pie, and Pie—each piece is perfectly symmetrical, and its weight carefully proportioned to that of the other pieces. There has, however, been lately struck flat money resembling that of other countries,—the dollar, half-dollar, ten and five-cent pieces, having a pagoda on the obverse, and the elephant, a sacred animal in Siam, on the reverse.

The coins of

CAMBODIA

resemble the cash of China, but are chiefly made of lead.

CHINA.

The coinage of China, according to the chroniclers of that country, dates back to the remotest ages before the Christian era, and consisted at first of oblong, razor-shaped pieces. The present style of coinage is said to have been adopted about 250 B. C. The *cash* pieces are of brass or copper, and cast, the square hole in the middle being for the convenience of placing them on strings. As the Chinese are accustomed to characterize the reigns of their monarchs by some particular phrase, instead of the monarch's name, this phrase is placed on the coins issued during his reign. Others of the characters mean "current money," while others are the mint marks of the officials by whom the coins have been issued.

In 1856 a native silver dollar was issued which has become already very rare. The gold coin resemble the cash.

In 1863 there were issued for the British colony of Hong Kong, copper coins having bust crowned with, VICTORIA QUEEN, and on the reverse, four Chinese characters in a circle of dots, with, outside, HONG KONG, ONE CENT, 1863. A very small coin was issued next year for the same colony; on the obverse, a square, perforated like the Chinese coins, with crown above, V. R. below, and date 1863–4 and 1866 on either side, with the words HONG KONG,

ONE MILL, round the circle, and on the reverse a Chinese character on each side of the square. There has also been issued in silver a dollar, half, quarter, ten and five-cent pieces, with the queen's head.

JAPAN.

The early gold coinage of Japan consisted of large, but very thin, oval pieces of pure gold, the surface being slightly corru-

GOLD AND SILVER ITZEBU OF JAPAN.

gated or waved, called the *Cobang*, with its rectangular quarter, the *Itzebu*, with the value written on them with Indian ink. The *silver* Itzebu and its quarter are also of the domino shape, while the brass or copper *Tempo* is thick and oval, with a hole in the centre; the *round* four and one *P'senny* pieces resemble the Chinese Cash.

The latest Japanese gold, silver and copper money is circular in shape, having on the obverse the royal arms, a large chrysanthe-

GOLD TWENTY YEN, JAPAN.

mum flower enclosed in a circle occupying the centre, and on the reverse a nondescript figure with Japanese characters in a border.

SILVER YEN OR DOLLAR OF JAPAN, 1871.

AUSTRALIA.

The gold fields of Australia have been so productive that England judged it desirable to establish a Colonial mint. In 1852, therefore, a gold sovereign was issued, bearing on the obverse a crown with date, and legend, GOVERNMENT ASSAY OFFICE, ADELAIDE, and on reverse, VALUE ONE POUND in the center, with weight of metal for a legend. Next year, two and a half ounce pieces were issued, having a large Kangaroo, with date and legend, PORT PHILIP, AUSTRALIA; with reverse, a large numeral of weight.

In 1855 the Sydney mint issued a sovereign, with queen's head and name, and on reverse, AUSTRALIA, within branches, and SYDNEY MINT above.

For

OCEANICA,

Generally, there are as yet no other distinct issues, English money circulating, while a large number of tokens of penny and halfpenny value, issued by store-keepers in the various settlements, are freely used. The Sandwich Islands may be regarded as an exception, their rulers having lately issued a copper cent, with bust of the king and native inscription, with date.

AFRICA.

There is no necessity for illustrating the coinages of the countries of North Africa, such as Egypt, Tunis or Tripoli, for all these, being dependencies of Turkey, either receive their coins from the Turkish mint or resemble in their inscriptions the Turkish devices.

Formerly, Algiers also belonged to Turkey, when its coinage resembled that of its neighboring States, but in 1830 it became a French possession and now receives its money from France.

Morocco has a coinage of its own, but for the most part uses Spanish coins.

WEST AFRICA.

On the West Coast of Africa, European nations have at different times planted trading or Colonial settlements. In 1791 the

SIERRA LEONE SILVER DOLLAR, 1791.

English Sierra Leone Company, trading to the west coast of Africa, and connected with the early Guinea Coast Company, issued a Dollar, half, 20 cent and 10 cent pieces in silver, and a one penny and a one cent piece, having a lion on the obverse, with legend, SIERRA LEONE COMPANY, and in the exergue, AFRICA. On the reverse are two hands joined, with value and date. Another issue was made in 1796.

To Portugal belong the Cape Verde Islands, Senegambia, some islands of Guinea, Angola, Benguela and Mozambique. For these there have been issued silver and copper pieces of so many *Macuta* value. The device is the arms of Portugal, resting on a crowned globe, with the monarch's name—as P. REGENS DOMINUS GUINEÆ, and on reverse, PORTUGUEZIA AFRICA, with value and date in the center.

LIBERIA

Was founded in 1820 by the American Colonization Society as a colony or settlement of free persons of color from the United States. In 1833 the Society issued a copper cent, with name and date of origin—1816, on the obverse and on the reverse a man planting a tree by the seashore, while the sun is rising from the waves, with date. In 1847, the settlement having adopted a republican form of government, was recognized as a free and independent State, and then issued coins of one and two cent value. On these coins, the obverse has a head of Liberty, wearing the Phrygian cap, and on a raised rim, REPUBLIC OF LIBERIA. On the reverse is a large palm tree on the seashore, with ONE or TWO CENTS, and date 1847 on the rim.

ST. HELENA.

This lonely island, famous only for being the prison of Napoleon, had a copper coinage struck for it by the East India Company. On the obverse is, ST. HELENA 1821, HALFPENNY, inclosed by a wreath, and on the reverse the arms of the Great Company.

REUNION.

In 1649 the French took the Isle of Bourbon from the Portuguese, changing its name to *Reunion* in 1789, and to *Isle Bonaparte* in 1809. In1720, they took posession of Mauritius, which was then named the Isle of France, but this, in 1810, was taken by the British and remains in their hands. For these islands, France issued, during the reigns of Louis XV. and Louis XVI., small silver and billon pieces, bearing the crowned arms of Anjou, with the King's name and title, and on the reverse, the value and date, with ISLES DE FR. ET DE BOURBON. On those issued of late years, we have on the reverse, value and date within branches, with the legend COLONIES FRANCAIS.

MAURITIUS.

In addition to all the English issues for particular localities, there was a silver coinage struck specially for Mauritius, but current through all the Colonies. On the obverse is a large shield with the royal arms, with legend GEORGIUS IV., D. G. BRITANNIARUM REX, and on the reverse the arms of the British Admiralty, an anchor and cable with crown above, with legend COLONIAR: BRITAN: MONET: 1822.

ENGLISH COLONIAL SILVER.

APPENDICES.

I.

SOVEREIGNS OF FRANCE,

WITH THE YEARS OF THEIR ACCESSION AND NAMES OF THE COINS WHICH THEY ISSUED.

Hugh Capet 987
Deniers and Oboles.

Carloman I 768
" II 879

Charebert 561

Charlemagne 768

Charles I—The Bold 840
" II—The Fat 884
" III 893
" IV—The Handsome 322
Gold—Agnel, Florin, Royal and Half.
Silver—Gros Tournois, ½ and ⅓ Gros, Denier Tournois.
Billon—Double Paris, Denier Paris, Double Denier, Obole Tournois.

Charles V 1364
Gold—Royals, Francs, Fleur de lis, Florins.
Silver—Gros Tournois.
Billon—White Gros, Denier and Double Tournois.

Charles VI 1380
Gold—Royal, Crown, Mouton, Chaise, Salut.
Silver—Gros Tournois.
Billon—Blancs, Double and Denier Tournois, Double and Denier Paris, Liard, Obole.
[Henry V. and VI. of England struck money in France and for France during this reign.]

Charles VII 1442
Gold—Crown, Franc, Royal, Mouton, Chaise.
Silver—Gros.
Billon—Large Blanc, Double and Denier Paris, Double and Denier Tournois, Obole.

Charles VIII 1483
Gold—Crown.
Silver—Gros.
Billon—White Crown, White Sun, Carolus, Liard, Hardi, Double and Denier Tournois, Maille, Denier Tourdelais.
[Coins were struck during this reign for Italy.]

Charles IX 1560
Gold—Crown.
Silver—Teston.
Billon—Double Sun, Paris, Sun Paris, Douzain, Liard, Double and Denier Tournois.

Charles X—Cardinal de Bourbon 1589
Gold—Crown.
Silver— ———
Billon— ———

Charles X 1824
Gold—Pieces of 100, 40, 20 and 10 Francs.
Silver—Five Franc, with its divisions.
Bronze—10 and 5 cents, struck for the colonies.

Charles Martel 737

Childebert I 511

" II 575

" III 695

Childeric I 716

" II 720

Clodion 427

Clodomir 511

Clotaire I 511

" II 584

" III 566

" IV 719

Clovis I 481

" II 638

" III 691

Dagobert I 628

" II 670

" III 711

Eudes or Hugh 887

Francis I 1515

Gold—Crown.

Silver—Teston.

Billon—Blancs, Liard, Double and Denier Tournois, Denier Bourdelat, Coronat.

Francis II 1559

[The coins of Henry II. were issued down to 1561.]

Gontram 561

Henry I 1031

Silver—Denier.

Henry II 1547

Gold—Crown, Henry.

Silver—Teston.

Billon—Gros de Nesle, Douzaine, Double and Denier Tournois.

Henry III 1574

Gold—Crown.

Silver—Franc, Teston, ¼ Crown.

Billon—Six Blanc, Douzaine, Liard, Double and Denier Tournois.

Henry IV 1610

Gold—Crown.

Silver—Franc, ½, ¼ and ⅛ Crown.

Billon—Douzaine and Liard.

Bronze—Double and Denier Tournois, Double Dauphinè.

John I 1316

Gold—Royal.

John II 1350

Gold—Crown, Fleur de lis, Mouton, Royal, Franc.

Silver—Gros Tournois.

Billon—Large White Crown, large White Fleur de lis, large White Star, Gros, Double and Denier Tournois, Double and Denier Paris, Obole.

Lothaire 954

Louis I—Le Debonnaire 814

" II 877

" III 879

" IV 936

" V 986

" VI 1108

Silver—Denier and Obole.

Louis VII 1137

Silver—Denier and Obole.

Louis VIII 1223

Silver—Denier and Obole.

Louis IX 1226

Gold—Chaise, Royal, Reine, Agnel, Franc or Crown.

Silver—Gros and Denier Tournois, Denier Paris.

Louis X 1314

Gold—Agnel.

Silver—Gros, Denier and Obole Tournois.

Billon—Denier and Obole Tournois

Louis XI 1461

Gold—Crown.

Silver—Gros.

Billon—Blanc, Denier Paris, Hardi, Maille, Denier Tournois, Denier Bourdelais.

Louis XII 1498

Gold—Crown of Queen Ann.

Silver—Gros, Teston.

Billon—Large White, Double and Denier Tournois, Liard, Hardi, Coronat, Patard.

Louis XIII 1610

Gold—Double, Single and Half Crown, Louis d'or.

Silver—Franc, Crown, Half and Quarter.

Billon—Douzaine.

Bronze—Double and Denier Tournois.

Louis XIV 1643

Gold—Crown, Louis and Louis d'or.

Silver—Six Franc, Fleur de lis, Crown and Quarter.

Billon—Six White, 4 and 2 Sols.

Bronze—Liard, Double and

Denier Tournois, pieces of 2, 4, 6 and 30 Denier.

Louis XV 1715
Gold—Quinzain, Louis, Half Louis.
Silver—Crown and Quarter, pieces of 10 and 20 Sous.
Billon—2 and 1 Sou.
Bronze—Sou, ½ and ¼.

Louis XVI 1774
Gold—2, 1 and ½ Louis.
Silver—Crown, ½, ¼ and $\frac{1}{10}$.
Billon—Pieces of 3, 15 and 30 Sous, Six Blanc.
Bronze—2, 1, ½ and ¼ Sou, Liard.

Louis XVII 1793
Assignats of 100, 400, 500 and 1500 Livres.

Louis XVIII 1814
Gold—Pieces of 20 and 40 Francs.
Silver—Pieces of 5 Francs and its divisions.
Bronze—

Louis Philippe 1830
Same as Charles X.

Merovæus 448

Napoleon Bonaparte 1804
Gold—20 and 40 Francs.
Silver—5, 2, 1, ½ and ¼ Franc.
Bronze—10 Centime.

Napoleon II 1821

Napoleon III 1852
Gold—
Silver—
Bronze—

Pepin—The Short 752

Pharamond 418

Philip I 1060
Silver—Denier and Obole.

Philip II 1180
Silver—Double and Denier Tournois, Double Paris and Obole.

Philip III 1270
Gold—Agnel, Royal, Denier and Crown Chaise.
Silver—Gros and Denier Tournois, Denier Paris.

Philip IV 1285
Gold—Large and Small Royals, Chaise, Agnel.
Silver—Gros, ½ and ⅓ Tournois.
Billon—Double and Denier Paris, Double and Denier Tournois, Bourgeois, Double and Single Obole or Maille.

Philip V 1316
Gold—Agnel.
Silver—Gros Tournois.
Billon—Denier Tournois.

Philip VI 1327
Gold—1 and 2 Royal Crown Paris, Angelot, Lion, Chaise, Pavillion, Florin, George.
Silver—Paris, Tournois, Fleur de lis, Crown.
Billon—Double and Denier Paris, Double and Denier Tournois, Obole.

Robert I 928
" II 996
Silver—Denier.

Rudolph 923

Siegebert I 561
" II 638

Theodebald 548

Theodebert I 534
" II 596

Thierry I 511
" II 596
" III 670
" IV 720

II.

ABBREVIATIONS ON ROMAN COINS,

WITH THEIR EXPLANATION, AND ENGLISH TRANSLATIONS.

A.

A. AULUS. Name of a personage; or ANNUS, a year.

A.A. ANNI, or ANNOS. The year, or years.

A.A. A.A.A. AUGUSTI. Two, or three Augustuses.

A.A.A.F.F. AURO, ARGENTO, AERE FLANDO FERIUNDO. An inscription in allusion to the *flandi* or planchets, of gold, silver and copper, from which the coins of the respective metals were struck, generally following the name of the monetary triumviri for the time being. The triumviri monetales were the three chief officers of the Roman mint.

ABN. ABNEPOS. Grand-nephew.

ACCI. ACCITANA. Accitana, a Roman colony in Spain, now Guadix, in Grenada.

ACCI.L.III. ACCITANA LEGIO III. The third Legion of Accitana.

ACT. ACTIACUS, ACTIA or ACTIUM. Actiacus or Actium, a town of Epirus, now Prevenza.

A. ACT. A. ACTIACUS APOLLO. The Actiatic Apollo.

AD. FRV. EMV. AD FRUGES EMUNDUS. For buying corn; alluding to the public purchases of corn for the people, for which money was expressly struck.

ADI. ADJUTRIX. Relief, alluding to a legion distinguished for some signal assistance afforded in time of need.

ADLOCVT. AUG. ADLOCUTIO AUGUSTI. Adlocution of Augustus, alluding to an address to the military.

ADLOCVT. COH. PRÆTOR. ADLOCVTIO COHORTIUM PRÆTORIANORUM. Adlocution to the Prætorian cohorts.

ADVENT. AUG. IUD. or MAV. or ACHA. or AFRIC. or ASI. or SIC. or GAL. or HISP. ADVENTUS AUGUSTI JUDEAE, or MAURITANIÆ, or ACHAIÆ, or AFRICÆ, or ASIÆ, or SICILIÆ, or GALLIÆ, or HISPANIÆ. The arrival of Augustus in Judæa, or Mauritania, or Achaia, or Africa, or Asia, or Sicily, or Gaul, or Spain.

AED. CVR. AEDILIS CURULIS. The curule aedile appointed by the Patricians.

AED. DIVI. AVG. REST. AEDES DIVI AUGUSTI RESTITUTAE. The divine temples restored by Augustus.

AED. P. AEDILITIA POTESTAS. The Aedile power.

AED. PL. AEDILITIA PLEBIS. Aedile of the people.

AED. S. AEDES SACRAE, or AEDIBUS SACRIS The sacred edifices, or to the sacred edifices, (in the dative case).

AEM. AEMILIUS, or AEMILIA. Name of a personage.

ÆQVIT. AVG. ÆQVITAS AUGUSTI The equity of Augustus.

AET. AETERNITAS. Eternity.

A. F. AULI FILIUS. The son of Aulus

A. N. AULI NEPOS. The nephew of Aulus.

AGRIP. F. AGRIP*pae* F*ilius*. The son of Agrippa.

AGRIPPA M. F. MA. C. CÆSARIS. AVGVSTI. AGRIPPA M*arci* F*ilia* MA*ter* C*aii* CÆSARIS AUGUSTI. Agrippa, the daughter of Marcus, and mother of Caius Cæsar Augustus (the emperor Caligula).

AL or ALE. ALE*xandria*. Alexandria.

ALIM. ITAL. ALIM*enta* ITAL*iae*. The provision of Italy, in allusion to the public purchase of corn, for distribution in Italy.

ALVIT. ALVIT*ius*. Name of a personage.

ANIC. ANIC*ius*. Name of a personage.

A. M. B. A*ntiochiae* M*oneta* officina secunda. Money of Antioch B, that is, of the second office or division of the mint; the officers being distinguished by A, B, for first and second; a system common in Roman monetary numerals.

AN. B. or ANT. B. AN*tiochiae* officina secunda. The second division of the mint of Antioch.

A. N. F. F. A*nnum* N*ovum* F*elicem* F*austum*. A happy and prosperous new year; wished to the Emperor.

ANN. DCCCLXXII. NAT. VRB. P. CIR. CON. ANNO DCCCLXXII. NAT*ali* URB*is* P*opulo* CIR*censes* CON*stituti*. In the year of the city, 872, the Circensian games were established for the people.

ANNONA. AVG. ANNONA AUG*usti*. The provision of Augustus, alluding to a yearly distribution of corn among the people.

ANT. P. ANT*iochiae* P*ercussa*. Struck at Antioch.

ANT. S. ANT*iochiae* S*ignata*. Struck at Antioch.

A. P. F. A*uro* P*opulo* F*eriundo* or A*rgento* P*opulo* F*eriundo*. Gold or silver (coins) struck for the people.

A. P. LVG. P*ecunia* LVG*duni* A. Money of Lugdunum, now Lyons in France; A of the first division of the mint.

APOL. MON. APOL*lo* MON*etalis*. The monetary Apollo.

APOL. PAL. APOL*lo* PAL*atinus*. The Palatine Apollo.

APOL. SALVT. CONSERVATORI. APOL*loni* SALUT*ari* CONSERVATORI. To Apollo, the Saviour and Preserver.

AQ. O. B. AQ*uiliæ* O*fficina* B. Of Aquilia, the second division of the mint.

AQ. P. S. AQ*uiliae* P*ecunia* S*ignata*. Money struck at Aquilia.

AQ. P. AQ*uiliae* P*ercussa*. Struck at Aquilia.

AQ. S. AQ*uilia* S*ignata*. Struck at Aquilia.

AQVA. M. AQUA M*arcia*. The Marcian water, alluding to water brought to the city through the care and liberality of Marcus.

AQVA. TRAJ. AQVA TRAJ*ana*. The Trajanian water.

AR. or ARL. AR*elate* or ARL*ate*. Arles.

ARA. PAC. ARA PAC*is*. The altar of peace.

ARAB. ADQVI. ARAB*ia* ADQUI*sita*. Arabia conquered.

ARMEN. CAP. ARMEN*ia* CAP*ta*. Armenia subjugated.

ARMENIA ET MESOPOTAMIA POTESTATEM P. R. REDACT. ARMENIA ET MESOPOTAMIA POTESTATEM P*opuli* R*omani* REDACT*ae*. Armenia and Mesopotamia reduced under the power of the Roman people.

ASI. ASIA. Asia.

A. SISC. A. SISC*iae*. Of Sescia A. signifying that it was of that town; struck in the first division of the mint.

AST. AST*igitana*. Astigitana, now Ecisa in Andalusia, Spain.

AVG. AUG*ur* or AUG*ustus*, or AUG*usta*, or AUG*ustalis*. Augur or Augustus, or Augusta, or of the august.

AVG. D. F. AUG*ustus* D*ivi* F*ilius*. Augustus, son of the deity.

AVGG. or AVGGG. AUG*usti*. Augustus: two or three G's after AV, signified that two or three emperors were reigning jointly.

AVR. PIA. SIDON. COLONIA. AUR*elia* PIA SIDON*is* COLONIA. Aurelius Pius, a colony of Sidon.

B.

B. B*erythus* or B*ono*, or B*raccara* or officina secunda. This letter B by itself, is used to signify either Berythus, a Phœnician town, or BONUS, the adjective good, or BRACCARA, or the second office of the mint, being sometimes used as a numeral, and signifying 2.

B. A. B*raccara* A*ugustalis*. The Augustalian Braccara, now Brague, a town in Portugal.

BAEBI. BAEBI*us* or BAEB*ia*. Bæbius, a man's name, or Bæbia, the name of a Roman family.

BALB. BALB*us*. Balbus the name of a personage.

BON. EVENT. BON*us* EVENT*us*, or BON*o* EVENT*ui*. A good event, or to a good event.

BRIT. BRIT*annicus* or BRIT*annia*. Britannia, or the country Britain.

BROC. BROC*chus*. Brocchus, the name of a personage.

B. R. P. N. B*ono* R*e*P*ublico* N*ato*. Appointed (to be struck) for the good of the public.

BRVN. BRVN*dusium*. Brundusium. a town in the kingdom of Naples.

B. SIRM. B. SIRM*ii*. B., struck at Sirmium in the second office of the mint, as signified by the numeral B.

B. S. LG. B (officina secunda) *signata* L*u*G*dunum*. The second (monetary office), coined at Lyons.

B. T. B*eata* T*ranquillitas*. Happy tranquility.

BVTHR. BUTHR*otum*. Buthrotum, now Butrinto in Epirus.

C.

C. *caius* or *caesar*. Caius or Caesar.

C. c*arthago* or c*ensor* or c*entum* or c*ives* or c*lypeus* or c*ohors* or c*olonia* or c*onsultum* or c*ornelius*. Carthage, or censor, or a hundred, or citizens, or a buckler, or a cohort, or a colony, or a decree, or Cornelius (name of a personage).

C. A. A. P. c*olonia* A*ugusta* A*roe* P*atrensis* or c*olonia* A. A*ugusta* P*atrensis* or c*olonia* A*grippina*. (Cologne) the august colony of Aroe Patrensis; or A (the first) august colony of Aroe Patrensis; or the Agrippine colony.

CABE. CABE*llio*. Cabellio, now Cavaillon, in France.

C. A. BVT. c*olonia* A*ugusta* BVT*hrotum*. The colony Augusta Buthrotum (of Butrinto, now of the same name in Epirus).

C. A. C. c*olonia* A*ugusta* c*aesarea*. The august colony of Caesarea.

C. A. E. c*olonia* A*ugusta* E*merita*. The colony Augusta Emerita, now Merida in Spain.

C. A. E. AVG. PATER. c*olonia* A*ugusta* E*merita* AUG*ustus* PATER. Augustus, the father of the colony Augusta Emerita, in Spain, now Merida.

CAES. CAES*area* or CAESAR. Caesarea, a town in Palestine, or Caesar

CAESS. or CAESSS. CAES*ares*. Caesars; ss signifying two, and sss three Caesars.

CAESAR. AVG. F. DES. IMP. AVG. COS. ITE. CAESAR AUG*usti* F*ilius* DE*signatus* IMP*erator* AUG*ustus* CO*nsul* ITE*rum*. Caesar, son of Augustus, chosen Emperor, Augustus, and Consul for the second time.

CAESAR. DIVI. F. CAESAR DIVI F*ilius*. Caesar, son of the God. This inscription most frequently occurs on the coins of Augustus Caesar, the adopted son of the deified Julius Caesar.

CAESAR. PONT. MAX. CAESAR PONT*ifex* MAX*imus*. Caesar the High Pontiff.

C.A.I. or C.I.A. c*olonia* A*ugusta* J*ulia*. The colony Augusta Julia, in Spain, now Cadiz.

CAL. CAL*aguris* or CAL*idius* or CAL*idia*. Calaguris, a town in Spain, now Calahora. Calidius, name of a personage. Calidia, name of a family.

C. A. O. A. F. c*olonia* A*ugusta* O*ca* A*ntoniniana* F*elix*. The happy colony Oca Augusta Antoniniana, in Africa, now Tripoli.

C. A. PI. MET. SID. c*olonia* A*urelia* PI*a* MET*ropolis* SID*on*. The colony Aurelius Pius, the metropolis of Sidon, in Syria.

C. A. R. c*olonia* A*ugusta* R*auracorum*, or c*olonia* A*ugusta* R*egia*. The colony Augusta Rauracum, in Switzerland; now Augst, near Basle; or the royal colony of Asta, in Spain.

C. C. Numeral letters signifying hundreds.

C. C. A. *Colonia Caesarea Augusta.* The colony Augusta Caesarea.

C. CAESAR. AVG. PRON. AVG. P. M. TR. P. IIII. P. P. *Caius* CAESAR AUG*usti* PRON*epos* AU*gustus* P*ontifex* M*aximus* TR*ibunitia* P*otestate* IIII. P*ater* P*atriae.* Caius Caesar, great grandson of Augustus; Augustus, High Pontiff, exercising the tribunitian power for the fourth time; father of his country.

C. C. COL. LVG. *Claudia Copia* COL*onia* LUG*dunum.* The colony Claudia Copia Lugdunum, now Lyons.

C. C. I. B. *Colonia Campestris Julia Babba.* The rural colony of Julia Babba, in Mauritania.

C. C. I. B. D. D. *Colonia Campestris Julia Babba Decreto Decurionum.* The rural colony of Julia Babba, by the decree of the Decurions.

C. C. I. H. P. A. *Colonia Concordia Julia Hadrumetina Pia Augusta.* The colony Concordia Julia Hadrumetina Pia Augusta, in Africa.

C. CIV. D. D. P. *Corona Civica Data Decreto Publico.* The civic crown awarded by public decree.

C. C. N. A. *Colonia Carthago Nova Augusta.* The colony Carthago Nova Augusta, in Spain.

C. C. N. C. D. D. *Colonia Concordia Norba Caesarea Decreto Decurionum.* The colony Concordia Norba Caesarea, by the decree of the Decurions, Caesarea Norba, a town in Lusitania.

C. R. *Centissima Remissa,* or *Circenses Restituti.* The hundredth remitted; or, The Circensian games restored.

C. C. S. *Colonia Claudia Salaria.* The colony Claudia Salaria.

C. CVP. *Caius* CUP*iennius.* Name of a personage.

CEN. CEN*sor.* Censor.

CENS. PER. CEN*sor* PER*petuus,* or CENS*oris* PER*missu.* Perpetual Censor, or by permission of the Censor.

CER. SACR. PER. OECVME. ISELA. CER*tamina* SACR*a* PER*iodica* OECUME*nica* ISELA*stica.* The sacred periodical oecumenic contests, called Iselastica.

CERT. QVIN. ROM. CON. CERT*amina* QUIN*quennalia* ROM*ae* CON*stituta.* The fifth year games of Rome established.

C. E. S. *Cum Exercitu suo.* With his army.

CEST. CEST*ius,* or CEST*ia.* Name of a personage or family.

C. F. *Caius Fabius.* Name of a personage.

C. F. *Caii Filius.* Son of Caius.

C. N. *Caii Nepos.* Nephew of Caius.

C. F. P. D. *Colonia Flavia Pacensis Develtum.* The colony Flavia Pacensis Develtum now Develto, a small town in Turkey.

C. G. I. H. P. A. *Colonia Gemella Julia Hadriana Pariana Augusta.* The colony Gemella Julia Hadriana Pariana Augusta, a town in Mysia.

C. I. C. A. *Colonia Julia Concordia Apamaea,* or *Colonia Julia Carthago Antiqua.* The colony Julia Concordia Apamaea; or the colony Carthago Antiqua, now Carthagena, in Spain.

C. I. C. A. GENIO. P. R. D. D. *Colonia Julia Concordia Augusta* GENIO *Populi Romani Decreto Decurionum.* The colony Julia Concordia Augusta to the genius of the Roman people by the decree of the Decurions.

C. I. A. D. *Colonia Julia Augusta Dertona.* The colony Julia Augusta Dertona.

C. I. AV. *Colonia Julia* AV*gusta.* The colony Julia Augusta, now Cadiz, in Spain.

C. I. AVG. F. SIN. *Colonia Julia* AU*Gusta Felix* SIN*ope.* The colony Julia Augusta Felix Sinope.

C. I. B. *Colonia Julia Balba.* The colony Julia Balba, in Mauritania.

C. I. C. A. P. A. *Colonia Julia Carthago Augusta Pia Antiqua,* or *Colonia Julia Corinthus Augusta Pia Antoniniana.* The colony Julia Carthago Augusta Pia Antiqua, in Spain, now Carthagena; or, the colony Julia Corinthus Augusta Pia Antoniniana, now Corinth, in Greece.

C. I. CAES. *caius julius* CAES*ar*. Name of a personage.

C. I. CAL. *colonia julia* CAL*pe*. The colony Julia Calpe, now Gibraltar, in Spain.

C. I. F. *colonia julia felix*. The colony Julia Felix.

C. I. G. A. *colonia julia Gemella Augusta*. The colony Julia Gemella Augusta.

C. I. I. A. *colonia immunis illice Augusta*. The free colony Illice Augusta.

C. I. IL. A. Q. PAPIR. CAR. Q. TER. MONT. II. VIR. Q. *colonia immunis* IL*lice Augusta quinto* PAPIR*io* CAR*bone quinto* TER*entio* MONT*ano* II. VIR*is quinquennalibus*. The free colony Illice Augusta, under Quintus Papirius Carbo and Quintus Terentius Montanus, the Duumvirs for five years.

C. I. N. G. *colonia julia Norba caesariana*. The colony Julia Norba Caesariana.

C. I. N. C. *colonia julia Nova carthago*. The colony Julia Nova Carthago, now Carthagena, in Spain.

CIR. CON. CIR*censes* CON*stituti;* or CIR*censes* CON*sessit*. The games of the Circus established; or, he celebrated the Circensian games.

C. I. V. *colonia julia valentia*. The colony of Julia Valentia, in Spain.

CL. CL*audius* or CL*audia* or CL*ypeus*. Name of a personage or family, or a buckler.

CLASS. PR. CLASS*is* PR*aefectus* or CLASS*is* PR*aetoriana*. The Praefect of the fleet, or the Praetorian fleet.

C. L. AVG. F. *caius Lucius* AUG*usti filius*. Caius Lucius, the son of Augustus.

C. L. CAESS. *caius et Lucius* CAES*ares*. Caius and Lucius, the two Caesars.

C. L. I. COR. *colonia Laus julia* COR*inthus*. The colony Laus Julia Corinthus, in Greece.

CL. V. CL*ypeus votivus*. The votive shield.

C. M. L. *colonia Metropolis Laodicea*. The colony Metropolis Laodicea.

CN. ATEL. FLAC. CN. POMP. FLAC. II. VIRIS. Q. V. I. N. C. CN*aeo* ATEL*lio* FLACC*o* CN*aeo* POMP*eio* FLACC*o* II. VIRIS *quinquennalibus victricis juliae Novae carthaginis*. Under Cneius Atellius Flaccus and Cneius Pompeius Flaccus, the Duumvirs for five years of the victorious Carthago Julia Nova.

CN. DOM. AMP. CN*aeius* DOM*itius* AMP*lus*. Name of a personage.

CN. DOM. PROCOS. CN*aeo* DOM*itio* PRO*consule*. Under Cnaeus Domitius, the Proconsul.

CN. F. CN*aei filius*. The son of Cnaeus.

CN. MAG. IMP. CN*aeus* MAG*nus* IM*perator*. Cnaeus the Great, the commander; that is, Cnaeus Pompey, the son of Quintius Pompey.

CO. DAM. METRO. *colonia* DAM*ascus* METRO*polis*. The colony Damascus Metropolis.

COH. PRÆT. VII. P. VI. F. CO*hortes* PRÆT*orianae* VII. *piae* VI. *fideles*. Alluding to the piety and fidelity of the Prætorian Cohorts, in the usual manner.

COH. I. CR. COH*ortis* I. CR*etensis*. Of the first cohort of Crete.

COH. PRÆ. PHIL. COH*ors* PRÆT*oriana* PHIL*ippensium*. The Prætorian cohort of the Philippians. A town in Macedonia, famous for the battle fought there, B. C. 38.

COL. AEL. A. H. MET. COL*onia* AEL*ia Augusta Hadrumetina*. The colony Aelia Augusta Hadrumetina, in Africa.

COL. AEL. CAP. COMM. P. F. COL*onia* AEL*ia* CAP*itolina* COMM*odiana pia felix*. The colony Aelia Capitolina Commodiana Pia Felix. The modern Jerusalem.

COL. ALEX. TROAS. COL*onia* ALEX*andriana* TROAS. The colony Alexandriana Troas in Phrygia, now Carasia.

COL. AMAS. or AMS. COL*onia* AMAS*trianorum* or COL*onia* AMS*trianorum*. The colony Amstrianorum in Paphlagonia, now Amstre.

COL. ANT. or ANTI. COL*onia* ANT*io-*

chia or ANTI*ochia*. The colony Antiochia in Asia.

COL. ARELAT. SEXTAN. COL*onia* ARELAT*e* SEXTAN*orum*. The colony Arelate Sextanorum, now Arles in France.

COL. AST. AVG. COL*onia* AST*igitana* AUG*usta*. The colony Astigitana Augusta, now Exija in Spain.

COL. AVG. FEL. BER. COL*onia* AU*gusta* FEL*ix* BER*ithus*. The colony Augusta Felix Berithus, now Beyroot.

COL. AVG. FIR. COL*onia* AUG*usta* FIR*ma*. The colony Augusta Firma Astigitana, now Exija in Spain.

COL. AVG. IVL. PHILIP. COL*onia* AU*gusta* JUL*ia* PHILIPP*ensis*. The colony Augusta Julia of Philippi, a town in Thrace.

COL. AVG. PAT. TREVIR. COL*onia* AUG*usta* PAT*erna* TREVIR*orum*. The colony Augusta Paterna Trevirorum.

COL. AVG. TROA. or TROAD. COL*onia* AUG*usta* TROA*densis* or TROAD*ensis*. The colony Augusta Troadensis, built on the site of the ancient Troy.

COL. AVGVSTA. EMERITA. COL*onia* AUGUSTA EMERITA. The colony Augusta Emerita, now the town of Merida in Spain.

COL. AVR. ANTONI. AVG. TROA. COL*onia* AUR*elia* ANTONI*niana* AU*gusta* TROA*densis*. The colony Aurelia Antoniniana Augusta Troadensis, founded on the site of Troy.

COL. AVR. KAR. COMM. P. F. COL*onia* AUR*elia* KAR*rhæ* COMM*odiana* P*ia* F*elix*. The colony Aurelia Karrhæ Commodiana Pia Felix, a town in Asia, now Carrhes.

COL. AVR. PIA. SIDON. COL*onia* AU*Relia* PIA SIDON. The colony Aurelia Pia Sidon.

COL. AVR. P. M. SIDON. COL*onia* AU*Relia* P*ia* M*etropolis* SIDON. The colony Aurelia Pia Metropolis Siddon, now Seid or Sayde in Syria.

COL. B. A. COL*onia* B*raccara* A*ugusta*. The colony Braccara Augusta, now Brague in Lusitania.

COL. BERIT. L. V. or VIII. COL*onia* BERIT*hus* L*egio* V. or VIII. The colony Berythus, now Beyroot in Phœnicia, the fifth or eighth legion.

COL. CABE. COL*onia* CABE*llio*. The colony Cabellio in France.

COL. CAES. ANTIOCH. COL*onia* CAE*sarea* ANTIOCH*ia*. The colony Caesarea Antiochia in Syria.

COL. CAES. AVG. COL*onia* CAES*area* AU*gusta*. The colony Caesarea Augusta.

COL. CAMALODVNVM. COL*onia* CAMALODUNUM. The colony Camalodunum, now Colchester.

COL. CASILIN. COL*onia* CASILIN*um*. The colony Casilinum, now Castellazzo.

COL. CL. PTOL. COL*onia* CL*audia* PTOL*omais*. The colony Claudia Ptolomais, now Acre in Phœnicia.

COL. DAMAS. METRO. COL*onia* DAMAS*cus* METRO*polis*. The colony Damascus Metropolis, the capital of Syria.

COL. F. J. A. P. BARCIN. COL*onia* F*lavia* J*ulia* A*ugusta* P*ia* BARCINO. The colony Flavia Julia Augusta Pia Barcino, now Barcelona in Spain.

COL. FLAV. AVG. COR. COL*onia* FLA*via* AUG*usta* COR*inthus*. The colony Flavia Augusta Corinthus in Greece.

COL. FL. PAC. DEVLT. COL*onia* FL*avia* PAC*ensis* DEVLT*um*. The colony Flavia Augusta Pacensis Deultum, now Zagara or Zagoria, a town in Thrace.

COL. H. COL*onia* H*eliopolis*. The colony Heliopolis.

COL. HA. MER. COL*onia* HA*driana* MER*curi*. The colony Hadriana Mercuri, now Fermo in Italy.

COL. HEL. I. O. M. H. COL*onia* HEL*iopolis* J*ovi* O*ptimo* M*aximo* H*eliopolitana*. The colony Heliopolis Jovi Optimo Maximo Heliopolitana.

COL. IVL. AVG. C. I. F. COMAN. COL*onia* JUL*ia* AUG*usta* C*laudia* I*nvicta* F*elix* COMAN*orum*. The colony Julia Augusta Claudia Invicta Felix Comanorum, now Comane in Cappadocia.

COL. IVL. AVG. FEL. BER. COL*onia* JUL*ia* AUG*usta* FEL*ix* BER*ythus*. The colony Julia Augusta Felix Berythus, now the town of Beyroot in Phœnicia.

COL. IUL. AVG. FEL. CREMNA. COLonia JULia AUGusta FELix CREMNA. The colony Julia Augusta Felix Cremna, now of the same name in Pamphilia.

COL. IVL. CER. SAC. AVG. FEL. CAP. OECVM. ISE. HEL. COLonia JULia CERtamen SACrum AUGustum FELix CAPitolinum OECVMenicum ISElasticum HELiopolitanum. The Julian colony; the Sacred Augustan Felician Contest; Œcumenic Iselastic Heliopolitan (certain games celebrated at the Julian colony of Heliopolis in Syria).

COL. IVL. CONC. APAM. AVG. D. D. COLonia Julia CONcordia APAMea AUGusto Decreto Decurionum. The colony Julia Concordia Apamea by the august decree of the Decurions.

COL. IVL. LAV. COR. COLonia JULia LAUS CORinthus. The colony Julia Laus Corinthus.

COL. IVL. PATER. NAR. COLonia JULia PATERna NARbonensis. The colony Julia Paterna Narbonensis, now Narbonne in France.

COL. ANT. COM. COLoniae ANToninianae COMmodianæ. The Antoninian and Commodian colonies.

COL. NEM. COLonia NEMausus, or NEMausensium. The colony Nemausus, or Nemausensium, now Nismes.

COL. NICEPH. COND. COLonia NICEPHorium CONDita. The Nicephorian colony, founded upon the Euphrates, in Mesopotamia.

COL. PATR. COLonia PATRensis, or PATRicia. The colony Patrensis, or Patricia. This latter town is now Cordova, in Spain.

COL. P. F, AVG. F. CAES. MET. COLonia Prima Flavia AUGusta Felix CAESarea METropolis. The colony Prima Flavia Augusta Felix Caesarea Metropolis, in Palestine.

COL. P. FL. AVG. CAES. METROP. P. S. P. COLonia Prima FLavia AUGusta CAESarea METROPolis Provinciæ Syriae Palestina. The colony Prima Flavia Augusta Caesarea Metropolis of the province of Syria, in Palestine.

COL. PR. F. A. CAESAR. COLonia PRima Flavia Augusta CAESARea. The colony Prima Flavia Augusta Caesarea, in Palestine.

COL. R. F. AVG. FL. C. METROP. COLonia Romana Felix AUGusta FLavia Caesarea METROPolis. The colony Romana Felix Augusta Flavia Cæsarea Metropolis, the capital of Syria.

COL. ROM. COLonia ROMulensis. The colony of Romula, now Seville, in Spain.

COL. ROM.LVGD. COLonia ROManorum LVGDunum. Lugdunum, the colony of the Romans, now Lyons.

COL. RVS. LEG. VI. COLonia RVSeino LEGio VI. The colony Ruseino, the sixth Legion, now Ruseino in France.

COL. SABAR. COLonia SABARiae. The colony of Sabaria, in Pannonia, now Sarwar in Hungary.

COL. SEBAS. COLonia SEBAStiae. The colony of Sebastia, in Palestine.

COL. SER. G. NEAPOL. COLonia SERvia Galba NEAPOLis. The colony of Servius Galba Neapolis, now Nablous in Palestine.

COL. TYR. METR. COLonia TYRus METRopolis. The colony Tyrus Metropolis.

COL. V. I. CELSA. COLonia Victrix Julia CELSA. The colony Victrix Julia Celsa, thought to be now Kelsa, in Spain.

COL. VIC. IVL. LEP. COLonia VICtrix JULia LEPtis. The colony Victrix Julia Leptis, in Africa, now Lebida.

COL. VIM. AN. I. COLonia VIMinacium ANno I. The Viminacian colony, in the first year.

COL. VLP. TRA. COLonia ULPia TRAjana. The colony Ulpia Trajana, now Kellen or Varhel, in Transylvania.

COM. ASI. ROM. ET. AVG. COMmune ASIae ROMae ET AUGusto. For the community of Asia, of Rome, by Augustus, meaning Roman money struck by Augustus for the use of the Asiatic provinces.

COM. IMP. AVG. COMes IMPeratoris AUGusti. The deputy of the august Emperor.

COMM. COMModus, or COMModiana. Commodus, an Empéror's name, or Commodiana, a colony.

CO. M. O. B. or CO. M. OB. *Constantinopoli Moneta Officina* B. or *Constantinopoli Moneta OBsignata.* Money struck at Constantinople, B. that is, of the second office or division of the Mint; the offices being distinguished by the letters A. B., for first and second, a system common in Roman monetary numerals; or, money struck at Constantinople.

CON. or CONS. or CONST. CONST*antinople.* Constantinople in Turkey.

CON. AVG. VIII. CON*giarium* AUG*usti* VIII. The eighth gift of corn of Augustus.

CONC. CONC*ordia.* Concord.

CONC. APAM. CONC*ordia* APAM*eae.* The Concord of Apamea, a town of Bithynia.

CONG. DAT. POP. CONG*iarium* DAT*um* POP*ulo.* A gift of corn to the people.

CONGIAR. PRIMUM. P. R. D. CONGIAR*ium* PRIMUM P*opulo* R*omano* D*atum.* The first gift of corn bestowed on the Roman people.

CONG. P. R. or CONG. PR. CONG*iarium* P*opulo* R*omano;* or, CONG*iarium* PR*imum.* The gift of corn for the Roman people; or, the first gift of corn.

CONG. TER. P. R. IMP. MAX. DAT. CONG*iarium* TER*tium* P*opulo* R*omano* IMP*ensis* MAX*imis* DAT*um.* The third gift of corn for the Roman people for great benefits.

CON. M. CON*stantinopolis* M*oneta.* The money of Constantinople.

CON. O. B. CON*stantinopoli* O*fficina* B. The money of Constantinople; officina B; that is, of the second office or division of the mint.

CON. OB. CON*stantinopoli* OB*signata.* Struck at Constantinople.

CONSENSU. SENAT. ET. EQ. ORDINIS. P. Q. R. CONSENSU SENAT*us* ET EQ*uestris* ORDINIS P*opuli*Q*ue* R*omani.* By the consent of the Senate, of the equestrian order, and of the Roman people.

CONS. O. A. CONS*tantinopoli* O*fficina* A. Of Constantinople, the office A., that is, of the first office or division of the mint.

CONS. P. A. CONS*tantinopoli* P*ercussa* A. Struck at Constantinople, office A. (See above.)

CONS. SUO. CONS*ervatori* SUO. To his preserver; a title given to several emperors.

COOPT. COOPT*atus.* Chosen, or adopted, or associated.

COOPT. IN. OMN. CONL. SVPRA. NVM. EX. S. C. COOPT*atus* IN OMN*e* CONL*egium* SUPRA NUM*erum* EX S*enatus* C*onsulto.* In all the colleges by the majority, and by Senatorial decree.

CO. P. F. CAE. METRO. CO*lonia* P*rima* F*lavia* CAE*sarea* METRO*polis.* The colony Prima Flavia Caesarea Metropolis, the capital of Palestine.

C. O. P. I. A. C*olonia* O*ctavianorum* P*acensis* J*ulia* A*ugusta.* The colony of Octavianorum Pacensis Julia Augusta.

CO. R. N. B. CO*nstantinopoli* R*omae* N*ovae* B. Struck at Constantinople, the new Rome, B.

COS. ITER. ET. TER. DESIGN. CO*nsul* ITER*um* ET TER*tium* DESIGN*atus.* Appointed consul for the second and third time.

COSS. CO*nsules.* Consuls.

COS. VI. CO*nsul.* VI. Consul for the sixth time.

C. PAET. C*aius* PAET*us.* *Caius* Paet*us*, name of a personage.

C. P. FL. AVG. F. G. CAES. METRO. P. S. P. CO*lonia* P*rima* FL*avia* AUG*usta* F*elix* G*ermanica* CAES*area*, METRO*polis* P*rovinciæ* S*yriae* P*alestina.* The colony Prima Flavia Augusta Felix Germanica Caesarea, Metropolis of the province of Syria in Palestine.

C. R. C*laritas* R*eipublicae.* The glory of the Republic.

CRAS. CRASS*us.* Crassus, name of a personage.

C. R. I. F. S. C*olonia* R*omana* J*ulia* F*elix* S*inope.* The colony Romana Julia Felix Sinope.

CRISPINA. AVG. COMMODI. CRISPINA AUG*usta* COMMODI*a.* Crispina Augusta, wife of Commodus Augustus.

C. SACR. FAC. C*ensor* SACR*is* FAC*undis.* Censor for performing the sacred duties.

C. T. T. C*olonia* T*ogata* T*araco.* The

colony Togata Taraco, now Tarragona in Spain.

C. V. *clypeus votivus.* The votive buckler.

C. VAL. HOST. M. QVINTUS. *caius* VAL*ens* HOST*ilianus* M*essius* QUINTUS. Caius Valens Hostilianus Messius Quintus, name of a personage.

C. VET. LANG. *caius* VET*tio* LANG*uido.* To Caius Vettius Languidus, name of a personage.

C. VI. IL. *colonia* VI*ctrix* IL*lice.* The colony Victrix Illice.

C. Q. P. P. *consul Quintum pater patriae.* Consul for the fifth time, Father of his country.

CVR. X. F. CUR*ator* X. F*landorum.* An officer for striking a certain class of coin.

C. V. T. *colonia victrix taraco.* The colony Victrix Taraco, now Tarragona in Spain.

C. V. T. T. ÆTERNIT. AVG. *colonia victrix Togata taraco* ÆTERNIT*ati* AUG*ustae.* The colony Victrix Togata Taraco to the Æternity of Augustus, now Tarragona in Spain.

D.

D. A. D*ivus* A*ugustus.* The divine Augustus.

DAC. DAC*ia.* DAC*icus.* Dacia or Dacicus.

DAC. CAP. DAC*ia* CAP*ta.* Dacia taken.

DACIA AVG. PROVINCIA. DACIA AUG*usti* PROVINCIA. Dacia, the province of Augustus.

DAMA. DAMAScus. Damascus in Syria.

D. C. A. D*ivus* C*æsar* A*ugustus.* The divine Augustus Cæsar.

D. C. C. N. C. D*ecuriones* C*oloniae* C*oncordiae* N*orbae* C*aesarianae.* The Decurions of the colony of Concordia Norba Cæsariana.

D. CL. SEPT. ALBIN. CAES. D*ecimus* CL*odius* SEPT*imus* ALBIN*us* CAES*ar.* Decimus Clodius Septimus Albinus Cæsar.

D. C. S. D*e* C*onsulum* S*ententia.* By the decree of the consuls.

D. D. N. N. D*omini* N*ostri* or D*ominorum* N*ostrorum.* Our Lords, or of our Lords.

DEBELLATOR. GENT. BARBAR. DEBELLATOR*i* GENT*ium* BARBAR*orum.* To the vanquisher of barbarous nations.

DECI. DECI*us* or DEC*ennalia.* Decius, or the decennial games.

DE. GERM. DE GERM*anis.* Of the Germans, that is, relating to that nation.

DEO. NEM. DEO NEM*ausus.* To the god Nemausus, the tutelar divinity of Nismes.

DERT. DERT*osa.* Dertosa.

D. F. D*ecimi* F*ilius.* The son of Decimus.

D. N. D*ecimi* N*epos.* The nephew of Decimus.

DNS. Dominus. Lord or Emperor.

DIANA. PERG. DIANA PERG*ensis.* Diana of Perga.

DICT. PER. DICT*ator* PER*petuus.* Perpetual dictator.

DII. PAT. DII PAT*rii.* The gods of the country.

DIIS. CVST. DIIS CVST*odibus.* To the guardian gods.

DIIS. GENIT. DIIS GENIT*alibus.* To the genital gods.

D. I. M. S. D*eo* I*nvicto* M*ithras* S*acrum.* Sacred to the invincible god Mithras.

DISCIPLINA, or DISCIPVLINA AVG. DISCIPLINA, or DISCIPULINA AUG*usta,* or AUG*usti.* The august discipline, or the discipline of Augustus.

DIVI. F. DIVI F*ilius.* The son of the god. This inscription generally appears on the coins of Augustus, the adopted son of Julius Cæsar, who was deified by the Senate.

DIVO. AVG. VESP. DIVO AVG*ustus* VESP*asiano.* To the divine Augustus Vespasian.

DIVO. AVG. DIVO AVG*usto.* To the divine Augustus.

T. DIVI. VESP. F. VESPASIANO. T*ito* DIVI VESP*asiani* F*ilio* VESPASIANO. To Titus Vespasian, the son of the divine Vespasian.

DIV. PIO. DIV*o.* PIO. To the divine Pius (Antoninus).

DIVVS. TRAIAN. AVG. PARTH. PATER. DIVUS TRAIAN*us* AUG*ustus* PARTH*icus* PATER. The divine Trajan Augustus Parthicus, the Father.

DOM. or DOMIT. DOM*itius,* or DOMI*tianus.* Domitius, or Domitian.

DOMITIA AVG. IMP. CAES. DIVI. F. DOMITIANI AUG. DOMITIA AVG*usta*

IMPeratrix CAESaris DIVI, Filii DOMITIANA AUGusti. Domitia Augusta, mother of the divine Cæsar, son of the august Domitian.

D. P. Divus Pius. The divine Pius, meaning Antoninus.

D. P. P. Dii Penates. The household gods, the Penates.

DR. CÆS Q. PR. DRusus CÆSar Quinquennalis PRaefectus. Drusus Cæsar, the five years præfect.

DRVSVS. CÆSAR. TI. AVG. F. DIVI AVG. N. DRVSVS CÆSAR TIberii AUGusti Filius, DIVI AUGusti Nepos. Drusus Cæsar, son of Tiberius Augustus, and grandson of Augustus Cæsar.

D. S. I. M. Deo Soli Invicto Mithrae. To Mithras, the invincible god of the sun.

DOM. N. First given to Licinius, Jr., 317 A. D.

E.

EGN. GAL. AVG. EGNatius GALlienus AUGustus. Egnatius Gallienus Augustus, name of a personage.

EID. MART. EIDibus MARTii. To the Ides of March.

EQ. COH. EQuestris COHors. The equestrian cohort.

EQ. M. EQuitum Magistri. The masters of the cavalry.

EQ. ORDIN. EQuitum ORDINis. The order of Knights.

ETR. ETRuscus. Etrurian.

EVR. EURopa. Europe.

EX. AR. P. EX ARgento Puro, or Probato, or Publico. Money made from fine silver, or the approved silver, or the public silver.

EX. CONS. EX CONSensu. By consent.

EX. D. D. EX Decreto Decurionum. By the decree of the Decurions.

EX. EA. P. Q. I. S. AD. AE. D. E. EX EA Pecunia Quae Jussu Senatus AD AErarium Delata Est. The money which, by the command of the Senate, has been remitted to the Treasury.

EXERCITVS. VAC. EXERCITUS VACceus. The Vaccenian army.

EXERCITVS. YSC. EXERCITUS YSCanus. The army of Isca.

EXERC. PERS. EXERCitus PERSicus. The Persian army.

EX. S. C. EX Senatus Consulto. By order of the Senate.

EX. S. D. EX Senatus Decreto. By decree of the Senate.

F.

F. Fabius, or Faciundum, or Fecit, or Felix, or Filius, or Flamen, or Fortunus. The name of a person, or the future participle of the verb to make, or the perfect tense of the same verb, made ; or, happy, or, a son, or, a high priest, or, fortune.

FAB. FABius. Fabius, a man's name.

FABRI. FABRIcius. Fabricius, a man's name.

FAD. FADius. Fadius, a man's name.

FÆCVND. FÆCUNDitas. Fruitfulness.

FAN. FANnia. Fannia, the name of a Roman family.

FATIS VICTRI. FATIS VICTRIcibus. To the victorious fates.

FAVSTINA. AVG. ANTONINI AVG. PII. P. P. FAUSTINA AUGusta ANTONINI AUGusti PII Patris Patriae. Faustina Augusta (the wife of) Antoninus Augustus Pius, father of his country.

F. B. Felicitas Beata. Blessed happiness .

F. C. Faciendum Curavit, or Frumento Convehendus. The making (of coin) superintended, or, conveying corn.

FELICITATI AUG. FELICITATI AUGustæ, or AUGusti. To the august happiness, or the happiness of Augustus.

FEL. PRO. FELicitas PROvinciarum. The happiness of the provinces.

FEL. TEMP. REP. FELix TEMPorum REParatio. The happy amendment of the age.

FER. D. FERonia Dea. The Goddess Feronia.

FIDEI LEG. FIDEI LEGionum. To the fidelity of the Legions.

FIDES MILIT. FIDES MILITum. The fidelity of the soldiers.

FID. EXERC. FIDes EXERCitus The fidelity of the army.

FL. FLamen, or FLavius. The flamen,

or high priest, or, Flavius, a man's name.
FLAM. D. FLAM*en* D*ivi*. The high priest of the god, the deified emperor.
FLAM. DIAL. FLAM*en* DIAL*is*. The high priest of Jupiter.
FLAM. MART. FLAM*en* MART*ialis*. The high priest of Mars.
FL. FEL. FL*aviae* FEL*icis*. Of the happy Flavian (Legion).
FOR. FOR*tuna*. Fortune.
FORT. P. R. FOR*tuna* or FOR*titudo* P*opuli* R*omani*. The Fortune, or the strength of the Roman people.
FORT. PRIM. FORT*una* PRIM*igenita*. The Fortune of the first-born.
FORT. RED. FORT*unae* RED*ux;* or FORT*unae* RED*uci*. The return of Fortune; or, to the return of Fortune.
FOVR. FOUR*ius*. Fourius, a man's name; FOURIA, a Roman Gens.
FRVG. AC. FRUG*es* AC*ceptae*. Supplies of corn received.
F. T. R. F*elix* T*emporum* R*eparatio*. The happy re-establishment of the times.
FVL. FUL*vius*. Fulvius, a man's name.
FVLG. FULG*urator*. (Jupiter) Fulgurator.
FVLM. FULM*inator*. (Jupiter) Fulminator.

G.

G. G*alinicus*, or G*audium*, or G*enius*, or G*ermanus*, or G*naea*. Galinicus, surname of Volusianus; or Joy, the name given to one of the Roman Legions; or the Genius of good or evil, a divinity; or Germanus, the name of a personage; or Gnea, a woman's name.
GADIT. GADIT*ana*. Gaditana, now Cadiz, in Spain.
GAL. GAL*indicus*, or GAL*erius*. Galindicus, or Galerius, both names of personages.
G. or GEN. AVG. G*enio* AUG*usti*. To the genius of Augustus.
G. COR. SVPER. G*nea* COR*nelia* SUPER*a*. Gnea Cornelia Supera, the name of an empress.
G. D. G*ermanicus* D*acicus*. Germanicus, Dacicus, titles bestowed on the emperors for their victories over the Germans and Dacians.
GEM. L. GEM*ina* L*egio*. The Double Legion.
GEN. COL. COR. GEN*io* COL*oniae* COR*inthiae*. To the Genius of the colony of Corinth.
GEN. ILLY. GEN*ius* ILLY*rici*. The Genius of Illyria, now Dalmatia.
GENIO. COL. NER. PATR. GENIO COL*oniae* NER*onianae* PATR*ensis*. To the Genius of the colony of Neroniana Patrensis.
GENIT. ORB. GENIT*rix* ORB*is*. Mother of the world, a title conferred on empresses.
GEN. LVG. GEN*io* LUG*dunensi*. To the Genius of Lugdunum, now Lyons.
GERM. CAPTA. GERM*ania* CAPTA. Germany conquered.
GER. P. GER*manica* P*rovincia*, or GER*maniae* P*opulus*. The German Province, or, the German people.
GL. E. R. GL*oria* E*xercitus* R*omani*. The glory of the Roman army.
GL. P. R. GL*oria* P*opuli* R*omani*. The glory of the Roman people.
GL. R. GL*oria* R*omanorum*. The glory of the Romans.
G. L. S. G*enio* L*oci* S*acrum*. Consecrated to the Genius of the place.
G. M. V. G*emina* M*inerva* V*ictrix*. The colony Gemina Minerva Victrix, in Italy.
GOTH. GOTH*icus*. Gothicus, a title given to several emperors.
G. P. G*ræcia* P*eragrata*, or G*ræciæ* P*opulus*. Greece traversed; or, the people of Greece.
G. P. R. G*enio* P*opuli* R*omani*. To the Genius of the Roman people.
GRAC. GRAC*chus*. Gracchus, name of a personage.
G. T. A. G*enius* T*utelaris* A*egypti*, or G*eminae* T*utator* A*fricae*. The tutelary genius of Egypt, or the protector of the two Africas.

H.

H. H*astati*. Hastati, a name given to a certain portion of the Roman army.

HADRIANVS AVG. COS. III. P. P. HADRIANUS AUG*ustus* CONS*ul* III. P*ater* P*atriae*. Hadrianus Augustus, Consul for the third time, father of the country.

HA. P. or H. P. HA*statorum* P*rincipum*. Of the Hastati and of the princes.

HEL. HEL*iopolis*. Heliopolis, the city of the sun, in Egypt.

HELV. PERT. HELV*ius* PERT*inax*. Helvius Pertinax, name of an emperor.

HER. HER*cules*, or HER*ennius*. Hercules, the name of a god, or Herennius, a man's name.

HERAC. HERAC*litus*. Heraclitus, a man's name.

HERC. COMMOD. HERC*uli* COMMOD*iano*. To Hercules Commodianus.

HERC. GADIT. HERC*uli* GADIT*ano*. To Hercules Gaditanus.

HERC. ROM. CONDIT. HERC*uli* ROM*ano* COND*itori*. To Hercules Romanus Conditor; the Roman Hercules, the founder.

HILARIT. TEMP. HILARIT*as* TEMP*orum*. The hilarity of the times.

HIP. HIP*pius*. Hippius, a man's name.

HISP. HISP*alis*, or HISP*ana*, or HISP*alus*; a town in Spain; or Spain; or Hispalus, the name of a person.

HO. HO*nor*, the divinity Honour.

HS. a sign for sestertium; the Sesterce, a piece of Roman money.

I.

I. I*mperator*, or J*ovis*, or J*uno*, or J*ussu*, or I, or 1. Imperator, or Jupiter, or Juno, or by the command, or the first, or one.

I. A. I*mperator* A*ugustus*, or I*ndulgentia* A*ugusti*. The emperor Augustus, or by the permission of Augustus.

I. C. I*mperator* C*aesar*, or J*ulius* C*aesar*. The Emperor Caesar, or Julius Caesar.

II. IMP. CC. PHILIPPIS. AVGG. II. IMP*eratoribus* Caesaribus PHILIPPIS AUG*ustis*. To the two Philips, Caesars, and Augusti.

III. VIR. A. A. A. FL. F. T*rium*VIR*i* A*uro* A*rgento* A*ere* F*lando* F*eriundo*. The three officers for striking the prepared metal into gold, silver, and brass coins.

I. IT. I*mperator* IT*erum*. Imperator for the second time.

II. VIR. QVINQ. DUUMVIR QUINQ*uennalis*. Duumvir for five years.

IMP. CAES. ANTONINUS AVG. P.P.P. IMP*erator* CAES*ar* ANTONINUS AUG*ustus* P*ius* P*ater* P*atriae*. The emperor Cæsar Antoninus Augustus, Pius, Father of the Country.

IMP. CAES. AVG. COMM. CONS. IMP*erator* CAES*ar* AUG*ustus* COMM*uni* CONS*ensu*. The emperor Caesar Augustus, (chosen) by the consent of the community.

IMP. CAES. C. VIB. VOLVSIANO. IMP*erator* CAES*ari* C*aio* VIB*io* VOLusiano. To the emperor Cæsar Caius Vibius Volusianus.

IMP. CAES. DIVI. TRAIANI. AVG. F. TRAIANI. HADRIANO. OPT. AVG. DAC. PARTHICO. P. M. TR. P .COS. P. P. IMP*eratori* CAES*ari* DIVI TRAJANI AUG*usti* F*ilio* TRAJANI HADRIANO OPT*imo* AUG*usto* DAC*ico* PARTHICO P*ontifici* M*aximo* TR*ibunitiae* P*otestate* CONS*uli* P*atri* P*atriae*. To the emperor Caesar Trajanus Hadrianus Augustus, son of the divine Trajanus Augustus, the Best, Dacicus Parthicus, High Priest, exercising the Tribunitian power, Consul, Father of the Country.

IMP. CAES. DIVI. VESP. F. DOMIT. AUG. P. M. TR. P. P. P. IMP*erator* CAES*ar* DIVI VESP*asiani* F*ilius* DOMIT*ianus* AUG*ustus* P*ontifex* M*aximus* TR*ibunitia* P*otestate* P*ater* P*atriae*. The emperor Caesar Domitianus Augustus, son of the divine Vespasianus, Pontifex Maximus, exercising the Tribunitian power, Father of the Country.

IMP. CÆS. G. M. Q. IMP*erator* CÆS*ar* G*neus* M*essia* Q*uintus*. The emperor Caesar Gneus Messius Quintus, name of a usurper.

IMP. CÆS. L. AVREL. VERVS. AVG. ARM. PART. IMP*erator* CÆS*ar* L*ucius* AUREL*ius* VERUS AUG*ustus* ARM*enicus* PART*hicus*. The emperor Caesar Lucius Aurelius Verus Augustus Armeniacus Parthicus; the dissolute associate of Marcus Aurelius.

IMP. CÆS. L. SEPT. SEV. PERT. AUG. TR. P. COS. IMPerator CÆSar Lucius SEPTimius SEVerus PERTinax AUGustus TRibunitia Potestate CONsul. The emperor Caesar Lucius Septimius Severus Pertinax Augustus, exercising the Tribunitian power, Consul.

IMP. CÆS. M. ANT. GORDIANUS. AFR. AVG. IMPerator CÆSar Marcus ANToninus GORDIANUS AFRICanus AUGustus. The emperor Caesar Marcus Antoninus Gordianus, Africanus, Augustus.

IMP. CÆS. M. OPEL. SEV. MACRINUS. AVG. IMPerator CÆSar Marcus OPELius SEVerus MACRINVS AUGustus. The emperor Caesar Marcus Opelius Severus Macrinus Augustus.

IMP. CÆS. NERVÆ. TRAIANO. AVG. GER. DAC. P. M. TR. P. COS. V. P. P. IMPeratori CÆSari NERVAE TRAJANO AUGusto GERmanico DACico Pontifici Maximo TRibunitia Potestate CONsul V. Pater Patriae. To the emperor Caesar Nerva Trajan, Augustus, Germanicus, Dacicus, high pontiff, exercising the Tribunitian power, consul for the fifth time, father of the country.

IMP. CÆS. P. HELV. PERTIN. AVG. IMPerator CÆSar Publius HELVius PERTINax AUGustus. The emperor Caesar Publius Helvius Pertinax Augustus.

IMP. C. C. VA. F. GAL. VEND. VOLVSIANO. AVG. IMPerator caesari caio VAlindico Finnico GALindico VENDendico VOLUSIANO AUGusto. To the emperor Caesar Caius Valindicus Finnicus Galindicus Vendendicus Volusianus Augustus, titles which Volusianus assumed after his conquests.

IMP. C. M. CASS. LAT. POSTVMVS. P. F. AVG. IMPerator caesar Marcus CASSius LATienus POSTUMUS Pius Felix AUGustus. The emperor Caesar Marcus Cassius Latienus Postumus, Pius, Felix, Augustus, Imperator, one of the thirty tyrants.

IMP. C. M. TRAIANVS. DECIVS. AVG. IMPerator caesar Marcus TRAJANUS DECIUS AUGustus. The emperor Caesar Marcus Trajanus Decius Augustus.

IMP. C. P. LIC. VALERIANVS. P. F. AVG. IMPerator Caius Publius LICnius VALERIANUS Pius Felix AUGustus. The emperor Caius Publius Licinius Valerianus Pius Felix Augustus.

IMP. ITER. IMPerator ITERum. Imperator for the second time.

IMP. M. IVL. PHILIPPVS AVG. IMPerator Marcus JULius PHILIPPUS AUGustus. The emperor Marcus Julius Philippus Augustus.

IMP. T. AEL. ANTONINO. IMPeratori Tito AELio ANTONINO. To the emperor Titus Aelius Antoninus.

IMP. T. CÆS. DIVI. VESP. F. AVG. P. M. TR. POT. COS. REST. IMPerator Titus CÆSar DIVI VESPasiani Filius AUGustus Pontifex Maximus Tribunitia POTestate CONSul RESTituit. The emperor Titus Caesar, son of the divine Vespasian, high pontiff, exercising the Tribunitian power, and Consul, restored.

IMP. VI. IMPerator VI. Imperator for the sixth time.

INDVLGENT. AVGG. IN. CARTH. INDULGENTia AUGustorum IN CARTHaginenses. The clemency of the two Augustus's in favor of the Carthaginians.

INDVLG. PIA. POSTVMI. AVG. INDULGentia PIA POSTUMI AUGusti. The pious clemency of Postumus Augustus.

IO. CANTAB. Jovi CANTABrico. To Jupiter Cantabricus.

I. O. M. D. Jovi Optimo Maximo DEDicatum. Dedicated to Jupiter, the best and greatest.

I. O. M. H. Jovi Optimo Maximo Heliopolis. To Jupiter, the best and greatest, of Heliopolis.

I. O. M. S. Jovi Optimo Maximo sacrum. Sacred to Jupiter, the best and greatest.

I. O. M. SPONS. SECVRIT. AVG. Jovi Optimo Maximo SPONSori SECURITatis AUGusti. To Jupiter, the best, the greatest, the sponsor of the security of Augustus.

I. O. M. S. P. Q. R. V. S. PR. S. IMP. CAES. QVOD. PER. EV. RP. IN. AMP. ATQ. TRAN. S. E. Jovi Optimo Maximo senatus PopulusQue Romanus vota suscepta PRo salute IMPeratoris CAESaris QUOD PER EUM

RESP*ublica* IN AMP*liori* ATQ*ue* TRAN*quilliori statu* E*s*t. The Roman people and Senate (have) offered thanksgivings to Jupiter, the best, the greatest, for his preservation of the Emperor Caesar, and that through him the republic is in a richer and more tranquil state.

I. O. M. V. C. *Jovi Optimo Maximo Victori Conservatori.* To Jupiter, the best, the greatest, the victorious, the preserver.

IOV. OLYM. JOV*i* OLYM*pio.* To Jupiter Olympius.

IOV. STAT. JOV*i* STAT*ori.* To Jupiter Stator.

IOV. TON. JOV*i* TON*anti.* To Jupiter, the Thunderer.

ISEL. OECVM. ISEL*astica* OECUM*enica.* The Iselastican and Oecumenican games (held sacred at Rome).

I. S. M. R. *Juno Sospita Magna Regina,* or *Juno Sospita Mater Romanorum.* Juno Sospita, the great queen; or, Juno Sospita, the mother of the Romans.

ITAL. ITAL*ia.* Italy.

ITAL. MVN. ITAL*icum* MUN*icipium.* The Italian municipality.

IVD. CAP. JUD*æa* CAP*ta.* Judea taken.

IVL. *Julius* or *Julia,* or *Julianus.* Julius, or Julia, or Julianus, all names of personages.

IVL. AVG. CASSANDREN. JUL*ia* AU*Gusta* CASSANDREN*sis.* Julia Augusta Cassandrensis, a Roman colony, formerly a town in Greece; Cassandros, supposed by some to have been founded by Cassander, one of the generals of Alexander the Great, who, on the death of that monarch, seized upon the administration of Greece.

IVL. AVG. GENIT. ORB. JUL*ia* AU*Gusta* GENIT*rix* ORB*is.* Julia Augusta, mother of the world.

IVLIA. AVGVSTA. C. C. A. JULIA AUGUSTA *Colonia Caesarea Augusta.* Julia Augusta, the colony of Caesarea Augusta.

IVLIA. IMP. T. AVG. F. AVGVSTA. JULIA IMP*eratoris Titi* AUG*usti Filia* AUGUSTA. Julia Augusta, daughter of the Emperor Titus Augustus.

IVL. V. MAXIMVS. C. JUL*ius Verus* MAXIMUS *Caesar.* Julius Verus Maximus Cæsar, name of a personage.

IVN. JUN*ior* or JUN*ius* or JUN*o.* The younger, or Junius (name of a personage); or Juno (the goddess).

IVN. MART. JUN*oni* MART*iali.* To Juno Martialis.

IVN. REG. JUN*o* REG*ina.* Juno, the queen.

K.

K is often used for C on coins struck in the Grecian provinces.

K. *Carthago* or *Kaeso.* Carthage, or Kaeso (a Christian name).

KAP. CAP*itolina.* Capitolina.

KAR. CAR*thago.* Carthage.

KAR. O. CAR*thaginensis Officina.* The Carthagenian monetary office.

KART or KRT. E. CART*hago officina quinta.* The fifth Carthagenian monetary office.

KON. or KONS. CONS*tantinopolis.* Constantinople.

L.

L. *Laus* or *Legatus* or *Legio* or *Lucius* or *Ludi.* The colony Laus, or an ambassador, or a legion, or Lucius, name of a personage, or the games.

L. C. *Lugdunum Colonia.* The colony Lugdunum, now Lyons in France.

LAPHR. LAPHR*ia.* Laphria, a surname for Diana.

L. AUREL. COMMO. GERM. SARM. *Lucius* AUREL*ius* COMMO*dus* GER*Manicus* SARM*aticus.* Lucius Aurelius Commodus Germanicus Sarmaticus, titles given him for the victories.

L. CAN. *Lucius* CAN*inius.* Lucius, Caninius, the name of a personage.

LEG. LEG*io.* A legion.

LEG. AUG. PR. PR. LEG*atus* AUG*usti* PR*o* PR*aetore.* The ambassador of Augustus for the prætor.

LEG. GEM. PAC or PARTH. or NEP. or VLP. LEG*io* GEM*ina* PAC*ifica* or PARTH*ica* or NEP*tunia* or ULP*ia.* The double legion Pacifica, or Parthica, or Neptunia, or Ulpia, all distinctive titles of this Roman legion.

LEG. I. ADI. P. F. LEG*io* I. ADJ*utrix* P*ia* F*idelis*. The first legion, Pia, Fidelis, Adjutrix. This legion probably obtained these names from coming up in a needful moment to the help of another legion.

LEG. II. PART V. P. V.F. LEG*io* II. PART*hica* V. P*ia* F*idelis*. The second legion Parthica, Pia for the fifth time, and faithful for the fifth time, distinctive honorary titles of this legion.

LEG. II. TRO. or TR. FOR. LEG*io* II. TRO*janus* or TR*ajanus* FOR*tis*. The second legion of Troy, or Trajanus Fortis.

LEG. III. PART. LEG*io* III. PART*hica*. The third Parthian legion. Legions, as in this case, often took the name of the country in which they had been eminently successful.

LEG. IIII. VI. P. VI. F. LEG*io* IIII. VI. P*ia* VI. F*idelis*. The fourth legion, pious for the sixth time, and faithful for the sixth time, distinctive titles repeatedly conferred.

LEG. M. XX. LEG*io* M*acedonica* XX. The twentieth Macedonian legion.

LEG. PRO. COS. or LEG. PRO. PR. or LEG. AVG. or LEG. A. P. LEG*atus* PRO CO*nsule* or LEG*atus* PRO PR*aetore*, or LEG*atus* AUG*usti*, or LEG*io* A*rmeniae* P*rovinciae*. Ambassador for the consul, or ambassador for the prætor, or the ambassador of Augustus, or the legion of the province of Armenia.

LEG. VII. CL. GEM. FIDEL. LEG*io* VII. CL*audia* GEM*ina* FIDEL*is*. The seventh faithful legion Claudia Gemina.

LEG. V. M. P. C. LEG*io* V. M*acedonica* P*ia* C*onstans*. The fifth Macedonian legion, pious and constant, distinctive titles of honor.

LEG. XI. CLAVDIA. LEG*io* XI. CLAUDIA. The eleventh legion Claudia.

LEG. XVI. FRE. LEG*io* XVI. FRE*gellae* or FRE*genae*. The sixteenth legion of Fregella, a town in Latium ; or Fregena, an ancient town of Tuscany.

LEG. XXX. NEP. VI. F. LEG*io* XXX. NEP*tuniana* VI. F*idelis*. The thirtieth legion Neptuniana, faithful for the sixth time.

LEN. CVR. X. F. LEN*tulus* CUR*ator* X. F*landorum*. Lentulus, an officer for striking a certain class of money.

LEP. LEP*idus* or LEP*tis*. Lepidus, name of a personage, or Leptis, name of a town.

L. H. T. L*ucius* H*ostilius* T*ubero*. Lucius Hostilius Tubero, name of a personage.

LIB. AVG. IIII. COS. IIII. LIB*eralitas* AUG*usti* IIII. consul IIII. The fourth liberality of Augustus, consul for the fourth time.

L. N. L*ucii* N*epos*. Nephew of Lucius.

L. F. L*ucii* F*ilius*. Son of Lucius.

LIBERALIT. AVG. LIBERALIT*as* AUG*usta* or AUG*usti*. The august liberality, or the liberality of Augustus.

LIBERIS. AVG. COL. A. A. P. LIBERIS AUG*usti* COL*onia* A*ugusta* A*roe* P*atrensis*. To the children of Augustus, the colony Augusta Aroe of Patras.

LIBERT. REST. LIBERT*as* REST*ituta*. Liberty restored.

LIB. II. or III. LIB*eralitas* II or III. The second or third liberality.

LIB. P. LIB*ero* P*atri*. To Liber, the father, Bacchus.

LIB. PVB. LIB*eralitas* PUB*lica*, or LIB*ertas* PUB*lica*. A public liberality, or public liberty.

LIC. COR. SAL. VALER. N. CÆS. LIC*inius* COR*nelius* SAL*oninus* VALER*ianus* N*obilis* CÆS*ar*. Licinius Cornelius Saloninus Valerianus Nobilis Cæsar.

LIC. or LICIN. LIC*inius* LICIN*ianus*. Licinius or Licinianus.

L. I. MIN. L*egio* I. MIN*ervium*. The first legion of Minerva, a town in Italy.

LOCVPLET. ORB. TERRAR. LOCUPLET*atori* ORB*is* TERRAR*um*. To the enricher of the universe.

LON. LON*gus*. Longus, name of a personage.

L. P. D. AE. P. L*ucius* P*apirius* D*esignatus* AE*dilis* P*lebis*. Lucius Papirius chosen Aedile of the people.

L. SEPTIM. SEVERVS. PIVS. AVG. P. M. TR. P. XV. COS. III. P. P. L*ucius* SEPTIM*ius* SEVERUS PIUS

AUGustus Pontifex Maximus TRIbunitia Potestate XV. COnsul III. Pater Patriae. Lucius Septimius Severus Pius Augustus, High Pontiff (exercising) the tribunitian power for the fifteenth time, consul for the third time, father of the country.

L. SEPTIM. SEV. PERT. AVG. IMP. PARTH. ARAB. PARTH. ADIAB. COS. II. P. D. Lucius SEPTIMius SEVerus PERTinax AUGustus IMPerator PARTHicus ARABicus PARTHicus ADIABENicus CONsul II. Pater Patriae. Lucius Septimius Severus Pertinax Augustus Imperator Parthicus Arabicus, Parthicus Adiabenicus, consul for the second time, father of the country.

L. VAL. Lucius VALerius. Lucius Valerius, name of a personage.

LVC. LUCanus or LUCrio or LUCdunum. Lucanus or Lucrio, names of personages, or Lugdunum, now Lyons.

LVC. P. S. LUCduni Pecunia Signata. Money struck at Lyons.

LVC. AEL. LUCius AELius. Lucius Aelius.

LVCILLÆ. AVG. ANTONINI. AVG. F. LUCILLÆ AUGustae ANTONINI AUGusti Filiae. To Lucilia Augusta, daughter of Antoninus Augustus.

LVD. SÆC. FEC. COS. XIIII. LUDos SÆCulares FECit consul XIIII. He celebrated the secular games; consul for the fourteenth time.

LVP. LUPercus. Lupercus.

LV. PC. S. LUGduni PECuni Signata. Money struck at Lyons.

M.

M. Maesia, or Marcus, or Memmius, or Mensis, or Minerva, or Moneta, or Municeps, or Munitae. Maesia, or Marcus, or Memmius, names of persons, or a month, or Minerva, or money, or municipal, or munitae, a fortified town.

M. A. Marcus Aurelius. Marcus Aurelius.

MA. CANI. MAnius CANInius. Manius Caninius (name of a person).

MA. C. AVG. MAgna (aedes) Caesaris AUGusti or MAcellum AUGusti. The great temple of Augustus, or, the market-place of Augustus.

M. ÆM. Marcus ÆMilius. Marcus Æmilius (a man's name).

MAG. DECENT. MAGnentius DECENTius. Magnentius Decentius.

MAG. PIVS. MAGnus PIUS. The great and pious, awarded to Cneius Pompey.

M. ANN. Marcus ANNius. Marcus Annius (a man's name).

M. ANT. IMP. AVG. COS. DES. ITER. ET TERT. Marcus ANToninus IMPerator AUGur CONsul DESignatus ITERum ET TERTium. Marcus Antoninus, imperator, augur, and consul for the second and third time.

M. ANTON. AVG. GERM. Marcus ANTONinus AUGustus GERManicus. Marcus Antoninus Augustus Germanicus.

M. ANTONINVS. IMP. COS. DESIG. ITER ET. TERT. III. VIR. REIP. C. Marcus ANTONINUS IMPerator CONsul DESIGnatus ITERum ET TERTium TRIUMVIR REIPublicae constiuendae. Marcus Antoninus, imperator (or commander), consul for the second time, and triumvir for the third time for establishing the Republic.

MARC. MARCia, or MARCus, or MARtius, Marcia, or Marcus, or Martius.

MARCIA OTACIL. SEV. AVG. MARCIA OTACILia SEVera AUGusta. Marcia Otacilia Severa Augusta.

MAR. PROP. MARS PROPugnator. Mars, the defender.

MAR. VLT. MARti ULTori. To Mars the avenger.

M. CASS. LAT. POSTVMVS. Marcus CASsius LATienus POSTUMUS. Marcus Cassius Latienus Postumus.

MAT. AVGG. MATer AUGustorum. Mother of the Augusti.

MAT. SEN. MATer SENatus. Mother of the senate.

MAT. PAT. MATer PATriae. Mother of the country.

MAT. DEVM. CONSERVAT. MATri DEUM CONSERVATrici. To the mother of the gods, the preserver, Cybele.

MAT. DEVM. SALVT. MATer DEUM SA-

LUTari. To the beneficent mother of the gods.

MATER. AVGG. MATER AUGUStorum. Mother of the Augusti.

M. ATIVS. BALBVS. PR. Marcus ATIUS BALBUS PRaetor. Marcus Atius Balbus, Praetor.

MATR. CASTROR. MATRi CASTRORum. To the mother of the camps.

M. AVF. Marcus AUFidius. Marcus Aufidius (the name of a personage).

M. AVR. or MAR. AVR. Marcus AURelius. Marcus Aurelius.

M. AVR. ANTON. Marcus AURelius ANTONinus. Marcus Aurelius Antoninus.

M. AVREL. ANTONINVS. AVG. ARMEN. P. M. Marcus AURELius ANTONINUS AUGustus ARMENiacus Pontifex Maximus. Marcus Aurelius Antoninus Augustus Armeniacus, high Pontiff.

MAX. MAXimus. Maximus.

M. C. I. Municipium Calaguris Julia. The city of Calaguris Julia, now Lahorre in Spain.

M. COMMODVS ANTONINVS AVG. BRIT. Marcus COMMODUS ANTONINUS AUGustus BRITannicus. Marcus Commodus Antoninus Augustus Britannicus.

MES. MESsius. Messius.

MET. METropolis. The Metropolis.

MET. METaccus. Metaccus.

MET. VLPIAN. PAN. METallum ULPIANum PANnonicum. Ulpian and Pannonian metal.

MET. DEL. METallum DEL. for DALmatianum. Metal of Dalmatia.

MET. NOR. METallum NORicum. Metal of Noricum.

M. F. Marci Filius. The son of Marcus.

M. N. Marci Nepos. The nephew of Marcus.

M. H. ILLERGAVONIA. DERT. Municipium Hibera ILLERGAVONIA DERToza. The municipal city of Hibera Illergavonia Dertoza.

MINAT. MINATius. Minatius.

MINER. VICT. MINERvae VICTrici. To the victorious Minerva.

M. K. V. Moneta Karthaginesis Urbis. Money of the city of Carthage.

M. L. Moneta Lugdunensis. Money of Lugdunum, Lyons.

M. LEP. C. REG. INST. Marcus Lepidus Civitatem REGinensium INStauravit. Marcus Lepidus repaired the town of Reginens.

M. L. Moneta Lugdunensium. The money of Lugdunum (Lyons).

M. MARC. Marcus Marcellus. Marcus Marcellus.

M. M. I. V. Municipes Municipii Julii Uticensis. The municipals of the municipal city of Julius Uticensis.

M. N. Moneta Narbonensis. Money of Narbonne.

MON. MONeta. Money.

MON. AVG. MONeta AUGusti. Money of Augustus.

MO. S. T. Moneta Signata Treveris. Money struck at Treves, a city in Germany.

M. POP. Marcus POPilius. Marcus Popilius (a man's name).

M. R. Municipium Ravennatum. The city of Ravenna, in Italy.

M. S. Moesiae Superioris. Of Upper Moesia.

M. S. AVGG. ET CAESS NOSTR. Moneta Sacra AUGustorum ET CAESarum NOSTROrum. Sacred money of our Augusti and Cæsars.

M. S. T R. Moneta Signata. TReveris. Money struck at Treves.

MVL. FEL. MULta FELicia. Many prosperities.

MVN. AVG. BILBILIS. C. CORN. REFEC. M. ELV. FRONT. II. VIR. MUNIcipium AUGusta BILBILIS Caio CORNelio REFECto Marco HELVio FRONTone DUUMVIRi. The town of Augusta Bilbilis, repaired under Caius Cornelius and Marcus Helvius Fronto, Duumvirs.

MVN. CLVN. MUNicipium CLUNia. The town of Clunia.

MVN. FANE. ÆL. MUNicipium FANEstre ÆLium. The town of Fanestre Ælium.

MVNICIP. STOB. MUNICIPium STOBensium. The town of Stobensium.

MVNIC. ITALIC. PER. AVG. MUNICipium ITALICense PERmissu AUGusti. An Italian municipality, by the permission of Augustus.

MVN. STOB., or STOBENS, or STOBENSIVM. MUNicipium STOBense or STOBENSium. The town of Stobensium, in Macedonia.

MVN. TVR. or MV. TV. MUN*icipium* TUR*cussae*. The town of Turcussa.

N.

N. *Natalis*, or *Nepos*, or *Nobilis*, or *Noster*, or *Numen*, or *Nummus*. The birth ; or, the nephew ; or, noble ; or, our ; or, money.

NAT. NA*talis*, or NA*tus*. The birth, or born.

NAT. VRB. CIRC. CON. NAT*ali* URB*is* CIRC*enses* CON*stituti*. The Circensian games instituted on the anniversary of the foundation of the city.

N. C. *Nero Caesar*, or *Nobilis Caesar*. Nero Cæsar, or noble Cæsar.

N. C. A. P. R. *Nummus Cusus A Populo Romano*. Money struck by the Roman people.

NEP. RED. NEP*tuno* RED*uci*. To the returning Neptune.

NEP. S. NEP*tuno Sacrum*. Sacred to Neptune.

NEPT. or NEPTVN. NEPTUN*alia*, feasts held in honor of Neptune.

NER. NER*o* or NER*va*. Nero or Nerva, both names of personages.

NER. I. Q. VRB. NER*o* I. *Quaestor* URB*is*. Nero, the first Quaestor of the city.

NERO. CLAVD. DRVSVS. GERMAN. IMP. NERO CLAUD*ius* DRUSUS GERMAN*icus* IMP*erator*. The emperor Nero Claudius Drusus Germanicus.

NERO. ET. DRVSVS. CAESARES. QVINQ. C. V. I. N. C. NERO ET DRUSUS CAESARES QUINQ*uennales Coloniae Victricis Juliae Novae Carthaginis*. Nero and Drusus quinquennial Caesars of the colony Victrix Julia, or Nova Carthago.

N. F. *Numerii Filius*. The son of Numerius.

N. N. *Numerii Nepos*. The nephew of Numerius.

NICEPH. NICEPH*orium*. Nicephorium, a colony in Mesopotamia.

NIG. NIG*er*. Niger, the surname of the emperor Pescennius.

NOB. C. NOB*ilis* or NOB*ilissimus Caesar*. Noble, or noblest Caesars.

N. T. *Numini Tutelari*. To the tutelar Deity.

N. TR. ALEXANDRIANÆ. COL. BOSTR. *Nervae* TR*ajanae* ALEXANDRIANÆ COL*oniae* BOSTR*ae*, or BOSTR*ensis*. Of the colony Nerva Trajana Alexandriana Bostra, or Bostrensis, a town in Palestine.

NV. NU*ma*. Numa Pompilius.

O.

O. *ob*, or *officina*, or *ogulnius*, or *optimo*. The preposition ob; the mint-mark showing where the money was manufactured ; Ogulnius, the name of a personage, or optimo "the best," a title of Jupiter, sometimes bestowed also upon the Emperor Trajan.

OB. C. S. or OB. CIV. SER. or O. C. S. OB. *Cives Servatos*. For the preservers of the citizens, speaking of a crown which was given to those who had saved the life of a Roman citizen.

ŒC. Œ*cumenia*. A name given to public games and combats.

OFF. III CONST. OFF*icinae Tertiae* CONST*antinopoli*. In allusion to money struck in the third monetary office at Constantinople.

OGVL. OGUL*nius*. Ogulnius.

OLY. OLY*mpius*. Olympius.

O. M. T. *Optimo Maximo Tonanti*. To the Thunderer, the best, the greatest.

OP. or OPT. PRIN. or PR. OP*timo* PRIN*cipi*. To the best prince.

OP. DIV. OP*i* DIV*inae*. To the divine Ops.

OPEI. OPEI*mius*. Opeimius.

OPEL. OPEL*ius*. Opelius.

OPI. DIVIN. TR. P. COS. II. OPI. DIVIN*ae* TR*ibunitia Potestate* CON*sul*. II. To the divine Ops ; exercising the tribunitial power, and consul for the second time.

OPPIVS. CAPIT. PROPR. PRÆF. CLA. OPPIUS CAPIT*o* PROPR*aetor* PRÆF*ectus* CLA*ssis*. Oppius Capito, governor and commander of the fleet.

ORB. TER. ORB*is* TER*rarum*. Alluding to the extent of the Roman empire.

OT. or OTACIL. OT*acilia* or OTACIL*ius*. Otacilia, the name of an empress, or Otacilius, the name of a personage.

P.

P. *Pater*, or *Patriae*, or *Per*, or *Percussa*, or *Perpetuus*, or *Pius*, or *Pontifex*, or *Populus*, or *Posuit*, or *Praefectus*, or *Primus*, or *Princeps*, or *Provincia*, or *Publius*, or *Publico*. Father, or of the country, or (the preposition) by, or struck, or perpetual, or pious, or pontiff, or the people, or he has placed, or praefect, or the first, or a prince, or a province, or Publius, or to the public.

P. A. *Pietas Augusti*, or *Augusta*. The piety of Augustus, or Augustan piety.

PAC. or PACI. PACI*fico*. To the pacific Mars.

PACE. P. R. TERRA. MARIQ. PARTA. IANVM. CLVSIT. PACE *Populi Romani* TERRA MARIQ*ue* PARTA JANUM CLUSIT. He has shut the temple of Janus, having procured peace for the Roman people upon land and sea.

P. ALITIO. L. MENIO. II. VIR. *Publio* ALITIO *Lucio* MENIO DUUMVIR*i*. Under the Duumvirs Publius Alitius and Lucius Menius.

PANNON. PANNON*iae*. For Pannonia.

PAPI. PAPI*rius*. Papirius, name of a personage.

P. AQ. *Percussa* AQ*uileiae*. Struck at Aquilia, a town in Italy, on the coast of the Adriatic.

P. AR. *Percussa* AR*elate*. Struck at Arelate, now Arles in France.

P. AR. AD. *Parthicus* AR*abicus* AD*iabenicus*. Parthicus Arabicus Adiabenicus, titles given to emperors for their conquests or victories obtained in these countries.

PAR. PAR*thicus*. Parthicus, a title given to the emperors for victories over the Parthians.

P. ARL. *Pecunia* AREL*atensis* or *Percussa* AREL*ate*. The money of Arles, or struck at Arles.

PAT. PAT*er* PAT*riae*. Father of the country.

PAX. AVG. PAX AUG*usta*. The Augustan peace.

PAX. P. ROM. PAX *Populi* ROM*ani*. The peace of the Roman people.

P. C. CÆS. *Pater Caii* CÆS*aris*. The father of Caius Caesar.

P. C. L. VALERIANVS. *Publius Cornelius Licinius* VALERIANUS. Publius Cornelius Licinius Valerianus, name of an emperor.

P. D. *Populo Datum*. Given to the people.

PELAG. PELAG*ia*. Pelagia, a title given to Venus.

PENATES. P. R. PENATES *Populi Romani*. The Penates of the Roman people.

PER. PER*missu*. By the permission.

PER. A. or PERPET. AVG. PER*petuus Augustus*, or PERPET*uus* AUG*ustus*. Perpetual Augustus.

PERM. DIVI. AVG. COL. ROM. PER*missu* DIVI AUG*usti* COL*onia* ROM*ulea*. The colony Romulea, by the permission of the divine Augustus.

PERM. IMP. COR. PERM*issu* IMP*eratoris* COR*inthi*. Of Corinth, by permission of the emperor.

PERM. IMP. GERM. PERM*issu* IMP*eratoris* GERM*anici*. By the permission of the emperor Germanicus, alluding to Domitian, who had that surname.

PERMISSV. L. APRONI. PROCOS. III. PERMISSU *Lucii* APRONI*i* PROCONS*ul* III. By permission of Lucius Apronius, proconsul for the third time.

P. R. P. *Pecunia Romae Percussa*. Money struck at Rome.

PERT. PERT*inax*. Pertinax, name of an emperor.

PESCEN. PESCEN*nius* Pescennius, name of an emperor.

P. F. *Pius Felix*, or *Pia Fidelis*, or *Primus Fecit*. Pious and happy, or pious and faithful, or first done.

P. F. *Publii Filius*, or *Pii Filia*. The son of Publius, or the daughter of the Pius, that is, of Antoninus Pius.

P. H. C. *Provinciae Hispaniae Citerioris*. Of the province of Spain Citerioris.

PH. COND. PH*ilippus* COND*itor*. Philip the founder.

P. I. or PRIN. IVVEN. *Princeps Juventutis* or PRIN*ceps* JUVEN*tutis*. The Prince of youth.

PIET. AVG. PIETas AUGusta. Augustan piety.

P. K. Percussa Karthagine. Struck at Carthage.

PLAE. TRAN. PLAEtorius TRANquillus. Plaetorius Tranquillus, name of a personage.

P. L. COR. SAL. Publius Licinius CORnelius SALoninus. Publius Licinius Cornelius Saloninus, name of an emperor.

P. L. O. N. Percussa Lugduni Officinâ Novâ or Nonâ. Struck at Lugdunum in the new, or ninth office.

P. M. Pontifex Maximus. The sovereign pontiff.

P. M. S. COL. VIM. Provinciae Moesiae Superioris COLonia VIMiniacum or VIMinacium. The colony Viminiacum, or Viminacium, in the province of Upper Moesia, now Widin, in Servia.

POL. POLlio. Pollio, name of a personage.

POM. POMpeius. Pompey.

PORT. OST. PORTus OSTiensis. The port of Ostia.

P. P. Pater Patriae. Father of the country.

P. P. AVG. Perpetuus AUGustus. Perpetual Augustus.

P. POMPON. CR. II. VIR. Publio POMPONio CRispo, or CRispino DUUMVIRO. Under the Duumvir Publius Pomponius Crispus, or Crispinus.

P. R. Percussa Romae. Struck at Rome.

PRÆ. CLAS. ET ORAE. MARIT. PRÆFectus CLASSis ET ORAE MARITimae. Præfect of the fleet and of the coasts.

PRÆF. GERM. PRÆFectus GERManorum. Præfect of the Germans.

PR. COS. PROconsul. Proconsul.

PRIMI. DECEN. PRIMI DECENnales. The first Decennials.

PRINCIP. IVVENT. PRINCIPi JUVENTutis. To the prince of youth.

PROB. PROBus. Probus, name of an emperor.

PROC. PROConsul. Proconsul.

PROC. SIC. PROConsul SICiliae. Proconsul of Sicily.

P. ROM. Percussa ROMae. Struck at Rome.

PRON. PRONepos. Grand-nephew.

PROP. or PRO. P. PROPraetor, or PROPraetore. Propraetor, or for the prætor.

PROQ. or PRO. Q., or P. provincia. PROQuaestor or PROQuaestore. Proquæstor, or for the quæstor.

PROV. DEOR. PROVidentiae or PROvidentiâ DEORum. To the providence, or the providence of the gods.

PROVIDENT SENAT. PROVIDENTia SENATus. By the foresight of the senate.

PR. S. P. PRovinciae Syriae Palestinâ. Of the province of Syria, in Palestine.

PR. VRB. PRaefectus URBis or PRaetor URBis. Præfect or prætor of the city.

P. S. Percussa Sisciae. Struck at Siscia, in Croatia, now Sisseg.

P. T. Percussa Treveris. Struck at Treves, in Germany, now Treves.

PVDIC. PUDICitia. Modesty.

PVPIE. PUPIEnus. Pupienus, name of an emperor.

Q.

Q. Quaestor or Quinarius or Quintus or Quinquennalis or Quod. A quæstor, or Quinarius (the name of a personage), or every fifth year, or quod, that.

Q. CAS. Quintus CASSius. Quintus Cassius, the name of a personage.

Q. C. M. P. I. Quintus Cecilius Metellus Pius Imperator. Quintus Cecilius Metellus Pius, Commander.

Q. DES. Quaestor DESignatus. Appointed a quæstor.

Q. HER. ETR. MES. DEC. NOB. C. Quintus HERennius ETRuscus MESsius DECius NOBilis Caesar. Quintus Herennius Etruscus Messius Decius, Noble Caesar.

Q. HISP. Quaestor HISPaniae. Quæstor of Spain.

Q. M. Quintus Marcius. Quintus Marcius, the name of a personage.

Q. O. C. FAB. Quinto Ogulnio (et) Caio FABio. To Quintus Ogulnius and to Caius Fabius.

Q. P. *quaestor praetoris.* Quæstor of the prætor.

Q. PAPIR. CAR. Q. TER. MON. *quinto* PAPIR*io* CAR*boni* (et) *quinto* TER*entio* MON*tano.* To Quintus Papirius Carbo and to Quintus Terentius Montanus.

Q. PR. or Q. PRO. C. or COS. *quaestor* PR*ovinciae,* or *quaestor* PRO *consule* or PRO *consulis.* Quæstor of the province, or quæstor of the proconsul.

Q. TERENT. CULLVEON. PRO. COS. III. *quinto* TERENT*io* CULLEON*i* PROCON*suli* Tertium. To Quintus Terentius Culleonis, proconsul for the third time.

QVAD. QUAD*ratus.* Quadratus.

QVADRAG. REM. QVADRAG*esima* RE*missa.* The quadragesima, a tax so called, remitted.

QVIN. ITER. QUIN*quennalis* ITER*um.* Quinquennial repeated.

Q. V. or QVOD. V. M. S. *quod viae munitae sint, or sunt.* That the roads may be defended.

Q. VRB. *quaestor* URB*is.* Quæstor of the city.

R.

R. *Remissa,* or *Roma,* or *restituit,* or *Romanus.* Remitted, or Rome, or he has restored, or Roman.

RA. RA*venna.* Ravenna, a city of Italy.

R. C. *Romani cives.* Roman citizens.

R. CC. *Remissa* C C. The two hundredth remitted.

RECEP. RECEP*ta.* Received.

REC. ORB. REC*tor* ORB*is.* Ruler of the world.

REF. REF*ecta.* Rebuilt or repaired.

RELIQVA. VETERA. HS. NOVIES. MIL. ABOLIT. RELIQUA VETERA HS. NOVIES MIL*le* ABOLIT. The state debt, to the value of nine thousand sesterces, abolished, by payment. HS. signifies sesterces.

RES. RES*titutus* or RES*tituit.* Restored, or he has restored.

REST. ITAL. REST*itutor* ITAL*iae.* The restorer of Italy.

REST. NVM. REST*ituta* NUM*idia* or NUM*mum* REST*itutum.* Numidia restored, or the money remitted.

REX. ARM. DAT. REX ARM*eniae* DAT*us.* A king given to Armenia.

REX. PART. DAT. REX PART*his* DAT*us.* A king given to the Parthians.

REX. PTOL. REX PTOL*emaeus.* King Ptolemy.

R. M. or REI. MIL. *Rei Militaris* or REI MIL*itaris.* Military affairs.

RO. *Romae.* To Rome.

ROM. ÆTER. ROM*ae* ÆTER*nae.* To eternal Rome.

ROMA. RENASC. ROMA RENASC*ens.* Reviving Rome.

ROM. COL. ROM*ulea* COL*onia.* The colony Romulea.

ROM. ET. AVG. ROM*ae* ET AVG*usto.* To Rome and to Augustus.

ROM. RESVRG. ROM*a* RESURG*ens.* Reviving Rome,

ROMVL. AVG. ROMUL*o* AUG*usto.* To Romulus Augustus.

ROMVL. CONDIT. ROMUL*o* CONDIT*ori.* To Romulus the founder.

RO. P. S. *Romae pecunia signata.* Money struck at Rome.

R. P. *Romae percussa.* Struck at Rome.

R. P. C. *Reipublicae constituendae.* For the re-establishing of the Republic.

R. S. *Romae signata.* Struck at Rome.

R. V. *Roma victrix.* Victorious Rome.

R. P. S. *Ravennae pecunia signata.* Money struck at Ravenna.

R. XL. *Remissa* XL. The fortieth remitted.

S.

S. *sacerdos,* or *sacra,* or *semissus,* or *senatus,* or *senator,* or *senior,* or *sextus* or *soli,* or *spes,* or *suscepto,* or *sisciae.* Priests, or things to be sacrificed, or the half of the Roman As, or the senate, or senator, or ancient, or Sextus (the name of a personage), or the sun, or Siscia (a town in Croatia).

S. A. SA*lus,* or SA*lus Augusti,* or SE*curitas Augusti,* or *signata Antiochiae.* Salus, the goddess of health, or the health or security of Augustus, or struck at Antioch, speaking of money.

SACERD. COOP. IN. OMN. COLL. or CONL. SVPRA NVM. SACERD*os*

COOP*tatus* IN OMN*ia* COLL*egia* (or CONL*egia*) SUPRA NUM*erum*. Supernumerary priests appointed in all the colleges.

SAC. F. SAC*ris* F*aciundum* or SAC*ra* F*aciens*. Sacrifices to the gods to be performed, or being performed.

SACR. PER. SACR*a* PER*iodica*. Periodical sacrifices.

SÆCVLAR. AVGG. SÆCULAR*es* AU*Gustorum*. Secular games of the Augusti.

SÆCVLAR. SAC. SÆCULAR*ia* SAC*ra*. Secular sacrifices.

SÆCVL. FRVGIF. SÆCUL*o* FRUGIF*ero*. To a fertile period.

SAG. SAG*untum*. Saguntum, a town in Spain.

SAL. SAL*us*, or SAL*duba*, or SAL*oninus*, or SAL*onina*. The goddess of health; or Salduba, a town in Spain; or Saloninus, or Salonina.

SAL. GEN. HVM. SAL*us* GEN*eris* HUM*ani*. The health of the human race.

SALL. BARB. SALL*ustia* BARB*ia* (Orbiana). Sallustia Barbia Orbiana. The names of an empress.

SALM. SALM*antica*. Salmantica, a town in Spain.

S. ARL. S*ignata* AREL*ate*. Struck at Arles, in France.

SARM. SARM*aticus*. Sarmaticus, a title given to an emperor for his conquests over the Sarmatians.

SAVF. SAUF*feia*, or SAUF*feius*. Sauffeia, the name of a Roman family, or Sauffeius, the name of a personage.

S. C. S*enatus* C*onsulto*. By decree of the Senate, which allowed money to be coined.

SCI. AF. SCI*pio* AF*ricanus*. Scipio Africanus.

SCIP. ASIA. SCIP*io* ASIA*ticus*. Scipio the Asiatic.

S. CONST. S*ignata* CONST*antinopoli*. Struck at Constantinople.

SCR. SCR*ibonia*, or SCR*ibonius*. Scribonia, the name of a Roman family, or Scribonius, the name of a personage.

SEC. or SÆC. SEC*uritas* SÆC*ulum*. Security, or the age.

SEC. ORB. SEC*uritas* ORB*is*. The security of the universe.

SEMP. SEMP*ronius*. SEMP*ronia*. Sempronius, the name of a personage, or Sempronia, the name of a family.

SEN. SEN*ior*. Elder.

SENTI. SENTI*a*. Sentia, the name of a Roman family.

SEP. COL. LAVD. SEP*timia* COL*onia* LAUD*icea*. The seventh year of the colony of Laudicea, for Laodicea.

SEPT. SEV. SEPT*imius* SEV*erus*. Septimius Severus.

SEPT. TYR. MET. SEPT*ima* TYR*us* MET*ropolis*. The seventh of the metropolitan city of Tyre, in Phœnicia.

SER. SER*vius*. Servius, the name of a personage.

SEREN. SEREN*us*. Serenus, the name of a personage.

SERVILI. SERVILI*a*. Servilia, the name of a Roman family.

SEV. SEV*erus*. Severus, the name of a personage.

SEX. F. SEX*ti* F*ilius*. The son of Sextus.

S. F. S*aeculi* F*elicitas*. The happiness of the age.

SICIL. SICIL*ia*. Sicily.

SIDER. RECEPT. SIDER*ibus* RECEPT*is*. Received among the constellations.

SIG. RECEPT. SIG*nis* RECEP*tis*. The standards being received.

SIL. SIL*ius*. Silius, the name of a personage.

S. I. M. S*oli* I*nvicto* M*ithrae*. To Mithras, the invincible sun.

SIR. or SIRM. SIRM*ium*. Sirmium, now Simach in Slavonia.

SISC. SISC*iae*. Of Siscia, alluding to money struck there.

SISC. P. SISC*iae* P*ercussa* (moneta). Money struck at Siscia.

S. M. A. S*ignata*, or S*acra* M*oneta* A*ntiochiae*. Money struck at Antioch, or the sacred money of Antioch.

S. M. A. P. S*acra* M*oneta* A*quileiæ* P*ercussa*. Sacred money struck at Aquileia.

S. M. HER. S*ignata* M*oneta* HER*acleae*. Money struck at Heraclea.

S. M. O. B. S*ignata* M*oneta* O*fficina*

secunda. Money struck in the second monetary office.

S. M. N. *sacra* or *signata Moneta Narbonae* or *Nicomediae.* Sacred money of Narbonne or Nicomedia, or struck at Narbonne or Nicomedia.

S. M. R. *signata Moneta Romae.* Money struck at Rome.

S. M. R. Q. *signata Moneta Romae officina Quarta.* Money struck at Rome in the fourth monetary office, expressed by the letter Q.

S. M. SISC. *signata Moneta SISCiae.* Money struck at Siscia.

S. M. TR. *signata Moneta TReveris.* Money struck at Treves.

S. M. T. S. B. *sacra Moneta TReveris signata, officina secunda.* Sacred money of Treves, B signifying of the second monetary office.

SP. SP*urius.* Spurius, the name of a personage.

SP. AVGVSTA. SP*es* AUGUSTA. The august hope.

SPES. P. R. SPES *Populi Romani.* The hope of the Roman people.

S. P. Q. R. ADSERT. LIBERT. *senatus PopulusQue Romanus* ASSERT*ori* LIBERT*atis.* The Roman senate and people to the assertor of liberty.

S. P. Q. R. A. N. F. F. *senatus Populus Que Romanus Anno Natali* (scilicet urbis) *Fieri Fecit* (optimo principi). Which may be freely interpreted, as struck by the senate and people of Rome, &c., in honor of the year of the birth of the best prince.

S. P. Q. R. IMP. CÆ. QVOD. V. M. S. EX. EA. P. Q. IS. AD. A. D. *senatus PopulusQue Romanus* IMP*erator* CÆ*sari* QUOD *Viae Munitae sunt* EX EA *Pecunia Quam* IS AD *Aerarium Detulit.* Money struck by the senate and people, &c., in order that the public roads might be maintained.

S. P. Q. R. IVLIÆ. AVGVST. *senatus PopulusQue Romanus* JULIÆ AUGUS*Tae.* The senate and Roman people to Julia Augusta.

S. P. Q. R. OPTIMO. PRINCIPI. *senatus PopulusQue Romanus* OPTIMO PRINCIPI. The senate and Roman people to the best prince.

S. P. Q. R. SVF. P. D. *senatus Populus Que Romanus* SUF*famenta* POP*ulo Data.* The senate and Roman people, a grant of corn given to the people.

S. P. Q. R. V. S. PRO. R. CÆS. *senatus PopulusQue Romanus vota solvunt* PRO *Reditu* CÆS*are.* The senate and Roman people make votive offerings for the return of Cæsar.

S. R. *senatus Romanus* or *salus Romanorum* or *spes Reipublicae* or *sacris Receptis,* or *Restitutis.* The Roman senate, or the health of the Romans, or the hope of the republic, or sacrifices received, or sacrifices revived.

S. T. *signata Treveris* or *securitas Temporum.* Money struck at Treves, or the security of the times.

STABIL. STABIL*itas.* Stability.

SYLL. SULL*a* or sylla. Sulla or Sylla, the name of a personage.

Ss. sestertium. The sestertii were pieces of money valued at two as and a half.

T

T. *Titus,* or *Treveris,* or *Tribunus,* or *Tutelaris.* Titus, name of a personage, or Treves, in Germany, or tribune, or tutelar.

T. AR. *Tertia ARelate.* Struck in the third monetary office of Arelate, now Arles.

T. CAES. DIVI. VESP. F. AVG. P. M. TR. P. P. COS. VIII. *Titus* CAES*ar* DIVI VESP*asiani Filius* AUG*ustus Pontifex Maximus* TR*ibunitiâ Potestate Pater Patriae Consul* VIII. Titus Caesar, son of the divine Vespasian, so styled, because he had been deified by the Romans; Augustus, high pontiff, exercising the tribunitian power, father of the country, consul for the eighth time.

TEMPL. DIV. AVG. REST. COS. IIII. TEMPL*um* DIV*i* AUG*usti* REST*itutum consul quartum.* The temple of the divine Augustus, restored, consul for the fourth time.

TER. TER*entius.* Terentius, name of a personage.

TES. TES*salonicae.* Of Thessalonica.

T. F. *Titi Filia* or *Temporum Felicitas.*

daughter of Titus, or the Felicity of the times.

T. FL. T*itus* FL*avius*. Titus Flavius, name of a personage.

T. G. A. T*utelaris* G*enius* A*egypti*. The tutelary genius of Egypt.

THEOPO. THEOPO*lis*. Theopolis, a name given to the city of Antioch in the reign of Justinian, Emperor of the East.

TI. TI*berius*. Tiberius, name of an emperor.

TI. N. TI*berii* N*epos*. Nephew of Tiberius.

TI. F. TI*berii* F*ilius*. Son of Tiberius.

T. M. AP. CL. T*itus* M*anlius* (et) AP*pius* CL*audius*. Titus Manlius and Appius Claudius, names of persons.

T. P. or TR. POT., or TRIB. POT. V. &c. T*ribunitia* P*otestas*, or TR*ibunitia* POT*estas* or TRIBUNITIA POTESTAS V. The tribunitian power, or exercising the tribunitian power for the fifth time.

TR. TR*everis*. Treveris or Treves.

TRAI. TRAJ*anus*. Trajan (name of a personage).

TRAN. TRAN*quillus*. Tranquillus, name of a personage.

TRANQ. TRANQ*uillitas*. Tranquility.

TREBAN. TREBAN*ius*. Trebanius, name of a personage.

TREBON or TREB. TREBON*ianus* or TREB*onianus*. Trebonianus, name of a personage.

TR. F. TR*ajana* F*ortis*. The legion Trajana Fortis, a distinctive title of this legion.

TRIVMPH. TRIUMPH*ator*. Triumpher.

TR. OBS. or O. B. S. TR*everis* OB*signata* or O*fficina* B. S*ignata*. Struck at Treves, in Germany, or struck in the office B.

TR. LEG. II. TR*ibunus* LEG*ionis* II. The military tribune of the second legion.

TR. P TR*everis* P*ercussa* or P*ecunia*. Struck at Treves, or the money of Treves.

TR. PL. D. TR*ibunus* PL*ebis* D*esignatus*. Chosen tribune for the people.

TR. V. M. TR*iumviri* M*onetales*. Monetary triumvirs.

T. T. T*revirorum*. (Coinages) of Treves.

TVL. H. or HOST. TUL*lus* H*ostilius* or HOST*ilius*. Tullus Hostilius, name of one of the kings of Rome.

T. R. S. TREVERIS SIGNATA.

V.

V. Q*uinque*, or V*erus*, or V*ictrix*, or V*ir*, or V*irtus*, or V*oto*, or V*otivus*, or U*rbs*. Five, or Verus, name of a personage, or virtue, or by the vow, or votive, or the city.

V. AET. V*irtus* AET*erna*. Eternal virtue.

VAL. or VALER. VAL*erius* or VALER*ianus*, names of personages.

VAR. RVF. VAR*ius* RUF*us*. Varius Rufus, name of a personage.

VEN. FEL. VEN*eri* FEL*ici*. To the happy Venus.

VENER. VICTR. VENER*i* VICTR*ici*. To Venus the victorious.

VENT. VENT*idius*. Ventidius, name of a personage.

VESP. VESP*asianus*. Vespasian, name of an emperor.

VETER. VETER*anorum*. Of the veterans.

VET. LANG. VET*tius* LANG*uidus*. Vettius Languidus, name of a personage.

V. I. V*ota* I*mperii*. The vows of the empire.

VIB. VIB*ius*. Vibius, name of a personage.

VIC. AVG. VIC*toria* AUG*usti*. The victory of Augustus.

VIC. GERM. VIC*toria* GERM*anica*. The Germanic victory.

VIC. PAR. M. VIC*toria* PAR*thica* M*axima*. The greatest Parthian victory.

VIC. S. VIC*toria* S*icilia*. The Sicilian victory.

VIC. BEATISSIM. CAESS. VIC*toria* BEATISSIM*orum* CAES*arum*. The victory of the most sacred Cæsars.

VIC. BRIT. P. M. VIC*toria* BRIT*annica* P*ontifex* M*aximus*. The British victory, the high Pontiff.

VICTOR. ROM. VICTOR*ia* ROM*anorum*. The victory of the Romans.

VICT. P. GAL. AVG. VICT*oria* P*arthica* GAL*lieni* AUG*usti*. The Parthian victory of the Emperor Gallienus Augustus.

VIII. VIII. Eight, generally this figure when it appears on silver coins signifies that they are worth eight As.

VII. VIR. EPV. VII. VIRI. EPU*lonum*. The Epulonean Septemvir, a sacred dignity among the Romans.

VIR. VIR*tus*. Virtue, or courage, or valor.

VI. VIR. A. VI. VIR. A*ugustus*. The Augustan Sexemvir or Sevir, a titular rank among the Romans.

V. N. M. R. *urbis* N*icomediae* M*oneta* R*estituta*. The restored money of the city of Nicomedia.

VOL. VOL*usius*. Volusius, name of a personage.

VOLER. VOLER*o*. Volero, name of a personage.

VOTA. PVB. VOT*a* PUB*lica*. Public vows.

VOT. DECEN. VOT*a* DECEN*nalia*. Decennalian vows.

VOT. XX. MVL. XXX. VOT*a* XX. MUL*tiplica* XXX. The vows for twenty years increased to thirty.

V. P. *vota* P*ublica* or *vota* P*opuli*. Public vows or vows of the people.

V. V. *vota* V. Quinquennalian vows.

X.

X. Decem. Ten, or Decennalia (feasts) or denoting the value of X Ases on a Roman denarius.

X. F. X. F*aciendum*. An officer appointed for striking silver money, X signifying the silver denarii, which were originally worth *ten* Ases.

XL. R. XL. R*emissa*. The fortieth, a tax so called, remitted.

XVI. XVI. The later denarii are marked thus; this coin was formerly only worth ten Ases, but rose to the value of sixteen, with which figures they were marked.

XV. XV. Money worth fifteen denarii.

XV. VIR. SAC. FAC. XV. VIR*i* SAC*ris* FAC*iundis*. Fifteen men appointed for performing the sacrifices.

XX. V. XX. *vota*. Thanks returned on the twentieth year.

LIST OF ROMAN FAMILIES THAT ISSUED COINS.

A few of these issues were in gold, a larger number in bronze, but by far the largest were in silver denarii.

Name of the Family.	No. of Known Varieties.
Aburia	5
Accoleia	1
Acilia	18
Aebutia	4
Aelia and Allia	24
Aemilia	43
Afrania	8
Allienus	1
Annia	28
Antestia or Antistia	12
Antia	3
Antonia	138
Appuleia *bronze*	3
Apronia *bronze*	5
Aquilleia	12
Ania	7
Asinia	6
Atia	1
Atilia	8
Aufidia	2
Aurelia	17
Autronia	1
Axia	8
Baebia	8
Betilienus	1
Cæcilia	
Cæcina	2
Cæsia	1
Calidia	1
Calpurnia	150
Canidia	2
Caninia	8
Carisia	23
Carvilia	23
Cassia	37
Cestia	6
Cipia	2
Claudia	43
Clovia	1
Cloulia	6
Cocceia	1
Coelia	21
Considia	13
Coponia	8
Cordia	5
Cornelia	121
Cornuficia	5
Cosconia	1
Cossutia	11
Crepercia	6
Crepusia	23
Critonia	1
Cupienna	3
Curiatia	5
Curlia	4
Didia	3
Domitia	19
Durmia	9
Egnatia	10
Egnatuleia	1
Eppia	2
Fabia	38
Fabricia	2
Fabrina	2
Fannia	2
Farsuleia	11
Flaminia	4
Flavia	3
Fonteia	30
Fufia	1
Fulvia	11
Fundania	5
Furia	10
Gallia	3
Gellia	3
Herennia	15
Hirtia	1
Horatia	4

Name of the Family.	No. of Known Varieties.
Hosidia	2
Hostilia	5
Itia	1
Julia	122
Junia	75
Licinia	31
Livineia	13
Lollia	21
Lucilia	1
Lucretia	11
Luria	7
Lutatia	3
Maecilia	4
Maenia	4
Maiania	3
Mamilia	18
Manlia	8
Marcia	42
Maria	46
Memmia	15
Mescinia	6
Mettia	8
Minatia	3
Mineia	3
Minucia	10
Mitreia	2
Mucia	2
Munatia	3
Mussidia	20
Naevia	27
Nasidia	3
Neria	1
Nonia	3
Norbanus	26
Numitoria	5
Numonia	3
Ogulnia	5
Opeimia	7
Oppia	9
Pacuvia	1
Papia	63
Papiria	16
Pedania	2
Petillia	2
Petronia	19
Pinaria	10
Plaetoria	57
Plancia	8
Plautia	9
Plolia	4
Poblicia	15
Pompeia	33
Pomponia	33
Porcia	26
Postumia	12
Procilia	2
Proculeia	2
Quinctia	12
Renia	1
Roscia	43
Rubellia	1
Rubria	10
Rustia	3
Rutilia	1
Salvia	4
Sanquina	4
Satrienus	22
Saufeia	5
Scribonia	6
Sempronia	22
Sentia	31
Sepullia	6
Sergia	1
Servilia	25
Sestia	4
Sicinia	3
Silia	4
Socia	3
Spurilia	1
Statia	2
Statilia	4
Sulpicia	32
Tarquitia	2
Terentia	14
Thoria	2
Titia	6
Titinia	2
Tituria	33
Trebania	4
Tullia	3
Valeria	34
Vargunteia	3
Ventidia	3
Vettia	1
Veturia	3
Vibia	70
Vinicia	4
Voconia	3
Volteia	34

NAMES

OF ALL OFFICIAL OR DISTINGUISHED ROMAN PERSONAGES BY WHOM COINS HAVE BEEN ISSUED, OR TO WHOM THEY HAVE BEEN ASCRIBED.

Cnaeus Pompeius. Born 106 B. C.; called by Sylla the Dictator, *Magnus,* a title that descended to his son and is found on his coins. Formed with Cæsar and Crassus, the first Triumvirate. Killed 48 B. C. G.—R.[6] S.—R.[1] R.[2]; Br.—R.[1] Some coins represent him with his sons Cnaeus Pompeius and Sextus Pompeius. There are some silver coins restored by Trajan.

CAIUS JULIUS CÆSAR. Born 100 B. C.; made Perpetual Dictator 44 B. C.; and assassinated the same year. G.—R.[1] R.[7] S.—C.—R[4] Br.—C. Many coins represent him with Marc Antony and Augustus.

Cnaeus Pompeius, son of Pompey the Great. Born — B. C.; killed 45 B. C. S.—R.[1] R.[7] Some coins represent him with his father Cnaeus Pompeius Magnus, and his brother Sextus Pompeius. He bore, like his father, the surname of Magnus.

Sextus Pompeius, second son of Pompey the Great. Born 65 B. C.; killed 35 B. C. G.—R.[6] S.—R.[1] R.[4] With and without his head. Some coins represent him with his father and brother, Cnaeus Pompeius Magnus and Cnaeus Pompeius the Younger.

Marcus Junius Brutus. Born 85 B. C.; assassinated Cæsar and died at Philippi 40 B. C G.—R.[3] S.—R.[4] R.[6] With and without portrait; with the heads of the two Brutuses. There are among these, some coins restored by Trajan.

Caius Cassius Longinus. Date of birth unknown; died at Philippi, 42 B. C. G.—R.[4] S.—R[1] R.[2] These coins do not bear the head of Cassius.

Marcus Æmilius Lepidus. Date of birth, unknown; joined Cæsar against Pompey, and with Octavius and Anthony formed the second Triumvirate; died 13 B. C. G.—R.[3] S.—R.[3] R.[5] Some coins represent him with Marc Antony and Octavius.

Marcus Antonius. Born 83 B. C.; died in Egypt 30 B. C. G.—R.[3] R.[3] S. C.—R.[5] Br. R.[1] R.[4]. With and without his head. Some coins represent him with Julius Cæsar, Lepidus, Cleopatra, Marc Antony (his son), Lucius Antonius, or Augustus.

Octavia, sister of Augustus, wife of Marc Antony. Died 10 or 11 B. C. G.—R.[8] This coin represents her with Marc Antony.

Marcus Antonius, son of Marc Antony and Fulvia. Killed 36 B. C. G.—R.[8] This coin represents him with Marc Antony, his father.

Cleopatra, queen of Egypt. Made queen 56 B. C.; killed herself 36 B. C. G.—R.[8] S.—R.[4] Br.—R.[4] Most of these coins represent her with Marc Antony. The gold coins are doubtful.

Caius Antonius, brother of Marc Antony, killed by Brutus 44 or 43 B. C. G.—R[6] Without portrait.

Lucius Antonius, brother of Marc Antony. Born —; died —. G.—R.[8] S.—R.[4] These coins represent him with Marc Antony, his brother.

Caius Octavius Caepas AUGUSTUS, nephew and heir of Julius Cæsar. Born 63 B. C.; declared Emperor 29 B. C.; obtained the name of Augustus 27 B. C.; died 14 A. D. G.—

C.—R.[8] S.—C.—R.[8] Br.—C.—R[8] Some coins represent him with Julius Cæsar, Lepidus, Agrippa, Tiberius, Julia, Caius and Julius, or Germanicus. There are many of his coins restored by Claudius, Nero, Titus, Domitian, Nerva, and Trajan. The coins of Augustus are numerous.

Livia Drusilla, second wife of Augustus. Born 57 B. C.; died 29 A. D. S.—C.—R.[4] The coins of this princess, struck in Rome, do not bear her head; she is represented as Justice, Piety, and Health. She is called *Julia Augusta,* on *Latin* coins; *Livia* on some *Greek* ones. Took the name of Julia after Augustus's death.

Marcus Vipsanius Agrippa, son-in-law of Augustus. Born 63 B.C.; died 12 B.C. G.—R.[8] S.—R.[6] R.[7] Br.—C.—R.[4] Some coins represent him with Augustus. There are second brass coins restored by Titus, Domitian, and silver by Trajan.

Julia, daughter of Augustus, wife of Marius Marcellinus, Marcus Agrippa, and, lastly, of Tiberius. Born 39 B. C.; died of starvation by command of Tiberius, A. D. 14. Her name appears on a coin of Augustus, with the heads of her sons, Caius and Lucius. There are only Greek coins of this princess.

Caius et *Lucius,* sons of Marcus Agrippa and Julia. Caius, born 20 B. C.; Cæsar, 17 B. C.; died 4 A. D.; Lucius, born 17 B. C.; Cæsar, the same year; died 2 A. D. These two princes are named together on the coins of Augustus. We do not find their portraits except on Colonial coins.

Agrippa Postumus, son of Marcus Agrippa and Julia. Born 12 B. C.; obtained the name of Cæsar 4 A. D.; killed by Tiberius, his brother, 14 A. D. Of this Prince no coins are known, except a Greek and one colonial.

TIBERIUS CLAUDIUS NERO, son-in-law of Augustus. Born 42 B. C.; obtained the title of Cæsar 4 A. D.; declared Emperor 14 A. D.; smothered, by order of Caligula, 37 A. D. G.—C.—R.[6] S.—C.—R.—[6] Br.—C.—R.[8] Some coins are without his head; other represent him with Augustus and Drusus the Younger. There are some coins restored by Titus, Domitian, and Trajan.

Nero Claudius Drusus, Junior, son of Tiberius. Born 13 B. C.; poisoned by his wife, Livia, 23 A. D. Br.—C.—R.[6] Most of the coins of this prince, and all those in silver, represent him on the reverses of Tiberius. Some of them are without his portrait. There are coins restored by Titus and Domitian.

Nero Claudius Drusus, Senior, brother of Tiberius. Born 38 B. C.; died 9 A. D. G.—R.[4] S.—R.[4] Br.—R.[2] There are some coins struck by Claudius, and others restored by Titus and Domitian.

Antonia, daughter of Marc Antony, and wife of Drusus Senior. Born 38 B. C.; poisoned by her grandson Caligula, 38 A. D. G.—R.[4] S.—R.[4]

Germanicus, son of Drusus Senior and Antonia. Born 15 B. C.; adopted by Tiberius and obtained the title of Cæsar 4 A. D.; was poisoned 19 A. D. G.—R.[4] R.[6] S.—R.[4] R.[6] Br.—C.R.[8] Nearly all the coins represent him with Augustus, Caligula, and Agrippina. There are coins restored by Titus and Domitian.

Agrippina Senior, daughter of Agrippa and Julia, wife of Germanicus. Born 15 B. C.; was starved to death by order of Tiberius 33 A. D. G.—R.[4] R.[8] S.—R.[4] Br.—R.[2] R.[8] Most of the coins represent her with Caligula and Germanicus. There are coins restored by Titus.

Nero and *Drusus,* sons of Germanicus and Agrippina. Nero born 7 A. D.; starved to death by Tiberius 31 A. D. Drusus born 8 A. D.; starved to death by Tiberius 33 A. D. Br.—C. They are represented together on horseback.

CAIUS, commonly called CALIGULA, son of Germanicus and Agrippina. Born 12 A. D.; declared Emperor 37 A. D.; killed by the Prætorian guards 41 A. D. G.—R.[4] R.[5] S.—R.[2] R.[4] Br.—C.

—R.[3] The name of Caligula was given to this Emperor, because he had worn from his infancy the Caliga, or military boot. Some coins represent him with Germanicus and his mother Agrippina. The title of *Imperator* is found on his Colonial coins alone.

Claudia, first wife of Caligula. Date of birth unknown; married 33 A. D.; died 36 A. D. No genuine coins. This first wife of Caligula is sometimes called by writers Junia Claudilla.

Caesonia, fourth wife of Caligula. Born —; married 39 A. D.; killed 41 A. D. No reliable coins known.

Drusilla, daughter of Caesonia. Born —; killed 41 A. D. The coins attributed to this princess are false.

Drusilla, sister of Caligula. Born 17 A. D.; died 38 A. D. There are *Greek* but no *Roman* coins of this princess, those which are attributed to her being false. Some say that there is the head of this princess on the reverse of a gold coin of Caligula.

Julia Livilla, sister of Caligula. Born 18 A. D.; killed 41 A. D. This princess is called by historians Julia or Livilla. No Roman coin can be attributed to this princess with certainty. Julia Livilla may be found on Greek coins.

Tiberius CLAUDIUS *Drusus*, son of Drusus Senior (the brother of Tiberius) and Antonia. Born 10 B. C.; declared Emperor 41 A. D.; poisoned by his wife Agrippina 54 A. D. G.—R.[1] R.[6] S.—C. —R.[3] Br.—C.—R.[4] Some coins represent him with Agrippina the Younger. Some of his coins were restored by Titus and Trajan. Claudius had three wives, Plautia Urgulanilla, Aelia Petina, and Valeria Messalina.

Valeria Messalina, third wife of Claudius. Born —; killed 48 A. D. No coins of this princess are known, except some Colonial Greek.

Agrippina the Younger, sister of Caligula and fourth wife of Claudius, her uncle. Born 16 A. D.; assassinated by her son Nero 59 A. D. G.—R.[2] S.—R.[1] R.[6] Br.—R.[8] Some coins represent her with Claudius and with Nero.

Claudia, daughter of Claudius and Plautia Urgulanilla. Born —; killed by Nero 65 A. D. We do not know of any Roman coins of this princess. Her name is to be found on a Colonial coin, and her portrait on two pieces—one a Colonial and the other of Alexandria.

Tiberius Claudius Britannicus, son of Claudius and Messalina. Born 42 A. D.; was poisoned by Nero 55 A. D. Br.—R.[8]

Lucius Domitius NERO, the younger son of Cnaeus Domitius Ahenobarbus and Agrippina the Younger; son-in-law and adopted by Claudius as heir, then took the names of *Tiberius Claudius* NERO *Drusus*. Born 37 A. D.; obtained the name of Cæsar 50 A. D.; declared Emperor 54 A. D.; killed himself 68 A. D. G.—C.—R.[4] S.—C.—R.[4] Br.—C.—R[6]. The coins of this emperor are numerous. Some of them represent him with Agrippina the Younger.

Octavia. Born 42 A. D.; first wife of Nero, by whom she was first divorced and then killed by opening her veins, 62 A. D. No Roman coins are known of this princess. There are, however, some Colonial Greek.

Poppaea Sabina, second wife of Nero. Born —; died 66 A. D., from the effects of a kick given her by Nero. We do not know of any coins of this princess except a silver Greek, which is doubtful, and two Colonial coppers of her daughter Claudia (also uncertain), which bear her name on the reverse.

Statilia Messalina, third wife of Nero. Born —: died A. D. Some Greek but no Roman coins are known of this empress.

Claudia, daughter of Nero and Poppaea. Born 64 A. D.; died the same year, aged 4 months. There are no coins of this princess except a leaden one, which bears her head on the reverse of a coin of Nero her father; also two doubtful Colonial bronzes, which bear her name.

Lucius Clodius Macer, Propraetor in Africa 68 A. D.; assumed to be Emperor on Nero's death, but put to death by order of Galba. S.—R.[6] R.[8] These coins were struck in Africa.

Servius Sulpicius GALBA. Born 3 B.C. declared Emperor 68 A. D.; assassinated by Otho 69 A. D. G.—R.[2] R.[4] S.—C.—R.[4] Br.—C.—R.[6] Some of these coins were restored by Titus and by Trajan.

Marcus Salvius OTHO. Born 32 A. D.; declared Emperor 69 A. D.; conquered by Vitellius and killed himself the same year. G.—R.[4] S.—R.[1] R.[3] There are only Colonial brass of Otho.

Aulus VITELLIUS. Born 15 A. D.; declared Emperor in Germany 69 A. D.; and put to death by Vespasian's soldiers the same year. G.—R.[4] R.[8] S.—C.—R.[4] Br.—R.[2] R.[5]

Lucius Vitellius, father of Aulus Vitellius. Born —; died 48 or 49 A. D. G.—R.[8] S.—R.[4] Some coins represent him with the Emperor Vitellius his son.

Flavius VESPASIANUS. Born 9 A. D.; declared Emperor 69, died 79. G.—C.—R.[5] S.—C.—R.[2] Br.—C.—R.[5] The coins of Vespasian are numerous; some of them represent him with his sons Titus and Domitian, others bear only their names. Some of the Roman coins of Vespasian were struck in Antioch in Syria. Some of these coins were restored by Trajan.

Flavia Domitilla, wife of Vespasian, Born —; died before her husband was made emperor. G.—R.[8] S.—R.[6] R.[8] Some coins represent her with Vespasian.

Domitilla, daughter of Vespasian and Flavia Domitilla. Born —; died before her father became emperor. Br.—R.[2] Without her portrait.

Polla, mother of Vespasian. Born —; died —. The coins attributed to the mother of Vespasian are false.

TITUS *Flavius Vespasianus,* son of Vespasian and Flavia Domitilla. Born 41 A. D.; obtained the title of Cæsar 69. Shared the sovereign power with his father, with the title of Emperor 71; became sole emperor 79; died 81. G.—C.—R.[6] S.—C.—R.[5] Br.—C.—R.[4] The coins of Titus are numerous; some represent him with Vespasian, Domitian, or with his daughter Julia. Arricidia (who is not named on any coin) and Marcia Furnilla were his wives.

Marcia Furnilla, second wife of Titus, Born —. Repudiated by Titus before his advancement to the throne. Died —. No Roman coins are known of Furnilla. There is a Greek coin attributed to her.

Julia, daughter of Titus and Furnilla. Born —; died —G.—C.—R.[8] S.—R.[4] R.[6] Br.—R.[2]

DOMITIANUS, son of Vespasian and Flavia Domitilla. Born 51 A. D.; obtained the name of Cæsar 69; declared Emperor 81; assassinated 96. G.—C.—R.[8] S.—C.—R.[8] Br.—C.—R.[4] The coins of this Emperor are numerous, and represent him with Vespasian, Titus, and with his wife Domitia.

Domitia Longina, wife of Domitian. Born —; died 140 A.D. G.—R.[6] S.—R[4] R.[6] Br.—R.[6] B.[8] Some coins represent her with Domitian and with his son.

Anonymus, son of Domitian and Domitia, Born 82 A.D.; died young. This child, whose name is not known, is represented on the coins with his mother.

Vespasianus the Younger, son of Flavius Clemens Domitianus. We know only of Greek coins.

Marcus Cocceius NERVA. Born 32 A. D.; declared Emperor 96; died 98. G.—R.[2] R.[6] S.—C.—R.[5] Br.—C.—R.[4] The coins of this prince are numerous. Some represent him with Trajan.

Marcus Ulpius Crinitus or *M. U. Nerva* TRAJANUS. Born 53 A. D.; associated in the Empire with Nerva, with the titles of Cæsar and Emperor, but without that of Augustus 97; declared sole Emperor 98; died 117. G.—C.—R.[6] S.—C.—R.[8]

Br.—C.—R.[6] Trajan restored many of the coins of the Roman Families, and of his predecessors. Many coins represent him with Nerva, his father, Plotina, or Hadrian. The coins of Trajan are very numerous; his coins are struck with the metals of different countries, such as Dalmatia, Pannonia, &c.

Plotina, wife of Trajan. Born —; died 129 A. D. G.—R.[4] R.[6] S.—R.[6] Some coins represent her with Trajan, Matidia, or Hadrian.

Trajanus Pater, father of the Emperor Trajan. Born — ; died 100 A. D. ; G.—R.[4] S.—R.[4] These coins represent him with the Emperor Trajan, his son.

Marciana, sister of Trajan. Born —; died 144 A. D. G.—R.[6] S.—R.[6] Br.—R.[6] Some of her coins bear the name of Matidia.

Matidia, daughter of Marciana. Born —; died in the reign of Antoninus Pius. G.—R.[6] S.—R.[6] Br—R.[8] Some coins represent her with Plotina, others bear the name of Marciana.

Publius Aelius HADRIANUS, son-in-law of Matidia and Trajan. Born 76 A. D.; adopted by Trajan 117; made Emperor the same year; died 138. G.—C.—R.[5] S.—C.—R.[8] Br.—C.—R.[6] Some coins represent him with Trajan, Plotina, Sabina, and Antoninus. The coins of this Emperor are numerous, many bearing the names of the different provinces over which he traveled.

Sabina, daughter of Matidia, wife of Hadrian. Born —; killed herself 137 A. D. G.—R.[3] S.—C.—R.[3] Br.—C.—R.[4] Some coins represent her with Hadrian.

AELIUS *Lucius Aurelius Cejonius Commodus Verus*. Adopted by Hadrian 135 or 136 A. D., by the name of *Lucius* AELIUS *Verus*; died 138 A. D. G—R.[4] R.[5] S.—R.[2] Br.—C.—R.[8]

Antinous, the favorite of Hadrian; died 130 A. D. There are only Greek coins of Antinous.

Titus Aurelius Fulvius Bojonius Arrius ANTONINUS PIUS. Born 86 A. D.; adopted by Hadrian and named Cæsar, 138 A. D.; declared Emperor the same year, taking the names of *Titus Ælius Hadrianus* A., receiving from the Senate the title of *Pius;* died 161 A. D. G.—C.—R.[3] S.—C.—R.[6] Br.—C.—R.[8] Some coins represent him with Hadrian, Faustina, Marcus Aurelius, and Lucius Verus. The coins of this Emperor are numerous.

Annia Galeria Faustina Senior. Born 105 A. D.; married Antoninus before his adoption by Hadrian, and died 141 A. D. G.—C.—R.[5] S.—C.—R.[5] Br.—C.—R.[5] Some coins represent her with Antoninus. The coins of Faustina, the mother, are numerous.

Marcus Galerius Antoninus, son of Antoninus Pius and Faustina; died young, before his father came to the throne. There are only Greek coins known of this child.

Marcus Annius Verus Catilius Severus MARCUS AURELIUS, son-in-law of Antoninus Pius. Born 121 A. D. ; adopted by Antoninus, 138, when he was adopted by Hadrian, with the name of Cæsar; made Emperor 161, taking the names of MARCUS AURELIUS ANTONINUS ; died 180. G.—C.—R.[2] S.—C.—R.[5] Br.—C.—R.[8] Some coins represent him with Antoninus, Faustina the Young, Lucius Verus, and Commodus. The coins of this Emperor are numerous.

Faustina the Younger, cousin and wife of Marcus Aurelius; died 175 A. D. G.—C.—R.[5] S.—C.—R.[2] Br. — C.—R.[6] Some coins represent her with Marcus Aurelius. The coins of Faustina the Younger are very numerous.

Annius Verus, the youngest son of Marcus Aurelius and Faustina. Born 163 A.D.; obtained the name of Cæsar 166; died 170. B.—R.[6] R.[8]

LUCIUS VERUS *Lucius Cejonius Commodus*, son of Ælius Cæsar, and son-in-law of Marcus Aurelius.

Born 130 A. D.; adopted by Antoninus Pius, without the title of Cæsar, 137; associated in the empire, with the titles of Cæsar and Augustus, by Marcus Aurelius, 151; poisoned 169. G.—C.—R.[3] S.—C.—R.[6] Br.—C.—R.[6] Some coins represent him with Antoninus and Marcus Aurelius. The coins of Lucius Verus are very numerous.

Annia Lucilla, the youngest daughter of Marcus Aurelius and Faustina, and wife of Lucius Verus. Born 147 A. D.: exiled 183 to Capreæ, by order of Commodus, and put to death soon afterwards. G.—R.[1] R.[2] S.—C.—R.[2] Br.—C.—R.[7]

Lucius, or *Marcus Ælius Aurelius* COMMODUS *Antoninus*, elder son of Marcus Aurelius and Faustina the Younger. Born 161 A. D.; obtained the name of Cæsar 166; associated in the empire, with the title of Emperor, 176; obtained the name of Augustus 177; declared sole emperor 180; strangled 192. G.—R.[5] R.[8] S.—C.—R.[4] Br.—C.—R.[8] Some coins represent him with Marcus Aurelius, Crispina, and Annius Verus. On some of his coins we meet with the head of a woman without any name. She is supposed to be his concubine Marcia. Commodus had a particular devotion for Hercules, and is often represented with the attributes of this Demigod, and is called the Herculean Commodus. The coins of this emperor are very numerous.

Bruttia Crispina, wife of Commodus. Born — ; banished to Capreæ, and there died, 183 A. D. G.—R.[6] S.—C.—R.[1]. Br.—C.—R.[7] Some coins represent her with Commodus.

Publius Helvius PERTINAX. Born 126 A. D.; declared Emperor by the Prætorians 192, but assassinated by the soldiers after a reign of 87 days. G.—R.[3]. R.[6] S.—R.[4] R.[6] Br.—R.[5] R.[7]

Titiana, wife of Pertinax. Born — : On the death of her husband she retired from public life, where she died. There are only Greek coin. of this Princess.

MARCUS DIDIUS *Severus* JULIANUS, Born 133 A.D.; purchased the purple on the death of Pertinax, but put to death after a reign of 66 days. G.—R[6] S.—R.[6] Br.—R.[2] R.[6]

Manlia Scantilla, wife of Didius Julianus. Born — ; retired from public life, on the death of her husband. G.—R.[8] S.—R.[6] Br.—R.[4] R.[7]

Didia Clara, daughter of Didius Julianus and Scantilla. Born 153 A. D.; died — ; G.—R.[8] S.—R.[6] Br.—R.[4]

Caius PESCENNIUS NIGER. Born — ; declared Emperor by the legions in Syria; killed by Severus, 194. G.—R.[8] S.—R.[5] R.[7] The Roman coins of Pescennius Niger were struck in Syria, probably at Antioch.

Decimus CLODIUS *Septimius* ALBINUS. Born —; named Cæsar, by Septimius Severus 193; being at that time Governor of Britain, he took the title of Emperor of Britain and Gaul, 196; defeated and killed by Septimius Severus 197; G.—R.[8] S.—R.[2] R.[4] Br.—R.[2] R[8] The Roman coins of Albinus with the title of Cæsar, were struck at Rome during the time that there existed an alliance between him and Septimius Severus, when the latter conferred upon Albinus the title of Cæsar. Those coins which bear the title of Emperor and of Augustus were struck in Gaul, and perhaps some of them in Britain after Albinus had taken the title of emperor.

Lucius SEPTIMIUS SEVERUS. Born 146 A. D.; declared Emperor 193; became master of the whole empire 197, when he took the surname of Pertinax; died 211. G.—R.[2] R.[6] S.—C.—R.[5] Br.—C.—R.[6] Some coins represent him with Julia Domna, Caracalla, and Geta. The coins of this emperor are numerous.

Julia Domna, daughter of *Bassianus*, wife of Septimius Severus. Born — ; starved herself to death on the death of Caracalla, 217. G.—R.[2] R.[8] S.—C.—R.[8] Br.—C.—R[8].

Some coins represent her with Septimius Severus, Caracalla, and Geta. The coins of this empress are numerous.

Marcus Aurelius Antoninus, (or Bassianus), commonly called CARACALLA, eldest son of Septimius Severus and Julia. Born 188 A.D.; obtained the name of Cæsar 196, when he took the name of Marcus Aurelius Antoninus; that of Augustus 198; Emperor with his brother Geta 211, whom he killed in his mother's arms; sole emperor 212; asssassinated by Macrinus, 217, G.—R.^{1} R,^{8} S.—C.—R.^{6} Br.—C.—R.^{7}. The name of Caracalla came from a new sort of garment which he introduced and frequently wore. Some coins represent him with Septimius Severus, Julia Domna, Geta, and Plautilla. The coins of this emperor are very numerous.

Fulvia Plautilla, married Caracalla 202 A. D.; banished to Lipari, 203; died there, 212. G.—R.^{6} S.—G.—R^{2}. Br.—R.^{3} R^{8}.

Lucius or *Publius Septimius* GETA, second son of Septimius Severus and Julia Domna. Born 189 A.D.; obtained the name of Cæsar 198, and that of Augustus 209; Emperor with his eldest brother Caracalla 211; assassinated by him in the arms of his mother 212. G.—R.^{4} R.^{6} S.—C.—R.^{4} Br.—C.—R.^{6} Some coins represent him with Septimius Severus, Julia Domna, and Caracalla. The coins of Geta are numerous.

Marcus Opelius Severus MACRINUS, Born 164 A. D.; declared Emperor 217; killed 218. G.—R. 4 R. 7 S.—R. 1 R. 5. Br.—R. 1 R. 8

Marcus Opelius Diadumenianus, son of Macrinus. Born 208 A.D.; obtained the names of Cæsar and of Antoninus, 217; and that of Augustus the same year; killed 218. G.—R. 8 S.—R2. R. 6 Br.—R. 2—R. 5 Many of his coins were struck at Antioch in Syria.

ELAGABALUS, *Varius Avitus Bassianus*. Born 205 A.D.; declared Emperor 218, when he took the names of Marcus Aurelius Antoninus; put to death 222. G.—R. 2 R. 8 S.—C.—R. 5 Br.—C.—R. 7. The name of Elagabalus was given to this Emperor because he was in his infancy made Pontiff to the God Elagabalus, (the Sun), at Emisa in Syria, his country. Some coins represent him with Aquila Severa, Annia Faustina, and Julia Soaemias.

Julia Cornelia Paula, first wife of Elagabalus. Died in private life. G.—R. 6 R. 8 S.—R. 1 R. 2 Br.—R. 3 R. 5 The name of Cornelia is only found on Greek coins.

Aquilia Severa, second wife of Elagabalus. Died after the Emperor. G.—R. 8 S.—R. 2 R. 4. Br.—R. 2 R. 4 Some coins represent her with Elagabalus.

Annia Faustina, third wife of Elagabalus. Born—; divorced as soon as she was married; died —. G.—R. 8 S.—R. 8 Br.—R. 6 The gold coin is doubtful, as it bears on the reverse a portrait of Elagabalus.

Julia Soaemias, mother of Elagabalus, and sister of Julia Mæsa; killed 222 A.D. G.—R. 6 S.—C. —R. 5 Br.—C.—R. 4 Some coins represent her with Elagabalus.

Julia Mæsa, sister of Julia Domna, aunt to Elagabalus. Born— ; died 223. G.—R^{6} S.—C.—R.^{4} Br.—C.—R.^{4}

ALEXANDER SEVERUS, *Bassianus Alexianus*, cousin of Elagabalus. Born 205 A.D.; adopted by Elagabalus with the name of Marcus Aurelius Alexander, 221 ; Emperor, 222, taking the name Severus; assassinated 235. G.—C.—R.^{8} S.—C.—R.^{8} Some coins represent him with Julia Mamaea and Orbiana. The coins of this prince are very numerous.

Memmia, second wife of Alexander Severus. No particulars are known respecting this princess, and the coin attributed to her is very doubtful.

Sallustia Barbia Orbiana, third wife of Alexander Severus. No details are known respecting this princess. G.—R.^{8} S.—R.^{2} R.^{8} Br.—R.^{1} R.^{8} Some coins represent her with Alexander Severus, and Mamaea. This princess is not spoken of by ancient authors: some consider her to have been the wife of Decius, although she appears on the coins with Alexander Severus.

Julia Mamaea, sister of Julia Soaemias, and mother of Alexander Severus. Assassinated with her son, 235 A. D. Some coins represent her with Alexander Severus and Orbiana. The coins of Mamaea are numerous.

Uranius Antoninus. Born — ; had himself proclaimed Emperor in Asia in the town of Emisa in Syia, during the reign of Alexander Severus; but was defeated and taken prisoner soon after. G.—R.^{8} One piece of Roman money is the only coin of his which is known ; it was struck inAsia, and probably at Emisa in Syria.

Caius Julius Verus MAXIMINUS I. Born 173 A.D. ; Emperor 235; assassinated 238. G.—R.^{6} R.^{8}S.—C.— R.^{7} Br.—C.— R.^{8} Some coins represent him with his son Maximus. On *Roman* coins we have only MAXIMINVS ; on *Colonial Latin*, IVLIVS MAXIMINVS. on *Greek*, the name in full CAIVS IVL. VERVS. MAXIMINVS.

Paulina, wife of Maximinus. No particulars are known respecting this princess. S.—R.^{4} Br.—R.^{2} R.^{4} We believe this princess to be the wife of Maximinus, from the great resemblance which the portrait of Maximus on his coins bears to hers, and the great likeness between the coins of Maximinus and Maximus and hers. All the coins of Paulina represent her consecration, so that it is believed she died before her husband.

Caius Julius Verus Maximus, son of Maximinus. Born — ; obtained the name of Cæsar 235 A. D. ; killed 238 A. D. G.—R.^{8} S.—R.$_{4}$ R.^{8} Br.—R.^{1} R.$_{8}$ Some coins represent him with his father Maximinus.

Junia Fadilla, betrothed to Maximus. All that is known of this princess is, that Maximinus wished to marry his son to her, being grand niece to the Emperor Antoninus, but this marriage was not effected, as the father and son were both killed. The coins attributed to this princess are false.

Titus Quartinus. Proclaimed himself Emperor in Germany during the reign of Maximinus ; killed soon after. There is a coin attributed to him, bearing on one side the inscription "Divo Tito," and on the reverse "Consecratio;" but this coin is one of those struck by Gallienus in honor of his predecessors who had been ranked among the gods

Marcus Antoninus GORDIANUS AFRICANUS I. (Pater). Born 158 A. D. ; proclaimed Emperor in Africa, and acknowledged by the Senate ; killed himself about forty days afterwards on hearing of his son's death. S.—R.$_{5}$ R.^{6} Br.—R.$_{3}$ R.^{8} These Latin coins were struck, without doubt, at Carthage.

Marcus Antoninus GORDIANUS AFRICANUS II. son of Gordianus Africanus I. Born 192 A. D. : Emperor with his father 238 ; killed about forty days afterwards. S.—R.^{6} Br.—R.^{4} These coins were, without doubt, minted in Carthage, like those of his father.

Decimus Caelius BALBINUS. Born 178 A. D. ; Emperor with Pupienus 238 : massacred after a reign of three months. G.—R^{8} S.—R.^{1} R.^{3} Br.—R.^{2} R.^{6}

Marcus Clodius PUPIENUS *Maximus*. Born 164 A. D. ; declared Emperor with Balbinus 238 ; massacred about three months afterwards. G.—R.^{8} S.—R.^{2} Br.—R.^{2} R.^{6}

Marcus Antonius GORDIANUS PIUS III., nephew of Gordianus Africanus. Born 222 A. D. ; Cæsar 538 ; Emperor the same year ; assassinated 244. G.—R.^{1} R.^{8} S.—C.—R.^{7} Br.—C.—R.^{6} The coins of this Prince are numerous.

Furia Sabina Tranquillina, wife of Gordianus III. Born — ; died after her husband. S.—R.^{8} Br. —R.^{8}

Marcus Julius PHILIPPUS I. Born 204 A. D. ; Emperor 244; killed in battle by Trajan Decius 249. G. —R.^{6} R.^{8} S.—C.—R.^{8} Br.—C.

—R.[6] Some coins represent him with Otacilia and Philip, his son. The coins of Philip are numerous.

Marcia Otacilia Severa, wife of Philip. Born —; died 249. G. —R.[5] R.[6] S.—C.—R.[5] Br.—C.—R.[7] Some coins represent her with Philip the father and son.

Marcus Julius PHILIPPUS II. Son of Philip and Otacilia. Born 237 A. D. Cæsar, 244. Associated in the empire with the title of Augustus, 247; killed 249. G.—R[4] R. S.—C.—R.[4] Br.—C.—R.[7] Some coins represent him with Philip the elder. The coins of this prince are numerous.

Marinus. Proclaimed Emperor in Moesia and Pannonia, 339 A. D.; killed soon afterwards. The coins which have been attributed to this prince are Greek, but their attribution is doubtful. These coins were minted in Arabia, and most likely belong to a relation of the Emperor Philip, and perhaps to his father.

Jotapianus. Proclaimed Emperor in Syria, 248 A. D.; put to death soon after. S.—R.[8] This coin was, without doubt, minted in Syria.

Tiberius Claudius Marius Pacatianus. This personage was proclaimed Emperor about this period, and is only known by his coins. S.—R[8]. It is thought from his coins that Pacatianus had himself proclaimed emperor in the reign of Philip or Trajanus Decius; that he reigned in Greece, because his coins were found there, or that he was proclaimed in Moesia and Pannonnia.

Sponsianus. Proclaimed Emperor about this period, and only known by his coins. G.—R.[7]

Caius Messius Quintus TRAJANUS DECIUS. Born 201 A. D.; Emperor, 249; drowned in a bog, 251. G.—R.[4] R.[5] S.—C.—R.[8] Br. —C.—R.[6] Some coins represent him with Etruscilla, Hostilius and Herennius.

Herennia Etruscilla (wife of Decius). This princess is only known by her coins. G.—R.[6] S.—C.—R.[1] Br. —C.—R.[5]

Quintus Herennius Etruscus Messius Trajanus Decius, son of Decius. Cæsar, 249; Augustus, 251; killed same year. G.—R.[8] S.—C.—R.[8] Br.—R.[2] R.[8]

Caius Valens HOSTILIANUS *Messius Quintus,* son of Decius. Cæsar, 249; Emperor with Gallus, 251; died same year. G.—R.[8] S.—C.—R.[2] Br.—R.[2] R.[6] Some coins represent him with Volusianus.

Caius Vibius TREBONIANUS GALLUS. Born 207; Emperor, 251; killed 254. Br.—S.

VOLUSIANUS, son of Gallus. Cæsar, 251; Emperor, 252; killed, 254. G.—R.[4] R.[6] S.—C.—R.[4] Br. *Ca*—C.—R.[7]

Caia Cornelia Supera, wife of Aemilianus. This princess is only known by her coins. S.—R.[8] Br.—R.[∞]

Publius Licinius VALERIANUS *Senior.* Born 190 A. D.; Emperor, 253; made prisoner by the Persians, 260; died 263. The coins of this Emperor are numerous.

Mariniana, believed to be the second wife of Valerian. This princess is only known by her coins. G. —R.[1] R.[3] S.—R.[2] R.[4]

Publius Licinius GALLIENUS son of Valerian, by his first wife. Emperor, 253; assassinated, 268. G.—R.[2] R.[6] S.—R.[6] Po.—C.—R.[5] Br.—C.—R.[5] R.[6] During the reign of Gallienus, many generals declared themselves emperors; and, as their number was about thirty, they have been called the Thirty Tyrants.

Cornelia Salonina, wife of Gallienus. Assassinated, 208. G.—R.[4] R.[6] S.—R.[6] Po.—C.—R.[2] Br.--C. —R.[4]

Publius Licinius Cornelius Saloninus Valerianus Gallienus, son of Gallienus. Born 242 A.D.; Cæsar, 253; put to death, 259. G.—R.[6] R[8] S.—R.[∞] Po.—C.—R.[4] S.—C.—R.[8] Some coins represent him with Galienus.

Quintus Julius Gallienus youngest son of Gallienus. No coins can be attributed to this prince with any certainty.

Valerianus Junior brother of Gallienus. Assassinated 268. The coins that were attributed to this prince have been restored to Saloninus.

Licinia Galliena, aunt to Gallienus. No particulars are known of this princess. The coins attributed to her are false.

Marcus Cassianus Latinius POSTUMUS *P.* (Pater). Proclaimed Emperor in Gaul, 258; killed in 267. G.—R.[4] R.[8] Po.—C. R.[8] S.—C.—R.[6] Some coins of Postumus bear also another head, which has long been considered to be that of his son. The coins of Postumus are numerous. All were struck in Gaul.

Julia Donata believed to be the wife of Postumus. Nothing is known of this empress, whose existence is hardly proved. The coins that have been published are false.

Postumus (Filius). Declared Augustus in Gaul 258; killed in 267. Nothing is known of this emperor, except that there are coins attributed to him, which truly belong to his father, and the heads which appear on the reverse of the coins of the latter, are probably those of Mars and Hercules. All the coins of Postumus the Younger (if any exist) were struck in Gaul.

Ulpius Cornelius Laelianus. Little is known of this personage, who caused himself to be acknowledged emperor in Gaul during the reign of Gallienus. G.—R.[8] Po.—R.[2] R.[5] Br.—R.[2] R.[5] Laelianus and the two following—Lollianus and Aelianus—according to their money, appear to be three different personages. It must be observed that a great number of coins attributed to these three are doubtful. The coins of Laelianus were struck in Gaul.

Lollianus. No details are known of this prince. Br.—R.[8]

Quintus Valens Aelianus. No facts are known of this emperor. Br.—R.[8]; See the observations on Laelianus.

Marcus Piauvonius Victorinus (Pater). Associated in the empire of Gaul by Postumus 265; killed 267. G.—R.[6] R.[8] Po.—C.—R.[3] Br. C.—R.[2] The coins of the Roman standard were struck in Gaul.

Victorinus (Filius). Made Cæsar in Gaul 267; died soon afterwards. The coins formerly attributed to this prince have been restored to his father.

Victoria or *Victorina*, mother of Victorinus Senior. Died according to general opinion in 268. Br.—R.[8] The coin that has been published of this princess is false.

Marcus Aurelius MARIUS. Proclaimed Emperor in Gaul in 267; killed after a reign of three days. G.—R.[8] Po.—R.[2] R.[3] Br.—R.[1] R.[6] Historians say that he was killed by one of his comrades, after a reign of three days; the comparative abundance of his coins prove they were minted before he assumed the title of emperor.

Caius Pesuvius Tetricus (Pater). Proclaimed Emperor in Gaul in 267; restored his provinces to Aurelian and retired into private life 273. G.—R.[6] R.[8] Po.—R.[2] Br.—C.—R.[6] Some coins represent him with his son. A great many of this emperor's coins are of the second brass, of barbarous execution, and bear illegible inscriptions. The coins of Tetricus and his son were all struck in Gaul.

Caius Pesuvius Pivesus Tetricus (Filius). Cæsar in Gaul 267; retired from public life on the abdication of his father 273. G.—R.[6] R.[8] Po.—R.[2] Br.—C.—R.[6] It is a question whether this emperor was ever made Augustus or not.

Cyriades. Proclaimed Emperor by the Legions in Asia in 257; killed 258. No coins are known.

MACRIANUS (Pater). Proclaimed Emperor in the East 261; was killed by his soldiers 262, with his two sons. The coins published as those of the father have been restored to his son.

Marcus Fulvius Macrianus (Filius). He was made Augustus during his father's reign. Po.—R.[2] R.[3] His coins were struck in the East, perhaps in Syria.

Quietus, brother of the preceding. Killed with his father and brother at Emisa. G.—R.[8] Po.—R[2] R.[3] Br.—R.[8] These coins were struck in the East.

Balista. Proclaimed Emperor in Syria 262 ; killed 264. The coins published of Balista are false.

Ingenuus. Proclaimed Emperor in Mæsia and Pannonia 262; killed in three months. Coins all doubtful.

Regalianus. Proclaimed Emperor in Mœsia 261; killed 263. S.—R.[8] These coins, if true, were struck in Mœsia.

Sulpicia Dryantilla, wife of Regalianus. Nothing is known of this princess. S.—R.[8] The fact of Dryantilla being the wife of Regalianus is doubtful.

Valens. Emperor in Achaia 261; killed the same year. The coins at present known of Valens are doubtful.

Piso Frugi. Emperor in Thessalia 261; killed same year. The known coins of this Emperor are false.

Alexander Aemilianus. Proclaimed Emperor by the legions in Egypt 262; killed the same year. The coins of Alexander are false.

Saturninus I. Proclaimed Emperor 263; died shortly afterwards. No authenticated coins are known of this tyrant.

Trebellianus. Proclaimed Emperor of in Isauria 264; killed soon afterwards. The coins attributed to this personage are false.

Celsus. Proclaimed Emperor of Carthage in 265; killed after a reign of seven days. No true coins are known of Celsus.

Marcus Acilius AUREOLUS. Proclaimed Emperor in Illyria and in Rhetia in 267; killed 268. G.—R.[8] Br.—R.[8] These coins were either struck in Rhetia, Italy Superior, or in Milan.

Sulpicius Antoninus. Proclaimed Emperor in Syria 267; died soon afterwards. No coins are known of Antoninus.

Marcus Aurelius CLAUDIUS GOTHICUS. Born 214 A. D.; Emperor in 268; died of the plague 270. G.—R.[6] R.[8] Br.—C.—R.[4] After the reign of Claudius no coins in billon are known, for at this period they were so thinly coated with silver that it has in most cases all worn off except when the coin is in singularly fine preservation.

Censorinus. Proclaimed Emperor at Boulogne 270; killed seven days after. The coins that have been published are false.

Marcus Aurelius Claudius QUINTILLUS, brother of Claudius Gothicus. Proclaimed Emperor near Aquileia 270; committed suicide eight days after. G.—R.[8] Br.—C. R.[8] The coins of Quintillus are too numerous to allow that his reign was so short as it is said by historians to have been; it is probable that he reigned about two months, as according to Zozimus.

Lucius Claudius Domitius AURELIANUS. Born 207 A. D.; Emperor 270; assassinated 275; G.—R.[2] R.[4] Br. — C.—R.[2] The coins of this emperor are numerous. Some coins represent him with Severina and Vabalathus Athenodorus.

Ulpia Severina, wife of Aurelianus. No details are known of this empress. G.—R.[3] R.[6] Br.—C.—R[2]

PRINCES OF PALMYRA.

SEPTIMUS ODENATHUS. King of Palmyra 261; associated in the empire by Gallienus 264; assassinated 266–7. There are no true coins known of this emperor.

SEPTIMIA ZENOBIA, last wife of Odenathus. Queen of Palmyra 261; vanquished by Aurelianus 273. There are some coins of this queen struck in Egypt, but there are no true autonomous coins.

Herodes, son of Odenathus by his first wife. Augustus 264; killed 267. The coins of this prince are false.

Timolaus, son of Odenathus and Zenobia. Named Augustus by his mother 266; taken prisoner by

Aurelian 273. He has no true coin of Roman mintage, but there is one Greek coin that belongs to him.

VABALATHUS ATHENODORUS, son of Zenobia. Emperor in Syria 266; taken prisoner by Aurelian 273; Br.—R.^{2}—R.^{6} These coins were struck in Syria.

Maeonius. Proclaimed Emperor 267; killed shortly afterwards. The coins attributed to Maconius are false.

ROMAN LINE *resumed.*

FIRMUS. Proclaimed Emperor in Egypt in 275; defeated and put to death the following year. The coins attributed to Firmus are false.

Marcus Claudius TACITUS. Emperor 275; assassinated 276; G.—R.^{2}R.^{4} Br.—C.—R.^{6} The coins of this emperor are numerous.

Marcus Annius FLORIANUS. Born 232 A. D.; Emperor 276; killed same year. G.—R.^{3} R.^{6} Br.—C.—R.^{2}

Marcus Aurelius PROBUS. Born 232 A. D.; Emperor 276; killed 282; G.—R.^{4} R.^{6} S.—R.^{8} Br.—C.—R.^{6} The issues of this emperor are so numerous and so diverse in their types, that the Abbé Rothlin had a collection of upwards of 2,000 coins, all differing in some minute respect.

Bonosus. Proclaimed Emperor of Gaul 280; died 281. There are no true coins of this emperor.

Saturninus. Emperor of Egypt and Palestine 280; killed shortly afterwards. The coins of Saturninus are false.

Proculus. Emperor of Cologne 280; put to death the same year. The coins of this emperor are false.

Marcus Aurelius CARUS. Born 230 A. D.; Emperor 282; killed by lightning 283. G.—R.^{2} R.^{6} S.—C.—R.^{6} Some coins represent him with Carinus.

Marcus Aurelianus NUMERIANUS. Born 254 A. D.; Cæsar, 282; Augustus, 283; died 284. G.—R.^{4} R.^{6} S.—C.—R.^{5} Some coins represent him with Carinus.

Marcus Aurelius CARINUS. Born 249 A. D.; Cæsar, 282; Emperor, 283; killed, 284. G.—R.^{3} R.^{8} Some coins represent him with Numerianus and Magnia Urbica.

Magnia Urbica. This princess is only known by her coin. G.—R.^{3} S.—R.^{2} R.^{6} Supposed to be the wife of Carinus.

Nigrinianus (son of Carinus). This prince is only known by his coins. G.—R.^{8} S.—R.^{6} R.^{8}

Marcus Aurelianus JULIANUS I. Proclaimed Emperor in Pannonia, 284; killed, 285. These coins were most probably struck in Italy Superior.

Caius Valerius DIOCLETIANUS. Born 245; Emperor 284; adopted Galerius, 292; abdicated, 305; died, 313. G.—R.^{2} R.^{5} S.^{8}—R.^{1} R. Br.—C.—R.^{6} The coins of this emperor are numerous. It was in this reign that the Roman empire was first divided by common consent among four emperors: two Augustuses and two Cæsars.

Marcus Aurelius Valerius MAXIMIANUS *Hercules.* Born 250; associated in the Empire with Diocletian in 286; gave to Constantius Chlorus the title of Cæsar; abdicated 305; retook the empire 306; abdicated afresh, 308; proclaimed himself emperor again in 309; strangled himself, 310. G.—R^{1} R.^{6} S.—R.^{1} R.^{6} Br—C. R.^{9} Some coins represent him with Galerius and Diocetian. His coins are numerous.

Eutropia, wife of Maximianus. No details are known of this princess. No true coins are attributed to her.

Amandus. Emperor in Gaul 285; killed 287. The coins published of this personage are very suspicious.

Aelianus. Emperor in Gaul 285; killed 287. The coins of this emperor are likewise doubtful.

Marcus Aurelius Valerius CARAUSIUS. Emperor in England 287; assassinated 289. G.—R^{8} S.—R.^{5} R.^{7} Br.—R.^{3} R.^{8} These coins were struck in England.

ALLECTUS. Emperor in England 293, killed in battle with the army of Constantius, 296; G.—R.^{8} S.—

R.[6] Br.—R[4] R.[6] These coins were struck in England.

Achilleus. Emperor in Egypt about 292; put to death soon afterwards. There are no true coins known of this personage.

Lucius Domitius Domitianus. Emperor in Egypt 305. Br.—R.[4] These coins were struck in Egypt.

Flavius Valerius CONSTANTIUS I. (Chlorus). Born 250; Cæsar, 292; Emperor 305; died 306. G.—R.[1] R.[5] S.—R.[1] R.[4] Br.—C. R.[6] Some coins represent him with Diocletian. His coins are very numerous.

Flavia Julia Helena, first wife of Constantius Chlorus. Born about 248 A.D.; died about 328; Br.—C.R.[5]

Flavia Maxima Theodora, second wife of Constantius Chlorus. S.—R.[6] Br.—C.

GALERIUS VALERIUS MAXIMIANUS. Adopted and named Cæsar by Diocletian, in 292; Augustus and Emperor in 305; died 311. G.—R.[2] R[6] S.—R.[2] R.[6] Br.—C. R.[6] Some pieces represent him with the Herculeian Maximianus and Constantius Chlorus. The coins of this prince are numerous.

Galeria Valeria, second wife of Galerius Maximianus. Put to death by Licinius in 315 A.D. G.—R[6] S.—R.[6] Br.—C. R.[4]

Flavius VALERIUS SEVERUS II. Named Cæsar by the Herculeian Maximian in 305 : Augustus and Emperor in 306; put to death in 307. G.—R.[4] R.[6] S.—R[4] Br. —C. R.[4]

Galerius Valerius MAXIMINUS DAZA, son of Galerius, named Cæsar by Diocletian in 305; given the title of the son of the Augusti in 307; proclaimed himself Emperor in the East in 308; defeated by Licinius and poisoned himself in 313 A. D. G.—R[3]. R[5]. S.—R.[4] R.[6] Br.—C. R[3]. The coins of this emperor are numerous. A part of these pieces in Roman coin must have been struck in the East, probably in Syria.

Marcus Aurelius Valerius MAXENTIUS, son of Maximianus Hercules. Born about 282 A. D. ; proclaimed himself Emperor at Rome in 306, and was drowned in the Tiber in 312 A. D. G.—R.[2] R.[6] S.—R.[6] R.[7] Br.—C. R.[6] One piece represents him with his son Romulus. The coins of Maxentius are very numerous.

Marcus Aurelius Romulus, son of Maxentius. Born about the year 306 A. D. ; named Cæsar in 307 ; Augustus in a short time afterwards ; died in 309. G.—R.[8] S.—R.[8] Br.—R.[4] R.[8] One coin represents him with Maxentius, his father.

Alexander. Proclaimed Emperor at Carthage in 306 ; defeated and put to death in 311 A. D. S.—R.[8] Br.—R.[6] R.[8] The Roman coins of Alexander were struck in Africa, and probably at Carthage.

Publius Flavius Claudius Galerius Valerius Licinianus LICINIUS, senior son-in-law of Constantius Chlorus. Born 263 A. D. ; named Cæsar and Augustus, and associated in the empire with Galerius Maximianus 307 ; conquered and taken prisoner by his brother-in-law, Constantine, afterwards the Great, and strangled in 223. G.—R.[2] R.[6] S.—R.[2] R[6] Po.—R.[2] Br.—C. R.[5] Some coins represent him with his son Licinius. The coins of this prince are very numerous.

Flavia Constantia, wife of the elder Licinius. Died 330 A. D. The pieces which were published of this princess were false.

Flavius Valerianus Licinianus. LICINIUS, junior, son of the elder Licinius. Born 315 A. D, ; named Cæsar 317 ; deprived of the title in 323 ; put to death in 326. G.—R.[4] R.[6] S.—R.[3] B. C. R.[6] Some pieces represent him with his father, Licinius Crispus, and with Constantine the Great.—The Roman coins of this R.[8] Br.—R.[4] R.[6] These pieces were probably struck in Pannonia.

Aurelius Valerius Valens. Named Cæsar, and perhaps Augustus, by Licinius in 314; but was deprived of his dignities and killed. The supposed coin is very doubtful.

Martinianus. Created Cæsar and Augustus at Byzantium by Licinius in 323; put to death two months afterwards. Br.—R.[6] These Roman coins were most probably struck at Nicomedia.

Flavius Galerius Valerius CONSTANTINUS *Magnus*, son of Constantius Chlorus and Helena. Born 274 A. D.; named Cæsar and Augustus in 306; deprived of the last title; again named Augustus by Maximianus in 307; then only son of the Augusti; given again the name of Augustus in 306: converted to the Christian religion in 311; made sole emperor in 323; changed the name of Byzantium to Constantinople, which he made the seat of his government, 336; died in 337. G.—R.[1] R.[6] S.—R.[4] R.[1] Br.—C. R.[6] Some pieces represent him with Crispus, Constantine the younger, and Licinius senior. The coins of this emperor are very numerous.

Flavia Maxima Fausta, wife of Constantine the Great, drowned in a warm bath, by her husband's order, in the year 326 A. D. G.—R.[8] S.—R.[4] Br.—C.— R.[5]

Flavius Julius Crispus, son of Constantine and Minervina. Born about 300 A. D.; named Cæsar in 317; put to death by order of his father in 326. G.—R.[3] R.[6] Br.—C.—R.[4]

Helena, wife of Crispus. This princess is only known by one coin. Br.—R.[6] It is not certain whether she was ever Crispus' wife or not.

Flavius Julius Delmatius, nephew of Constantine, named Cæsar in 335; obtained in the division, Thrace, Macedonia, and Achaia in 335; killed 337. G.—R.[6] S.—R.[4] Br.—R.[1] Some pieces represent him with Constantine. It is doubtful whether these pieces were struck in Constantinople or in the provinces which he obtained in the division.

Hanniballianus, brother to Delmatius. Made King of Pontus, Cappadocia and Armenia in the year 335; died 337. Br.—R.[6] It is not known whether these pieces were struck in Constantinople or in the dominions of his sovereignty.

Flavius Claudius Julius CONSTANTINUS II. eldest son of Constantine and Fausta. Born 316 A. D.; named Cæsar 317; obtained in the division in 335, Gaul, Spain, and England; on his father's death, in 337, named Emperor and Augustus; defeated and killed in 340. G.—R.[3] R.[5] S.—R.[2] R.[4] Br.—C.—R.[3] The coins of this emperor are numerous. These coins probably, or at least a part, were struck in the countries assigned to him in the division.

Flavius Julius CONSTANS I. youngest son of Constantine the Great and Fausta. Born about 320 A. D.: named Cæsar in 333; obtained in the division in 335, Italy, Illyria, and Africa; called Emperor and Augustus in 337; on his brother's death, in 346, made Emperer of the East and assassinated in 350. G.—C.—R[6] S.—R.[1] R.[5] Br.—C. —R.[7] The coins of this emperor are numerous.

Saturninus. This personage is only known by one coin; he was proclaimed Emperor under the reigns of Constans I. or II. The piece produced is doubtful.

Flavius Julius CONSTANTIUS II., second son of Constantine the Great and Fausta. Born 317 A. D.; named Cæsar in 323; obtained in the division in 335, the East; named Augustus in 337; on the murder of Constans, became master of all the Empire in 350; died 351. G.—C.—R.[8] S.—R.[1] R.[5] Br.—C. R.[3] The coins of this emperor are numerous.

Fausta, wife of Constantius II. Br.—R.[6] It is doubtful whether she was ever the wife of Constantius or not.

Flavius Popelius NEPOTIANUS *Constantinus*, son of Eutropia, sister of Constantine the Great. Proclaimed Emperor at Rome in 350; killed after a reign of 28 days. Br.—R.[7] These pieces were probably struck at Rome.

Vetranio. Proclaimed Emperor in Pannonia in 350; abdicated after reigning 10 months; died 356; G. —R. 8 S.—R.[8] Br.—R.[4] R.[6] These pieces were probably struck in Pannonia.

Nonius. Historians do not mention this personage. The pieces attributed to this Nonius are doubtful.

Flavius Magnus MAGNENTIUS. Born about 303 A. D.; proclaimed Emperor at Augustodunum, the modern Autun, 350; and killed himself in 353. G.—R.[2] R.[7] S.—R.[4] R.[7] Br. —C. R.[2] These pieces were either struck in Gaul or Italy.

Magnus Decentius, brother of Magnentius. Named Cæsar in 351; and strangled himself in 353. G.—R.[4] R.[7] S.—R.[4] R.[7] Br.—C. R.[4] These pieces were struck in Gaul or in Italy.

Desiderius, brother of Magnentius. Named Cæsar in 351; stabbed by his brother in 353; but not killed as it was thought. The published pieces of this prince are false.

Flavius Claudius Julius Constantius Gallus. Born 325 A. D.; named Cæsar in 351; condemned to death and executed in 354. G—R.[3] R.[5] S.—R.[2] R.[4] Br.—C. R.[3]

Constantina, daughter of Constantine the Great, wife first of Hanniballianus and secondly of Constantius Gallus. Died 354 A.D. The published pieces of this princess are very doubtful.

Sylvanus. Proclaimed Emperor at Cologne, in 355; killed after a reign of twenty-eight or twenty-nine days. The published pieces of Sylvanus are false.

Flavius Claudius JULIANUS II. Julian the Apostate, son of Julius Constantius, the brother of Constantine the Great. Born 331 A. D.; named Cæsar in 355; proclaimed Emperor at Paris, 360; sole Emperor, 361; killed in a battle against the Persians in 363. Gold.—R.[2] R.[4] S. —C.—R.[6] Br.—C.—R.[4] The coins of Julian are very numerous.

Flavia Helena, wife of Julian II.; died 360. G.—R.[8] Br.—C.

Flavius JOVIANUS. Born 331 A. D.; Emperor in 363; died 364. G.—.R[3] R.[8] S.—R.[2] R.[8]. Br.—C.—R.[2]

Flavius VALENTINIANUS I. Born 321 A. D.; Emperor in 364; died 375, G.—C. R.[4] S.—C.—R.[2] Br.—C. R.[3] The coins of Valentinian were struck partly at Rome, and partly in the East.

Valeria Severa, first wife of Valentinian I. Died in the reign of Gratian. The published pieces are false.

Flavia Justina, second wife of Valentinian I. Born—A. D.; died 387. The published pieces are false.

Flavius VALENS, brother of Valentinian. Born 328 A. D. Associated in the Empire and given the name of Augustus in 364; had the East for his division; was burnt to death in 378. G.—C.—R.[6] S.—C. —R.[5] Br.—C.—R[2].

Albia Dominica, wife of Valens. Died in the reign of Theodosius the Great. The published piece of this princess is false.

Procopius. Born about 344 A. D.; proclaimed Augustus at Constantinople, in 365; defeated by Valens and put to death in 366. G.—R.[7] S.— R.[5] Br.—R.[6] R.[7]

GRATIANUS, son of Valentinian I. and Severa. Born 350 A. D. Named Augustus at Amiens in 361; Emperor in 375; killed in 389. G.— C.—R.[8] S.—R.[5] Br.—C.—R[9] The coins of this prince were struck in the West and probably in Gaul and Italy.

Constantia, wife of Gratian. Born 362 A. D.; died 482. The published pieces of this princess are false.

Flavius VALENTINIANUS II. son of Valentinian I. Born 371 A. D. Named Augustus and associated in the Empire, 375; had for his share Italy, Illyria, and Africa; Emperor of all the Western Empire 383; was assassinated in 392. G.—C.— R.[9] S.—C.—R.[6] Br.—C.R[5] The coins of Valentinian II. cannot all be attributed with certainty, and may be confounded with those of his father, or those of Valentinian III. These coins were probably struck in Italy.

THEODOSIUS MAGNUS I. Born 346 A. D. Named Augustus, and associated in the Empire, by Gratian in 379: succeeded Valens in the government of the East. Died at Milan 395. G.—C.—R.[1] S.—C.—R.[2] Br.—C.—[2]

Aelia Flaccilla, first wife of Theodosius I. Died 388. G.—R.[5] S. R.[5] Br.—R.[1]

MAGNUS MAXIMUS, assumed the name of Augustus in Britain, in 383; acknowledged Emperor; seized upon Italy in 387, and was put to death in 388. G.—R.[1] R.[2] S.—R.[1] R.[5] Br.—C. These pieces were struck in Britain, Gaul, or Italy.

Flavius Victor, son of Magnus Maximus. Named Augustus in 383; put to death in 388. G.—R.[5] S.—R.[2] Br.—R. These pieces were struck in Gaul.

Eugenius, proclaimed Augustus 392, ruled in the Western provinces. Killed 394. G.—R.[8] R.[4] S.—R.[2] S.[8] Br.—R.[7]

ARCADIUS, son of Theodosius the Great. Born 377; made Augustus in 383; Emperor of the East in 395; died in Constantinople 408. G.—C.—R.[6] S.—R.[1] R.[2] Br.—C.—R.[3]

Eudocia, or *Eudoxia,* wife of Arcadius. Died 404. The pieces attributed to this princess have been restored by Eckhel to Eudocia, the wife of Theodosius II.

HONORIUS, the youngest son of Theodosius the Great and Flaccilla. Born 384; named Augustus 393; Emperor of the West 395; died at Ravenna 423. G.—C.—R.[7] S.—C.—R[6] Br.—C.—R.[3] These pieces were probably struck at Rome.

CONSTANTIUS III., named Augustus, and associated with Honorius in the Empire of the West in 421; died the same year. G.—R.[6] R.[7] S.—R.[7] These pieces were struck in Italy.

Galla Placidia, daughter of Theodosius, widow of Ataulf or Adolpus, king of the Goths, 414; wife of Constantius III. in 417; died in 433. G.—R.[5] R.[7] S.—R.[4] R.[5] Br.—R.[5] R.[7] These pieces were struck in Italy.

Flavius Claudius CONSTANTINUS III. Augustus in England and Gaul 407; taken prisoner and put to death 411. G.—R.[2] S.—R.[2] Br.—R.[6] The coins of this prince have frequently been confounded with those of Constantine I. and II. These coins were struck in Gaul. Constantinian coins with AVGGG or AVGGGG belong to this prince.

CONSTANS II., son of Constantinus III. Augustus in Gaul 408; assassinated in 411. S.—R.[5] These pieces were probably struck in Gaul.

MAXIMUS. Emperor in Spain 409; abdicated 411. S.—R.[5] These pieces were probably struck in Spain.

JOVINUS. Emperor at Mayence 411; beheaded by the Goths 413. G.—R.[4] S.—R.[2] Br.—R.[8] These coins were struck in Gaul.

SEBASTIANUS, brother of Jovinus. Associated in the sovereign power by his brother in 412; beheaded in 413. S.—R.[5] These coins were struck in Gaul.

PRISCUS ATTALUS. Made emperor by Alaric at Rome 409; deprived of that title; reassumed it in Gaul 410; died in the isle of Lipari. G.—R.[4] S.—R.[4] R.[8] Br.—R.[4] R.[6] These pieces were struck at Rome.

THEODOSIUS II., son of Arcadius and Eudocia. Born 401; Augustus 402; Emperor of the East 408; died 450. G.—C.—R.[2] S.—R.[3] R.[5] Br.—R.[4] R.[6] These coins must not be confounded with those of Theodosius I.

Eudoxia, wife of Theodosius II. Born about 393 A. D.; died 460. G.—R.[3] R[5] S.—R.[4] Br.—R.[4] Some of the coins of this princess have been attributed falsely to Eudocia, wife of Arcadius.

JOHANNES. Born 383; Emperor at Rome 423; died 425. G.—R.[3] R.[6] S.—R.[3] R.[5] Br.—R.[3] These coins were struck in Rome.

PLACIDIUS VALENTINIANUS III., son of Constantine III. Born 419; Emperor 425; assassinated 455. G.—C.—R.[5] S.—R.[2] R.[4] Br.—R.[2] R.[3] These coins were struck in Rome.

Licinia Eudoxia, wife of Valentinian. Born 423; died —. G.—R.[5] These coins were struck in Italy.

Justa Grata Honoria, sister of Valentinian. Born 417; Augustus 433; died 454. G.—R.[5] R.[6] S.—R.[6] These coins were struck in Italy.

ATTILA, King of the Huns. Born—; King 434; died 453. There are no true autonomous coins of this king.

PETRONIUS MAXIMUS. Born 395; Emperor at Rome 455. Killed same year. G.—R.[4] S.—R.[4] Br.—R.[8] All these were struck at Rome.

MARCIANUS. Born 391; Emperor of the East 450; died 457. G.—R.[2] R.[6] S.—R.[4] Br.—R.[6]

Aelia Pulcheria, sister of Theodosius II., wife of Marcianus. Born 399; died 453. G.—R.[6] S.—R.[4] Br.—R.[6]

Marcus Mæcilius AVITUS, Emperor 455; abdicated and became bishop of Placentia 456. G.—R.[4] Br.—R.[6]

LEO I. Born —; Emperor of the East 457; died 474. G.—C.—Br.—R.[4]

Aelia Verina, wife of Leo I. Born —; died 484. G.—R.[5]

Julius MAJORIANUS. Born —; Emperor 457; assassinated 461. G.—R.[1] R.[2] S.—R[3] Br.—R.[4] R.[5]

Libius SEVERUS III. Born —; Emperor 461; poisoned 465. G.—R.[2] S.—R.[2] Br.—R.[8] These were struck in Italy.

Procopius ANTHEMIUS. Emperor 467; assassinated 472. G.—R.[2] S.—R.[7] Br.—R.[6]

Aelia Marciana Euphemia. Born —; died —. G.—R.[6] These were struck in Italy.

Anicius Olybrius. Born —; Emperor of the West 472; died same year. G.—R.[5] R.[6] S.—R.[6] Pl.—R.[8] These were struck in Italy.

Placidia, daughter of Valentinianus, wife of Olybrius. Born —; died. Her portrait is only found on the coins of her husband.

Glycerius. Born —; Augustus at Ravenna 473; dethroned 474; died 480, *Bishop of Salona.* G.—R.[4] S.—R.[7] These coins were struck in Italy.

LEO II. Born about 459 A. D.; Emperor 437; Emperor of the East 474. G.—R.[4] These pieces represent him with Zeno.

ZENO, son-in-law of Leo I., and father of Leo II. Born 426 A. D.; associated in the Eastern Empire with his son, Leo II., 474; sole Emperor in the same year; deposed by Basiliscus 476; re-established 477; died 491. G.—C.—S.—R.[2] Br.—R.—R.[1] R.[2]

BASILISCUS, brother of Verina, wife of Leo I. Born —; Emperor of the East 476; dethroned by Zeno and died of hunger 477. G.—R.[2] R.[3] S.—R.[4] Br.—R.[6] Some pieces represent him with Marcus his son.

Aelia Zenonis, wife of Basiliscus. Born —; starved with her husband 477. G.—R.[5]

Marcus, son of Basiliscus. Born —; Augustus and associated in the Empire 476; starved to death with his parents 477. This prince only on the coins of Basiliscus.

LEONTIUS I. Born—; Augustus at Tarsus in Cilicia in 482; conquered and put to death 488. G.—R.[3] These pieces were struck in Asia Minor.

JULIUS NEPOS. Born—; Emperor of the West 474; driven from Rome 475; assassinated 480. G.—R.[1] R.[2] S.—R.[4] Br.—R.[8] These pieces were struck in Italy.

ROMULUS AUGUSTUS. Born —; Emperor of the West 475; dethroned by Odoacer, King of the Heruli, who proclaimed himself King of Italy, and thus terminated the Empire of the West 476. G.—R.[4] Br.—R.[8] These pieces were struck in Italy.

THE GOTHIC PRINCES OF ITALY, AFRICA, &c.

Theodoricus, the Ostrogoth. Born —; occupied Pannonia and Illyria; invaded Italy, defeated Odoacer, and was crowned King 493; died 526. S.—R.[1] Br.—R.[4] Some coins represent him with Anastasius and Justin. The coins of t is prince were undoubtedly struck in Italy.

Baduila, an uncertain king. Historians do not mention this king, and he must not be confounded with Baduela, or Baduila, a Gothic king.

Theia, or *Thela*, an uncertain king. Not known in history. He is only found on the coins of Anastasius.

Athalaricus, grandson of Theodoric. Born —; King of the Goths 526; died 534. S.—R.[1] R.[2] Br.—R.[1] R.[3] These coins were struck in Italy.

Theodohatus. Born —; King of the Goths in Italy 534; killed 536. S.—R.[2] Br.—R.[1] R.[4]

Witiges. Born —; King of the Goths 536, conquered by Belisarius 540; died soon after on the Persian frontier. S.—R.[2] Br.—R.[3]

Hildibadus. Born —; King of the Goths in Italy 540; killed 541. No coins are known of this barbarian.

Araricus, or *Eraricus*. Born —; King of the Goths in Italy 541; killed same year. No coins are known of this prince.

Baduela, or *Baduila*. Born —; King of the Goths in Italy 541; defeated by Narses, Justinian's general, 552. S.—R.[4] Br.—R.[3] R.[6] This prince is called by the Greeks Totila. These coins were struck in Italy.

Theias. Born —; King of the Goths in Italy 552; defeated by Narses 553; his death put an end to the Gothic princes in Italy. No coins are known of this prince.

VANDAL KINGS.

Gunthamundus. Born —; Vandal King in Africa 484; died 496. S.—R.[6]

Trisamundus. Brother of the last Vandal King in Africa 496; died 523. S.—R.[4] These Vandal coins are also classed in the coins of the peoples, and towns, and were struck in Carthage.

Hildericus. Cousin of Trisamundus; Vandal King in Africa 523; dethroned 530. S.—R.[6]

Gelimarus, or *Geilamir*. Cousin of Hildericus; Vandal King in Africa 530; defeated by Belisarius 534, which put an end to the Vandal princes in Africa. S.—R.[4]

Theodebertus. Born —; King of Austrasia 534; killed in hunting, 548. The coins of Theodebert belong, perhaps, to the coins of Gaul, (Merovingian line), but they are here classed with the Roman emperors, because this king took the title of Augustus.

EASTERN OR BYZANTINE EMPIRE.

ANASTASIUS I. Born 430 A. D.; succeeded to the Eastern Empire, on marrying the widow of Zeno, 491; was killed by lightning in the year 518. G.—C.—S.—R.[1] R.[2] Br.—C.

JUSTINUS I. Born 450; Emperor 518; died in 527. G.—C.—R.[4] S.—R. R.[3] Br.—C. There are some coins which bear this emperor on the obverse, and the head of either Theodoric or Athalaric, kings of the Ostrogoths, on the reverse.

Euphemia, wife of Justinus I. No decided dates are known of this princess. Some pieces have been falsely attributed to her.

VITALIANUS. Proclaimed Emperor in 514; assassinated 520. G.—R.[8]

JUSTINIANUS I., nephew of Justinus. Born 483; associated in the Empire 527; sole Emperor 528; died 565. G.—C.—R.[8] S.—R.[1] R.[4] Br.—C. Many coins represent him with Athalaric, Theodohatus, Witiges, and Baduila, king of the Goths.

JUSTINUS II. Born at a date unknown; Emperor of the East 565; died in 578. G.—C.—R.[6] S.—R.[5] Br.—C.—R.[8]

Sophia, wife of Justin II. Born 545; died in the reign of Maurice. Br.—R.[6] R.[8]

TIBERIUS II. (CONSTANTINUS), son-in-law of Justinus; associated in the Empire 574; sole Emperor of the East 578; died in 582. G.—R.[2] R[3] S.—R.[2] R[4] Br.—C.

MAURICIUS TIBERIUS, son-in-law of Tiberius II. Born 539; made Emperor 582; and put to death together with his wife and children by Phocas 602. G.—C.—R.[3] S.—R.[3] R.[4] Br.—C.—R.[3] Some coins represent this emperor with his wife Constantina and his son Theodosius.

Constantina, wife of Maurice. Date of birth unknown; killed with her husband and children 602. The portraits of this princess are found only on the coins of Maurice.

Theodosius, son of Maurice. Date of birth unknown; associated in the Empire 590; killed with his parents 602.

PHOCAS. Date of birth unknown; succeeded to the throne 602; was beheaded 610. On coins this emperor's name is written FOCA, or FOCAS. Some coins represent him with his wife Leontia.

Leontia, wife of Phocas. Date both of birth and death unknown. The portrait of this empress is found only on coins of Phocas.

HERACLIUS I. Born about the year 575; dethroned Phocas and became Emperor 610; died in 641. G.—C.—R.[1] S.—R.[3] Br.—C.—R.[3] On some coins are found together portraits of this emperor and of his son Constantine IV.

Flavia Eudocia, first wife of Heraclius. Date of birth unknown; died 612. No coins are known of this empress.

HERACLIUS II., son of Heraclius and Flavia. Born 612; Emperor with his brother Heracleonas in 641; was poisoned in the same year. G.—R.[5] S.—R.[3] R.[5] Br.—R.[2] R.[4] Some coins represent this monarch with his father Heraclius, his wife Gregoria, Heracleonas, his brother, and Constans his son.

Gregoria, wife of Heraclius II. Date of both birth and death unknown. There are no portraits found of this princess except on the coins of her husband.

Martina, second wife of Heraclius I. Date of birth unknown; made regent with her son Heracleonas, 641; was exiled. No coins are known of this empress.

TIBERIUS III., son of Heraclius and Martina. Date of birth unknown; created Cæsar in 640; associated with Heracleonas in the Empire 641; year of death unknown. No coins are known of this Emperor.

CONSTANS II., son of Heraclius II. and Gregoria. Born 630; associated in the Empire with his uncles Tiberius III. and Heracleonas in 641; sole Emperor in the same year; assassinated in 668; G.—R.[1] R.[4] S.—R.[3] R.[4] Br.—R.[2] R.[3] Some coins of this Emperor have portraits of a female, supposed to be his wife, whose name is unknown, and also portraits of his sons Constantine IV., Heraclius, and Tiberius.

CONSTANTINUS IV., surnamed Pogonatus, son of Constans II. Date of birth unknown, associated with his father 654; sole Emperor 668; died in 685. G.—C.—.[2] S.—R.[2] R.[3] Br.—R[2] R.[4] Some of his coins bear portraits of his father.

Heraclius and Tiberius, brothers of Constantine IV. Named Cæsars 659; associated in the Empire by their brother in 668, and put to death in 674. Portraits of these princes are found only on the coins of Constans II., their father.

JUSTINIANUS II. (Rhinotmetus), son of Constantine IV. and Anastasia. Born 670, created Augustus 682; reigned alone in 685; dethroned after great tyranny in 695; restored in 705 by the Bulgarians; dethroned anew and killed 711 by Bardanes. G.—R.[1] R.[3] S.—R.[7] Br.—R.[6] Some coins represent him with his son Tiberius IV.

TIBERIUS IV., son of Justinian II. and Theodora. Born 701; declared Cæsar and Augustus in 706; put to death in 711. The portrait of this prince is only found on the coins of Justinian, his father.

LEONTIUS OR LEO II. Date of birth unknown; usurped the throne against Justinian II., 695; dethroned and placed in a monastery 698; after having had his nose and ears cut off, put to death in 705. G.—R[8]

Br.—R.[8] Coins have been attributed to this monarch which rightfully belong to Leo I.

TIBERIUS V. (Absimarus). Date of birth unknown; proclaimed Emperor 693; put to death by Justinian II., 705, G.—R.[1] R.[2] S.—R.[6] Br. —R[7].

FILEPICUS (Bardanes). Put Justinian II. to death, and was proclaimed Emperor in 711; dethroned and deprived of his sight, 713; died shortly afterwards. G.—R.[2] R.[3] S.—R.[6]

ANASTASIUS II. Date of birth unknown; proclaimed Emperor, 713; abdicated in favor of Theodosius III. in 716, but shortly afterwards taken and put to death. G.—R.[2] R.[3] S.—R.[6] It was about this time that a mixture of Greek and Latin letters was introduced in the inscriptions of the coins.

THEODOSIUS (Adramytenus) III. Date of birth unknown; proclaimed Emperor, 715; abdicated in 717 for a monastery. G.—R.[5] S.—R.[6]

LEO III. (Isaurus.) Date of birth unknown; proclaimed Emperor 717; died in 741. G.—C.—R.[1] S.—R.[3] Br.—R.[2] Many coins of this emperor represent him with his son Constantine VI., and his grandson Leo IV.

CONSTANTINUS V. (Copronymus), son of Leo III. and Maria. El.—R[2] R.[8] S.—R.[3] Br.—R.[5] Some coins represent him with Leo IV. and Artavasdus.

Irene, first wife of Constantine V. Date of birth unknown; died in 750. No coins are known of this empress.

Maria, second wife of Constantine V. Date of birth unknown; died, 751. No coins are known of this empress.

Eudocia, third wife of Constantine V. Date of birth and death unknown. No coins are known of this empress.

ARTAVASDUS, son-in-law of Leo III. Date of birth unknown; rebelled against Copronymus and was proclaimed Emperor, 742; next year was made prisoner, and exiled, after having had his eyes put out, in 743. G.—R.[8] El.—R.[8] Br.—R.[8] Some coins represent him with his son Nicephorus and Constantine V.

Nicephorus, son of Artavasdus and Anna, sister of Constantine V. Date of birth unknown; associated with his father, 742; made prisoner and exiled after having had his eyes put out, like his father, in 743. The portrait of this prince is found only on coins of Artavasdus.

Christophorus and *Nicephorus*, sons of Constantine V. and Eudocia. Dates of their birth unknown; created Cæsars in 769; exiled after having had their tongues and eyes burned out; put to death by order of Irene, 797. No coins are known of these princes.

LEO IV. (Chazarus), son of Constantine V. (Copronymus) and Irene. Born 750; created Augustus 751; reigned alone 775; died in 780. G.—R.[5] Br.—R.[4]

Irene, wife of Leo IV. Date of birth unknown; made regent of the Empire during the minority of her son Constantine VI. in 780; caused his eyes to be put out for the purpose of reigning alone; was imprisoned in the Isle of Lesbos by Nicephorus Logotheta 802; died in 803. G.—R.[5] S.—R.[6] Br.—R.[8]

CONSTANTINUS VI., son of Leo IV. Born 771; made Augustus in 776; reigned with his mother 780; died after having had his eyes put out by order of his mother, 797. G.—R.[6] S.—R.[7] Br.—R.4.R.8

NICEPHORUS I. (Logotheta.) Date of birth unknown; proclaimed Emperor 802; killed 811. G.—R.3 Br.—R.8 Some pieces represent him with his son Stauracius. During the reign of Nicephorus the *Second Empire of the West* commenced,—that of Charlemagne and his successors.

Stauracius, son of Nicephorus I. Date of birth unknown; associated in the Empire in 803; abdicated the throne with his father, 811; died 812. G.—R.3 Br.—R.8 Some pieces represent this emperor with his father Nicephorus.

MICHAEL I. (Rhangabe or Curopalata), son-in-law of Nicephorus. Date of birth unknown; elected Emperor 811; abdicated 813; died 845. G.—R.[3] S.—R.[4] Br.—R.[4] Some coins represent him with his son Theophylactus. Those coins of Michael I., upon which his son is not represented, can be equally attributed to the other emperors of the same name.

THEOPHYLACTUS, son of Michael. Date of birth unknown; associated in the Empire, 811; entered into a monastery after having been mutilated by order of Leo V. G.—R.[4] Br.—R.[4] The coins of this prince represent him with his father.

LEO V. (Armenius.) Date of birth unknown; proclaimed Emperor in 813; assassinated in 820. Br.—R.[6] These coins bear the portrait of his son Constantinus VII.

CONSTANTINUS VII., son of Leo V. Date of birth unknown; associated with his father 813; mutilated and exiled by order of Michael II. 820. Br.—R.[6] Some coins represent him with his father, Leo V.

MICHAEL II. (Balbus.) Date of birth unknown; proclaimed Emperor on the death of Leo V. 820; died 829. G.—R.[2] R.[3] S.—R.[7] Br.—R.[1] Some coins represent him with his son, Theophilus.

THEOPHILUS, son of Michael II. G.—R.[2] R.[3] El.—R.[2] S.—R.[5] Br.—C.—R.[3] There exists a coin bearing the busts of Theophilus, and of a prince named Constantine, who probably was his son, but the piece is doubtful. There are some pieces which were formerly attributed to Theophilus which are now restored to Michael III.

Theodora, wife of Theophilus. Date of birth unknown; acted as regent to her son, Michael III., 842; was shut up in a monastery by order of her son, 857. Her coins bear portraits of Michael III. on the reverse.

MICHAEL III., son of Theophilus. Born 836; succeeded his father, 842, under his mother; reigned alone 857; died 867. G.—R.[3]R.[7] S.—R.[5] Br.—R.[7] Some pieces represent him with Theodora, his mother, Thecla, his sister, his son, and Basilius I.

Constantinus was formerly supposed to have been the son of Theophilus, but was really the son of Michael III. This prince is unknown in history. G.—R.[4] Some coins represent him with Theophilus, but most with Michael III.

Thecla, daughter of Theophilus. Date of birth unknown; shut up in a monastery with her mother in 857. G.—R.[8] S.—R.[5] The coins of this princess represent her with her brother, Michael III.

BASILIUS I. (Macedo.) Date of birth unknown; associated in the Empire by Michael III. in 866; reigned alone in 867; died 886. G.—R.[3] R.[4] S.—R.[6] Br.—C. Some coins represent him with his sons, Constantine IX., Leo VI., and Alexander. There are some coins falsely attributed to Basilius I., which really belong to Basilius II.

CONSTANTINUS VIII., son of Basilius I. Born about 853; associated in the Empire 868; died 879. G.—R.[2] R.[4] S.—R.[5] Br.—C. Some coins represent him with his father, Basilius I.

LEO VI. (Sapiens), second son of Basilius. Born 865; associated in the Empire 870; reigned with his brother Alexander in 886; died 911. G.—R.[2] R.[6] S.—R.[3] Br. R.[1] R[3]. Some coins represent him with Basilius I., his son Constantine X., and his brother Alexander.

Zoe (Carbonopsina), the wife of Leo VI. Date of birth unknown; regent over her son Constantine X., 912; shut up in a monastery by her son 919. Br.—R.[1] R.[3] Her coins represent her with her son Constantine XI.

ALEXANDER, third son of Basilius. Born 870; reigned with his brother Leo VI. in 886. Died in 912. G.—R.[4] Br.—R.[2] Some of his coins represent him with his father Basilius I. and his brother Leo VI.

Romanus I. (Lecapenus.) Date of birth unknown; associated in the empire with Constantine X. in 919; seized, dethroned, and exiled by his son Stephen in 944; died in 946. G.—R.^{3} R.^{5} His coins bear the names of Christopher, Stephen, and Constantine XI., son of Leo VI.

Christophorus, son of Romanus I. Date of birth unknown; associated in the Empire 920; died 931. G.—R.^{3} R.^{5} Br.—R.^{3} Some coins represent him with his father Romanus I.

Stephanus, second son of Romanus. Date of birth unknown; associated in the Empire in 931; dethroned and exiled his father 944; exiled by Constantine XI. in 945; died 964. The name of this Prince is only found on the coins of his father.

Constantinus IX., third son of Romanus. Date of birth unknown; made Augustus in 945; put to death shortly afterwards. This prince is found only on the coins of his father.

Constantinus X., Pophyrogenitus, son of Leo VI. and Zoë. Born 905; succeeded his father, 911; first under the regency of Alexander his uncle, and then of his mother Zoë; reigned alone 945; died 952. G.—R.^{3} R.^{4} S.—R.^{6} Br.—R.^{1} R.^{3} Some coins represent him with his father, Leo VI., his mother Zoë, his son Romanus II., and with Romanus I., his colleague.

Romanus II., son of Constantine X. Born in 938; succeeded his father 959; died 963. G.—R.^{3} R.^{4} S.—R.^{6} Br.—R.^{3} Some coins represent him with his father Constantine. These coins are not of certain attribution.

Theophano, second wife of Romanus II. Date of birth unknown; regent for her sons Basilius and Constantine in 963; she married the same year Nicephorus II., caused him to be assassinated in 969; exiled by John Zimisces; recalled by her sons in 975; died 980. S.—R.^{4}

Nicephorus II. (Phocas). Born in 912; proclaimed Emperor 963; assassinated by his wife 969. G.—R.^{6} S.—R.^{6} Br.—R.^{3}—R.^{4} Some coins represent him with Basilius II.

John I. (Zimisces). Date of birth unknown; proclaimed Emperor 969; died from poison 975; S.—R.^{6} Br.—C.—R.^{1} It is in this reign, for the first time, that the figure of Christ is placed upon the coins instead of the portrait of the emperor. Some of the coins of this reign are of doubtful attribution.

Basilius II., son of Romanus II. and Theophano. Born 956; created Augustus 960; reigned with his brother Constantine XI. after the death of John Zimisces in 975; died 1025. G.—R.^{3} R.^{5} S.—R.^{5} R.^{6} Br.—C. Some coins represent him with his brother Constantine. Some coins are attributed to Basilius I. which rightly belong to this monarch.

Constantinus XI., youngest son of Romanus II. Born 961; reigned with his brother Basilius 975; sole emperor 1025; died 1028. G.—R.^{3} R.^{5} S.—R.^{5} R.^{4} Br.—C. Concave, or cup-shaped coins called *Bracteates*, came into use at this time.

Romanus III. (Argyrus). Married Zoë, daughter of Constantine XI. Born 973; emperor 1028; smothered by Zoë in 1034. There are no certain coins of this emperor.

Michael IV. (Paphlago). Date of birth unknown; married Zoë and succeeded to the throne 1034; retired into a monastery and died there 1041. There are no certain coins of this emperor.

Michael V., son of Maria, sister of Michael IV. Date of birth unknown; succeeded to the throne 1041; shut up by his aunt in a monastery, after having had his eyes put out, 1042. There are no coins known of this emperor.

Constantinus XII. (Monomachus.) Married Zoë and commenced his reign 1042; died 1054. G.—R.^{4} S.—R.^{7}

Zoë, daughter of Constantine XI. and wife of Romanus III., Michael

IV., and Constantine XII. Born 978; poisoned her first husband 1034; after the death of her second, in 1041, adopted her nephew Michael V. (Calaphates); when exiled by him she caused the people to rise against him, and had his eyes put out; reigned two months with her sister Theodora in 1042; espoused in the same year Constantine XII.; died 1050. The coins that have been published of this empress are not to be found in any cabinet.

Theodora, sister of Zoë. Born 981; at first she became a nun but was proclaimed Empress with her sister Zoë in 1042; and preserved the title of Augusta during the reign of Constantine XII.; after his death, in 1054, reigned alone till 1056. G.—R.[3] R.[6]

MICHAEL VI. (Stratioticus). Emperor in 1056; forced to abdicate 1057; died 1059. There are no certain coins of this emperor.

ISAACIUS I. (Comnenus.) Proclaimed Emperor 1057; abdicated in favor of Constantine XIII. in 1059; died in 1061. G.—R.[5] Br.—R.[5]

CONSTANTINUS XIII. (Ducas.) Born 1007; proclaimed emperor 1059; died 1067. G.—R.[3] S.—R.[1] Pl.—R.[8]

Eudocia Dalassena, first wife of Constantine XIII., afterwards of Romanus IV. After the death of Constantinus, in 1067, she governed in the name of her sons; married Romanus and proclaimed him Emperor 1068; shut up in a monastery by her son Michael VII. in 1071; died after the year 1096. G.—R.[5] Br.—R[7] Some coins represent her with her sons, Michael VII., Constantinus and Andronicus, and her second husband, Romanus IV.

ROMANUS IV. (Diogenes). Married Eudocia who proclaimed him Emperor 1068; prisoner of the Turks, 1070; set free and had his eyes put out by order of Michael VII.; shut up in a monastery 1071, where he soon after died. G.—R.[3] R.[7] Br.—R.[3] Pl.—R.[8] Some coins represent him with Eudocia. Michael VII., Constantinus and Andronicus.

MICHAEL VII. (Ducas), son of Constantinus XIII. Succeeded his father with his brothers Constantinus and Andronicus, under the regency of their mother, in 1067; gave up the throne to Romanus; re-ascended it but was dethroned in 1071, and retired into a monastery; became Bishop of Ephesus; died in the reign of Alexius Comnenus. G.—R.[4] R.[8] S.—R.[5] Some coins represent him with his wife Maria.

Maria, wife of Michael VII. and afterwards of Nicephorus Botoniates III. Retired into a monastery with her first husband in 1078; espoused Nicephorus 1080, and retired for the second time into a monastery in 1081. G.—R[4] B.—R[7] This empress is found only on coins of Michael VII.

Constantinus (Ducas Porphyrogenitus), son of Constantine XIII. and Eudocia. Made Emperor with his brothers Michael and Andronicus, under the regency of his mother, in 1067; abdicated 1078; died 1082. G.—R.[5]—R.[7] Br.—R[8] Pl.—R.[8] Coins ascribed to this prince are either of Eudocia or of Romanus IV.

Andronicus, third son of Constantine XIII. Associated in the Empire with his brothers; died young. G.—R.[7] P.—R.[8] The coins that represent this prince are of Romanus IV.

CONSTANTINUS, son of Michael VII. and Maria. Born 1874; shut up in a monastery by Nicephorus III., 1078; died in the reign of Alexius Comnenus. There are no certain coins of this prince.

NICEPHORUS III. (Botaniates). Born ——; proclaimed Emperor 1077; by the aid of the Turks he dethroned Michael VII., 1078; dethroned by Alexius Comnenus, 1081; retired into a monastery and died shortly afterwards. G.—R.[4] Br.—R.[2]

ALEXIUS I. (Comnenus). Born 1048; proclaimed Emperor in 1081;

died 1118. G.—R.[2] S.—R.[4] Br.—R.[4]

JOHN II. (Comnenus Porphyrogenitus), son of Alexius I. Born 1088; Emperor 1118; died 1143: G—R.[2] R.[8] S. R.[3] Br.—R.[2]

MANUEL I. (Comnenus Porphyrogenitus Ducas), son of John II. and Irene, daughter of Ladislaus of Hungary. Born 1120; made Emperor 1143; died 1180. G.—R.[3] S. R.[4] R.[5] Po.—R.[4] Br.—C.—R.[2]

ALEXIUS II. (Comnenus), son of Manuel I. and Maria. Born 1167-9; Emperor under the regency of his mother Maria, 1180; strangled by command of his cousin Andronicus Comnenus in 1183. G.—R.[6] Br.—R.[4] One coin represents him with Andronicus I.

ANDRONICUS I. (Comnenus), son of Isaac, brother of John II. Seized upon the throne, 1183; dethroned and torn in pieces by the people, 1185. G.—R.[4] S.—.[2]

ISAAC II., son of Andronicus Angelus. Elected Emperor 1185; deposed and imprisoned by his brother Alexius III., 1195; re-established by the Crusaders, 1203; died 1204. G.—R.[4] S.—R.[4] Br.—R.[2]

ALEXIUS III. (Angelus), brother of Isaac II. whom he dethroned, mutilated and imprisoned. Seized upon the throne 1195; deposed by the French and Venetian Crusaders 1203; shut up in a monastery after having had his eyes put out. There are no certain coins of this prince. However it is possible that some of those attributed to Alexius I. really belonged to Alexius III.

ALEXIUS IV. (Angelus), son of Isaac II. Associated with his father, who had been restored by the Crusaders, 1203; dethroned and strangled by Alexius Murzuphlus, 1204. The same observation as above may be made here.

ALEXIUS V. (Murzuphlus). Seized upon the throne 1204; put to death by the Crusaders, who established a new empire at Constantinople.

FRENCH EMPERORS.

Baldwin I., son of Baldwin VIII., Count of Flanders and Margaret of Alsace. Elected Emperor by the Crusaders in 1204; conquered and taken prisoner by the Bulgarians 1205; died 1206. Br—R.[8]

Henry, brother of Baldwin. Regent during his brother's captivity 1205; Emperor 1206; died 1216.

Petrus de Courtnay, Count of Auxerre. Elected Emperor 1216; crowned at Rome by Pope Honorius II., 1207; taken prisoner by Theodorus Angelus, Prince of Epirus; died 1218; during his captivity his wife Jolande governed in his stead. No coins are known of this emperor.

Robert, son of the preceding. Emperor, 1221, after an interregnum; died 1228. No coins are known of this emperor.

Baldwin II., brother of Robert. Elected Emperor, 1228; dethroned by Michael Paleologus, who put an end to the empire of the French in the East, and re-established the Greek empire at Constantinople, 1261; died 1272. No coins are known of this emperor.

GREEK EMPIRE OF THESSALONICA.

THEODORUS I. (Lascaris), husband of Anna Comnena, daughter of Alexius III. Born 1176; retired into Asia after the taking of Constantinople by the Crusaders; conquered Bithynia and was declared Emperor at Nice 1205; died 1222. The coins that could be attributed to Theodore I. and III., not being of certain attribution, may be more safely attributed to Theodorus II.

THEODORUS II., son of John Angelus Comnenus, King of Epirus; took the title of Emperor at Thessalonica in Macedonia 1223; vanquished and taken prisoner by the Bulgarians 1230; had his eyes put out; recovered his liberty but abdicated in favor of his son John, who was dethroned by John III. (Vatatzes). Ar.—R.[5] Br.—R.[3] The coins of this emperor were probably struck in Macedonia and Epirus. Those which belong to Theodore I. and III. were undoubtedly struck in Bithynia.

JOHN III. (Vatatzes), son-in-law to Theodorus I. Born 1193; succeeded to the empire 1222; died 1255. Br.—R.[8] These coins were struck in Bythynia.

THEODORUS III. (Lascaris Junior), son of John III. Born 1223; succeeded his father 1255; died 1259. No certain coins are known of this prince.

JOHN IV. (Lascaris), son of Theodorus III. Born 1251; succeeded his father 1259; divided the Empire with his brother Michael VIII.; kept prisoner in a castle after having had his eyes put out 1261. No coins are known of this emperor.

BYZANTINE EMPERORS RESTORED.

MICHAEL VIII. (Paleologus). Proclaimed Emperor with his brother 1259; sole Emperor in 1261; died 1282. G.—R.[7] Br.—R.[8] After this reign the Greek coins were again struck at Constantinople. One coin represents him with his son Andronicus.

ANDRONICUS II., son of Michael VIII. Born 1258; named Emperor 1273; succeeded his father 1282; dethroned by his grandson Andronicus III. 1328; died 1332. G.—R.[4] S.—R.[6] Br.—R.[4] Some coins represent him with his son Michael IX.

MICHAEL IX. (Paleologus), son of Andronicus II. and Anna, daughter of Stephen of Hungary. Born 1277; associated with his father 1295; died 1320. G.—R.[4] Br.—R.[4]

ANDRONICUS III., son of Michael IX. Born 1295; associated in the Empire with his grandfather, whom he dethroned, 1325; died 1341. No certain coins are known of this emperor.

JOHN V., son of Andronicus III. and Ann of Savoy. Born 1332; succeeded his father 1341; dethroned by his son Andronicus IV. 1371; re-established by the Sultan Bajazet 1373; died 1391. No coins are known of this emperor.

JOHN VI. (Cantacuzenus). Regent 1341; proclaimed colleague of John V. 1347; renounced the throne 1355. Pl.—R.[8] Of doubtful attribution.

ANDRONICUS IV., son of John V. Associated in the throne with his father, whom he dethroned; abdicated 1373 in favor of his brother Manuel. No coins are known.

MANUEL II., brother of Andronicus IV. Born 1348; succeeded his brother 1373; died 1425. No coins are known of this prince.

JOHN VII. (Paleologus). Associated with his uncle Manuel in the empire 1399; renounced the throne 1402; died in a monastery. No coins are known of this emperor.

JOHN VIII., son of Manuel II. Born 1390; declared Augustus 1419; succeeded his father 1425; died 1448. G.—R.[8] This coin is doubtful.

Constantinus XIV., son of Manuel II. Born 1403; succeeded his brother 1448; killed in the taking of Constantinople by the Turks, 29th of May, 1453, (the 2206th year from the foundation of ancient Rome). Thus ended the empire of the Cæsars. G.—R.[5] The coins of this emperor are doubtful.

INDEX.

Chiefly of the Cities or Countries mentioned in this Work, that have issued Coins.

R

S

T

U

V

W

Z

www.ingramcontent.com/pod-product-compliance
Lightning Source LLC
LaVergne TN
LVHW020240110826
845151LV00003B/982

9781425529758